TRANSFORMING PROVINCIAL POLITICS

The Political Economy of Canada's Provinces and Territories in the Neoliberal Era

Over the past thirty-five years, Canada's provinces and territories have undergone significant political changes. Abandoning mid-century Keynesian policies, governments of all political persuasions have turned to deregulation, tax reduction, and government downsizing as policy solutions for a wide range of social and economic issues. *Transforming Provincial Politics* is the first province-by-province analysis of politics and political economy in more than a decade, and the first to directly examine the turn to neoliberal policies at the provincial and territorial level.

Featuring chapters written by experts in the politics of each province and territory, *Transforming Provincial Politics* examines how neoliberal policies have affected politics in each jurisdiction. A comprehensive and accessible analysis of the issues involved, this collection will be welcomed by scholars, instructors, and anyone interested in the state of provincial politics today.

(Studies in Comparative Political Economy and Public Policy)

BRYAN M. EVANS is an associate professor in the Department of Politics and Public Administration at Ryerson University.

CHARLES W. SMITH is an assistant professor in the Department of Political Studies at St Thomas More College, University of Saskatchewan.

Studies in Comparative Political Economy and Public Policy

Editors: MICHAEL HOWLETT, DAVID LAYCOCK (Simon Fraser University), and STEPHEN MCBRIDE (McMaster University)

Studies in Comparative Political Economy and Public Policy is designed to showcase innovative approaches to political economy and public policy from a comparative perspective. While originating in Canada, the series will provide attractive offerings to a wide international audience, featuring studies with local, subnational, cross-national, and international empirical bases and theoretical frameworks.

Transforming Provincial Politics

The Political Economy of Canada's Provinces
and Territories in the Neoliberal Era

EDITED BY BRYAN M. EVANS
AND CHARLES W. SMITH

UNIVERSITY OF TORONTO PRESS
Toronto Buffalo London

© University of Toronto Press 2015
Toronto Buffalo London
www.utppublishing.com
Printed in the U.S.A.

ISBN 978-1-4426-4334-5 (cloth)
ISBN 978-1-4426-1179-5 (paper)

Library and Archives Canada Cataloguing in Publication

Transforming provincial politics : the political economy of Canada's
provinces and territories in the neoliberal era / edited by Bryan M. Evans
and Charles W. Smith.

(Studies in comparative political economy and public policy)
Includes bibliographical references.
ISBN 978-1-4426-4334-5 (bound). – ISBN 978-1-4426-1179-5 (pbk.)

1. Provincial governments – Canada.   2. Neoliberalism – Canada.
I. Evans, Bryan M., 1960–, author, editor   II. Smith, Charles W., 1976–,
author, editor   III. Series: Studies in comparative political economy and
public policy

JL198.T73 2015   320.971   C2014-907760-2

University of Toronto Press acknowledges the financial assistance to its
publishing program of the Canada Council for the Arts and the
Ontario Arts Council, an agency of the Government of Ontario.

Canada Council   Conseil des Arts
for the Arts   du Canada

ONTARIO ARTS COUNCIL
CONSEIL DES ARTS DE L'ONTARIO
an Ontario government agency
un organisme du gouvernement de l'Ontario

University of Toronto Press acknowledges the financial support of the
Government of Canada through the Canada Book Fund for its
publishing activities.

We would like to dedicate this book to Graham White and John Conway. Graham and John are outstanding scholars of Canadian provincial politics and political economy. This volume emerges from their pioneering efforts to bring greater attention and understanding to the complexities of provincial and territorial politics. Political science and sociology in Canada are stronger disciplines because of their contributions.

Contents

Part Two: Neoliberalism and the Decline of Central Canada

Part Three: Neoliberalism and the "New West"

Part Four: New Opportunities and Old Problems: The North

Acknowledgments

It goes without saying that a work of this nature is the product of a collective effort by many dedicated people. We truly owe a debt of gratitude to our contributors for their expertise in preparing each chapter. As politics in the provinces and territories never stands still, we would also like to acknowledge their patience and skill as we continuously asked them to closely follow each election and update their already substantial chapters over the past two years. This volume is a dedication to their keen observations of current events surrounding questions of politics and political economy.

We would like to both thank our respective institutions – St Thomas More College, University of Saskatchewan, and Ryerson University – for their intellectual, collegial, and financial support in seeing this project through to completion. At St Thomas More College we would like to particularly thank David McGrane for his helpful comments on the project as a whole and Joanne Illingworth for her helpful guidance in preparing grant applications for financial support. We also received editorial support from exceptional undergraduate researchers, Emily Lafreniere, Aleida Oberholzer, and Amanda Bestvater, who skilfully assisted in preparing the bibliography. We suspect it will not be long before they too are making substantial contributions to the study of provincial and territorial politics and political economy. At Ryerson University, we would like to thank president Sheldon Levy in particular, for his support of this work. In Toronto he is viewed as a "city builder," and that he is, but it is also well known throughout the country that Ryerson has been fundamentally transformed under his leadership. His interest in this project is testimony to his attention to things big and rather small!

We also owe a significant debt to Daniel Quinlan at the University of Toronto Press. Daniel demonstrated keen optimism for this project from the very beginning and was thoroughly supportive of the volume as it went through the numerous stages of publication. His keen eye for detail also added significant insight into the direction of the project. We would also like to thank the dedication shown by the peer reviewers to each chapter in this manuscript. Their expertise and advice made each chapter stronger and more precise.

Finally, we would like to thank our friends and family for their continued support and guidance. Charles would particularly like to thank Allison for her love and patience in editing this volume. It could not have been accomplished without her support. Charles would also like to thank the inspiration that his twin sons Dylan and Jonah provide him every day. They are a constant source of joy and happiness and provide an important reminder to strive for a more just and better world. Bryan is grateful for the support and encouragement of several friends and colleagues, including John Shields and Steve McBride, who endured the trials and tribulations of various revisions. And, of course, we are eternally grateful to the bartenders at the Communist's Daughter.

TRANSFORMING PROVINCIAL POLITICS

The Political Economy of Canada's Provinces
and Territories in the Neoliberal Era

Introduction: Transforming Provincial Politics: The Political Economy of Canada's Provinces and Territories in a Neoliberal Era

BRYAN M. EVANS AND CHARLES W. SMITH

Over the past thirty-five years, politics in Canada's provinces and territories has undergone significant transformations. Quite simply, the provincial and territorial states of 2014 bear little resemblance to their 1970s counterparts. Under the auspices of neoliberal globalization, regional power blocs have been formed and reformed in such a way that natural resource extraction is taking on both national and global importance. Traditionally, Canadian political economists argued that Canada's economic underdevelopment derived, in part, from an over-reliance on commodity extraction.[1] Today, however, governments and multinational corporations promote natural resource extraction as a driver of Canadian competitiveness abroad. The economic power of commodity production has placed new influence in the hands of provincial and territorial governments, most notably in the West and the North. Meanwhile, the traditional manufacturing strength in Ontario and Quebec continues to decline in both real and absolute terms. Rather than promote greater public investment in manufacturing or technological research and development, however, governments of all political persuasions promote further trade liberalization, tax reduction, deregulation, and balanced budgets as long-term policy solutions to a host of social and economic concerns.

These economic transformations have shifted the ideological terrain in which political parties compete for government power. The electoral hegemony of the Conservative and Liberal parties – while readily apparent in most provinces and territories – is challenged by unthreatening social democratic contenders in several provinces, while more radical alternatives either simply do not exist or, as in the case of Québec Solidaire, are rather limited. Whereas left-wing social democracy once challenged the forces of the market, the New Democratic Party (NDP) and the Parti Québécois (PQ) increasingly promote market-driven policies in order to foster long-term economic development, high-wage value-added jobs, and delivery of public services.[2] These same governments also promote seemingly counter-intuitive policies, limiting the capacity of workers to organize, bargain, or strike, while containing the influence of social movements and non-governmental organizations on the policymaking functions of the state. Ultimately, these transformations have placed downward pressure on popular organizations that traditionally advance activist government in the promotion of equality, full employment, and social inclusion.

How have these transformations occurred? The chapters in this book seek to answer this question from a political economy perspective. Political economy provides a rich array of analytical tools to scrutinize and explain how economic, political, and ideological forces within society produce and replicate themselves. By its nature, such an examination is "historical and dynamic, since it seeks to locate the motion of society in the forces of change as production and reproduction transform."[3] Using this framework, the book endeavours to explain how the forces of neoliberalism have shaped Canadian provincial and territorial politics since the 1970s. By relying on what Pierson and Skocpol term a "long-term perspective," the book also examines how struggles over new forms of accumulation have altered the terrain of economic, political, and ideological policymaking.[4] Such a historical exploration allows researchers to avoid the causational traps that often occur in research concentrating on short-term policy studies, rationalist political behaviour, or positivist electoral analysis. Rather, each author explains the transformation in provincial and territorial politics by mapping, as Colin Hay has identified, "the complex interaction of causal processes to produce structural and behavioural change – whether continuous or discontinuous, incremental or punctuating, evolutionary or revolutionary."[5] By examining long-term neoliberal transformations, the chapters in the book demonstrate that a profound class shift has occurred in each province/territory that overwhelmingly benefits the most powerful groups in society.

Each chapter illustrates the long-term shifts in provincial/territorial politics through a critical examination of neoliberalism. As a political phenomenon, neoliberalism is often associated with globalization, as both paradigms have dramatically reshaped how people interact with the state, the market, technology, and each other.[6] Although identifying a precise point of origin of the neoliberal revolution can be an exasperating exercise, it can broadly be agreed that neoliberalization began as a response to the general crisis of capitalist accumulation in the late 1970s.[7] The crisis challenged the post-war economic order (loosely defined as Keynesianism or Fordism) in North America and Western Europe, characterized by national forms of capitalist accumulation existing alongside numerous versions of full-employment policies, welfare regimes, in historical terms, comparatively high and secure levels of unionization, and progressive taxation.[8] Neoliberal ideas (and the actual processes of neoliberalization) emerged as a political project aimed at disentangling the state from redistributive and collectivist policies associated with the post-war economic order in the advanced capitalist countries. The implications of this political revolution also reasserted the class power of economic and political elites.

The Canadian process of neoliberalization began slowly and, like its counterparts in the United States and Western Europe, was driven by the economic crisis of the 1970s. In this period, the federal Liberal government of Pierre Trudeau fluctuated between two policy paradigms in response to the shifting economic context. On the one hand, confronting high unemployment and high inflation, it flirted with neoliberal economic reforms as a means of addressing the general crisis of accumulation and the subsequent stagflation that occurred after the worldwide oil shocks in 1973. Under Trudeau's watch, the Bank of Canada imposed monetarist "shocks" that slowed the economy with a dramatic interest rate hike that witnessed declining growth, waves of home foreclosures, and double-digit unemployment. On the other hand, the Liberals also explored neo-Keynesian policies such as wage and price controls and corporatist structures to facilitate multi-class and cross-sectoral social dialogue. Part of Trudeau's plan to stimulate the ailing economy included dramatic restructuring of collective bargaining rights (especially for public-sector workers), cuts to federal spending, and altering the level and coverage of public services, while also centralizing the power of the Prime Minister's Office and other central agencies to limit internal political opposition.[9] Although the Trudeau Liberals never fully embraced the neoliberal project, the party set in motion a series of ideas that later formed the nucleolus of Brian Mulroney's political project in the 1980s.

Perhaps the most notable shift for both prominent Liberals and Conservatives was the recommendation to adopt free trade from Trudeau's Royal Commission on the Economic Union and Development Prospects

for Canada (the Macdonald Commission).[10] For the Mulroney government, a Canada–United States Free Trade agreement (CUFTA) allowed
for the "freeing" of domestic capital from burdensome protectionist
policies and opened the Canadian market to more direct competitive
pressures. These policies were designed to attract foreign direct investment (especially from multinational corporations), and, perhaps most
importantly for the Conservatives, guarantee Canadian capital access
to the American market (unsuccessfully).[11] Perhaps equally important
for the Conservatives (and for the Americans), the CUFTA also acted
as quasi-constitutional document binding future governments from
taking policy actions to economic problems that might upset the neoliberal consensus, including nationalizing key commodities such as oil
and gas.[12] Along the lines of freeing the market, Mulroney also implemented several changes to the federal tax code (including the introduction of a flat sales tax – the Goods and Services Tax [GST]) and curtailed
collective bargaining rights for federal workers. The government also
implemented a series of downsizing measures through budget cuts,
outsourcing, and privatization of Crown corporations.

Mulroney's devastating defeat in 1993 was the culmination of economic restructuring that began to sweep through Canada's industrial
heartland in the late 1980s. The result was, in part, a realignment of
the Canadian party system. Yet somewhat paradoxically, given the 1988
election campaign in which the federal Liberals opposed free trade,
Mulroney's inability to complete many of the neoliberal reforms he
began – such as radically downsizing the federal welfare state – was
embraced and deepened by the Liberal governments of Jean Chrétien
and Paul Martin in the 1990s and early 2000s. Perhaps the most obvious
example of the Liberal Party's transformation was its enthusiastic signing of the North American Free Trade Agreement (NAFTA) in 1994. For
the federal Liberals, NAFTA further strengthened the property rights
of both national and international business investors in Canada.[13] The
Liberals also engaged in aggressive restructuring of the Canadian welfare state through historically unprecedented cuts to social programs,
reductions in federal-provincial transfers, and further decreasing the
tax burden for Canada's wealthiest citizens.[14] The Conservative government of Stephen Harper is expanding (and deepening) these processes
of neoliberalization, albeit with a more draconian and authoritarian
virulence than has characterized previous governments.[15]

Given the ascendancy of neoliberalism, the paucity of research and
analysis focused on the political economy of provincial and territorial

states is both surprising and unfortunate. To be sure, there is a rich tradition in Canadian political science comparing regional variations of different provincial states to broader questions of institutional objectives, political culture, and public policy creation.[16] Other collections focus specifically on political party competition in an attempt to map different ideological traditions onto questions of political culture and policy design.[17] One of the most important collections directly analysing the interconnections between political economy, political change, and the provincial state remains Michael Howlett and Keith Brownsey's *Provincial State in Canada*.[18] In the 2001 edition, Brownsey and Howlett make a convincing argument that the study of the provincial and territorial state from a political economy tradition is virtually non-existent. That collection, which broadly examines the historical trajectory of provincial and territorial economies through the post-war era of "province building" to the turn of the century, provides important insight on the transformation of the sub-national state in the early stages of neoliberal globalization. It is our hope that this collection builds on the significant foundation established by Brownsey and Howlett's work, with specific focus on the process of neoliberalization in the provinces and territories since the 1970s.

We believe a critical analysis of neoliberalism and the provincial/territorial state is essential for a variety of reasons. First, the continued constitutional role assigned to Canada's ten provinces for the delivery and regulation of popular and important public services such as health care, education, labour relations, environmental regulation, and social services, to name but a few, suggests that we cannot understand how neoliberalism has been introduced in Canada without examining the provinces and territories. Second, beyond the areas of public policy, provincial and territorial states continue to be the front line for ideological debates over economic accumulation (and redistribution), as well as shaping the spectrum of political legitimization and coercion. One has to look no further than the clash between Toronto police and G20 protesters in 2010 (and the coercive law passed by the McGuinty government to aid the crackdown); the tension between thousands of student protesters with Quebec police over access to publicly funded universities in 2012; or the ongoing debates over labour law reform in British Columbia, Saskatchewan, Ontario, and Quebec throughout the 2000s (to name but a few) to recognize that the actions of the provincial/territorial states give us important insight into the ongoing neoliberalization in Canada. Third, the changing regional dynamics of Canada's political economy need close examination if we are to understand the shifting ideological terrain in which political parties compete for government power. The dominance of commodity extraction in the West, the decline of the central manufacturing hub in Ontario and Quebec, and the changing economic conditions in the North and Atlantic Canada have all had a profound impact on how political and economic power shapes the everyday lives of Canadians.

Historically, the study of Canadian political economy has played an essential role in unpacking how divided societies were able to construct national policies to sustain long-term capital accumulation within the rubric of a single state.[19] Recognizing the spatial roots of Canadian national policies, as Janine Brodie has shown, is "an expression of and a response to phases of capitalist accumulation and class conflict [as] they imprint themselves on the geographic landscape in the character of economic activity and in political conflict."[20] Using this insight, we can begin to unpack how political and economic forces have shaped the Canadian provincial and territorial state through phases of capitalist restructuring. Inasmuch as Canadian governments were able to create the conditions for the "golden age" of post-war capitalism, for instance, it was constructed through ongoing regionally situated conflict between capitalists and workers' movements, and between the federal and provincial states themselves, resulting in the creation of new political and economic institutions, regulations, social programs, and workers' protections. In fact, Jane Jensen has argued that Canada's version of post-war Fordism was different from that of most of the Western world because it was shaped more by struggles between powerful provincial states than through a class-divided party system.[21] Jensen's insights suggest that the provincial state should be at the centre of study for Canadian political economists.

Although the building of the Canadian welfare state was uneven (and certainly not exceptional in the Western world), it was provincial governments that established the institutional foundations of Canada's post-war welfare state, presiding over the massive growth in schools, universities, hospitals, social programs, and the public services in the 1960s and 1970s, albeit in response to federal initiatives and incentives. The progression in these areas created the conditions for future economic and political conflict, which took on multiple forms. For instance, the politics of class and language defined regional tensions with Quebec and the rest of Canada, while Ontario grappled with institutional compromises between workers and industrialists to deepen (and expand) its branch-plant manufacturing sector. At the same time, Atlantic and Western Canada both struggled to acquire greater control over their natural resource industries. The territorial governments – always a mystery to the vast majority of Canadians – maintained their historic underdevelopment, partially through government mismanagement and partially through colonial attitudes directed at the First Nations and Inuit and Metis populations of those areas. On these broad economic questions, the provinces and territories were active participants in the extension of large-scale projects, which included public investments in natural resource extraction, manufacturing, public health and auto insurance, growth and professionalization of the public service, transportation, energy, and communications. In many cases, the close alliances that provinces maintained with leading industries and private interests in their respective jurisdictions accelerated the decentralization of political and economic power already characterizing Canadian federalism.[22]

When the federal government moved to restructure the economic and financial commitments associated with Canada's version of postwar Keynsianism in the 1980s and 1990s, it effectively downloaded responsibility for curtailing redistributive policies and public expenditures onto the provinces and territories. Given these developments, the chapters in this volume hope to contribute towards building greater understanding and appreciation for the political economy of Canada's provinces and territories, given that the ideas of neoliberalism have now become normalized into the political and policy fabric of each province and territory. In so doing, we hope the book will spark a broader interest in the study of Canadian political economy and specifically that of the provincial and territorial state.

Disentangling Neoliberalism

Understanding political economy in the current era requires an understanding of the concept of neoliberalism. On the surface, neoliberalism is simply an economic system that promises greater economic freedom by unleashing competitive forces designed to encourage individual entrepreneurial initiatives. In order to promote this specific form of freedom, neoliberals actively foster an ideal type of "free" market through the support of free trade, enhanced private property rights, deregulation – particularly in the financial industry – and privatization of public assets.[23] At its most basic, neoliberalism seeks to apply a market approach to governance and as such represents an ideological shift in the role of government in economic and social development. It is based on principles of competition, laissez-faire, efficiency, productivity, profitability, and individual autonomy.[24] In other words, neoliberalism views the state's sole role as facilitating "conditions for profitable capital accumulation on the part of both domestic and foreign capital."[25] Consequently, a number of very real effects on the state, policy, and role of government ensue. In particular, it has major effects institutionally, the hollowing out of certain regulatory capacities of the state, and the concentration of political power in the executive.[26]

The promotion of these economic, political, and institutional transformations places downward pressure on public institutions that act as barriers to trade, which include Crown corporations, public welfare systems (employment insurance, workers' health and safety regulations, etc.), and public services. State policies, however, are only the beginning. Neoliberalism as an economic system also seeks to limit the ability of workers to collectively challenge the power of employers. This opposition occurs through the loosening of restrictions on capital mobility, placing downward pressure on wages, weakening labour laws, making workplaces more flexible under the auspices of "lean production" while also promoting competition and competitiveness in order to discipline workers. The adoption of such reforms across Western societies has fundamentally transformed the economic priorities of almost all capitalist states.

To be sure, all economic transformations depend on multiple pressures from outside traditional markets. The transformation towards neoliberalism in the United States, for instance, will look vastly different from that in Canada, France, or Germany. Yet, when examining the broad history of neoliberal ideas, several characteristics are noticeable. In his exploration of neoliberalism in Canada, Gary Teeple has identified several areas that generally accompany the process of neoliberalization. Perhaps most important is the advancement of private property rights in order to reinforce the notion that markets alone can provide solutions to complex social problems.[27] Along the same lines, neoliberals have lobbied for "free" economic zones; pushed for deregulation, privatization, and tax restructuring; overwhelmingly focused on the politics of state debt; promoted government downsizing and the restructuring of local government; called for the dismantling of social welfare programs; restricted civil liberties that challenge social reform; promoted the building of new prisons to address social unrest and appeal to conservative populism; placed severe limits on union rights; and ultimately restricted the basic foundations of liberal democracy.[28]

These characteristics of neoliberalism do not exist independently of the state. In fact, it is one of the great contradictions of neoliberalism that it must capture, restructure, and then limit the democratic capacities of the state in order to build and protect (sometimes violently) the conditions for so-called free markets. In other words, neoliberalism is not about diminishing the role of the state but rather of reorienting its roles and functions to serve capital. The state's role, including that of sub-national states, is "to build institutions for the market."[29] It is the dependence on states to impose (and defend) neoliberalism from above that makes it an ongoing experiment prone to false starts, growth, restructuring, pushback, and crisis. These characteristics also make neoliberalism very uneven across both space and time. In Canada, each provincial and territorial jurisdiction has gone through its own neoliberal experiment, which needs to be understood, as Jamie Peck has argued, "as a form of reconstruction, representing a conjunctural episode or moment in the contradictory *evolution* of neoliberal practice."[30] For Peck, the analytical and political challenge is to understand how these forms of reconstruction have been integrated to achieve what he calls "a form of evolutionary consolidation."[31] This book is a first step towards achieving that goal in Canada's provinces and territories.

The chapters presented here seek to understand the creation, administration, and extension of neoliberalism across Canada's provincial and territorial states. In examining the adoption of neoliberalism by political parties and social forces across the country, each author offers important insights into the tensions and contested process of neoliberalization in each jurisdiction. In so doing, the authors contribute to the larger analysis of examining how neoliberal forces "roll back" postwar gains through deregulation and dismantling in the 1970s and 1980s while also mapping the emergence of active "roll-out" strategies, which Peck argues were the active use of state policies and institutions to build and defend neoliberalism in the 1990s and 2000s.[32] As these processes unfolded, each province and territory was forced to respond to forces from without (foreign investors, federal government restructuring) and from within (changing class structures, political realignments, democratic changes).

Neoliberalization and the Provincial/Territorial State: The Plan of the Book

In mapping the process of rollback and roll-out neoliberalism, each chapter tells a unique story. In so doing, the book does not offer a clear or single thread of analysis explaining the neoliberal transformation across the country. Such a task would be impossible, given the vast differences in political history, regional political economy, institutional make-up, balance of class forces, and party systems in each province and territory. Rather, each author emphasizes unique political, economic, social, and institutional explanations to understanding the broad neoliberal transformations in each provincial/territorial state. In each chapter, the long-term perspectives offer important insight into how provincial/territorial politics have been influenced by different political and economic forces. In some cases, there has been a resurgence of new forms of accumulation (as in the West and the North), while in other cases there has been a long-term economic decline that has yet to be fully addressed by political or economic elites (as in Ontario). Yet, recognizing the complexity of holistic political economy explanations, each chapter explores several themes that are essential to understanding the process of neoliberalization in Canada.

First, the process has changed how wealth is accumulated and redistributed. In most cases, these forms of redistribution have emphasized market-driven policies to further economic growth. Market-driven policy solutions, however, have commodified state services in ways that prioritize economic competitiveness over social equality. Generally, market-driven policy changes seek to transform state institutions, as Colin Leys has argued, to make the state serve the broad interests of business, mimic its internal operations along private sector "efficiencies," and shield government from democratic pressure from below.[33] In essence, market-driven reforms seek broad social, economic, and political transformation. The chapters on Saskatchewan, Manitoba, Ontario, Quebec, and Nova Scotia examine in many various ways how the process of neoliberalization has coalesced around market-driven state restructuring – by Conservative, Liberal, and social democratic governments – whose consequences have accelerated poverty and social inequality in those provinces.

Following similar observations that have been made throughout the advanced capitalist countries, the authors demonstrate that in the post-war era, the redistribution of wealth occurred through a generous welfare state and strong institutional support for collective bargaining. Most of these changes were financed through progressive forms of taxation and stable rates of business taxation.[34] Wealth was also redistributed through steady rates of unionization, allowing workers to use their collective power to extract a greater share of the economic surplus from employers.[35] Since the 1980s, however, both forms of redistribution have been altered in favour of policies that benefit individual wealth accumulation over collective freedoms (including the rights to bargain and strike) or an expanding social wage for the working classes.[36] A consequence has been the increased polarization between public and private sector workers, falling rates of unionization, and a restructuring of employment in favour of precarious part-time work relationships over long-term, full-time employment.

Second, the book highlights a concrete transformation of political parties, mapping an ideological morphing of the Keynsian left-right divide. In essence, the changing process of capital accumulation through the 1980s, 1990s, and 2000s contributed to a shifting of the philosophical space traditionally occupied by political parties. All of the chapters speak to the changing ideological "centre," which is now firmly embedded within a neoliberal framework. As many of these provinces are overwhelmingly dependent on natural resource commodities to drive economic growth, the politics of class always remain close to the surface. As many chapters in this book further demonstrate, the implications of political (and cultural) changes surrounding class have had dramatic implications for Canada's Conservative and Liberal parties but have also transformed the social democratic NDP and the PQ in Quebec.[37] In the 1980s, it was not entirely surprising that neoliberalism gained influence in the populist right platforms of the British Columbia Social Credit Party, or the Progressive Conservatives in Alberta, Saskatchewan, and Manitoba, or the Liberal Party in New Brunswick and Quebec. As the political spectrum changed, however, neoliberalism increasingly altered how the NDP and PQ acted in opposition and later in government. Indeed, as the chapters on British Columbia, Saskatchewan, Manitoba, Ontario, Quebec, and Nova Scotia amply demonstrate, one defining characteristic of neoliberalism in the provinces has been the aggressive restructuring that has occurred under the political rule of Canada's traditional social democratic parties.

Third, over the past thirty-five years, Canada's provinces and territories have been ruled (more or less) by centre-right political coalitions. The dominance of centre-right governments has resulted in significant institutional transformations that have dramatically accelerated market-driven politics. In some cases, as the chapter on Alberta demonstrates, this institutional reality has led to an intersection of political and economic power that weakens democratic alternatives in the province. The case of the Albertan "one-party state" is an extreme example of convergence between a ruling political party and market forces. In Alberta, the dominance of the Conservatives has led to a virtual merger of Conservative insiders and large private actors with an extremely powerful executive controlling the legislative process and public appointments. These conditions have allowed the Conservatives to impose neoliberalism from above with little resistance from the opposition or media. Alberta exemplifies how the process of neoliberalization institutionalizes the policy process in a way that gives access only to political consultants, business, and other partisan policy "experts."

While not as extreme, many other provinces have characteristics similar to the Alberta model. In fact, the rise of neoliberalism has led to a centralization of political power in almost all executive offices across the country. These changes give the premier and his or her office tight controls over appointments to the public service in order to further consolidate economic and political power. These trends have accelerated the capacity of neoliberal governments to utilize privatization, outsourcing, and contracting-out to private-sector partners with little internal opposition. As these reforms become embedded, the process of neoliberalization has given governments further ability to control the public agenda and further down-size the welfare state while also insulating the executive from popular movements demanding progressive reform. The chapters on BC, Ontario, New Brunswick, Newfoundland and Labrador, and Prince Edward Island highlight this unique transformation.

Fourth, the transformation of provincial/territorial politics has not occurred without significant social changes. Each chapter highlights the tension between the forces of neoliberalism and resistance from labour unions. This is not surprising, as the crisis of labour has been a defining feature of neoliberal transformations throughout the 1990s and 2000s.[38] In British Columbia, Saskatchewan, Manitoba, Ontario, Quebec, New Brunswick, Nova Scotia, Prince Edward Island, and Newfoundland and Labrador the unions have been a significant focal point in the politics of neoliberalism. Almost universally, however, labour unions have been forced to make significant concessions in order to maintain some of the gains from the Fordist era.

Social transformations have also occurred in relations to Canada's Aboriginal peoples. While it is insufficient to equate questions of equity, fairness, and justice for Aboriginal peoples only to neoliberal transformation, changing economic realities play an important role in questions over land and resources, especially in the North. In the northern territories of Yukon, Northwest Territories, and Nunavut the questions of market-based resource allocation, self-government, and federal government control remain dominant. While the Yukon is perhaps the most "province like," it has issues in land claims, federal devolution, and infrastructure development similar to those in the NWT and Nunavut. An ongoing theme in the North suggests that the unwillingness of the federal government to address outstanding land claims has led to high levels of poverty, social inequality, and underdevelopment. While the prospect of multinational investment in large resource projects has led some Aboriginal communities to benefit, others remain trapped by the now long-standing problems of federal mismanagement. With its large Inuit and Metis populations, Nunavut remains deeply impoverished while continuing to address persistent questions of infrastructure development and the implementation of self-government. Across the North, the experience thus far suggests that territorial and federal governments determined to implement market-oriented reforms continue to marginalize First Nations, Inuit, and Metis peoples in the territories. The tension between demands for self-government and what is an internal colonial relationship will continue to be the key fracture line defining the struggles of Aboriginal peoples in the North and the rest of Canada for some time to come.

The era of neoliberalism is now into its fourth decade, and only now, in the wake of the Great Financial Crisis of 2008, are its inherent contradictions beginning to emerge. While Canada and its provinces may not be Greece, Italy, or Spain, the list of fault lines will grow, and there can be no doubt that the discourse of Canadian exceptionalism – the perspective of the country's political and business elites that Canada has largely avoided the worst of the crisis – cannot be sustained.[39] As governments respond to the ongoing fiscal crisis, this will be most acutely observed in the provinces as they turn towards public-sector austerity by again placing balanced budget orthodoxy at the centre of their policy agenda. How (or even if) this turn towards austerity will again reshape or transform the provincial and territorial landscape is an open-ended question. The themes highlighted in this volume provide a rich historical perspective on the rolling out of neoliberalism at the sub-national level as well as a more contemporary context and analysis of the economic, political, and social implications of neoliberal transformation in Canada. To be sure, the chapters presented here offer only a snapshot of Canada's neoliberal revolution over the past three decades. Yet, given the significant transformations that have occurred over this period, the chapters also offer important insight into the social problems that continue to plague neoliberal governments. It is our hope that this book offers a small contribution to highlighting those problems in a way that future political and economic transformations may one day replace the neoliberal paradigm with one based on social and economic justice for all Canadians.

NOTES

1 Neil Bradford and Glen Williams, "What Went Wrong? Explaining Canadian Industrialization," in *The New Canadian Political Economy*, ed. Wallace Clement and Glen Williams, 54–76 (Montreal and Kingston: McGill-Queen's University Press, 1989).

2 See the essays in Bryan Evans and Ingo Schmidt, eds., *Social Democracy after the Cold War* (Edmonton: Athabasca University Press, 2012).

3 Wallace Clement, "Introduction: Whither the New Canadian Political Economy?," in *Understanding Canada: Building on the New Canadian Political Economy*, ed. Wallace Clement (Montreal and Kingston: McGill-Queen's University Press, 1997), 3.

4 Paul Pierson and Theda Skocpol, "American Politics in the Long Run," in *The Transformation of American Politics: Activist Government and the Rise of Conservatism*, ed. P. Pierson and T. Skocpol, 3–16 (Princeton: Princeton University Press, 2007).

5 Colin Hay, *Political Analysis* (New York: Palgrave, 2002), 149.

6 David Harvey, *A Brief History of Neoliberalism* (Oxford: Oxford University Press, 2005).

7 Gary Teeple, *Globalization and the Decline of Social Reform: Into the Twenty-First Century* (Toronto: Garamond, 2000), chap. 4.

8 Alain Lipietz, *Mirages and Miracles: The Crisis of Global Fordism* (London: Verso, 1987).

9 See François Houle, "Economic Strategy and the Restructuring of the Fordist Wage–Labour Relationship in Canada," *Studies in Political Economy* 11 (1983): 127–47.

10 For an overview (including Mulroney's embrace of free trade), see Gregory J. Inwood, *Continentalizing Canada: The Politics and Legacy of the Macdonald Commission* (Toronto: University of Toronto Press, 2005).

11 Stephen Clarkson, *Uncle Sam and US: Globalization, Neoconservatism and the Canadian State* (Toronto: University of Toronto Press, 2002).

12 Stephen McBride, "Quiet Constitutionalism: The International Political Economy of Domestic Institutional Change," *Canadian Journal of Political Science* 36 (2003): 251–73.

13 Ian Robinson, "Neoliberal Trade Policy and Canadian Federalism Revisited," in *New Trends in Canadian Federalism*, ed. François Rocher and Miriam Smith, 2nd ed. (Toronto: Broadview, 2003), 203.

14 Stephen McBride, *Globalization and the Canadian State*, 2nd ed. (Halifax: Fernwood, 2005), 99.

15 See Teresa Healy, ed. *The Harper Record* (Ottawa: Canadian Centre for Policy Alternatives, 2008).

16 See Christopher Dunn, ed., *Provinces: Canadian Provincial Politics* (Peterborough: Broadview, 2006); Rand Dyck, *Provincial Politics in Canada: Towards the Turn of the Century* (Toronto: Prentice-Hall, 1996); Martin Robin, ed., *Canada's Provincial Politics* (Toronto: Prentice-Hall, 1978); David J. Bellay, Jon H. Pammett, and Donald C. Rowat, eds., *The Provincial Political Systems: Comparative Essays* (Agincourt: Methuen, 1976).

17 See R. Kenneth Carty, William Cross, and Lisa Young, eds., *Leaders and Parties in Canadian Politics: Experiences of the Provinces* (Toronto: HBJ, 1992); David J. Elkins and Richard Simeon, eds., *Small Worlds Provinces and Parties in Canadian Political Life* (Toronto: Methuen, 1980). For a snapshot of a small group of provinces, see Jared J. Wesley, *Code Politics: Campaigns and Cultures on the Canadian Prairies* (Vancouver: UBC Press, 2011).

18 K. Brownsey and M. Howlett, eds., *The Provincial State in Canada: Politics in the Provinces and Territories* (Toronto: Broadview, 1992 and 2001).

19 Reg Whitaker, "Images of the State," in *The Canadian State: Political Economy and Political Power*, ed. L. Panitch, 28–70 (Toronto: University of Toronto Press, 1977).

20 Janine Brodie, *The Political Economy of Canadian Regionalism* (Toronto: Harcourt Brace Jovanovich, Canada, 1990), 1.

21 Jane Jensen, "'Different' but Not 'Exceptional': Canada's Permeable Fordism," *Canadian Review of Sociology and Anthropology* 26 (1989): 69–94.

22 Garth Stevenson, *Unfulfilled Union: Canadian Federalism and National Unity*, 5th ed. (Montreal and Kingston: McGill-Queen's University Press, 2009), chap. 4.

23 See Harvey, *Brief History of Neoliberalism*, 2. Also see Greg Albo, Sam Gindin, and Leo Panitch, *In and Out of Crisis: The Global Financial Meltdown and Left Alternatives* (Oakland: PM, 2010), 27–8; and Greg Albo, "The 'New Economy' and Capitalism Today," in *Interrogating the New Economy: Restructuring Work in the 21st Century*, ed. Norene J. Pupo and Mark P. Thomas (Toronto: University of Toronto Press, 2010), 4.
24 Wendy Larner, "Neoliberalism: Policy, Ideology, Governmentality," *Studies in Political Economy*, 63 (2000): 5–25.
25 Harvey, *Brief History of Neoliberalism*, 7.
26 Greg Albo, "Neoliberalism, the State, and the Left: A Canadian Perspective," *Monthly Review* 54 (2002): 46–55. See also Bob Jessop, "Hollowing Out the 'Nation-State' and Multi-Level Governance," in *A Handbook of Comparative Social Policy*, ed. Patricia Kennett, 11–26 (Northampton: Edward Elgar Publishing, 2004).
27 Teeple, *Globalization and the Decline of Social Reform*, chap. 5.
28 Ibid.
29 World Bank, "The State in a Changing World," *The World Development Report 1997* (Washington DC: World Bank, 1997).
30 Jamie Peck, *Constructions of Neoliberal Reason* (Oxford: Oxford University Press, 2010), 6. (Emphasis in original.)
31 Ibid.
32 Jamie Peck and Adam Tickell, "Neoliberalizing Space," *Antipode* 34 (2002): 384.
33 Colin Leys, *Market-Driven Politics: Neoliberal Democracy and the Public Interest* (London: Verso, 2001), 3.
34 See Andrew Glyn, *Capitalism Unleashed: Finance Globalization and Welfare* (Oxford: Oxford University Press, 2006).
35 Thom Workman, *If You're In My Way, I'm Walking: The Assault on Working People since 1970* (Halifax: Fernwood, 2009), chap. 2.
36 Leo Panitch and Donald Swartz, *From Consent to Coercion: The Assault on Trade Union Freedoms*, 3rd ed. (Toronto: Garamond, 2003).
37 See the essays in William K. Carroll and R.S. Ratner, eds., *Challenges and Perils: Social Democracy in Neoliberal Times* (Halifax: Fernwood, 2005).
38 See Kim Moody, *Workers in a Lean World* (London: Verso, 1997). More recently, see the essays in Stephanie Ross and Larry Savage, eds., *Rethinking the Politics of Labour in Canada* (Halifax: Fernwood, 2012).
39 "Every G20 Nation Wants to Be Canada, Insists PM," *Reuters*, 25 September 2009, http://www.reuters.com/article/2009/09/26/columns-us-g20-canada-advantages-idUSTRE58P05Z20090926.

PART ONE

Resistance and Neoliberal Restructuring in Atlantic Canada

1 Newfoundland and Labrador, 1979–2011: Contradiction and Continuity in a Neoliberal Era

SEAN T. CADIGAN

Neoliberalism has been one of the most prominent ideological responses to the economic and social crises associated with globalization since the late 1970s. Neoliberals have emphasized the importance of communities, regions, or nation states becoming more competitive in the global economy, extolling the free market, and advocating the privatization of government services, wide-ranging deregulation, and the "shrinking and hollowing out of the state in terms of industrial and welfare policies."[1] Canadian federal neoliberal policies have focused on free trade, retrenchment in fiscal and monetary policies, privatization, and the downloading of costs for many social programs onto the provinces. In Atlantic Canada, neoliberal provincial policies were similar to federal ones but included an intensive "assault on working people."[2]

Provincial governments' engagement in the "assault" on labour unions persists. Neoliberals reject much of post-1945 Fordism: the commitment to capitalist development through mass production and mass consumption abetted by the welfare state and the constraints of industrial legality. Governments have instead attacked the rights of working people to bargain collectively. In the private sector, employers fostered "lean production": lowering their overhead costs by industrial restructuring that made their workforces more flexible, insecure, and poorly paid. In the public sector, neoliberal policies reduced government expenditures by privatizing and cutting programs, contracting out, laying off or not replacing workers, and undermining compensation, especially by wage freezes and cuts to benefits. Governments favoured back-to-work legislation, imposed settlements, and declaring more public workers as the providers of essential services in their assault on public-sector workers.[3]

In Newfoundland and Labrador, neoliberalism has dominated provincial labour relations over the past thirty years, mimicking anti-union politics in many other provinces despite apparently different local contexts. Attacks on labour have occurred in provinces where the political system is much more polarized, as demonstrated in the chapters on British Columbia and Saskatchewan. Of course, the case of historically centrist Ontario (chapter 6) and the experience of the Common Sense Revolution is an example of historical moments where an abrupt rupture takes place where pragmatic centrism is displaced by rigid neoliberal ideological conviction.[4] In Newfoundland and Labrador confrontations with public-sector unions occurred against the backdrop of imposed "lean production" methods in important industrial sectors such as forestry. However, focusing on the relationship between provincial governments and their unionized employees reveals the broader dynamic and hegemonic nature of neoliberalism. Neoliberals have attempted to build local support by emphasizing that people might take charge of the manner in which globalization has affected them locally.[5] Neoliberal governments have also incorporated unions in strategic partnerships with employers so long as their goal is to enhance participation in international markets. Newfoundland and Labrador governments have pursued both strategies, but their most important tactic has become to play on a sense of provincial grievance about long-term economic underdevelopment through often neo-nationalist conflicts with the federal government and multinational corporations, especially in the offshore oil sector.

From 1979 to 2003, the province's poor economy meant that governments engaged in a conventional assault on public-sector unions. Under premier Danny Williams (2003 to 2010), the government continued to beset public-sector workers. The advent of impressive offshore oil revenues meant that the premier appeared to contradict the long-term pattern of the assault on labour, but Williams pursued a subtler neoliberal agenda. In some cases, such as in a pay equity settlement with healthcare workers in 2006, the government saddled unions with the direct costs for administering compensation. From 2006, the Williams government spent more money on public-sector workers, but a significant aim of new collective agreements was to entrench a more market-oriented approach to compensation. A template settlement with the Canadian Union of Public Employees (CUPE) was the first manifestation of this new market orientation. Finally, the provincial government's bargaining has attempted to foster divisions among the members of collective bargaining units. In the case of the Newfoundland and Labrador Nurses Union (NLNU), the government secured a collective agreement in 2009 at the expense of benefits for extended earnings losses by nurses injured on the job. The government also attempted to undermine the Newfoundland and Labrador Medical Association (NLMA) by cutting side deals with some of its members and questioning the right of the association to speak on behalf of its members in bargaining. In many ways, the premiership of Kathy Dunderdale (2010–14) represented a continuation of Williams's policies, especially on negotiations with its public workers.

The Context of Neoliberalism in Newfoundland and Labrador

Ongoing economic, environmental, and social crises in Newfoundland and Labrador's traditional primary resource sectors fostered neoliberalism in the province. Part of one of the world's earliest global industries, the cod fishery had unevenly transformed into a hybrid of labour-intensive, small-boat inshore fisheries and more capital-intensive offshore fisheries and plant processing. Significant alternative rural employment to production for continental fresh/frozen markets never materialized. Throughout the 1960s and 1970s, the provincial government permitted more fish plants to open as a means of economic development. The provincial and federal governments encouraged small-boat fishers to invest in larger boats and more efficient fishing gear, and the result was tremendous over-capacity in the fishing industry. Over-fishing ensued and contributed to the moratoria on ground fisheries in 1992.

Although the federal government provided limited compensation programs to fishers and plant workers who lost employment after 1992, they could not stem significant emigration in the twenty years that followed. Newer fisheries for species such as snow crab have developed, but they are more capital-intensive operations, making it difficult for individuals to enter the market. The fewer fishers who survive in these new commodity markets have become small-scale capitalists, despite their representation by the Canadian Auto Workers – Fishers, Food, and Allied Workers. At the federal level, post-1992 fisheries management became more explicitly neoliberal, emphasizing the downloading of more management responsibility onto representatives of fishers and fish companies through participatory co-management bodies.[6]

As in British Columbia and Quebec, the forestry industry, at least in the pulp and paper mill towns of Grand Falls (now the amalgamated town of Grand Falls–Windsor) and Corner Brook, also experienced neo-liberal restructuring and an assault on labour. Industrial forestry began in earnest with the opening of a massive pulp and paper complex in Grand Falls in 1909 and one in Corner Brook in the 1920s. Throughout the 1950s, the companies of both towns shared a paternalistic approach in their relationships with their workers and unions. Both companies offered wages, job security, and working conditions that compared favourably with those available to most people throughout Newfoundland. While this company paternalism melded into post-war Fordism, it was partially at the expense of the far greater number of poorly paid loggers who supplied the mills. The paper companies often advanced credit to allow individual loggers to purchase power saws, thereby increasing their ability to cut and earn more in the prevailing piece-rate system in the forests. However, this early form of mechanization permitted a reduction of the logging labour force by two-thirds between 1951 and 1971. As the demand for newsprint fell after 1980, local paper companies tried to remain competitive through drastic restructuring, which included shuffling corporate ownership; reductions in employment levels and benefits; more contracting out; and a shift to unorganized workers in logging. Mechanized harvesting has eliminated jobs while stressing wood supplies. In Bowater's case, it withdrew from Corner Brook in 1984.[7]

Oil is the most important natural resource commodity currently shaping the political economy in the province. From the first exploration for oil offshore in the late 1960s, the dream of an oil and gas boom dominated Newfoundland and Labrador: premier Brian Peckford initially came to power in 1979 as the voice of younger Newfoundlanders and Labradorians who wanted more provincial control over natural-resource development, and he fought for maximum provincial benefits from offshore oil development. The year Peckford became premier was also when Chevron Standard Limited had its first major oil find at the Hibernia oil well, located 350 kilometres east of St John's on the Grand Banks. Yet poor international prices for oil and a bitter jurisdictional dispute with Ottawa over the offshore-oil sector delayed the development of oil production until the early 1980s.

Although the Newfoundland government had lost its jurisdictional dispute with the federal Liberal government of Pierre Trudeau, the Peckford government and the federal Progressive Conservative government of Brian Mulroney signed an agreement in 1985 to jointly manage the development of offshore hydrocarbon resources. The agreement accepted the Newfoundland and Labrador government's equal say over the management of offshore oil and gas resources through a Canada-Newfoundland Offshore Petroleum Board. The agreement also recognized the province's right to collect revenues from the exploitation of those resources as if it took place on land. Soon after this Atlantic Accord, the provincial and federal governments announced that Mobil Oil would establish oil production at the Hibernia site by using fixed concrete platforms. Furthermore, the federal government agreed to contribute 75 per cent of a $300 million development fund to allow the province to prepare for industrial development. The developments in the offshore oil sector contributed significantly to Peckford winning a general election in April, but it would be another twelve years before commercial oil production was ready.[8]

With actual oil production still far in the future, Newfoundland and Labrador continued to face serious economic problems. Vulnerable to threats of industrial shutdowns during a time of international recession, the government assaulted organized labour. In 1984, the government had passed Bill 37 to void a Labour Standards Board decision in favour of Wabush iron ore miners, members of the United Steelworkers of America. The board had found that Wabush Mines had failed to give proper notice to miners in 1981 during a layoff and had ordered it to pay $750,000 in back wages. Similar cases were pending against Fisheries Products International and Advocate Mines at Baie Verte. The bill eliminated the need for more notice and appeased Kruger Corporation, which was considering purchasing the Bowaters mill at Corner Brook. Although the province offered Kruger $64 million in financial assistance, the company agreed to take over the mill only because Bill 37 relieved it of $6.7 million in back wages that had been owed to improperly laid-off Bowaters workers.[9]

Global recession, hurting primary-sector industries, and the beginning of federal retrenchment meant that the Peckford government did not have the resources to deal with burgeoning social problems. At the same time that British Columbia and Saskatchewan were imposing their own neoliberal rollbacks (chapters 8 and 10), the Peckford government began rolling out its own draconian attack on public employees. The government fought with the Newfoundland Association of Public Employees (NAPE) over Bill 59, an Act to Amend the Public Services

(Collective Bargaining) Act, 1983, passed in 1984. This bill permitted the government to designate up to 49 per cent of public-sector union members as essential public employees and limited their right to strike, especially by outlawing rotating strikes. Having failed in challenging Bill 59 in the Supreme Court of Newfoundland, 5,500 public-sector workers went on strike on 3 March 1986. They returned to work after a month, but 5,000 went on strike again in September when the government made clear it was going to take full advantage of Bill 59. The Canadian Labour Congress (CLC) became involved, and Bill 59 eventually earned the criticism of the International Labor Organization (ILO) of the United Nations.[10]

Its popularity waning, the Progressive Conservative government agreed to demands by NAPE, CUPE, the NLNU, the International Brotherhood of Electrical Workers (IBEW), and the Association of Allied Health Professionals (AAHP) to adjust the pay scale to equitably compensate health-care workers. The pay equity measure was not enough to ameliorate the acrimony lingering from the public-sector strike of 1986, which contributed to the Progressive Conservatives' defeat at the hands of Clyde Wells's Liberals in the 1989 general election. Although the Hibernia project was about to begin, the provincial economy was still in trouble. Unlike the more populist Peckford, Wells was a dedicated neoliberal, committed to the private sector and government retrenchment as the best means to promote economic development. Particularly disturbing for the mostly female workers in health care, the government cancelled the payment adjustments that would have secured the promised equity for 5,300 women in the health-care sector, arguing that the province's financial troubles at the time justified it. In 1991, the Wells government's austerity program challenged public-sector unions. The provincial budget contained massive cutbacks in government spending and wage freezes for public employees. In many cases, the government reneged on union contracts.[11]

Led by NAPE, the public-sector unions relentlessly followed the premier with a "Clyde Lied" campaign and decried the government's introduction of Bill 16, the Public Sector Restraint Act. A coalition of unions mounted a legal fight against the Wells government, but it defended the budget because it could not afford a $114 million deficit, of which it was saving about $55 million by its actions. Although the union movement's solidarity in opposition to Wells was unprecedented, it failed to deter the government's continued austerity measures in subsequent budgets. Despite granting small public-sector wage increases, the succeeding government of Brian Tobin continued to wage public battles with its unions, especially the nurses.[12]

Better labour relations appeared to be developing in the growing offshore-oil sector. During the construction phase of the Hibernia platform (which began in 1985), the Newfoundland and Labrador government used a special project order to facilitate a collective agreement between a consortium of unions, the Oil Development Council (ODC) and an association of employers for the project, the Hibernia Employers' Association (HEA). The key agreements for all parties were no strikes, lockouts, or other job actions, and the submission of disputes for expedited settlement or arbitration.[13] The members of the ODC came to believe that the multiparty agreement was too complicated for future organization of platforms and rigs, arguing instead that one union organize these workplaces at sea in the interest of safety and orderly development. Such a view accorded with that of Morgan C. Cooper, who had been appointed by the Tobin government to make recommendations for labour relations in the offshore sector. Cooper's subsequent report drew on the tripartite leanings of the Labour Relations Working Group (LRWG), formed in 1996 and composed of senior government, employer, and union representatives. The LRWG accepted the legitimacy of collective bargaining so long as unions cooperated with employers and government in producing a secure environment conducive to private-sector growth. Cooper's report argued that unions had come to accept perspectives such as that outlined by the LRWG, including giving up the right to strike for arbitration in a first-contract situation. As a result of the report, the government designated the Hibernia platform as a unionized project by an amendment to the Newfoundland and Labrador Labour Relations Act in 1997. Eventually, the amendments and subsequent Newfoundland and Labrador Labour Relations Board rulings allowed the Communications, Energy and Paperworkers Union of Canada (CEP) to organize the Hibernia workers in 2001.[14]

The government's actions facilitated unionization in an industry notorious for its opposition to collective bargaining, and assisted the CEP in what would otherwise have been a potentially divisive and confusing multi-employer and multi-bargaining unit industry. For all this, the CEP, like the unions involved in the LRWG, had accepted significant limitations on their collective bargaining rights (particularly the right to strike in a first-contract situation) in the interest of fostering industrial development. Such limitations were part of the Fordist post-war settlement, but their extension into the neoliberal era represented a considerable undermining of organized labour's autonomy. By 2001, the serious economic problems that continued to face Newfoundland and Labrador led officials from the provincial government into partnership with representatives of the business community and of the province's major labour organizations, including the Newfoundland and Labrador Federation of Labour (NLFL), the NLNU, the NLTA, and the Newfoundland and Labrador Building and Construction Trades Council. These representatives constituted a Strategic Partnership Study Group, which developed a Strategic Partnership Initiative (SPI). The goal of the SPI was to promote collaboration rather than confrontation between government, business, and organized labour, prioritizing strategic policy over collective bargaining as the way to improve society and the economy. The province's labour movement took a view similar to that of the union federations in Quebec: it was better to cooperate with employers and the government to preserve some voice for labour in a public discourse shaped by neoliberal precepts about market competitiveness.[15]

Neoliberal Shifts in an Oil Windfall Economy, 2003–14

From the Peckford government to the last Liberal administration of Roger Grimes, public-sector unions experienced the hallmarks of the "lean state": back-to-work legislation, layoffs, wage freezes, and significant limitations on their right to strike in periods of retrenchment. When Danny Williams's Progressive Conservatives won the general election of 2003, provincial public workers faced a premier who sought to consolidate the government's assault on the public-sector unions.[16] Revenue and economic development flowing from offshore oil production stimulated the provincial economy somewhat over the next year, but Newfoundland and Labrador still had a massive public debt and a growing annual deficit, which the new premier was determined to bring under control. On 5 January 2004, Williams announced a projected increase in the province's deficit from $666 million to $827 million. In the premier's mind, this fiscal situation meant no wage increases for public-sector unions in the near future. The address brought an immediate response from a coalition of labour organizations: NAPE (now known as the Newfoundland and Labrador Association of Public and Private Employees), the NLTA, CUPE, NLNU, Royal Newfoundland Constabulary Association

(RNCA), Association of Allied Health Professionals (AAHP), IBEW, Newfoundland and Labrador Federation of Labour (NLFL), and the CLC. Together, these unions met to coordinate a response, criticized the government's usage of a wage freeze to open collective bargaining, and forecasted a massive public-sector strike.[17]

The premier did not back off. Williams's apparent election promise of no significant cutbacks in the provincial civil service was not what public-sector unions had hoped. Finance minister Loyola Sullivan's spring budget planned for major jobs cut and a two-year wage freeze to help reduce the provincial deficit by $280 million. Leo Puddister, the president of NAPE, called the budget a "'major attack' on workers." The finance minister defended his government by saying that most of the job losses would be through attrition and retirement rather than through actual layoffs. The government targeted 4,000 positions for elimination, but only 217 layoffs actually took place, with other positions being eliminated by non-replacement of vacated positions.[18] At midnight, 31 March, about 20,000 members of NAPE and CUPE went on strike when the unions and the government failed to agree on wage increases. The unions had bargained for 1.5 per cent wage increases in 2004 and 2005, to be followed by 3 per cent increases over the next two years. Williams's government offered a two-year wage freeze followed by a 2 per cent increase in each of the next two years, and contemplated back-to-work legislation. Wayne Lucas, the provincial president of CUPE, asserted that the government was attempting to break the unions.[19]

As the strike wore on, the government faced demonstrations and vocal public opposition, and CUPE and NAPE had the support of the provincial labour movement, including the nurses' union and teachers' association. While much of the clerical staff of the government was on strike, the host of licensed practical nurses, laboratory and X-ray technicians, and school and hospital custodial staff on the picket line became a serious public inconvenience. As early as 5 April, the premier speculated that back-to-work legislation might be necessary, and took this action on 26 April. The government forced public-sector workers to accept the two-year wage freeze, and offered 2 and 3 per cent per year increases over the next two years. The imposed settlement cut workers' sick leave benefits by about half and promised penalties of about $25,000 per day for union leaders who encouraged their members to disobey the legislation, and fines of $250,000 for any union that continued to strike.[20]

Williams's reputation among the public-sector unions suffered as a result of what the ILO later called "harsh" back-to-work legislation. Canadian newspapers referred to the government's measure as "the toughest back-to-work legislation in Canada" and quoted Wayne Lucas as calling Williams a "miserable louse."[21] The whole affair suggested that Williams was vulnerable to losing public support. A number of well-publicized opinion polls indicated that the public blamed Williams for mistreating public-sector workers.[22] Although the labour relations scene looked bad for Williams, the public-sector unions failed to maintain pressure on his government. A local newspaper editorial pointed out that, with most of a four-year mandate ahead, the premier had plenty of time to take measures that would make the public forget what his government had done to NAPE and CUPE.[23]

Williams sidestepped public anger about his treatment of the public-sector unions by fighting with the federal government and oil companies. In the fall of 2004, Williams engaged in a public battle with prime minister Paul Martin over the federal government's clawing back of offshore oil revenue through reductions in equalization payments. The premier engaged in the classic dodge of picking a fight with Ottawa, but he also burdened Martin with some of the responsibility for the provincial debt problems that had led to the wage freeze earlier in the year. Williams tapped a strong political undercurrent of provincial discontent with federal policies, following his predecessors in blaming Ottawa's early neoliberal retrenchment policies for downloading extra financial burdens onto the province and thus prompting some of Newfoundland and Labrador's cutbacks.[24]

By 2005, the premier rehabilitated his public image by taking the guise of a scrappy defender of Newfoundland and Labrador interests – just the sort of provincial premier to take on the federal government and big oil companies. Williams adopted a more conciliatory approach to public-sector unions and surprised everyone by his stance on the long-standing pay equity dispute early in 2006. In October 2004 the Newfoundland and Labrador government had won a unanimous ruling from the Supreme Court of Canada backing its decision not to pay a 1997 arbitration ordering the government to honour a pay equity settlement for women workers in the health-care sector.[25] The Supreme Court ruled that the provincial government's deficit problems meant that it did not have to redress the violation of these women's equity rights until it had the financial means to do so. The Supreme Court's decision "introduced a 'fiscal crisis' exception to the basic proposition that dollars should not trump human rights."[26] In doing so, the Supreme Court held up a more individualistic and market-based concept of equality over a substantive view that valued the potentially redistributive function of the state in sharing wealth. Women from the NLFL, NAPE, the Provincial Advisory Council on the Status of Women, and the National Action Committee on the Status of Women called on Williams to pay the approximately $80 million that was due to about 6,000 women in the health-care sector, arguing that equal pay for equal work was a fundamental human right.[27]

On 23 March 2006, Williams took many in the province by surprise through an apparently magnanimous announcement of a $24 million *ex gratia* payment to resolve the pay equity issue. Williams stated that the issue was a "black mark" against Newfoundland and Labrador, and that he was responding to a suggestion from the original five unions involved in the controversy that such a payment would improve public-sector labour relations.[28] The deal was a good one for the province; some estimates put the cost of making the deferred payments with compound interest much higher than $80 million. Almost immediately, some representatives from women's centres in the province questioned the right of the unions to accept a settlement that meant women who originally thought they deserved as much as $20,000 in their equity settlements would now get only between $1,200 and $1,300.[29]

Williams's about face on pay equity appeared to suggest that the fiscal crisis noted by the Supreme Court was lifting. The pay equity decision reflected the fact that offshore oil development was finally generating significant economic growth: international market conditions led to unprecedented high prices for oil, even as production in Newfoundland increased.[30] As a result, in 2005–6 the Newfoundland and Labrador government recorded its first budget surplus. In 2008, Statistics Canada proclaimed that Newfoundland and Labrador had entered a new era of prosperity on the strength of its oil exports.[31] Much of this good economic fortune has been attributed to the cyclical but steady rise in total oil revenue (see figure 1.1). Oil projects accounted for more than $5 billion in royalties between 1997 and 2008, and by 2009 such funds accounted for roughly 28 per cent of the province's revenue, supplemented by growing revenue from iron-ore and nickel mining.

Figure 1.1. Revenue from "Oil Boom": Newfoundland and Labrador, 2000–9

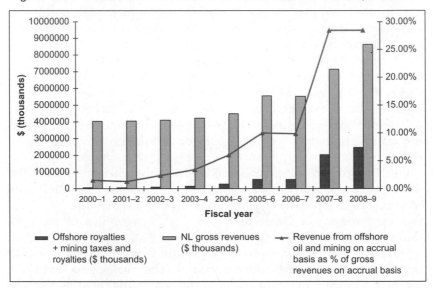

Sources: Public Accounts of Newfoundland and Labrador 1997–8 to 2008–9, volume 1; 2010 Provincial Budget 2009–10 revised and 2010–11 forecast

Yet the improving fiscal situation of the province did not end neo-liberal labour policies; rather, these policies took a new form. The Williams government insisted that unions administer the decision over who received pay equity money. This condition downloaded the cost of what Carol Furlong of NAPE called a "mammoth undertaking" onto the labour organizations. Over the next few years, NAPE and the other unions involved had to unravel the taxation implications of the payments with the Canada Revenue Agency, sort out a formula for paying everyone fairly, and ensure that payments reflected the individual classifications of the many workers who were involved. In later commenting on how time-consuming it was to ensure that the payments took place properly and to prevent future lawsuits by workers, Furlong remarked ruefully, "I can understand now why the premier handed it over to us."[32] The pay equity settlement was consistent with the overall process of neoliberalization in the province because the government cut much of its financial liability to working women while also privatizing the expense of administering the settlement.

Although the equity agreement created problems for the unions concerned, it appeared to be an example of how Newfoundlanders and Labradorians were going to benefit from Williams's blending of populism, regionalism, neoliberalism, and nationalism in the search for greater financial benefits from Ottawa and oil companies. The premier had a talent for using public battles with outside interests to maintain political popularity. A public skirmish with Paul McCartney over the seal hunt on CNN in 2006, for example, was popular within the province. However, Williams's public battles with international oil companies over better royalties and an equity stake in developments such as the Hebron oilfield made him into a star. In January 2007, the *Globe and Mail*'s *Report on Business* referred to Williams as "Danny Chavez" in an attempt to compare him to the populist-leftist Hugo Chavez of Venezuela. Although Williams may have resented the comparison, it emphasized the premier's desire to stand up for the province's economic interests. While prime minister Paul Martin had agreed to a new Atlantic Accord to prevent the province from losing oil revenue to equalization claw backs, prime minister Stephen Harper's decision not to honour the new provision in 2006 gave Williams another outsider to campaign against. With oil revenues and his popularity rising, the premier was able to announce in the late summer 2007 that oil companies had yielded to his demands for an equity stake in the Hebron–Ben Nevis oilfield and the White Rose oilfield expansion. His Progressive Conservatives won the 2007 election with forty-eight out of fifty-two seats in the House of Assembly and almost 70 per cent of the popular vote.[33]

The windfalls of oil nevertheless led public-sector unions to expect that the provincial government would ease its neoliberal agenda. Unions that had supported NAPE and CUPE in their 2004 strike also hoped that Williams's work on the Atlantic Accord would improve conditions for their members. The NLNU, for example, had responded to the legislated end of the NAPE-CUPE strike by deciding not to serve notice of its intention to bargain. Under provincial law, the lack of notice meant that the nurses' collective agreement extended by one year from June 2004. The AAHP made the same decision, as did teachers in the NLTA, whose contract would have expired in August 2004. The NLNU concentrated on lobbying the province for better funding of health care and hoped that the accord would provide more revenue to allow this funding to take place. In the NLTA's view, the agreement between Martin and Williams would provide another $2 billion or so in revenue to Newfoundland and Labrador, making a wage freeze unnecessary. Finance minister Loyola Sullivan argued, however, that the province still had an overall debt of $11.5 billion and as a result, the NLNU eventually accepted a small salary increase of 0 per cent in the first year of its new collective agreement and 3 per cent in each of the following two years.[34]

The growing boom in revenue from oil and mining meant that the public-sector unions began to court the Williams government, hoping for more spending on policies that would address their concerns and provide better compensation for their members. The spring 2007 budget significantly increased the minimum wage to $8 per hour. Reg Anstey, president of the NLFL, praised the budget for its $25-million fund to attract business, $6.7 million for investment in skilled trades development, income tax, and fees cuts, and money for health and education.[35] A bitter opponent of the government just three years before, Wayne Lucas, president of CUPE, began to laud the government's increases to the minimum wage and improvements to the pension plan for public employees, and noted that the premier "has given public sector workers a reason to be optimistic about the upcoming round of provincial bargaining."[36] Danny Williams supported improved wages for these workers during the election campaign in 2007. Over the next few years, the provincial government also raised the minimum wage to $10 per hour, the highest in the country, and invested in labour-market development and poverty-reduction strategies to support the entry of more people into the workforce. The SPI has evolved into a full government agency and serves as a forum in which the labour movement, employers, and the government may "discuss human resource issues."[37] As Peter Graefe demonstrates in chapter 5, the Newfoundland government's social policy resembled that of the Parti Québécois government in Quebec in the late 1990s, which proposed that policy should be more market-friendly and competitive and should concentrate on open labour-market participation by assisting vulnerable groups such as children living in poverty.[38]

Despite this apparent largesse, Williams, cloaked in nationalist garb, remained a keen supporter of neoliberalization in the province. For example, although his minister of fisheries, Tom Rideout, was critical of Fisheries Products International's attempt to force wage rollbacks at its processing plant in Marystown, Williams argued that workers should feel lucky to have jobs, even at lower wages, in such a "competitive labour market."[39] However, the premier saw the political capital in taking on a multinational corporation, particularly when it was clear that its operations in the province were likely to fold. Such was the case with the AbitibiBowater paper mill at Grand Falls–Windsor. Its forerunner, Abitibi-Consolidated Inc., had reviewed its mills at Stephenville and Grand Falls–Windsor in 2005. It ultimately decided that power costs at the Stephenville mill made it too uncompetitive, and in the absence of significant concessions from its unionized workers, it closed the mill in 2007. The company wanted to close one of the paper machines at the Grand Falls–Windsor plant, but provincial legislation tied its timber rights to the machine's continued operation. Abitibi-Bowater blamed much of the troubles of its remaining plant on high labour costs.[40] In 2008, the CEP local rejected a company-restructuring plan, which asked for cuts in pensions and benefits in addition to lay-offs, leading the company to announce that it would shut down the plant. The province responded with legislation to take back the water, timber, and land rights that had been provided to companies since the original 1905 charter.[41]

The government partially justified this expropriation by saying that it was not about to see a multinational corporation continue to benefit from provincial natural resources such as hydro power when it was putting so many people out of work. In the same year as the government appeared to be standing up for the working people of Grand Falls–Windsor and the surrounding area, it cemented a collective agreement with one of its most vocal opponents from the 2004 public-sector strike. In 2008, the government signed an agreement with CUPE, giving an 8 per cent wage increase to its members in provincial hospitals and school boards in the first year of a four-year deal, with 4 per cent raises in each of the next three years. Overall, CUPE workers received an approximately 20 per cent wage increase over four years. Ninety-five per cent of those CUPE members who voted ratified the deal, which also included increases in shift differential pay and standby premiums as well as special benefits for specific groups of workers, such as a better clothing allowance for Housing and School Board employees.[42]

NAPE was unhappy with what it perceived to be concessions made for the wage increases in what became known as the CUPE template. CUPE members had accepted a reduction in benefits for injured workers, but the provision that most bothered NAPE was CUPE's recognition of the government's prerogative to use market differential payments to recruit and/or retain workers in more remote parts of the province or in areas in which skills were hard to find. On 4 November, NAPE issued a public statement that CUPE's concession meant that it had accepted that the provincial government did not have to give equal pay for equal work. The next day, CUPE delegates to a convention of the NLFL walked out in protest against what it saw as the disrespectful tone of the NAPE statement, and Wayne Lucas denied that his union had engaged in concessionary bargaining. In fact, Lucas defended the government's position, stating that localized labour shortages justified market differentials in pay. NAPE maintained that the CUPE template meant significant concessions for NAPE members, but it accepted much the same deal in December, ratifying it in February 2009.[43]

The premier warned any other public-sector unions seeking more that even the conditions of the CUPE template might be taken off the table if the economy worsened. The NLTA stepped into line quickly, accepting essentially the same deal as CUPE's,[44] but the province's nurses were another matter. Williams warned that the nurses' union would have to accept the CUPE template, but the NLNU had special demands. In May, the NLNU's president, Debbie Forward, criticized the provincial budget for doing little to encourage nursing education and recruitment in the province, and recommended that the government guarantee full-time, permanent jobs to all graduating nurses.[45] The NLNU did not believe that the CUPE pay raise template would be enough to solve the unique problems facing the province's nurses. Forward argued that the government should have been negotiating on a number of issues, including a wage raise of 12 per cent per year in a two-year contract that would make nursing wages in Newfoundland and Labrador competitive with the rest of Canada. However, the government would also need to provide funds for hiring extra support staff to fulfil the non-nursing work nurses had taken on.[46]

In November 2008, Williams suggested that the government might even have to withdraw the template for the nurses because of dropping oil prices.[47] Angry that the NLNU was unwilling to accept the CUPE deal as a template, the new minister of finance, Jerome Kennedy, declared that the nurses had to accept the government's offer or face being legislated back to work under an imposed settlement. One press commentator called Kennedy's threat "a total mockery of the collective bargaining process, of pre-empting the nurses' right to strike."[48] Despite its stance on the nurses' demands, the Williams government continued to accumulate political capital by its struggle with AbitibiBowater. In the spring of 2009, the government stepped in to pay workers when the corporation suspended the pension benefits and severance pay it owed them, earning much public support from Wayne Lucas for doing so. On 19 May, on the eve of a possible strike by the NLNU, Williams announced that his government would make good on the money owed by AbitibiBowater, and that the funds would come out of the compensation for expropriation.[49] It is notable that Williams offered more help to the largely male constituency of unions who could be portrayed as yet more Newfoundland victims of an external nemesis than he had given to the largely female workers in the case of the pay-equity settlement of 2006.

Whether or not there was an explicitly gendered basis for Williams's particular form of neoliberalism awaits further analysis, but he and his senior ministers were clearly angry with the continued opposition of the predominantly female membership of the NLNU. In February 2009, the NLNU asked the government to consider an 8 per cent per year wage increase in a two-year contract.[50] However, the nurses' union could not accept, as had CUPE, contract language that would allow employers to pay higher wages to recruit nurses to the province and to retain them in more remote areas. The NLNU argued that this "market adjustment language ... would allow government to pay an individual nurse higher wages or benefits than other nurses already working in the same area in order to recruit or retain that individual." The union further rejected a government demand for an "extended earnings loss provision" that would provide it with the right "to terminate nurses deemed to be permanently disabled, as a result of work, after two years of them receiving full extended earnings loss benefits."[51] The government refused binding arbitration as a means of breaking the deadlock with the NLNU, and Jerome Kennedy argued that a 9 May rejection of the government's final offer by the NLNU membership meant that a strike was inevitable.[52] Twelfth-hour negotiations on the night of 19 May nonetheless produced an agreement that the NLNU could live with: it took the government's final offer of the salary template and agreed that the government could use bonuses to recruit and retain nurses. However, the nurses yielded the interests of their injured members by agreeing to the extended earnings losses provision.[53]

The final example of the manner in which, under Williams's leadership, the province disregarded the principles underlying collective bargaining lay in disputes with the Newfoundland and Labrador Medical Association.[54] The background was a 2008 enquiry into faulty breast-cancer testing, during which a group of pathologists and oncologists threatened to resign their positions. Particularly troubling was the threat by the province's only three cervical and ovarian cancer specialists to resign and leave the province if something was not done.[55] The controversy was public and emotional, and the government moved to break the impasse by offering the pathologists and oncologists hefty pay increases, which raised their pay about 42 per cent above that of other salaried specialists in the province. The premier knew that his "side deals" with the specialists would not go unnoticed by their fellow doctors.[56]

In the spring of 2010, the NLMA membership rejected $81 million in proposed pay raises from the government. The NLMA argued that all of its members who were salaried specialists should be paid the same as the oncologists and pathologists, and that all of its members should have parity with their counterparts in other parts of Canada.[57] Williams attacked the right of the NLMA to bargain on behalf of its members and, in November, his government attempted its pay-equity tactic by suggesting that the NLMA take the $81 million and divide it among its members according to their area of specialization. The president of the NLMA refused, stating that the government was simply trying to pit doctors against each other.[58] The premier had acknowledged in 2008 that there was a risk of setting a precedent through his side deal with pathologists and oncologists. However, he began to accuse Rob Ritter, the executive director of the NLMA, of reneging on a promise in 2008 that the association would not consider the deals as precedents.[59]

Dismayed by the government's approach, fourteen medical specialists tendered their resignations, arguing that they deserved the same pay as the oncologists and pathologists had received in 2008. On 8 November 2010, Jerome Kennedy, now health minister, released the salaries of those resigning, prompting a local newspaper to condemn the minister for his attempted public shaming of the doctors.[60] On 25 November, relations between the government and the NLMA began to thaw with Williams's announcement of his resignation. Upon hearing of the resignation, Dr Patrick O'Shea suggested that Williams should go out with a settlement by providing essential-services legislation with an accompanying right to binding legislation to doctors in exchange for their giving up the right to strike,[61] and his offer served as the basis for a settlement in short order. The province raised its money offer by 26 per cent, and the NLMA membership yielded in return their right to strike in future for binding arbitration. O'Shea noted that a key part of the deal was the ending of the "two-tier pay system" for specialists created by Williams in 2008.[62] The new premier, Kathy Dunderdale, ordered her ministers to find an end to the dispute. Thirteen of the fourteen doctors who had tendered their resignations decided to stay. A later St John's newspaper editorial, in commenting on the better relationships between the provincial government, the NLMA, and public-sector unions, attributed previously poor relationships to Williams's refusal to take collective bargaining with the NLMA seriously, misunderstanding "the fundamental precept of a union" as he "cooked up a side deal with oncologists and hoped other specialists would simply shrug it off."[63]

Throughout the disputes with the nurses' union and the NLMA, the aggressive public posturing of Williams and Jerome Kennedy was reminiscent of the climate of "fear and intimidation" in labour relations that was a facet of political life in British Columbia, Alberta, and Saskatchewan in the 1980s and 1990s (see chapters 8, 9, and 10). Although Newfoundland and Labrador has never developed the type of "one-party state" that emerged in Alberta, it also has yet to develop any serious political contender on the left. While many provinces, such as British Columbia and Ontario, substantially undermined the position of organized labour since the late 1980s, politics in Newfoundland and Labrador has been far more defined by provincial conflicts with the federal government. Williams had become exceptionally popular through such conflict, and it gave his government the basis for a confrontational approach to labour relations. However, this line of attack did not give permission to the government to be too heavy handed in its dealings with organizations such as the NLNU and the NLMA that represented working people in the province.[64]

Premier Dunderdale's more conciliatory approach to public-sector collective bargaining may account for some of the success of the Progressive Conservatives in the 2011 provincial general election. Despite her predecessor's public battles with nurses and doctors, there is little reason to believe that the labour movement has been dissatisfied overall with the Progressive Conservatives' new version of neoliberalism. Although Newfoundland and Labrador has long had the highest union density among employed people of any province in Canada, ranging from roughly 37 per cent to just over 40 per cent from 1999 to

2010, this has never translated into political support for the New Democratic Party. Prominent labour leaders, most notably Nancy Riche, former secretary-treasurer of the CLC and NAPE member, worked for the NDP provincially, but many other labour leaders have served with either the provincial Liberals or Progressive Conservatives. Roger Grimes, for example, who served as president of the NLTA, was a prominent member of Clyde Wells's Liberal governments. In 1996, Joan Marie Aylward, who had just finished five and a half years as president of the NLNU, joined Grimes and the Liberals. Although he failed to secure the party's nomination for the District of Bellevue in 2007, Fraser March, the former president of NAPE and provincial ombudsperson, attempted to run for the Liberals in 2007. Trevor Taylor, a former member of the executive board of the FFAW and failed NDP candidate in the federal election of 2000, won a by-election for the Progressive Conservatives in 2001 and won re-election in 2003. Grimes, Aylward, and Taylor all held significant Cabinet posts in their respective governments.[65]

While the president of the NLFL, Lana Payne, was a prominent spokesperson for the NDP, the labour federation was officially neutral during the 2011 general election. The NDP did improve its standing in the House from one seat to five, but the party failed to oust the Liberals, who elected six members, as the Official Opposition. Although the NDP finished second in total share of the popular vote with almost 25 per cent (as compared to the Liberals' 19 per cent) it was not able wrestle long-held seats away from the Liberals. There were close calls, such as the near-victory of NDP candidate Julie Mitchell over the incumbent and fisheries minister Clyde Jackman in the District of Burin-Placentia West. A groundswell of local FFAW members' anger about a major fish plant closure and related exports of unprocessed fish to China failed to give Mitchell the extra forty-one votes she required to topple Jackman. Despite such local battles, the impressive share of the popular vote (56 per cent) garnered by the Dunderdale Conservatives suggests that they retained the loyalty of much of organized labour's membership throughout the province.[66] While Dunderdale's government attempted to reach out to new supporters, it also ran into a series of problems in its handling of hydro blackouts in late 2013. When she resigned as premier and as a member of the House of Assembly in February 2014, her riding swung to the Liberals. Whether this represents a transformation of provincial politics in Newfoundland and Labrador continues to be an open-ended question.

Conclusion

The Williams government's loosening of the purse strings, starting with the pay equity settlement of 2006 and extending through the CUPE template of 2008, appeared to contradict the long assault on labour that had begun during Brian Peckford's premiership and continued through Williams' confrontation with NAPE and CUPE in 2004. Although he continued to engage in bitter disputes with the NLNU and the NLMA, Williams enjoyed unprecedented popular support until he resigned in 2010. For many Newfoundlanders and Labradoreans, Williams was their little scrapper: the tough little guy taking on Ottawa and the oil companies that wanted to exploit offshore resources. By taking on these foes, Williams appeared to be securing more of the oil revenues that could be spread around the province, including on better deals with public-sector workers.

This contradiction is superficial; much of Williams's actions continued the neoliberal assault on labour in Newfoundland and Labrador, especially on public-sector workers. As all the chapters in this volume demonstrate, this is not a unique strategy in Newfoundland and Labrador but rather a central feature of neoliberal restructuring across the country. Under Williams, however, neoliberalism took a unique form. Throughout the 2000s, the provincial government began to use some of its windfall revenues to fund typically neoliberal policies aimed at improving participation in the labour market, a policy reinforced through its support of strategic partnerships with a willing and complacent labour movement, weakened by almost thirty years of defending itself. Williams's particular form of neoliberalism was also able to solve issues like pay equity by actually downloading the costs onto NAPE and the other public-sector unions concerned. The premier later tried the same tactic in his bitter dispute with the NLMA. Williams was much more solicitous of laid-off workers and pensioners who were abandoned by AbitibiBowater, because championing their cause meant that the premier could serve as their white knight jousting with a foreign corporate dragon rather than fighting with unions who were, in any event, weakened by the effective loss of important locals in central Newfoundland. Throughout his tenure as premier, the downsizing and restructuring associated with lean production in fisheries and forestry continued unabated. The oil boom generated significant revenue, but it had little impact on rural unemployment, poverty, and out-migration associated with the more pervasive neoliberal dimensions of globalization that affected these sectors.

In the public sector, the government used its better financial resources to advance another type of neoliberal labour policy. Although the CUPE template of 2008 provided public-sector workers with pay increases that would have been the envy of workers elsewhere in Canada, it permitted the introduction of market principles into pay scales and required, as in its application to the deal with the NLNU, that unions sacrifice the interests of at least some of their injured membership who were on leave from their jobs. Throughout their negotiations, nurses lived constantly under the threat of back-to-work legislation and an imposed settlement. This threat, along with Williams's attempt to undermine the NLMA's ability to bargain collectively, suggests that, although the windfall era had made it more devious, Premier Williams's labour policy was no less neoliberal than that of his predecessors.

NOTES

1 Philip G. Cerny, George Menz, and Susanne Soederberg, "Different Roads to Globalization: Neoliberalism, the Competition State, and Politics in a More Open World," in *Internalizing Globalization: The Rise of Neoliberalism and the Decline of National Varieties of Capitalism,* ed. Philip G. Cerny, George Menz, and Susanne Soderberg (Houndmills: Palgrave Macmillan, 2005), 3.
2 The quotes are from Thom Workman, *If You're in My Way, I'm Walking: The Assault on Working People since 1970* (Halifax: Fernwood, 2009), 23; see also Workman, *Social Torment: Globalization in Atlantic Canada* (Halifax: Fernwood, 2003), 29–54. On Canadian trends, see Stephen McBride, "Domestic Neoliberalism," in *Working in a Global Era,* ed. Vivian Shalla, 257–77 (Toronto: Canadian Scholars', 2006). The term *assault* originates from Leo Panitch and Donald Swartz, *From Consent to Coercion: The Assault on Trade Union Freedoms,* 3rd ed. (Aurora, ON: Garamond, 2003).
3 Workman, *If You're in My Way,* 23; Leo Panitch, "Neoliberalism, Labour, and the Canadian State," in *Working in a Global Era: Canadian Perspectives,* ed. Vivian Shalla, 347–78 (Toronto: Canadian Scholars', 2006).
4 As nearly every chapter in this volume observes, an essential feature of the turn to neoliberalism is an attack on the public sector. In part, the pervasiveness of this characteristic is a function of the political objective of neoliberalism to erode and/or transform the production and delivery of public services.
5 Cerny, Menz, and Soederberg, "Different Roads to Globalization," 3–21.

6 Sean T. Cadigan, "The Moral Economy of Retrenchment and Regeneration in the History of Rural Newfoundland," in *Retrenchment and Regeneration in Rural Newfoundland*, ed. Reginald Byron, 14–42 (Toronto: University of Toronto Press, 2002); Rosemary E. Ommer, with the Coasts under Stress Research Project Team, *Coasts under Stress: Restructuring and Social-Ecological Health* (Montreal and Kingston: McGill-Queen's University Press, 2007), 68–93; on recent neoliberal fisheries management, see Dean Bavington, *Managed Annihilation: An Unnatural History of the Newfoundland Cod Collapse* (Vancouver: UBC Press, 2010), 40–4, 79–80.

7 This restructuring led to leaner forms of production in the paper mills. See Glen Norcliffe, *Global Game, Local Arena: Restructuring in Corner Brook* (St John's: ISER, 2005); Ommer, *Coasts under Stress*, 104–10; Peter R. Sinclair, Martha MacDonald, and Barbara Neis, "The Changing World of Andy Gibson: Restructuring Forestry on Newfoundland's Great Northern Peninsula," *Studies in Political Economy* 78 (2006): 177–99; Mark McLaughlin, "Power Tools as Tools of Power: Mechanization in the Tree Harvest of the Newfoundland Pulp and Paper Industry," *Newfoundland Studies* 2, no. 21 (2006): 235–54. The preceding paragraph is based on Sean T. Cadigan, "Boom, Bust and Bluster: Newfoundland and Labrador's 'Oil Boom' and Its Impacts on Labour," in *Boom, Bust, and Crisis: Labour, Corporate Power and Politics in Canada*, ed. John Peters, 68–83 (Halifax: Fernwood Publishing, 2012).

8 Sean T. Cadigan, *Newfoundland and Labrador: A History* (Toronto: University of Toronto Press, 2009), 260–70; J.D. House, "Premier Peckford, Petroleum Policy, and Popular Politics in Newfoundland and Labrador," *Journal of Canadian Studies* 17, no. 2 (1982): 20.

9 G.S. Kealey, *The History and Structure of the Newfoundland Labour Movement* (St John's: Royal Commission on Employment and Unemployment, Newfoundland and Labrador, 1986), 202–9; Norcliffe, *Global Game*, 97–104.

10 Panitch and Swartz, *From Consent to Coercion*, 123–5.

11 Susan M. Hart, "The Pay Equity Bargaining Process in Newfoundland: Understanding Cooperation and Conflict by Incorporating Gender and Class," *Gender, Work and Organization* 9, no. 4 (2002): 355–71; Judy Fudge, "Substantive Equality, the Supreme Court of Canada, and the Limits to Redistribution," *South African Journal of Human Rights* 23, no. 2 (2007): 235–52.

12 Claire Hoy, *Clyde Wells: A Political Biography* (Toronto: Stoddart, 1992), 297–314; Brian Tobin, with John L. Reynolds, *All in Good Time* (Toronto: Penguin Canada, 2002), 165–7. Much of the discussion in the preceding paragraphs was originally developed in Cadigan, *Newfoundland and Labrador*, 271–81.

13 Gregory S. Kealey and Gene Long, *Labour and Hibernia: Conflict Resolution at Bull Arm, 1990–92* (St John's: ISER, 1993); Robert

Hatfield, "Extreme Organising: A Case Study of Hibernia," *Just Labour* 2 (2003): 19.

14 Sean Cadigan, "Organizing Offshore: Labour Relations, Industrial Pluralism and Order in the Newfoundland and Labrador Oil Industry, 1997–2006," in *Work on Trial: Cases in Context*, ed. Judy Fudge and Eric Tucker, 143–71 (Toronto: Osgoode Society and Irwin, 2010).

15 The recommendations for the SPI came from a study group composed of the NLFL, the St John's Board of Trade, Newfoundland and Labrador Chamber of Commerce, the Newfoundland and Labrador Employer's Council, and the provincial Department of Industry, Trade and Rural Development. See Strategic Partnership Study Group, *Strategic Partnership: How Business, Labour and Government Collaborate to Produce Europe's High Performance Economies* (St John's: Strategic Partnership Study Group, 2002). On the Quebec situation, see Peter Graefe, "Quebec Nationalism and Quebec Politics, from Left to Right," in this volume.

16 On the periodization of restraint, retrenchment, and consolidation, see David Camfield, "Renewal in Canadian Public Sector Unions: Neoliberalism and Union Praxis," *Relations Industrielles* 62, no. 2 (2007): 282–304.

17 Tara Bradbury Bennett, "Unions Vow to Unite in Collective-Bargaining Showdown," *Western Star*, 7 January 2004.

18 Government of Newfoundland and Labrador, "Workforce Adjustment Strategy Implemented," news release, 1 May 2004, http://www.releases .gov.nl.ca/releases/2004/exec/0511n01.htm.

19 Bradley Bouzane and Barb Sweet, "Budget Was a 'Major Attack' on Workers: NAPE Boss," *Western Star*, 31 March 2004; Anthony Germain, *The House*, CBC Radio, 3 April 2004, 09:00 EST; Bouzane and Sweet, "Labour's Love Lost: Union Leaders Outraged by Job Reductions," *Telegram*, 31 March 2004.

20 Terry Roberts, "Back-to-Work Order Imminent: Unions: Premier Conniving to Force End to Walkout, Puddister Claims," *Telegram*, 11 April 2004; "Back-to-Work Bill Tabled; Legislation Expected to Pass This Week; Stiff Penalties Await Any of 20,000 Newfoundland Civil Servants Who Defy It," *Chronicle-Herald*, 27 April 2004.

21 See, for example, the comments section of the *Thunder Bay Chronicle-Journal*, 1 May 2004, although the commentary supported the government's bargaining position.

22 Tara Bradbury Bennett, "Poll Results Show Favour for Wage Increases, Say Public Sector Unions," *Western Star*, 6 February 2004; Bradley Bouzane, "Poll Indicates Majority Supports Unions in Event of Labour Dispute," *Western Star*, 30 March 2004.

23 "Making Threats and Keeping Promises," *Telegram*, 27 April 2004.

24 Norma Greenaway, "Newfoundlanders Throw Support behind 'Danny Millions,'" *Western Star*, 11 November 2004. On the history of federal neoliberal policies in Canada, see Bryan Evans and Charles W. Smith, "Introduction: The Transformation of Provincial Politics: The Political Economy of Canada's Provinces and Territories in a Neoliberal Era," this volume.

25 Supreme Court of Canada, *Newfoundland (Treasury Board) v NAPE*, [2004] 3 SCR 381.

26 Fudge, "Substantive Equality," 237.

27 "Coalition Vows to Fight Pay-Equity Decision," *Telegram*, 10 December 2004; Jean Edwards Stacey, "Unions Launch Petition, Urge Premier to 'Do the Right Thing' on Pay Equity," *Telegram*, 9 March 2005.

28 Jamie Baker and Tara Bradbury Mullowney, "Williams Corrects 'Black Mark' on Province with $24-Million Pay Equity Payment," *Western Star*, 24 March 2006.

29 "Pay Equity: Co-ordinator Believes Unions Should Have Held Out for a Better Deal," *Aurora*, 3 March 2006.

30 For more on the relationship between international market conditions and the Newfoundland and Labrador offshore sector, see Peter R. Sinclair, "An Ill Wind Is Blowing Some Good: Dispute over Development of the Hebron Oilfield off Newfoundland," 2008, http://www.ucs.mun.ca/~oilpower/documents/illwind.pdf.

31 "Canada's New Provincial Powerhouses," *Globe and Mail*, 16 May 2008.

32 "Health-care Workers Face Wait for Pay-Equity Funds," *CBC Newfoundland and Labrador*, 4 July 2006, http://www.cbc.ca/news/canada/newfoundland-labrador/story/2006/07/04/pay-equity.html?ref=rss.

33 Alex Marland, "The 2007 Provincial Election in Newfoundland and Labrador," *Canadian Political Science Review* 1, no. 2 (2007): 75–85; Marland, "Masters of Our Own Destiny: The Nationalist Evolution of Newfoundland Premier Danny Williams," *International Journal of Canadian Studies* 42 (2010): 155–81.

34 Deana Stokes Sullivan, "Nurses Eyeing Atlantic Accord Talks," *Telegram*, 17 January 2005; Rob Antle, "Unions Wonder How Accord Money Will Affect Contract Talks," *Western Star*, 5 February 2005; Antle, "Province, Nurses Reach Agreement: Deal Follows Template of Previous Contracts," *Telegram*, 24 October 2006.

35 Moira Baird, "Something for Everyone: Budget Strikes Positive Chord with Business and Labour," *Packet*, 30 April 2007.

36 "Things Are Looking Up, Union Leader Says," *Telegram*, 1 September 2007.
37 The quote is from Reg Anstey's farewell speech as the president of the NLFL in 2008, *Beacon*, 13 November 2008. Officially "The Labour Market Sub-Committee of the Strategic Partnership Initiative (SPI)," http://www .labourmarketcommittee.ca/index.htm.
38 On the Quebec situation, see Graefe, "Quebec Nationalism and Quebec Politics."
39 Craig Jackson, "Fish Plant Worker 'Disgusted' by Premier's Comments," *Western Star*, 13 September 2006.
40 Moira Baird, "Paper Mills under Review," *Telegram*, 27 January 2005; Baird, "No Quick Fix for Mills: Union," *Telegram*, 29 January 2005; "Abitibi Subsidy Worth the Cost: Williams," CBC Newfoundland and Labrador, 27 October 2005; Rosie Gillingham and Craig Jackson, "Union Head Confident Merge Won't Affect Grand Falls-Windsor Mill," *Telegram*, 30 January 2007; "Nobody Wants to Read This, But … Former Mill Manager Weighs In on Problems, Solutions for Grand Falls-Windsor Operation," *Advertiser*, 28 April 2008.
41 Terry Roberts and James McLeod, "Government Stripping AbitibiBowater: Legislation Repatriates Company's Land and Water Rights and Expropriates Hydro-Generating Stations," *Telegram*, 3 December 2010.
42 "CUPE Deal Will Be Template for Other Unions: Williams," CBC Newfoundland and Labrador, 25 April 2008, http://www.cbc.ca/news/ canada/newfoundland-labrador/story/2008/04/25/williams-cupe .html; "CUPE Releases Details of Deal with Williams Government," CUPE, Newfoundland and Labrador Division, http://nl.cupe.ca/News/CUPE _releases_detail.
43 Wayne Lucas, "Here's Why CUPE Signed," *Telegram*, 20 December 2008; "NAPE Reaches Tentative Agreements for 11 Units," National Union of Public and General Employees (NUPGE), 24 December 2008, http://www .nupge.ca/news_2008/n24de08a.htm.
44 "Newfoundland Premier Warns Unions against Asking for Too Much," Canadian Press, 19 October 2008; "Williams Issues Warning to Unions as Economy Worsens," CBC Newfoundland and Labrador, 25 November 2008, http://www.cbc.ca/news/canada/newfoundland-labrador/ story/2008/11/25/williams-economy.html; Nadya Bell, "NLTA Reaches Agreement with Province; Kennedy Says NAPE Discussions Going Well, Not Talking to Nurses," *Telegram*, 16 December 2008.
45 Peter Walsh, "Nurses, Minister Feud: Health Minister Strikes Back at Nurses' Union," *Telegram*, 2 May 2008.

46 Clayton Hunt, "Nurses Want Conciliation," *Pilot*, 14 May 2008.
47 James McLeod, "Low Oil Prices Doesn't Change Issues: Forward," *Western Star*, 27 November 2008.
48 Bob Wakeham, "Shabby Treatment of Nurses Is Indefensible," *Telegram*, 31 January 2009.
49 Corrina Baggs, "CUPE Joins CEP as a Show of Solidarity," *Advertiser*, 7 May 2009; Moira Baird, "Formal Notice: Premier Says Province Will Make Sure Abitibi Workers Get Their Severance," *Telegram*, 18 April 2009; Dave Bartlett, "Timing of Announcement Political: Opposition; Help for Former Abitibi Workers Announced on Eve of Nurses' Strike," *Telegram*, 20 May 2009.
50 "N.L. Finance Minister Rejects Latest Offer from NLNU," CBC Newfoundland and Labrador, 2 February 2009, http://www.cbc.ca/news/health/story/2009/02/02/nurses-pitch.html?ref=rss.
51 Gary Kean, "City Nurses Join in Rally," *Western Star*, 20 May 2009.
52 Everton Mclean, "'He Will Lose': Government's Stance 'Will Destroy Health Care,' Nurses' Union President Says," *Telegram*, 10 May 2009; "Kennedy Questions Rank-and-File Nurses' Commitment to Strike," CBC Newfoundland and Labrador, 11 May 2009, http://www.cbc.ca/news/health/story/2009/05/11/kennedy-nurses-vote-511.html?ref=rss.
53 "All-Nighter Yields Last-Minute Deal in N.L. Nurses Dispute," CBC News, 20 May 2009, http://www.cbc.ca/news/canada/newfoundland-labrador/story/2009/05/20/tentative-nurses-deal-520.html.
54 While unions in Newfoundland and Labrador generally bargain on behalf of their members under the legal authority of the *Newfoundland and Labrador Labour Relations Act* (RSNL 1990, Chapter L-1), the NLMA bargains collectively for physicians under the authority of the *Medical Act, 2011* (SNL 2011, Chapter M-4.02, s 5) and the *Corporations Act* (RSNL 1990, Chapter c-36).
55 "Newfoundland Oncologists Threaten to Leave Province," CTV – Canada AM, 1 August 2008.
56 Dave Bartlett, "Deals for Doctors a Sign of What's to Come," *Western Star*, 29 September 2008; Sue Bailey, "Doctors vs the Newfoundland Government: Dispute over Pay, Workload Gets Nastier," Canadian Press, 10 November 2010.
57 Barb Sweet, "Doctors Go Public with Contract Proposals," *Telegram*, 24 March 2010; "NLMA Waiting on Government Response for Next Move: Government Says More Doctors Working in Province than Ever Before," *Telegram*, 30 April 2010.

58 "N.L. Pitting MDs against Each Other: Doctors," CBC News, 15 November
    2010, http://www.cbc.ca/news/canada/newfoundland-labrador/n-l
    -pitting-mds-against-each-other-doctors-1.872760; Barb Sweet, "Doctors Go
    Public with Contract Proposals," *Telegram*, 24 March 2010; "NLMA Waiting
    on Government Response for Next Move: Government Says More Doctors
    Working in Province Than Ever Before," *Telegram*, 30 April 2010; "Against
    Each Other: Doctors," CBC News, 15 November 2010, http://www.cbc
    .ca/news/canada/newfoundland-labrador/story/2010/11/15/nl-offer
    -divisive-1115.html.
59 Steve Bartlett, "'Things Are Getting out of Hand': Premier Concerned by
    Doctors' Rhetoric," *Telegram*, 18 November 2010.
60 "Picking Battles," *Telegram*, 10 November 2010.
61 Deana Stokes Sullivan, "Essential Service Legislation for Doctors? NLMA
    Head Suggests Binding Arbitration Entrenched in Law Could Resolve
    Dispute," *Telegram*, 27 November 2010.
62 "Doctors Reach Tentative N.L. Contract Deal," CBC Newfoundland and
    Labrador, 16 December 2010, http://www.cbc.ca/news/health/story/
    2010/12/16/nl-doctors-deal-1216.html.
63 "State of the Unions," *Telegram*, 10 December 2010.
64 On the situation in Alberta, see Steve Patten, "The Politics of Alberta's
    One-Party State," in this volume. On British Columbia, see Dennis Pilon,
    "British Columbia: Right-Wing Coalition Politics and Neoliberalism," and
    on Ontario, see Bryan Evans and Charles W. Smith, "The Transformation
    of Ontario Politics," in this volume.
65 This discussion of labour leaders' participation in the provincial
    Progressive Conservatives and Liberals is by no means exhaustive. On
    Grimes and Aylward, see their House of Assembly biographies at http://
    www.releases.gov.nl.ca/releases/2001/exec/biographies.htm. On Taylor,
    see "Taylor Ready 'to Enter New Season of Public Service,'" *Western Star*,
    31 March 2011; on Fraser March, see "Pike Takes Liberal Nomination in
    Bellevue," CBC News, http://www.cbc.ca/news/canada/newfoundland
    -labrador/story/2007/07/05/pike-bellevue.html?ref=rss. Sadly, Riche
    passed away during the 2011 campaign.
66 See "Newfoundland & Labrador Votes 2011," CBC News, http://www
    .cbc.ca/news2/canada/nlvotes2011/; and "Newfoundland & Labrador
    Votes 2011: Burin-Placentia West," CBC News, http://www.cbc.ca/
    news2/canada/nlvotes2011/#/7.

2 Politics on Prince Edward Island: Plus ça change ...

PETER MCKENNA

The tiny province of Prince Edward Island (PEI), population 144,000, has long been known for its brownish "spuds," sandy beaches, fabled story of Anne of Green Gables, and yes, electoral scandals. Given its traditional, largely rural-based and small-c conservative political landscape, the province has lagged behind other provincial jurisdictions in Canada in political and socio-economic development.[1] And it goes without saying that politics on PEI is intensely personal and unique – where sitting provincial MLAs often know many of their constituents on a first-name basis, know how their parents and grandparents customarily voted, and where ridings can be won or lost by only a handful of votes.[2]

In more ways than one, PEI is a "have-less" province (vulnerable to changes in the federal Equalization Program), with a relatively poor economic or industrial base (and a GDP of barely $5 billion), and a largely depressed socio-economic landscape. Farming, fishing, and tourism are the central foundations of PEI's economic architecture – where prices and well-heeled tourists depend upon external commodity changes and a fickle travelling public.[3] Indeed, the island is more dependent upon tourist dollars (the largest single employer in the province for some 15,000 islanders) than any other province in Canada, and thus subject to the deleterious impact of any downturn in the national and global economy. Between 2005 and 2010, PEI's tourism industry has struggled, with both tourism revenues and day-visits down by a substantial amount.[4] Moreover, potato sales – the province's most important export crop – have been declining since early 2000, primarily in response to changing U.S. import regulations and altering consumption patterns of a nutrition- and fat-conscious public throughout North America.

Through periods of national economic downturn, wrenching global restructuring, and neoliberal thinking, politics on PEI has not registered a corresponding transformation. Of course, this is not to suggest that PEI is an island onto itself and thus largely immune or insulated from turbulent economic change. Policy adjustments are made periodically, government cutbacks and frozen departmental budgets are imposed, and new ways of thinking about balancing the provincial books are attempted – but it is all done in a reluctant, piecemeal, and almost apologetic fashion. Change on PEI, however large or small, is not something that most islanders – or those whom they elect to govern them – are comfortable with. This all stems from a largely parochial political culture that has remained essentially static since the province first joined Confederation in 1873.

Given PEI's rather parochial political system, it is worth examining a series of probing, analytical questions. First, how has this static situation manifested itself in the province's political system, especially its electoral outcomes and public policy decisions (especially those in the contentious area of legalized gaming)? Second, how can one account for the fact that political, economic, and social transformation does not come easily in the "Garden Province" or "Gentle Island"? Third, has the province's general cohesiveness, at least in some important ways, minimized the impact of neoliberal socio-economic change? Given the province's general cohesiveness, the chapter concludes with some observations on why the more things change on PEI, the more they tend to stay the same – particularly from a political standpoint.

PEI Politics: The Contextual Framework

Before delving into specific examples of how neoliberal thinking has influenced two key areas of public policy – a 1994 public-sector salary rollback and province-sponsored gambling – one needs to grapple first with the underlying social, economic, and political characteristics that define and shape PEI. It is only by situating these public policy decisions within this larger context that one can fully understand why these government initiatives were undertaken in the first place. While it does not account for many of the particular provincial-level explanatory variables, the overall domestic setting does establish the wider parameters within which these micro or idiosyncratic factors were permitted to unfold. In short, it is hard to imagine the mix of individual, group, and bureaucratic variables coming into play at all in the absence of these overarching macro policy determinants.

It is worth recalling that PEI residents have the dubious distinction of living on the lowest incomes in Canada, placing them just behind Nova Scotia and New Brunswick. In 2007, median total family (two persons or more) income stood at $59,500 (compared to the national average of $70,800), and many families continue to struggle to eke out a basic existence on the island.[5] Less than 6 per cent of the population earns more than $35,000 annually, with some 20 per cent having family income of less than $25,000.[6] Complicating matters even further have been persistently high levels of unemployment (and underemployment) – lingering around 11 per cent officially in 2012. Similar data suggest that the unofficial unemployment rate on PEI hovers somewhere between 14 and 16 per cent.[7] All of this, of course, has to be seen in the context of high levels of part-time employment, significant numbers of seasonal workers, and a greater reliance on social assistance such as employment insurance benefits.

Consequently, PEI is very much dependent upon federal transfers – mostly in the form of regional development grants, Employment Insurance (EI) entitlements, and even sponsorship funds. Federal government monies, whether through the Equalization Program disbursements or health and social transfer payments, consistently account for some 40 per cent of provincial government revenues.[8] This dependence also includes federal employment creation (some 4,000 federal employees) – such as the head office for Veterans Affairs in Charlottetown, the Goods and Services Tax Centre in Summerside, and the federal Addictions Institute in Montague. In the absence of this federal engagement, there is little doubt that the provincial deficit ($75 million for 2012–13) and overall debt (which stood at roughly $2 billion in 2012) numbers would skyrocket.

Through good and bad economic times, islanders have maintained their strong ties to the land and a largely traditional way of life. Religion once played a dominant social and political role in defining how the island was governed. Today, its religious past no longer dominates provincial politics, but it still hovers (often unspoken) just below the political radar.[9] Accordingly, islanders turn out in substantial numbers for wakes and funerals, regular church attendance remains high, and the provincial Conservative Party still does well in largely Protestant areas of the province ("down east") – as the Liberals do in traditionally Roman Catholic rural regions ("up west"). Both provincial parties cultivate workers and voters from their respective religious flocks and therefore can ill-afford to raise the ire of the church community needlessly.[10]

PEI's vibrant church community goes hand-in-hand with its largely rural way of life. Indeed, PEI is the most rural province in Canada – with roughly 55 per cent of its population living in small rural communities – clinging to long-standing values like traditionalism, hard work, and community – which are manifested in an uneasiness towards people "from away" and a public belief in the sanctity of the family farm.[11] Needless to say, the combination of religion and rural life has fortified a more parochial or conservative disposition among the province's population.

The rural, conservative dynamic of the province was well highlighted in the 1986 provincial election. Tellingly, a dominant issue of the campaign revolved around the building of a plant in Charlottetown by Toronto-based Litton Industries. The governing Progressive Conservatives, under the leadership of Premier Jim Lee, had hoped that the Litton announcement – and the promise of new jobs – would boost his sagging election fortunes. But the announcement of a high-tech urban plant slated to build military radar devices created an unwelcomed storm of political controversy on the island. While Lee pointed to the need for PEI to diversify its economic base and to create new opportunities, citizens were not amused. It was viewed by some as a "non-island" product and a real threat to the island way of life (especially in the rural parts of the province), which would somehow trigger a rural-to-urban shift in the population base. Liberal leader Joseph Ghiz tried to capitalize on this controversy by arguing that the Lee government had failed to revitalize the agricultural sector, had not done enough for the fishery and job creation, and had allowed the rural roots of the province to decay. As part of his rural development platform, Ghiz promised to preserve the island way of life, its traditional values, and the sacredness of family farms. At a campaign stop in the rural town of Kinkora, Ghiz was quick to note, "When farming is in trouble, our island is in trouble."[12]

PEI's Traditional Political Culture

Politically speaking, PEI's small-c conservative bent still infuses provincial politics. Indeed, PEI was the first province in Canada to enact Prohibition in 1906 and continues to deny abortion services to island women. Yet almost every aspect of island life – given its economic weaknesses, small size, tiny population, and only twenty-seven electoral districts (many of those averaging 2,500 eligible voters) – is heavily politicized. In fact, partisan politics is in the blood of most islanders – and many grow up socialized and conditioned by political developments. Families have been attached to the same party for generations, often voting for that party (either Liberal or Progressive Conservative) consistently and religiously in both provincial and federal elections.[13]

Islanders tend to be engaged fervently in the political process – while maintaining a resistance to change – and continue to display a keen knowledge and interest in things political. As is often said on PEI, nothing can bring out the crowds like raucous political party events and solemn wakes or funerals.[14] For this reason, voter turnout on PEI is the highest in Canada, with the average for both provincial and federal elections reaching over 80 per cent.[15] Indeed, voter participation for the September 2003 provincial election – which happened on the day after Hurricane Juan's 140-kilometre-an-hour winds left the province reeling – was actually 80 per cent (down from the 85 per cent in 2000).[16]

Similar to Newfoundland and New Brunswick, the island's dominant conservative political culture has reinforced a two-party political system. Indeed, it is often said that islanders are born either Liberal or Progressive Conservative.[17] Those organic linkages are reinforced by large and efficient organizational structures, while MLAs are expected to till the electoral ground regularly.[18] The traditional parties tend to know the voting preference of almost every constituent in any riding on the island and dominate the entire election process right down to the individual poll clerks. In comparison, the island New Democrats and the Green Party each garner less than 5 per cent of the popular vote and struggle mightily because of a lack of class consciousness, a weak union movement, a rural and traditional political culture, poor financial resources, and ingrained voting patterns.[19] And the upstart Island Party, formed in early 2010, is unlikely to survive until the next provincial election in 2015.[20] Not surprisingly, then, patronage politics or the "politics of acquisition" (government contracts, political appointments, and local public works projects) continues to be a central part of PEI political life – but because of a series of minor scandals, appears to be less so under the Liberal government of Robert Ghiz.[21]

The politics of public works and infrastructure development – which encompasses road construction and pavement, highway snow removal and sanding, and the distribution of driveway gravel – is just one manifestation of patronage politics in PEI. According to one prominent island politician, the favourite saying about patronage politics is simple: "If it moves, pension it; if it doesn't move, pave it."[22] Clearly, political "treating" or favours help to grease the political wheels in the province, attracting candidates, party funds, workers, and voters, and, in part, helping to deliver election victories. But the days of blatant patronage – as opposed to the more subtle form now practised on PEI – are probably over, as voters have grown increasingly less tolerant of this type of political practice.[23]

During the April 1986 provincial election campaign, then-Liberal Party leader Joseph Ghiz pledged not to continue the tradition of parcelling out political "goodies."[24] But only a few months after the election, there was substantial evidence that Ghiz's government was heavily invested in the politics of patronage. Indeed, the PEI Human Rights Commission received over 100 complaints from former seasonal government workers who claimed that they had been dismissed for political reasons. Premier Ghiz found out quickly that the strongest opposition to unplugging the patronage machine came mostly from those within his own party – who argued that eliminating the time-honoured practice would lead to political suicide at the polls.

Ghiz eventually stepped down after more than six years in the premier's chair. In early 1993, Catherine Callbeck replaced Ghiz, becoming the first woman premier elected in a general provincial election in Canada. By mid-November 1996, however, the PCs were again swept into power with a majority government (winning eighteen seats) under the leadership of Pat Binns. Besides pledging change and the rebuilding of communities, Binns promised to deal with the province's difficult employment situation, stand up to Ottawa, and change the way government operates in PEI. But the election was particularly noteworthy for three reasons: it brought to an end ten years of Liberal Party rule; it ushered in the new system of twenty-seven single district ridings; and it witnessed the first island New Democrat elected to the provincial legislature.[25]

Public-sector unions in PEI represent 26.6 per cent of the province's total labour force, and in addition, public-sector union members make up 83 per cent of all union members in the province, and they use this strength to make their presence felt in the political arena. They have been outspoken on a bevy of issues – from purported changes to pensions and salaries to reforms to the Employment Insurance (EI) system. From a provincial standpoint, local unions have expressed opposition to changes (along the lines of a collaborative care approach) to PEI's health-care system and any embrace of a "business model," fearing possible layoffs for nurses and other health-care professionals and reduced services. In the spring of 2013, the unions stopped the government from proceeding with a scheme to link provincial MLA salaries to increases in remuneration for public-sector employees.[26]

Given the conservative and insular nature of island politics, local interest groups, the media, and even the general public can exercise some political influence on certain issues. Because some districts can be decided by a very small shift in votes, the politicization of an issue can sway political decision-makers. Funding for new hospital services, a reversal of a new government initiative in the farming sector, or a decision to end the "can ban" (which allowed the sale of plastic and aluminium cans of soda pop on store shelves instead of only bottles) have all occurred to placate certain public constituencies that have sought to influence the political process. Conversely, though, if civil society groups and the public remain largely silent or indifferent towards an issue, it can open up room for a government to manoeuvre more easily. But when domestic groups do shape public policy decisions, it is often because the provincial government is reluctant to dig in its heels and oppose them – or it is shrewdly looking for domestic political cover.

Questions over domestic political power dominate PEI because of the strength of the provincial state. Often policy decisions are made behind Cabinet doors with very little public consultation and simply presented to islanders as a fait accompli.[27] Indeed, the closing of a prominent hog plant in Charlottetown in 2008, the phasing out of eight secondary schools in 2009, the introduction of a new early childhood development program in 2010 and the 2012–13 "Plan B" realignment of the Trans-Canada Highway all generated substantial public opposition. But the Liberal government was able to weather the storm, control the media frame, divert public attention to more positive spending initiatives, and keep opponents off balance. Simply put, nothing happens on PEI from a political standpoint without the direct involvement of the provincial government or its full endorsement. PEI remains a society in which high-profile policy decisions are deliberated, introduced, and administered with little input from the general public. This is now quite similar to neoliberal policymaking in British Columbia, Alberta, Saskatchewan, and Ontario, where declining voter participation and disenfranchisement is part of a wider disengagement from formal electoral politics. As those chapters demonstrate, the changes are due largely to both the homogenizing effect of neoliberalism on policy options presented by different parties and the centralization of power in the executive of the provincial state. In the age of neoliberalism, this has resulted in deep divisions over the long-term directions of the PEI provincial state.

Salary Rollbacks and Public-Sector Protests

While PEI's economy is certainly unique in many ways – as its relative immunity to the global financial downturn of 2008 onward has amply demonstrated – it could not escape the financial and fiscal pressures of the late 1980s and early 1990s.[28] Yet when other governments in Canada were slashing social programs, closing hospital beds, and download-ing costs to municipalities, PEI was adopting a more cautious approach to unbridled neoliberal capitalism and laissez-faire economics.[29] To be sure, it was unable to insulate itself from deep and serious fiscal pres-sures brought on by sustained deficit financing and growing provin-cial debt loads. As in other provinces in Canada, it became increasingly clear – at least to those who were wedded to a neoliberal philosophy – that PEI would have to get its financial house in order to placate the bond-rating agencies, the currency speculators, and nervous foreign investors.

In her first budget presented before the 1993 election campaign, Pre-mier Callbeck introduced tough financial measures and promised to balance the provincial books by 1996. This was the first warning sign of what was in store for islanders in budget cutting and deficit-elimina-tion.[30] Indeed, the April 1994 budget created a political tsunami in PEI, with public-sector workers bearing the brunt of government austerity. . Similar to those in BC, Alberta, Saskatchewan, Ontario, New Brunswick, Nova Scotia, and Newfoundland and Labrador, public-sector workers on the island had their salaries rolled back by 7.5 per cent for anyone earning more than $28,000 (and 3.5 per cent for those making below that figure).[31] While there was some discussion of scaling back generous provincial MLA pensions – much to the chagrin of former premier Joe Ghiz – it was the decision to reduce the salaries of provincial judges that angered elites in the province. But before campaigning on the austerity budget in the next election, Callbeck resigned and turned over the reins of the party to Keith Milligan – who was soundly defeated by PC leader Pat Binns in the 1996 election.[32]

The salary rollback, known disparagingly as the "7.5 percent solu-tion," was controversial because almost one in ten islanders relied on a paycheque from the provincial government. To add insult to injury, the

Liberal government had just concluded negotiations with the public-sector unions only months before imposing its austerity agenda. The unions, which did not have a tradition of militancy in the province, were incensed that the Callbeck government ignored or broke those same collective agreements. As far as the unions were concerned, if the government was looking to balance its budget, it should do so by increasing personal and corporate taxes.[33]

On 11 May 1994 the union leadership organized a major public march that brought protestors to the doorstep of the provincial legislature in Charlottetown. Speakers for the unions addressed the 5,000 angry public servants and stated that the rollback was unfair and that the collective bargaining process had to be honoured.[34] In a particularly telling scene, once Question Period had ended at Province House, all government MLAs scurried back to the nearby Coles Building via the underground tunnel to avoid the demonstrators. Much to the dismay of the Callbeck Liberals, these sheepish actions were all caught on tape by CBC cameras, highlighting the precarious political situation in the province.[35] Later, a rattled Premier Callbeck came out to address the angry crowd and was met immediately by a chorus of boos and jeers and a handful of eggs after she turned into the legislature. She later explained that her government had little choice but to make the cuts, especially given a purported reduction in transfers from Ottawa, declaring to protesters that "this government has a responsibility to all Islanders to get our deficit under control."[36]

It was clear that the respective public sector unions would not take this sitting down – as rumblings emerged of challenging the rollback in the courts and instituting unscheduled walkouts and illegal strikes in the days and months to come. As an aside, provincial court judges obtained a ruling from the Supreme Court of Canada that the salary reduction was unconstitutional, "since it was made by the legislature without recourse to an independent, objective and effective process for determining judicial remuneration."[37] In the end, the Liberal government stood by its decision, while paying a heavy price at the polls as provincial civil servants (and a small bloc of swing voters) punished them on election day.[38]

Although the public-sector salary rollback was never officially removed by governmental fiat, new wage agreements were later signed with the Binns government. What was also interesting about the "7.5 percent solution" was how it affected civil society groups in PEI. In general, the news media covered the story as they would any other political development (as front-page news), but the slant varied some-what across the island. The local CBC station was critical in its cover-age – as was the maverick coverage in the *Eastern Graphic*. However, the island's major newspaper, the *Guardian*, took an editorial stance in favour of the rollbacks (and opposed any possible tax hikes) – remark-ing in one editorial that the 1994 budget was "aggressively moderate" and warned in another about the prospect of New Zealand's much-exaggerated mid-1980s financial crisis materializing on PEI if tough fis-cal action was not taken.[39] The Summerside *Journal-Pioneer* also tended to favour the Callbeck government, wondering whether islanders would be able to muster any sympathy for well-heeled civil servants.[40]

Other groups in PEI remained mostly quiet – including the farmer unions, the churches, and the voluntary sector. Perhaps not surprisingly, business groups such as the Greater Charlottetown Chamber of Com-merce supported the government's austerity agenda, while the unions indi-cated that they would withhold their discretionary expenditures to local retailers as part of their protest.[41] As for the general public, the sentiments were mixed, with students protesting the cuts, and letters to the editor tending to favour the public-sector teachers, nurses, and doctors. Of course, some believed that unionized provincial civil servants and teachers/professors were already overpaid and underworked – and they were most assuredly not in favour of increased personal or consumption taxes.[42]

Gambling Comes to the "Gentle Island"

Another major change to come to the island in the 1990s and 2000s was casino gambling. Across the island, there were noises of both dissent and support on the decision of the Joe Ghiz government to introduce province-sponsored gambling (specifically the highly lucrative video lottery terminals or "slots").[43] Unlike other provinces across Canada, PEI was one of the last to embrace gambling revenues as a reliable means of taming growing budget deficits and averting painful belt-tightening.[44] By early 2004, media reports began to speculate about the possibility of a new gambling facility – possibly on the property of the historic provincial exhibition grounds – being built in PEI. Given the fact that there was no casino (or even a strip club, for that matter) on PEI at that time – and that VLTs were actually pulled from corner grocery stores in the late 1990s after a referendum in Charlottetown – it is worth explor-ing why this contentious public policy decision was implemented and even expanded upon by succeeding PEI governments.[45]

As was to be expected, there was an expansive and sometimes contentious debate within the Conservative caucus over the "racino" (or racetrack with a gaming entertainment centre) proposal. Some rural members, in part for religious reasons, expressed serious concerns about the moral and ethical issues surrounding government involvement in a revitalized "gaming" facility, while others spoke about the anticipated social fallout from gambling addiction. Even the option of simply allowing the harness-racing sector to die a slow death was not purged from the internal policy discussions.[46] But others pointed to the need to sustain the industry no matter what, since it was thought to represent a key segment of island history and folklore.[47]

Significantly, PEI had been experiencing growing and persistent budget deficits in the early 2000s, as was the case with many other provinces during that period. For the budget year 2003–4, the Binns government forecasted a shortfall of some $125 million – with its 2004–5 numbers showing a deficit of some $56 million.[48] These are striking figures for a small province largely dependent upon federal transfer payments, agricultural and fisheries monies, and revenue from tourism. In order to get its financial house in order, the government undertook a comprehensive program review, made cuts to some programs and services, implemented an early retirement package for public-sector employees, and sought a reduction in government grants and subsidies.[49]

The harness-racing sector did not escape these cuts, and thus its subsidy of almost $1 million (mostly for purse pools) was eliminated. But rather than leave the industry to survive on its own, the Binns government agreed to establish a racino-type gaming facility at the historic Charlottetown Driving Park (now the Red Shores Casino). The steady stream of revenues from the 200-plus VLTs would then be distributed between the provincial government, the Atlantic Lottery Corporation, and the harness-racing lobby. A good portion of those monies would go to doubling the purses for each race card – as a means of attracting new horse-racing fans and rejuvenating the industry.

Intimately connected to all of this were the ever-present political considerations, which in this case were substantial. Throughout much of 2004 and 2005, the Binns government was struggling with a series of seemingly unending bad news stories, beginning with the failed oil drilling tests of Meteor Creek (even though the premier once predicted that it would lessen the province's dependence on outside energy sources), the closure of hospital facilities and emergency services, and a general perception of financial mismanagement (along with the questionable use of government-issued credit cards by Cabinet ministers). Most damaging to the government, though, was the sudden collapse of Polar Foods (a fish-processing company that operated several plants across the province with assistance of million-dollar government loans).[50] The government was also plagued by the critical findings of the provincial auditor general on Polar Foods, which ended up costing island taxpayers some $31 million and sending the ruling Conservatives tumbling in the polls.[51] For purposes of political survival, then, there was simply no way that the government was going to countenance the demise of the harness-racing industry at the same time.

Clearly, pressure from the harness-racing sector was important, as horse-owners made a persuasive case to members of the Binns government (and to the opposition Liberal Party). In written and oral presentations, industry representatives stressed the positive benefits from an economic, agricultural (the CDP grounds are where the provincial farm exhibition takes place every August), and tourism standpoint.[52] The whole agricultural sector is still important economically and politically on PEI, and one needs to tread lightly whenever matters affecting it arise. In addition, frequent references in the media were being made to the unsubstantiated $20 million in economic activity, the hundreds of jobs, and the valuable connection of horse racing to the province's tourism. At public forums organized by the harness-racing lobby, industry representatives stressed the need for government intervention because of their declining economic fortunes, their inability to compete with other entertainment options, and the deteriorating state of the Charlottetown Driving Park itself.[53]

Much was made of the storied history and heritage associated with the harness-racing scene on largely agricultural PEI, reaching back to the mid-1800s.[54] In a province that depends heavily on tourism dollars, the high-profile Old Home Week celebrations – the premier horse-racing event in Atlantic Canada – is still synonymous with this cherished history. Others pointed to the need to draw in more tourists through upgraded harness racing, to the hundreds of jobs involved, and to the fact that it accounted for some $20 million in economic activity.[55] Lurking in the background, of course, were claims that horse-owners on PEI had deep pockets, a strong and vocal organizational capacity, and powerful political connections to both the Liberals and ruling Progressive Conservatives.[56]

After an initial period of silence and resignation, opponents to the racino proposal began to challenge the harness-racing lobby, the provincial government, and the Atlantic Lottery Corporation. A citizens' group – appropriately dubbed Racino Watch – emerged in the fall of 2004, establishing a website, issuing press releases, and organizing public meetings. It took issue with the expected personal suffering and hardship from VLT addiction, the lack of public consultation, and the secretive nature of the whole decision-making process itself (since few had actually seen the business plan for the new racino, and Access to Information Requests were proving difficult).[57] Eventually, it called for the removal of VLTs from local bars and restaurants in Charlottetown (so as to house them all in one facility), unsuccessfully lobbied the opposition Liberal Party, and petitioned the government to conduct a study on the scope of existing gambling-related problems in the province (since the last one was conducted in 2001).

However, unlike the groundswell of public displeasure with VLTs in the mid-1990s (which triggered their ultimate removal from local convenience stores), the response from ordinary islanders was largely muted. In fact, the silence from religious denominations, local business representatives, and mental health professionals was deafening. There were sporadic letters to the editor expressing deep concern over the number of VLTs, some critical op-ed pieces, and the occasional negative segment on the local CBC television station. But the overall media reaction, especially in the province's leading newspaper, the *Guardian*, was positively disposed towards the racino proposal.

While there was some critical coverage in the pages of the *Guardian*, the editorial stance was decidedly positive. Perhaps reflecting the small-c conservative bent of the paper, one editorial nicely summarized its predisposition when it noted, "There's no business reason why the harness industry shouldn't have a chance to try to achieve independence through VLTs."[58] And after the official announcement was made in August 2004, the newspaper was even more gushing in its praise of the racino concept: "The provincial government had no choice but to endorse plans for an influx of video lottery terminals as a means of boosting the Island's two racetracks. Quite simply, the positives far outweigh the negatives."[59]

Furthermore, the reaction from the religious community – to the surprise of many – was both infrequent and tepid.[60] One government MLA said that he received just one call of a religious nature on the racino decision.[61] Still Reverend Charles Wagner was quoted as saying, "The kind of facility that government is talking about would just be a trap for people ... Can we not find a way of saving horse racing that doesn't do so at the cost of ruining people's lives?"[62] There were occasionally other critical letters to the editor and opinion pieces to the *Guardian*, but there appeared to be a general sense of powerlessness and resignation among the religious denominations.

Similarly, the general public tended to react as if it was a "done deal," and that there was little, if anything, that it could do to change things. At one public meeting, the best that critics of the racino proposal could muster was to bring out roughly two-dozen interested citizens.[63] Unlike issues that directly affect the pocketbook, the racino was seen as mostly a problem for a small segment of the population. It may have been simply another case of islanders trusting their politicians on this one and accepting gambling in exchange for a nostalgic commitment to saving horse-racing on PEI (as was done in the case of Ontario).

For its part, the opposition Liberal Party, led by Robert Ghiz, largely avoided the racino issue. While the precise reasons for doing so are not clear, it did seem that his four-person caucus at that time was split on the question. The provincial Liberals undoubtedly believed that with an election just a few years away, it would not make sense to rock the harness-racing boat. For political reasons the opposition Liberals decided not to pursue the controversial racino issue with any vigour in the provincial legislature, deciding instead to let the ruling Conservatives off the hook and to ignore the negative implications of increased problem gambling.

The Binns government itself always maintained that the new racino, given its fiscal difficulties, was the correct public policy decision to make. While the premier largely stayed away from commenting publicly on this matter (and many suspected that he was privately uncomfortable with the concept), he still maintained support for the new gaming complex (mostly for financial or fiscal reasons). For the most part, though, it was the provincial treasurer, Mitch Murphy, who pushed hard to have the racino proposal accepted and implemented. In fact, when the government first floated news of the racino, he was absolutely adamant: "It's going to be very difficult for the industry to survive in its present form."[64] He was clearly a pivotal driving force behind the idea of supporting the harness-racing sector, as was indicated when he was wildly applauded by its members in August 2004 after announcing plans for a new racino in Charlottetown. In fact, discussions about some form of gaming arrangement with the Atlantic Lottery Corporation for the Charlottetown Driving Park had already begun when Murphy was the agriculture minister (and prior to the damage inflicted by Hurricane

Juan in 2003). It is fair to say that the decision to build the racino would not have been made without the full backing of key political figures (and that fundamental political reality – more so on PEI than in other provincial jurisdictions – is perfectly consistent with the Callbeck salary rollback of 1994). In the words of one provincial MLA, "Nothing gets done on PEI unless the premier and the provincial treasurer okay it."[65]

The personal power of the premier was on full display in the 2011 provincial election. Indeed, by early October 2011, the election on Prince Edward Island was actually over before it began. And notwithstanding the hard-fought campaign of the Olive Crane–led Progressive Conservatives, the final outcome was hardly in doubt – a majority Liberal government (with the Robert Ghiz Liberals winning twenty-two out of twenty-seven ridings).[66] Just one day before the election writ was dropped, a public opinion survey placed the Ghiz Liberals almost thirty points ahead of the opposition PCs. Even on tiny PEI, that was an insurmountable lead for the Liberals, and too high an electoral mountain for the other political parties to climb.

What those polling numbers also showed was a lukewarm response to the personality and leadership qualities of the PCs' Olive Crane. It was curiously reminiscent of former federal Liberal leader Michael Ignatieff, who had a difficult time not only connecting with voters, but also convincing them that he was prime ministerial material. For whatever reason, Ms Crane just never caught on with island voters, though she promised to stay on until the next provincial election (even after party strategists sought to remove her in November 2012 and again in February 2013). But her inability to gain traction was not the result of any lack of effort, major campaign gaffe, or a poor TV debate performance. In fact, she did reasonably well in the public debate formats (even in the face of intense pressure to exceed expectations), ran a largely error-free campaign, and aggressively pushed her campaign platform.

Crane did seek to exploit what opportunities presented themselves, such as critiquing the Ghiz Liberals on the perceived rural-urban divide on PEI, where Ghiz's urban biases were pegged as largely neglecting the province's agricultural communities. But her attacks were mostly focused on the controversial Provincial Nominee Program (PNP) – where would-be immigrants sought to fast-track their Canadian citizenship by investing anywhere from $100,000 to $200,000 in island businesses – which had been mired in scandal and innuendo for more than three years. It became a noisy part of the campaign battle in mid-September, when a story broke on the front pages of the *Globe and Mail* about envelopes of money changing hands between PEI government bureaucrats and wealthy Chinese immigrants.[67] It was not long before rehashed charges of bribery and fraud became a central campaign issue, with the provincial Liberals bearing the brunt of the accusations.

The Liberals quickly went into damage control and unleashed a spin-doctoring campaign that blamed the messengers, or, in this case, the three former provincial officials who witnessed first-hand some of the dubious business surrounding the PNP. The Liberal war room desperately tried to discredit the whistle-blowers and then unwisely leaked confidential e-mail correspondence from the public servants. Clearly, the Liberal Party's bare-knuckle response was a major over-reaction (given the results of the election) and obviously sent the wrong message to the public and workers in the broader public service.

For her part, the harsh language of Ms Crane was quickly unleashed, when she glared at Robert Ghiz during the televised debate and said his performance around the PNP was "a disgrace." The day after the campaign ended, one newly elected PC member was blunt in his assessment: "My win had more to do with the premier. I was hearing at the door people hate Robert Ghiz and I believed them and they showed that tonight."[68] It was symptomatic of an unusually aggressive campaign (with admittedly mild attack ads, a negative undertone, and a personalization of electoral politics), the likes of which islanders had never seen.

By voting day, however, none of it really mattered. In fact, the *Globe and Mail's* intervention may have worked in favour of the governing Liberals, since independent-minded islanders do not take kindly to "outside" interference in their political affairs. And when voters were asked to rank the top issues in the campaign, the PNP came in fifth place (after health care and education), garnering the interest of a lowly 5 per cent of the electorate.[69] One other factor working in Ghiz's favour was the utter failure of the smaller third parties – like the Greens (registering 4.4 per cent of the vote), the Island New Democrats (garnering 3.2 per cent), and the upstart Island Party (barely polling at 0.9 per cent) – to register in any meaningful way on the political radar.

The year 2011 is memorable for a number of reasons. It represented the lowest voter turnout in sixty-five years at just 76 per cent. Although neoliberalism has challenged PEI in different ways, falling voter turnout remains a strong symptom of voter disengagement in almost all provinces and territories. More substantially, however, PC leader Olive Crane was defeated not by her campaign or her party's platform, but by the ineluctable forces of electoral history and island political culture.[70] Over the last seventy-five years, virtually every government on PEI that secured a first mandate was given a second (and even a third) in the succeeding provincial elections. And the Ghiz Liberals did not defeat themselves or give the electorate a reason to remove them from office. As a good many islanders said to themselves over the course of this campaign, "It's still the Liberals' turn." But if recent history is any indicator, all bets will be off for the next election slated for spring 2015.

The controversial 2012 provincial budget – which reflected ongoing neoliberalization – sought to reduce the size of government (slashing hundreds of public servants and seasonal workers) and to offer tax benefits to the private sector. As in other provinces, notably British Columbia and Ontario (see chapters 10 and 6), the issue of harmonizing the provincial and federal sales tax emerged. At the centre of the budget was the unexpected inclusion of a controversial Harmonized Sales Tax (HST), which would provide an injection of much-needed revenues to government coffers, including $39 million in transitional assistance from Ottawa.[71] Similar to those in British Columbia, PEI residents were strongly opposed to the HST (a 14 per cent sales tax) for imposing too high a cost on low-income islanders, including high electricity bills, and for making it even more financially difficult for workers and the poor.[72] Opposition leader Olive Crane asked the Ghiz government pointedly, "Most Islanders are already stretched to the limit. The bottom line is, this government is going to take $32 million out of the pockets of ordinary Islanders from the HST and the increased fees. It's unprecedented … how does the deputy premier believe that it's fair to pick the pockets of ordinary Islanders?"[73] In the end, however, the lure of increased provincial revenues – especially in difficult and trying budgetary times – proved too attractive for the cash-strapped PEI government.

In addition, pressures to introduce the new tax came from the business community, which argued that it was placed at an unfair disadvantage vis-à-vis other companies in Atlantic Canada that already had the tax and also benefited from the HST rebate program. The PEI Business Federation, which had been pressing the provincial government for years on this matter, was "delighted" by the planned April 2013 implementation of the sales tax.[74] Reflecting similar neoliberal arguments throughout the country, representatives from agriculture, tourism, and road-builders/heavy construction were also in favour of its introduction, pointing to increased competitiveness, a reduction in business input costs, and the establishment of a 14 per cent HST rebate on equipment purchases.[75] Elaine Thompson of the Tourism Industry Association of Prince Edward Island (TAIPEI) spoke for many businesses on PEI when she noted: "Since 2006, TAIPEI has lobbied government for a taxation system that levels the playing field for the Island tourism industry and the implementation of a Harmonized Sales Tax to increase our competitiveness."[76] To many islanders (including outspoken public-sector union representatives), though, it seemed more likely that the Ghiz government was shifting the tax burden away from corporate interests and onto the shoulders of ordinary citizens.

Conclusion

There is no disputing the fact that PEI politics remains unique, storied, non-ideological, and intensely personal. While one is tempted to say that not much changes on PEI, it would be more accurate to suggest that precious little changes politically on the island. In large part, this is because the political economy of PEI, irrespective of external shocks and globalization, does not change much at all. But it can also be explained by the relative permanency of the political, party, and electoral structures on the island as evidenced by the decisive vote against electoral reform in November 2005. What we see confirmed in these pages is a political culture that remains stubbornly consistent, status quo–like, and infused by historical experience, tradition, and rural community values.

A case could be made that both the 7.5 per cent salary rollback and the racino/casino decisions underscore the fact that the "myth of the Garden" still has some resonance on PEI. Trimming the public sector in 1994, which is largely urban-based and unionized, was consistent with a parochial mindset, the lack of a robust political constituency and influential labour movement, a desire to reduce the vulnerability of the province to outside forces (e.g., bond-rating agencies), and a predilection for fiscal conservatism (as the 2012 cuts also illustrate). Moreover, the government, the provincial bureaucracy, civil society groups, and the general public all saw the racino largely in terms of sustaining harness racing on the island, which is consistent with a traditional economy and set of values, a pastoral ideal, and a rural and agricultural way of life. This lingering image, as long-time island observer David Milne explained, "would appear to be the central paradox of Island politics; the more that change has caught up with the province and proceeded to dismantle the 'Island way of life,' the more stubbornly do Islanders (and sentimental outsiders) resist dissolution in the name of the past."[77]

In addition, controversial public policy decisions highlight the degree to which key politicians and policymakers can have enormous influence over the final outcome of political disputes. Without the firm backing of Premier Callbeck and Treasurer Wayne Cheverie, and even in the face of some caucus resistance, there is little doubt that the public-sector cuts would have been approved in 1994. Similarly, there is no disputing that provincial treasurer Mitch Murphy was instrumental in pushing through the racino proposal and, most likely, approval would not have been granted had there been a different person in this position. To be sure, it would have been rejected by the government had Premier Binns and Treasurer Murphy not championed it – and even vigorously pushed it around the Cabinet and caucus table.[78] Simply put, the overwhelming dominance of the provincial state in PEI affairs was once again confirmed by these divisive public policy initiatives (and others, like closing public schools and trimming heath-care services in the province).

One of the more interesting questions surrounding these decisions was the role, or lack thereof, of ordinary islanders. Not only was the public not consulted on these controversial matters, but when it was informed, it tended to follow a seemingly subdued response. Perhaps this general silence and apathy speaks volumes about PEI's traditional political culture and cohesiveness. Of course, whatever public discontent or backlash there is, governments on PEI are prepared to weather any storms no doubt reassured by the fact that they would be short-lived and mostly ineffectual. Why, though, was the public's voice so muted on this issue? What does this say about politics on PEI? While there is no definitive explanation, it does seem that islanders were prepared to give the benefit of the doubt to both the Callbeck and Binns governments. And since the majority of citizens on PEI were not directly affected by the salary rollback or casino gambling, they could afford to tune out much of the public discussion. Both decisions also appeared to reflect a growing sense of powerlessness, resignation, and a "well, what can I do?" attitude among islanders towards government in general – which seems to be a key part of what a neoliberal framework can foster.

In addition, it seems clear that the PEI government can, if it so wishes, aggressively push through public policy decisions with little fear of public backlash. It is questionable, moreover, if there would even be a public outcry should the incoming PEI government move to implement a similar cost-cutting rollback or to rely more heavily upon the gambling revenue stream (or to even entice

Litton Industries back to the island). In the end, both Liberal and Progressive Conservative governments believe that they can implement these decisions knowing full well that there would be some social and political fallout, but no significant electoral repercussions. Like other provincial jurisdictions in Canada, PEI has been merely following other provinces in attempting to improve its deficit picture, gain additional revenues, and implement belt-tightening measures – ostensibly dispatching concerns about the health and well-being of their own citizens to the sidelines.

This all raises an important question: has the gradual encroachment of a more market-centred approach to public policy on PEI fundamentally altered its politics? The short answer is yes and no. Clearly, the dual quests for deficit reduction and debt management have effectively given politicians and governments a ready-made excuse or even political cover to largely ignore painful societal change. While this obsession with the balancing of books has not currently altered politics on PEI, it is starting to chip away at the long-standing special relationship between local politicians and individual island voters. It may still be too early to tell how this will affect PEI's political culture or the next government – since Robert Ghiz stepped aside for personal reasons in early 2015 – but the trend is towards subjugating people's interests on the island to the bureaucrats in the provincial Finance Department. Indeed, as a neoliberal lens firmly insinuates itself in political and bureaucratic circles, one could well expect an increase in government-societal clashes in public policy (probably over cuts to health care and education). Though admittedly difficult to quantify, it has already brought a harder edge to politics on PEI, which was on full display in the 2011 provincial election. Indeed, if that election tells us anything, it seems that the province has become less caring, more closed and non-transparent (i.e., the implementation of the HST in 2013). These changes reflect the deeply ingrained and personalized politics surrounding the myths of "the Pastoral Garden Province," "the Million-Acre Farm," and even "the Gentle Island," which are sure to be challenged in the coming years.

NOTES

1 While the rural-urban split is still roughly 60:40, the number of islanders forced to abandon rural (and farming) life is on the rise.
2 Because of the smallness of the polity, politics on PEI is unique in many ways – and so, too, is the province's place in the federation. Former premier

Robert Ghiz once confided to me that he was always amazed by the fact that PEI is treated like any other province, has equal weight from a constitutional standpoint, and his input was given due consideration like all the others' around the first ministers' table.

3 Rand Dyck, "Prince Edward Island," in *Provincial Politics in Canada: Towards the Turn of the Century*, ed. Rand Dyck (Scarborough, ON: Prentice-Hall, 2003), 26–43. For a more recent treatment on island political life, see Wayne MacKinnon, "Muddling Through: The Prince Edward Island Legislative Assembly," Canadian Study of Parliament Group, December 2010, 1–42.

4 In the summer of 2010, the province sought to boost these numbers by bringing in the popular TV program *Live with Regis & Kelly*, which cost taxpayers some $750,000 for four days of coverage. Dave Stewart, "Over 12,000 Tickets Requested for Regis and Kelly Shows," *Guardian (Charlottetown)*, 3 June 2010. More recently, the provincial government has sought to diversify the economy by focusing on four key industrial sectors: bioscience, aerospace, information technology, and energy self-sufficiency. See Nicholas Oakes, "The Man with a Plan," *Atlantic Business Magazine* (March–April 2010).

5 Government of Canada, *Income in Canada* (Ottawa: Statistics Canada, 2007), 42–4.

6 Government of Canada, *Understanding the Early Years: Early Childhood Development in Prince Edward Island* (Ottawa: Human Resources and Skills Development Canada, November 2001). The Centre for the Study of Living Standards places PEI's gross national income per capita at $34,778 in 2011. See Elspeth Hazell, Kar-Fai Gee, and Andrew Sharpe, *The Human Development Index in Canada: Estimates for the Canadian Provinces and Territories, 2000–2011* (Ottawa: Centre for the Study of Living Standards, May 2012), 65.

7 Government of Canada, *Labour Market Update* (Ottawa: Human Resources and Skills Development Canada, January 2005). The province raised the minimum hourly wage to only ten dollars in April 2012.

8 On this subject, see Robert J. Jackson and Doreen J. Jackson, *Politics in Canada: Culture, Institutions, Behaviour and Public Policy* (Toronto: Pearson Prentice Hall, 2006), 96–7. For 2010–11, federal equalization payments to PEI totalled some $330 million – and remained at that level for 2011–12.

9 Dennis King, "Religion in Politics May Lose a Lot under P.E.I.'s New Electoral Reform," *Guardian (Charlottetown)*, 3 May 1994.

10 Interestingly, PEI remained the only province in Canada to preclude year-round Sunday shopping until the Ghiz government changed the law in

late November 2010 – with the Speaker casting the deciding vote in favour (fourteen to thirteen) of removing the restrictions. Typically, shops were open for business on the Victoria Day Sunday (mostly afternoons after the weekend masses) and closed down again after Christmas. See editorial, "Another Great P.E.I. Debate Bites the Dust," *Guardian (Charlottetown)*, 2 December 2010.

11 Dyck, "Prince Edward Island," 27. Of course, the number of farms on PEI has decreased dramatically – dropping by 28 per cent in the last fifteen years – from thousands in the early twentieth century to roughly 1,600 today. Jim Day, "Farmers Warn IRAC of Major Impact if Two-Tiered Power Rate System Removed," *Guardian (Charlottetown)*, 15 June 2010. Furthermore, the province's fierce attachment to independence, a stubborn streak of self-reliance, and an aversion to outside interference are all a function of what some describe as "islandness." There is also a common refrain on PEI: "For Islanders, the entire population of the entire world is divided neatly into two groups: those from here, and those from away." David Weale, "Overheard on the Island," *Guardian (Charlottetown)*, 22 June 2010.

12 Quoted in CBC Television, "Family Politics," *CBC National News / The Journal*, 18 April 1986.

13 Dyck, "Prince Edward Island," 32–3. While my students at UPEI rarely speak about voting the same way as their grandparents, suggesting that things may be changing ever so slightly, the familial connection to voting intentions is still present. But voting on the basis of personal reason or for the individual candidate is slowly gaining ground on PEI.

14 There is an old adage on PEI: "If you don't get out to vote on the Island, you're either very angry or very dead." Quoted in David Weale, *Whatever You Say: The Talk of Islanders, 1975–2005* (Charlottetown: Tangle Lane, 2005), 59.

15 Dyck, "Prince Edward Island," 33.

16 Facing Liberal Opposition Leader Robert Ghiz for the first time, Binns won a third majority government in the 2003 election – garnering twenty-three seats to the Liberals' four. But he failed to secure a record fourth government in the May 2007 election, in which Robert Ghiz won a decisive victory by garnering twenty-three ridings, while the Binns caucus was reduced to just three seats.

17 When asked during the 1986 provincial election how he was going to vote, one man deadpanned, "If I didn't vote Liberal, my ancestors would come back and haunt me." Quoted in CBC Television, "Family Politics," *CBC National News / The Journal*, 18 April 1986.

18 It is also important to note that these two parties are mainly pragmatic and programmatic political vessels and most assured are not ideologically driven.

19 See Ian Stewart, *Roasting Chestnuts: The Mythology of Maritime Political Culture* (Vancouver: UBC Press, 1994), 36–63. The island NDP did, however, garner more popular support than the struggling official Opposition Progressive Conservatives in a series of public opinion surveys in 2012–13.

20 A June 2010 survey by Corporate Research Associates put public support for the Island Party at 1 per cent. Wayne Thibodeau, "Liberal Support Drops in Poll," *Guardian (Charlottetown)*, 4 June 2010.

21 Since 2009, the lingering issue of the Provincial Nominee Program has swirled around the province. Ostensibly the program was intended to encourage increased immigration to the province. Yet the controversy stems from the government's offer to expedite Canadian visas to those immigrants looking to invest $200,000 or more in PEI businesses. While the list of companies that received the "units" of investment has not been officially identified, there is speculation that some of those companies have been friends of the Liberal government of Robert Ghiz. As PC opposition MLA Jim Bagnall explained, "If government was handing out PNP units to help their own political party and their own political people then, yes, that information should be brought forward." Quoted in Teresa Wright, "Bagnall Disappointed PNP List Not Released," *Guardian (Charlottetown)*, 5 June 2010. Also see, Wright, "Privacy Commissioner to Decide on PNP List," *Guardian (Charlottetown)*, 3 June 2010.

22 This section draws heavily from Wayne MacKinnon, *The Life of the Party: A History of the Liberal Party in Prince Edward Island* (Summerside: Williams and Crue, 1973), 60–76.

23 In early January 2007, Liberal party leader Robert Ghiz disavowed one of his nominated candidates – who had spoken at his nominating meeting about dispensing the political pork to the Liberal faithful once in power – and had him replaced over the objections of the local district party machine.

24 After winning a majority government in 1986, Joe Ghiz – who played a major role in the Meech Lake constitutional debate – was re-elected with a second majority in 1989. The PC party was reduced two MLAs in the House, while the Liberals took thirty seats.

25 Interestingly, the original meeting of the Cooperative Commonwealth Federation was held in Bedeque, PEI, in 1936. During an emotional scrum with the media on election night 1996, newly elected party leader Herb

Dickieson – who campaigned on a slogan of "Fairness for Islanders" – said, "It's wonderful. And it has certainly been a long time in coming on PEI." Quoted in CBC Television, "Painting the Province Blue and Redrawing the Map," CBC News (Charlottetown), 18 November 1996. In the 2000 provincial election, Binns extended his majority to twenty-six ridings – leaving the Liberals with just one seat. By a slim margin, Dr Dickieson was defeated in his district in the western part of the province. Since Dickieson's defeat, no other NDP candidate has set foot in the provincial legislative assembly.

26 See Teresa Wright, "Premier Backpedals on Scrapping Commission," *Guardian (Charlottetown)*, 5 April 2013.

27 Referencing that PEI has a traditional political culture is not to suggest that civil society – including an array of agricultural, tourism, fishing, volunteer, and business associations – is not seriously engaged in the political process. To be sure, they are important players in PEI, but the nature and impact of their involvement is at the discretion of the provincial government. Still, the government's reluctance to abandon the traditional industries of farming, fishing, and tourism (and to embrace neoliberalism wholeheartedly) speaks to their political importance (including their connections to political parties) in shaping the media agenda. For more on what constitutes "active civic engagement," see Theda Skocpol and Morris Fiorina, eds., *Civic Engagement in American Democracy* (Washington, DC: Brookings Institution Press, 1999).

28 This is not to suggest that PEI was completely unscathed by the recession, but there was no significant increase in unemployment or massive job losses. Chandra Pasma, "Recession Creates Poverty for PEI," *Guardian (Charlottetown)*, 4 June 2010.

29 As in other provinces, PEI saw substantial increases in food bank use – especially among the working poor, two-parent families, and young adults. There was also growth in the number of homeless shelters in Charlottetown and those relying on charities and churches to get by.

30 According to one former deputy minister at the time, Callbeck was deeply concerned about the province's credit rating and overall debt situation. According to him, "Had Premier Callbeck not acted to make her mid-course correction to the public accounts, we can only surmise what the current financial situation of the province would be now, if indeed we could have continued as a province. Not only would the public debt be insurmountable, but also the current year's deficit would be of an entirely different order of magnitude." John Eldon Green, "Callbeck's Sense of Duty," *Guardian (Charlottetown)*, 29 November 2003. In the words of the

then-education minister Keith Milligan, "At the time, we had a $65 million deficit. The two choices were either everybody was part of the solution, which was the 7.5 percent, or there was going to be 500 or 600 employees that were just going to lose their jobs outright and sent home to nothing." Quoted in Wayne Thibodeau, "Public Sector Wage Cutbacks Was Wrong Decision," *Guardian (Charlottetown)*, 8 November 1999.

31 See Rand Dyck, "Prince Edward Island," 43.

32 In his first bout of patronage, Binns summarily fired 800 government workers on the highways and replaced them with loyal PC supporters.

33 According to the then-president of the PEI Union of Public Sector Employees, Sandy MacKay, the unions had already agreed in the negotiated collective agreements to no pay hikes for a two-year period. But the Liberal government – come hell or high water – was determined to squeeze the public sector for some $23 million in salary rollbacks. See Sandy MacKay, "Let's Resolve the Myths about the 7.5 Percent Rollback Once and for All," *Guardian (Charlottetown)*, 21 January 2004. The unions never accepted the argument that the province was under any financial distress – even pointing to a substantial increase in equalization payments from Ottawa.

34 Barb McKenna, "Callbeck Faces Angry Employees," *Guardian (Charlottetown)*, 12 May 1994.

35 "Protesting Callbeck's Cuts," *CBC Radio Archives*, 11 May 1994. Protesting civil servants, nurses, and teachers yelled in unison, "No more cuts!" and carried placards reading "7.5% Hurts Everyone: This Must Never Happen Again." One speaker shouted passionately, "I can't do it alone. You can't do it alone. But together, we could stop them."

36 Ibid. Also see Ron Ryder, "P.E.I. Public Sector Unions Recall 1994 Wage Rollback," *Guardian (Charlottetown)*, 18 May 2004. Of course, PEI was following in the footsteps of Nova Scotia, which had cut back public sector salaries by 3.5 per cent in the early 1990s. Public policymaking on PEI – as was amply demonstrated in the gaming sector as well – is often borrowed from what is happening in neighbouring provinces like Nova Scotia and New Brunswick.

37 Part of SCC's ruling indicated that the salary rollback negatively affected the perception of the provincial judges' impartiality and independence from government. This information was drawn from interviews in June 2010 from David Bulger, an adjunct professor of political science at the University of Prince Edward Island in Charlottetown. Also see Doug Beazley, "Highest Court Rejects Judges' Salary Rollback," *Guardian (Charlottetown)*, 19 September 1997.

38 In a May 1994 interview with the *Guardian*, Callbeck explained her decision this way: "Certainly, I regret that we had to go at the collective bargaining but the other choice was to break the province financially … The bottom line is we haven't got the money and if we are going to get this province on a financial secure footing, we have to make difficult decisions. I believe we made the right decision." Quoted in Jim Day, "Premier Convinced Rollback Right Move," *Guardian (Charlotetown)*, 13 May 1994.

39 Editorial, "Budget Pill Eases Pain," *Guardian (Charlottetown)*, 13 April 1994; editorial, "Explain Options to All Islanders," *Guardian (Charlottetown)*, 6 May 1994.

40 Editorial, "Turning the Heat Up," *Journal-Pioneer (Summerside)*, 13 May 1994; editorial, "Uncertainty Hovers," *Journal-Pioneer (Summerside)*, 4 May 1994.

41 Jim Day, "Government Workers' Purses Will Remain Closed May 2," *Guardian (Charlottetown)*, 26 April 1994.

42 Jim Day, "General Public Fails to Show as Unions Rally over Rollbacks," *Guardian (Charlottetown)*, 4 May 1994.

43 See Peter McKenna, *Terminal Damage: The Politics of VLTs in Atlantic Canada* (Halifax: Fernwood, 2008), 155–206.

44 For a fuller treatment of this, see James F. Cosgrove and Thomas R. Klassen, eds., *Casino State: Legalized Gambling in Canada* (Toronto: University of Toronto Press, 2009).

45 In late 2009, the Robert Ghiz government agreed to have the Charlottetown facility changed from a "racino" (or a horse racetrack with VLTs) to a full-blown "casino." While there is little evidence that the Charlottetown casino has actually made any money since opening in August 2005, it continues to operate and to inflict significant social harm on the citizenry of this province.

46 But there was always the lingering political issue of what would happen to the Charlottetown Driving Park (CDP) – a major landmark in the city – if the industry was unable to fend for itself.

47 This point came up repeatedly in confidential interviews with MLAs, Cabinet ministers, government officials, and interested citizens in the spring of 2005.

48 See Wayne Thibodeau, "Province Boosts Fees to Battle Huge Deficit," *Guardian (Charlottetown)*, 31 March 2004; and Thibodeau, "PEI Deficit $125 Million," *Guardian (Charlottetown)*, 2 February 2005.

49 See Wayne Thibodeau, "Debt Crippling Province: AG," *Guardian (Charlottetown)*, 7 April 2005; and Thibodeau, "Government Wields Axe to All of Its Departments," *Guardian (Charlottetown)*, 8 April 2005.

50 It is worth mentioning that fish plant closures (and openings) on PEI are nothing new. But as wrestling ballooning budget deficits to the ground takes on greater saliency post-2012, the provincial government has grown increasingly reluctant to prop them up with taxpayers' monies. It is becoming obvious to islanders that struggling businesses will not be able to turn to the provincial government for assistance, as was often the case in the past.

51 See Wayne Thibodeau, "Premier's Support Declines," *Guardian (Charlottetown)*, 8 December 2004.

52 See Ron Ryder, "High Stakes," *Guardian (Charlottetown)*, 19 June 2004. One horse owner was quoted as saying, "We really need to have a way of putting more money up. If we don't we're going to keep losing our best drivers and trainers to Ontario and the United States. Owners won't be able to afford to stay in either and it will just go downhill."

53 See Dave Stewart, "Harness Industry Defends Way of Life," *Guardian (Charlottetown)*, 26 November 2004; and Jim Day, "Public Shows Support for Racino," *Guardian (Charlottetown)*, 7 December 2004.

54 See Russ Doyle, "'Last, Last Chance,'" *Guardian (Charlottetown)*, 6 April 2004; and Charlie Ballem, "Opening of Charlottetown Driving Park," *Guardian (Charlottetown)*, 3 November 2004.

55 See John Eldon Green, "Harness Racing: Breeders, Trainer and Drivers Don't See It as Mere Sport," *Guardian (Charlottetown)*, 16 June 2004. There were also concerns about the poor financial returns to horse owners and the possibility of them leaving for greener pastures in Ontario.

56 Confidential interviews with members of the Conservative government caucus, 10–20 June 2005.

57 See Ron Ryder, "Racino Critics Want Discussion of Social Effects," *Guardian (Charlottetown)*, 6 October 2004.

58 Editorial, "Government Must Make Call on 'Racinos,'" *Guardian (Charlottetown)*, 14 August 2004.

59 Editorial, "A Deal Too Good to Turn Down," *Guardian (Charlottetown)*, 25 August 2004.

60 It is instructive to note that many churches were instrumental in having VLTs removed from island corner stores in the late 1990s.

61 Confidential interview with a caucus member of the Conservative government, 10 June 2005.

62 Quoted in Ron Ryder, "High Stakes," *Guardian (Charlottetown)*, 19 June 2004.

63 See "Poll Shows Horse Race on Racinos," *Guardian (Charlottetown)*, 23 August 2004. One unscientific web poll that was taken in August 2004 showed twenty-seven people in favour of the racino – while thirty-one opposed the new facility.

64 Wayne Thibodeau, "CDP Casino May Come by Next Summer," *Charlottetown Guardian*, 19 March 2004.

65 Confidential interview with a member of the Binns government, 13 June 2005.

66 Wayne Thibodeau, "Two in a Row," *Guardian (Charlottetown)*, 4 October 2011; and Thibodeau, "Liberal Support Jumps as Election Call Nears," *Guardian (Charlottetown)*, 6 September 2011.

67 Bill Curry, "Ottawa Calls for Probe of Immigration Program," *Globe and Mail*, 15 September 2011. In a May 2012 interview with the Charlottetown *Guardian*, federal citizenship and immigration minister Jason Kenney strongly denied that there was any political interference by the Harper government in the October 2011 provincial election. See Teresa Wright, "P.E.I.'s PNP 'serious failure': Kenney," *Guardian (Charlottetown)*, 23 May 2012.

68 Quoted in Steve Sharratt, "Rural Backlash Shows Its Colours," *Guardian (Charlottetown)*, 4 October 2011.

69 Wayne Thibodeau, "Health, Not PNP, No. 1 Issue for Voters: Pollster," *Guardian (Charlottetown)*, 30 September 2011.

70 She was subsequently replaced – some would say unceremoniously forced out – by the party establishment in February 2013 and replaced by interim party leader Steven Myers.

71 Teresa Wright, "HST Coming to P.E.I. Next Year," *Guardian (Charlottetown)*, 19 April 2012. Interestingly, the HST was introduced to islanders on 1 April 2013, the same month that the HST was rescinded in British Columbia.

72 By contrast, in Ontario the consumer tax was implemented with relative ease.

73 Quoted in Teresa Wright, "Crane Says HST, Fee Hikes Will Cost $32M," *Guardian (Charlottetown)*, 4 May 2012.

74 See, Staff, "PEI Business Federation 'Delighted' by HST," *Journal-Pioneer (Summerside)*, 26 April 2012.

75 Staff, "Agriculture Industry Will Benefit from HST," *Guardian (Charlottetown)*, 14 May 2012; and Mitch MacDonald, "Islanders Hear Other Side of HST," *Guardian (Charlottetown)*, 5 May 2012.

76 Quoted in Staff, "Tourism Industry Sees Positive Action in 2012 Budget," *Guardian (Charlottetown)*, 21 April 2012.

77 See David Milne, "Prince Edward Island: Politics in Beleaguered Garden," in *The Provincial State in Canada*, ed. Keith Brownsey and Michael Howlett (Peterborough, ON: Broadview, 2001), 112.

78 In addition, the role of key bureaucrats in both finance and agriculture – especially those who actually controlled the flow of information to key political figures – was important in sensitizing members of the government to the harness-racing side of the argument.

3 Nova Scotia: Fiscal Crisis and Party System Transition

PETER CLANCY

This chapter explores the Nova Scotia provincial experience in the neo-liberal era. It is a story of new political contradictions playing out against a backdrop of prior social arrangements. Not surprisingly, a small provincial society in the Maritimes numbering less than a million people encountered neoliberalism in its own distinct way, and the responses have been similarly singular. For one thing, capitalism in Nova Scotia has historically been markedly uneven and its component parts disconnected. A heavy-industry enclave at Sydney was structurally separate from the service sector metropole of Halifax-Dartmouth and the petty-bourgeois social relations of the small towns and rural areas. For another, the province consists of a network of subregions with traditions of social coherence at the county or inter-county level, cemented by commercial ties, community elites, and local identities. It has fallen largely to the provincial state to manage the compound tensions within this Nova Scotia social formation, particularly in the contemporary era.

Over the past three decades Nova Scotia has experienced dramatic transformations. In the 1980s it was often characterized as part of a traditional Maritimes culture where party patronage greased the electoral fortunes of two nineteenth-century holdover parties, skilled in brokering traditional social difference rooted in religion, ethnicity, and locale.[1] This system was reinforced by an incomplete social penetration by capitalist social relations, which slowed the rise of the new solidarities associated with commercial and industrial growth.[2] A consequence was a provincial political culture centred on "subject" orientations where high levels of mass political "interest" were countered by low senses of "efficacy" (ability to have an effect), a combination that generated a "subject" as opposed to a "participant" outlook on political affairs.[3]

There is still some truth in these characterizations. However, the intervening quarter century brought profound changes that render the traditional portrait of Nova Scotia partial at best. In the intervening time Nova Scotia has seen an accelerating demographic shift from the small town and rural areas towards metropolitan Halifax. It has also seen the traditional brokerage political model sag under its own weight, fractured by revelations of financial malfeasance and petty ineptitude. Also the fiscal underpinnings of provincial governance have been challenged by successive deficit crises – in the early 1980s, the 1990s, and most recently in the 2008 global financial meltdown. Strong social protests sprang up in response to these crises. In addition, deep structural pressures were released by free trade agreements, fiscal retrenchments, and program rationalizations. The state-owned heavy-industry complex in Sydney was dismantled, the primary resource economy experienced multiple dislocations (in fisheries, forestry, and mining), and public services have been reshaped in the central fields of education, health, and local government. In all cases, economic restructuring triggered opposition, ranging from plant closure protests to the defence of local schools and hospitals to green action initiatives and anti-Ottawa campaigns. These combined forces have accentuated the uneven and contradictory political pressures in the province.

The chapter begins with a brief historical overview of the provincial system to the early 1980s. This is followed by an account of the transformation from Nova Scotia's "normal" politics during the post-war capitalist expansion to the "new" challenges of a small open province facing neoliberal globalization in the current era. Three distinct responses are identified and linked to the past three decades. The chapter then explores one prominent transect of political change, the emergence of a transitional, three-party system in the late 1990s. It continues with an exploration of the Nova Scotia New Democratic Party (NDP), culminating with its election in 2009 and its extraordinary defeat in 2013 by the provincial Liberal Party.

Historical Legacy

Nova Scotia was a Confederation partner in 1867, though the decision was surrounded by a sharp debate over the costs and benefits of joining the British North American union. The struggle between the rival economies of sail and rail – between a trade-oriented economy linking Halifax with the Caribbean, the United States, and the United

Kingdom, against an industrial economy based in regional towns like Amherst, New Glasgow, and Truro – persisted through several decades. The "golden age" of Nova Scotia capitalism in the decades following the national policy tariff of 1879 brought significant prosperity, though it was in retreat by the time of the First World War.[4] By this time, however, a number of regional industrial towns were well grounded across the province.[5] The turn of the century corporate merger wave saw regionally owned enterprise bought by outside capital and an uneven industrial retreat.

The interwar period was one of contradictory force fields. Politically, Nova Scotia participated in a variety of protest movements. The Winnipeg General Strike of 1919 had an echo in the factory town of Amherst. The Farmer-Labour Party formed the official opposition at Province House in 1920. More broadly, the 1920s were a decade of worker protest and organizing struggles. In a different way, the Maritime Rights Movement challenged certain political biases of the National Policy towards central Canadian commerce, demanding structural remedies to regional business weakness.[6] The Great Depression set loose a panoply of new political currents ranging from farmer and labour union-organizing initiatives to the cooperative movement associated with Rev. Moses Coady and the appearance of new parties like the Cooperative Commonwealth Federation (CCF).

A belated governmental response to such pressures can be seen in the tenures of Liberal premier Angus L. Macdonald between 1933 and 1940 and 1946 to 1953. He personified many of the cross-pressures then shaping Nova Scotia.[7] From humble origins in rural Cape Breton, his life was altered fundamentally by college education and wartime service. By the time the Depression hit, Macdonald was a respected legal academic and member of Halifax society. A political and business liberal by inclination, he nonetheless authored the first modern trade union act in the province and recognized from an early date that the Government of Canada had the opportunity to rework federalism in response to societal change.

Robert Stanfield led the Conservatives to power in 1956 on a program of economic catch-up through the exercise of new provincial state capacities. Borrowing from European experience in Britain, France, and Sweden, this involved a striking range of novel economic instruments for a small province. The three leading initiatives included an industrial development agency (Industrial Estates Ltd), a program of targeted sectoral planning (Voluntary Economic Planning), and a mildly corporatist exercise in employer-union consultation (Joint Labour-Management Study Committee).[8] Notably all three measures were geared more towards the advance of industrial capitalism than towards small rural enterprise. Their uneven impacts and failures to flourish following Stanfield's time in office suggest that Nova Scotia's social base may not have been ready for such interventions.

At the same time, the Government of Canada provided critical underpinnings in the form of federal spending, intergovernmental transfers, and regional infrastructure investment that stabilized a society with suppressed market-driven growth. Most critically, the multi-year financing for social programs and the unconditional equalization grants, together with a variety of regional investment programs, formed crucial backstops. Ottawa also experimented with a fascinating series of programs during the post-war decades.[9] Reliance on federal transfers, however, made Nova Scotia vulnerable to political changes in Ottawa, as constraints on federal transfers triggered instabilities in Nova Scotia.

Through it all, the party system predominated. The Liberals and Conservatives alternated in office, while the CCF/NDP maintained nominal representation in the legislature after 1941 on a vote share that seldom exceeded single digits. For the traditional parties, the formula for electoral success was to combine numbers in small-town and rural Nova Scotia where the bulk of constituencies were found.

Global Capitalism

By the 1970s a new form of capitalism was taking root in Nova Scotia. This was a tentative and uneven process and its shape was far from clear. Some firms, industries, communities, and institutions were initially more sheltered than others. Floating currencies affected the province's export industries like fish, forest, and mineral products. The economic crisis of stagflation bred labour union militancy and dampened inward investment. The terms of profitability began to turn away from manufacturing and in favour of first primary commodities and later finance. If the decade of the 1970s marked the demise of managed capitalism in the Keynesian mould (see introductory chapter), the 1980s underlined the uncertainty on what would follow – deeper recessions, serial fiscal crises, and globalizing trade and capital movements, among others. It is worth noting that these forces registered somewhat differently on the periphery than in Ontario, Quebec, or British Columbia. In Nova Scotia, annual gross domestic product (GDP) has broadly tracked that of Canada as a whole over the generation since 1982, though Nova Scotia missed the peaks in 1988, 1993, and 2003. Provincial unemployment has tracked national levels as well, albeit from a level 1–3 per cent higher than Canada at large.[10]

Politically, Nova Scotia has seen at least three distinct development strategies over these decades, each associated with a sponsoring government. The first belongs to the Buchanan Conservatives in the 1980s, the second with the Savage Liberals in the 1990s, and the third with the Hamm/MacDonald Conservatives in the 2000s. Each is discussed below. These strategies are not all encompassing, in the sense that they did not exhaust the respective governments' range of actions. However they are sufficiently prominent to signify a deliberate and coherent line of thinking and action.

Strategy 1: Pursuit of Growth Pole Prosperity

The Buchanan era was in some respects paradoxical. On one hand was the apparent political continuity of old-line party politics. John Buchanan ran up repeated legislative majorities, triumphing in four consecutive elections in 1978, 1981, 1984, and 1988.[11] Yet the Buchanan Conservative era coincided with this eruption of volatile capitalism. The governing formula is telling – a personalized leadership, an untroubled reliance on deficit finance, a "new day" rhetoric associated with anticipated offshore petroleum prosperity, and a determined exploitation of federal economic development supports.

There were limits, of course, to each of these plans. The province of Nova Scotia became a debt leader in Atlantic Canada and found that credit-rating agencies compared it unfavourably to neighbouring provinces like New Brunswick. The early euphoria of Sable Shelf petroleum discoveries faded along with the National Energy Program after 1985. The Canada–Nova Scotia economic development sub-agreements, numbering more than a dozen in all, were time-limited and vulnerable to termination as the Mulroney Conservatives grappled with fiscal shortfalls of their own.[12] And industries ranging from fisheries to forestry to coal and steel came under pressure as the decade progressed.[13] Only two years into Buchanan's final term, the bottom fell out in 1990, with accumulating scandals leading to an airlift appointment to the Senate of Canada.

Buchanan's longevity can be explained in good part by the dexterity with which the Nova Scotia government managed issues at a sectoral and regional level. John Buchanan was a consummate "project" politician, eschewing grand narrative in favour of "retail" (street-level) political results. For example, Buchanan enacted the "Michelin bill," which modified the application of provincial labour law to lure investment and to help the multinational tire manufacturer resist unionization. Michelin made clear that it would not countenance a unionized workforce at its new North American facilities. While the Conservatives could not rescind the trade union statute, they could amend it to raise the threshold for unionization. By the bill's terms, a union could be recognized in a multi-plant firm only if a majority of workers at all plants approved. Three separate plants were opened in Nova Scotia, two of them in predominantly rural counties where union affinities proved, as expected, to be weak.

In industrial Cape Breton (Buchanan's birthplace) the federally owned coal company Devco and the provincially owned steel company Sysco were the anchor enterprises. Both had been nationalized in 1967 when the privately owned DOSCO closed abruptly. The Buchanan government worked continually to secure federal modernization funds for Sysco, eventually transforming the original blast furnace steel works into an electric arc mini-mill with a rail-finishing mill attached. The province then lobbied assiduously for rail contracts to supply the federally owned CNR.

The other ongoing target of political attention was the offshore Scotian Shelf, where oil and gas discoveries suggested that a dynamic new energy sector was in the offing. In 1982 Buchanan struck a crucial offshore agreement with Ottawa that authorized joint federal-provincial management of the offshore resource, with entrenched guarantees for Nova Scotia royalty revenues and business preferences. Although the exploration cycle ebbed and flowed over the decade (and beyond), the Sable offshore gas project fuelled an expansionary economic cycle after 1996.

Buchanan was always mindful of the federal government's direct economic impact in Nova Scotia, as employer, builder, and financier. The largest "business" in the province was the Department of National Defence, with massive naval facilities in Halifax and other smaller bases in the Annapolis Valley, the Eastern Shore, and Cape Breton. Federally administered port authorities were similarly significant, from the Halifax container ports to the small boat fishing harbours that dotted the provincial shores. In addition the federal Atlantic Canada Opportunities Agency or ACOA was established in 1985 to provide a suite of financing options for business location or expansion.

Buchanan's strategy geared to private business project sponsorships was destined to deliver mixed results. The province often found itself on the margins of federal jurisdiction, as when Ottawa undertook to restructure the fish-processing industry in the early 1980s. Equally, when a tidal wave of stagflationary pressure hit the light industrial sector in the 1980s, the Government of Nova Scotia had few policy tools to respond. Finally there were inherent dangers associated with prominently sponsored projects. The most agonizing of these was the Westray coal mine at New Glasgow, where a lethal underground explosion in 1992 raised trenchant questions about the adequacy of provincial regulatory oversight.[14]

Strategy 2: Reinventing Government in the Savage Years

In Nova Scotia, the 1990s began with the crumbling of an old order and continued in 1993 with the arrival of a crisis management brigade. Similar to his Liberal counterparts in Newfoundland, PEI, and New Brunswick, Dr John Savage took office with a determination to do politics differently. The Nova Scotia Liberals repudiated the patronage solidarities associated with Buchananism. Although there was little in the 1993 campaign to suggest that Savage planned to deliver more than a mildly reformist administration, the new Cabinet encountered a separate reality.[15] Nova Scotia had yet to recover from the 1990–2 recession, and the estimated 1992–3 budget deficit of more than $600 million meant that the province was out of credit room.

Savage relied on an inner Cabinet of a half dozen ministers who were assigned to the pivotal departments: Finance, Education, Health, Economic Development, and Municipal Affairs. The first priority was to develop a multi-year revenue and expenditure plan that aimed for a budget balance by the end of the first term of office. However, this was not a classic neoliberal assault on the public sector by a group of market ideologues similar to Sterling Lyon in Manitoba, Grant Devine in Saskatchewan, Ralph Klein in Alberta, or Mike Harris in Ontario. Rather, Savage himself was a social Liberal, a Dartmouth physician who had been involved in a number of progressive medical treatment programs. He harboured a visceral dislike of traditional party patronage and spoils (which he associated with old-line Maritime politics) and accepted the progressive potential of the public sector as an economic and social stabilizer.[16]

This led the Liberal government to a particular approach to government restraint – tackling the crippling budget deficit with tax increases and systemic expenditure cuts, to be sure, but also seeking to "reinvent" public services delivery in the process. One favoured instrument was the regionalization of service delivery, through new school and health authorities. Part of the thrust here was to break the perceived strangleholds of entrenched elites, by altering the mix of political voices on new school councils and regional health boards. Another change involved the creation of entirely new services such as a provincial paramedic and ambulance service and new economic development authorities at the county level. Still another dimension was the adoption of public-private partnerships for new capital works, a measure already popular with neoliberals in other provinces.

This was never going to be an easy project to deliver. The anti-patronage stance embittered many rural Liberals who had suffered through the Buchanan era with the conviction that seasonal jobs and local projects would eventually come their way. When anti-patronage was coupled with plans for the closure of small rural schools and hospitals that were seen as pillars of country communities, the scale of resistance intensified. Added to these pressures were public-sector wage freezes that were part of the Liberal restraint program and the Savage Liberals had catalysed a panoply of resistant interest groups. John Savage's political personality fed the flames of resistance here, for he seemed incapable of expressing regret for the circumstances and empathy for the dislocations being visited on Nova Scotians, instead adopting a dismissive "there is no alternative" stance.

The Savage years, then, represent a one-term Liberal government that brought a particular form of neoliberal politics to Nova Scotia. The provincial political culture was not prepared for the Liberal program. Savage was not adept at legitimizing his program, and his self-conscious band of Cabinet reformers were fully cognizant of the risks this entailed. In 1997 when Savage recognized that he had become a lightning rod for discontents, he fell on his sword and resigned, in the hope that a successor could secure a second, consolidating term. However the Liberal Party traditionalists confounded this hope by selecting federal backbench MP Russell MacLellan as the new leader. Inexperienced in provincial politics and Cabinet government, MacLellan spent his brief tenure trying to "walk back" key measures of the Savage program.

In sum, the single-term Savage Liberal government questioned virtually all of the familiar tenets of Buchananism. In large part this was the product of a shifting fiscal reality that made some form of restructuring inevitable. The particular shape and texture of this program was the Savage Cabinet's construct. In so doing it brought a particular form of neoliberalism to Nova Scotia – not hostile to an activist state in principle, but dedicated to an overhaul of existing arrangements. As was also true in Newfoundland, the Savage years had another crucial impact: galvanizing a new political awareness and solidarity among organized public-sector workers. Unlike in the other Atlantic provinces, however, these changes pushed public workers closer to the provincial union movement, whose leaders were already organizationally affiliated to the NDP. But with the parallel weakening of the old-line parties, the realignment of public-sector professionals towards the NDP (along with the Halifax urban public more generally) was over-determined.

Strategy 3: Neoliberal Market-Driven Growth after 1999

By the turn of the millennium, Nova Scotia had a new Conservative majority government and a fiscal surplus, a product of the Savage budget policies and the economic recovery after 1993. Premier John Hamm's five and a half years in office may be best remembered for his "campaign for fairness," which consisted of a call for Ottawa to honour the spirit of the 1980s offshore oil and gas accords and de-couple petroleum royalties from federal equalization payments.[17] Hamm is also remembered for a second signature issue, his debt-reduction measures. By statute, the province was obliged not only to balance its budget each year but also to allot any surplus to paying down consolidated debt. This manoeuvre was as much a symbolic expression of neoliberal governing philosophy as a substantive measure, as the actual surpluses were modest.

Another telling indicator of economic outlook that emerged during this same period was the "Atlantica" strategy for Nova Scotia development, which emerged in the early 2000s and was championed by the right-of-centre think tank known as the Atlantic Institute for Market Studies (AIMS). In a series of presentations to political and business audiences, and a set of backgrounders released by AIMS, Atlantica was described as a potentially dynamic cluster of provinces and states. Encompassing the four Atlantic provinces and Quebec south of the St Lawrence River, together with the northern tier states of Maine, New Hampshire, Vermont, and northern New York, it represented an energy and transport corridor between Asian export powers and the northeastern seaboard.[18]

Intellectually this was part of a renewed interest in Canada-U.S. borderlands in the wake of the twin continental trade deals of 1988 and

1994. The kernel of the Atlantica argument was that as east-west econo-mies declined, north-south "corridors" offered important economic and political alternatives. According to this argument, the new north-east cross-border cluster region would cement trade and investment ties for the next generation. But the window of opportunity was judged short, and the alternative was for the province/region to be left behind.

During the 2001–7 period, a regional business coalition began to emerge behind the "gateway" aspects of the strategy, which drew media attention along with the support of potential beneficiary firms and sectors. The "energy corridor" dimension fit with the scramble for liquefied natural gas or LNG import terminals in Nova Scotia and New Brunswick, and the offshore exploration boom then underway on the Scotian Shelf. The marine port and trans-shipment dimension described Halifax as an Atlantic gateway for a new generation of container ships and traders seeking efficient access to North American markets. In 2004 the Halifax Gateway Council brought together infrastructure provid-ers, business advocacy groups, and government agencies.[19] The Atlan-tic Canada Chambers of Commerce sponsored Atlantica conferences in 2006 and 2007 to consolidate business awareness, and the Government of Nova Scotia announced its own "gateway initiative."[20]

The trajectory of Atlantica took a significant turn in October 2005 when Ottawa announced a Pacific Gateway Initiative with substantial new funding for transportation infrastructure renewal. Though it took place in the waning months of the Martin Liberal minority, the possibility of parallel programs for other borderland regions was certainly implied. This was fulfilled by the Harper Conservatives' 2007 budget and its $2.1 billion allotment for Gateway and Border Crossings.[21] Nova Scotia polit-ical minister Peter MacKay was assigned Atlantic Gateway responsibili-ties, and a formal federal-provincial structure was announced to handle project applications. Sensing the significance of this statist turn, AIMS warned that the private sector momentum risked being overwhelmed by a non-strategic "project scattering" across the Atlantic region.[22]

This was not a misplaced concern. Rival provinces began queuing up with their own nominations, and the policy discourse shifted from the singular to the plural. By 2008 there were multiple "Gateway Councils," and in 2008 Ottawa set up a private-sector Gateways Advisory Council. If the political urgency of this strategy was sapped by inter-provincial tensions and federal boosterism, it was dealt a fatal blow by the 2008 financial meltdown. Trade flows slumped sharply and the pressures for port expansion evaporated. In any event, the unprecedented credit freeze meant that there was no ready capital available. The closing of the Atlantica window (and its fragility as a commercial growth plan) was confirmed by premier Darrell Dexter in 2009 when he declared, "We recognize the global economic downturn significantly changed the value proposition of the Atlantic Gateway."[23]

Political debates over fiscal fairness, debt payments, and trade-led growth strategies underline a continuing search for economic "trigger" policies. During this time, however, the social fabric of Nova Scotia was being re-spun as many people were displaced from traditional economic communities tied to natural resources. Data for the period 1996–2006 paint a stark picture. Three Cape Breton Island counties and neighbouring Guysborough County suffered population declines of 10 per cent or more during this period. Only Halifax County grew at more than 5 per cent, while the adjacent "commuter" counties of Colchester, Hants, and Kings grew at 0–5 per cent, and the other ten counties declined by 1–10 per cent. In effect a massive shift of residency was underway, as metropolitan Halifax emerged as an unassailable growth pole while the regional towns and cities grappled with stagnation.

Some of the partisan and electoral implications of this population shift will be seen below. However, one intriguing trend is the widening distinctiveness between three regional electorates – in the small-town mainland, Cape Breton Island, and the greater Halifax metropole. This "three Nova Scotias" pattern held up, in vote-share terms, through the seven elections to 2009. Greater Halifax became a New Democrat fortress, with the Liberals and Conservatives alternating for a distant second place. Cape Breton was an area of Liberal strength, with the Conservatives marginal and the New Democrats only recently competitive. The "rural mainland" remained an area of Conservative advantage, with the exception being the 2009 election.

The NDP in a Transitional Party System

A social democratic party has been present in Nova Scotia for more than half of the province's history, first as the Cooperative Commonwealth Federation and then as the New Democratic Party. Only since the mid-1990s, however, has it emerged as a viable contender for power. This coincides with the emergence of a competitive three-party system, which is linked to the forces described above.

The CCF contested its first Nova Scotia provincial election in 1937 but the electoral breakthrough came in 1941. With an endorsement from the United Mine Workers District 26 in Sydney, three CCF members were elected from labour districts. In 1945 the CCF vote doubled in Nova Scotia to 14 per cent. Two Sydney-area members were returned and formed the official opposition for a term. However, it would be more than thirty years before this share of the vote was won again. The two Cape Breton seats were held in 1949 and 1953, and a single seat followed in 1956 and 1960. During the Stanfield election of 1956 the CCF vote fell to its lowest level ever of 3 per cent, and the electoral limits of the Cape Breton industrial enclave were well evident.

In 1963 the party leadership fell to James H. Aitchison, an academic at Dalhousie University. This brought an abrupt shift of direction from urban Cape Breton to urban Halifax, with disappointing results. Not only did the leader fail to win election, but also the Nova Scotia NDP (so renamed in 1961) failed to gain a single seat during a period when Robert Stanfield was at the peak of his powers. After the second failed campaign in 1967 and a provincial vote of a mere 5 per cent, an NDP leadership review ended Aitchison's interlude.

In a contest won by the narrow margin of four votes, Jeremy B. Akerman, a twice-unsuccessful Cape Breton candidate, defeated Dalhousie law professor Keith Jobson for the provincial leadership. Akerman brought the party back into the legislature in 1970 (along with Sydney colleague Paul MacEwan). In 1974 a third New Democrat was elected from industrial Cape Breton, and the province-wide NDP vote topped 13 per cent. A fourth Sydney MLA joined them in 1978 when the party polled 15 per cent, its highest provincial share to date.

Yet this trend of apparent consolidation was soon shattered. Akerman resigned the leadership in 1980. Even more damaging, the NDP Provincial Council was then the site of a spectacular public rift between some Halifax-based New Democrats and Cape Breton MLA Paul MacEwan. The upshot was MacEwan's expulsion from the party, despite the fact that the (Cape Breton–based) NDP caucus voted to keep MacEwan in its legislative group. Former NDP federal leader David Lewis was brought in to mediate with mixed results.[24]

The 1980–1 period proved to be deeply wrenching to the NDP organization. An autumn leadership convention selected Halifax social worker Alexa McDonough over two Cape Breton MLAs by a resounding margin. In December, the two MLAs voted MacEwan out of their group. In the then-bipolar world of NDP party politics, the Halifax wing was back in command.

However, the 1981 election revealed the depths of the accumulated weakness. While McDonough was successful in Halifax Chebucto, she was the only member to be elected. Running as an Independent, Paul MacEwan was returned from Cape Breton Nova. While the province-wide NDP vote jumped to a record 18 per cent, the regional fracture between Cape Breton and Halifax began to deepen. Of the top ten NDP finishes in 1978, seven were from the Sydney area. Three years later only two Sydney seats remained on this list, while seven of the leaders were now from Halifax-Dartmouth and one from Kings County in the Annapolis Valley.

Further polarization lay ahead. In 1984 MacEwan formed the Cape Breton Labour Party and fielded fourteen candidates. While this was a brief and quixotic gesture (MacEwan was its only MLA), he remained in the legislature for more than fifteen years, sitting as an Independent (1988) and later as a Liberal (1993, 1998, 1999). During this time his renegade presence was a constant reminder of the internal NDP rupture and what seemed, for many, as the repudiation of Cape Breton by the "champagne socialists" of Halifax.

Alexa McDonough led the Nova Scotia NDP through fourteen years and four elections. During that time, voter support in mainland Nova Scotia grew significantly and the aggregate vote resumed its 1970s share.[25] By 1993 there were sixteen ridings in which the New Democrat vote exceeded the party's provincial aggregate of 18 per cent and a half dozen that were genuinely competitive in three-way contests. However, the legislative caucus never exceeded three members. At the same time, support in Cape Breton fell to third-place status, and candidate selection problems there mounted, reflecting a significant repositioning of the Nova Scotia NDP. McDonough shifted the party away from a traditional industrial labourist orientation and towards a middle-class/working-class urban coalition centred on social reform. Her tenure also coincided with the emergence of public-sector unions as the centre of gravity in the Nova Scotia Federation of Labour and, by affiliate extension, the NDP. However, the 1988 election result was disappointing.[26]

The next quantum shift in NDP voter support coincided with the Nova Scotia fiscal crisis of the 1990s and the severe structural restraints visited by the Savage Liberal government of 1993–8. As occurred in Newfoundland, Ontario, Quebec, Manitoba, and Saskatchewan in the 1990s, the wage freezes and program cuts (including proposed school and hospital closures) extended across the entire public sector, and the Savage Cabinet reaped a whirlwind of strike actions, interest group attacks, and community protests. While the combined audacity and rigidity of this strategy made John Savage a single-term premier, it also forced a reorientation of electoral (particularly urban voter) priorities in favour of the last "uncontaminated" party – the NDP.[27]

Ironically, McDonough resigned her position in November 1994 and within months entered the contest for the federal NDP leadership. Following an interim stint by Sackville MLA John Holm, the "other" Halifax MLA Robert Chisholm was selected as provincial leader in 1996. In some ways the 1998 provincial campaign was the party's modern breakthrough moment. The two old-line parties were both critically weakened by successive terms in office. Neither party entered the campaign from a position of strength, and the electorate proved volatile, particularly in urban areas of mainland Nova Scotia. The NDP total vote exploded from 18 per cent (1993) to 34 per cent. Moreover the New Democrats benefited from a very high efficiency rating in converting votes into seats in three-way races. Of the twenty-two seats where the NDP vote exceeded the party's province-wide share, they were successful in nineteen.

This breakthrough was broadly maintained in subsequent elections until 2013, and the core of this "class of 1998" continued to anchor the legislative party for the next decade. For the first time the New Democrats entered the new House of Assembly as the Official Opposition, as the Liberals were reduced to minority government status propped up by the Conservatives. The NDP, however, proved unable to fully consolidate its breakthrough. The Russell MacLellan Liberal minority government fell within fifteen months, and at the ensuing election the New Democrats dropped back to eleven MLAs. At the same time the John Hamm Conservatives formed a majority government. While this setback was widely attributed to the damaging disclosure of a youthful drunk driving conviction of NDP leader Chisholm, the 1999 results had deeper origins. At that time, the NDP was competitive (in terms of constituency vote share) in only two-fifths of the province, and the vote splits were less rewarding than a year earlier.

Shortly thereafter Chisholm resigned the NDP leadership. If the 1998 election results spoke to how inter-party positioning defines electoral opportunity structures, the 2000 NDP leadership succession spoke to the delicate intra-party dynamics that link leader, caucus, and membership. Three candidates challenged for the succession, and in an outcome not uncommon in convention politics, the NDP delegates opted for a consensus second choice. Helen MacDonald had been elected in a 1997 by-election but was defeated in the general a year later. As new party leader, she failed to win the ensuing by-election, and her brief tenure ended in resignation pressed by the caucus.

When Darrell Dexter took the reins of leadership, the NDP had endured three years of turmoil and had failed, organizationally, to build on its 1998 electoral breakthrough. It was a delicate moment, as the Conservative government now enjoyed a majority under a popular new leader. Dexter was able to consolidate the party's position as the official opposition, aided by key NDP staff appointments for chief of staff and party secretary.[28]

The resilience of the Nova Scotia NDP as an electoral formation was confirmed by the results of the 1999, 2003, and 2006 general elections, in which the party deepened its legislative representation of eleven, fifteen, and twenty respectively with vote shares of 30, 31, and 34 per cent.[29] Moreover the New Democrats broke out of their metro Halifax enclave with several victories in Sydney as well as the town ridings of Yarmouth and Pictou West and the rural ridings of Queen's, Guysborough, Shelburne, and Eastern Shore.

The party's electoral breakthrough also injected a profound caution into the strategic calculus of the Nova Scotia NDP elite. Party strategists believed that elections were easily lost by an absence of leadership clarity (witness failed Liberal premier Russell MacLellan) or an absence of policy coherence (witness failed Conservative premier Rodney MacDonald). Equally elections could be won through articulation of modest programs and calm avuncular leadership, as exemplified by Conservative premier John Hamm. These cautious attributes well fit Darrell Dexter's political personality as a "conservative progressive" or an "incrementalist."[30]

Bluenose Socialism: Coming into Government

In many respects, the 2009 election was won long before the writ was issued. Three months after Rodney MacDonald gained his minority Conservative government in June 2006, the NDP's share of decided voter intention rose from 34 to 37 per cent, and it did not fall below that mark for the next three and a half years.[31]

As the MacDonald government spun towards conclusion, the NDP crafted an electoral platform of amorphous simplicity under the slogan "Darrell Dexter: For Today's Families." It centred on seven commitments: create secure jobs across a variety of sectors; keep emergency rooms open and reduce health-care wait times; help young people stay in the province; remove the harmonized sales tax (HST) from home energy; fix rural roads; help seniors stay at home; and live within our financial means by controlling deficits.[32] Obviously each of these addressed a major social concern. As written, however, this program was minimalist in the sense that each commitment was defined by a series of concrete measures that voters were invited to audit. In any event, it proved sufficient to maintain NDP support levels against "fearful socialist" attacks from the right.[33]

The question arises about the degree of social democracy or even labourism reflected in the NDP program. Critics to the left find very little here and regard Dexter (like his counterpart Gary Doer in Manitoba, see chapter 7) as a long-time adherent to a neoliberal Blairite "Third Way." Matt Fodor, for instance, cites the Dexter campaign rhetoric on "living within our means" as evidence that the New Democrats offer little more than a "more humane version of neoliberalism."[34] Furthermore, Larry Haiven sees the Dexter government emulating the 1991 Roy Romanow government in Saskatchewan (see chapter 8) in its utilization of the deficit as a Trojan horse for draconian expenditure cuts. The Nova Scotia Centre for Policy Alternatives outlined an alternative budget strategy that rejected the centrality of deficit reduction for the duration of the present recession.[35] Dexter's professed admiration for Gary Doer's Manitoba NDP (see chapter 7) administration suggests further support for this case. In fact, the minimalist Nova Scotia NDP election platform represented not only a turn to pragmatic retail electoral politics but also an expression of the policy-narrowing effect of neoliberalism as is demonstrated throughout this book. In general, policies seeking a more fundamental rebalancing of social and economic power and opportunities are no longer prominent.[36] However, in the context of the party system transition that the NDP sought to drive, a broader political advantage could certainly be discerned.

New Democrats in Office

The distinction between holding office and holding power is conceptually critical and it can usefully guide a discussion of the Dexter government that was sworn in on 19 June 2009. Winning office involves the selection of ministers and assignment of portfolios, the convening of Cabinet, issuance of a Throne Speech and a budget, and generally serving as the executive voice of provincial authority. In doing this, the NDP offered some distinguishing features. A small Cabinet of twelve members required that many ministers doubled up on portfolio responsibilities. The Cabinet also comprised an experienced set of politicians, some with a decade at Province House, albeit in the official opposition. The party took office with a limited set of campaign commitments, though some (including a year-one balanced budget and a guarantee of twenty-four-hour hospital emergency room service) were destined to prove politically difficult. The transition brought a sense of political cleansing and popular optimism that some commentators likened to New Labour's 1997 election victory in the United Kingdom.

Power, on the other hand, involves the capacity to achieve policy objectives, particularly in the face of rival and opposing interests. The 2009 election result included some modest contributing attributes in this regard. It was only the second majority government to emerge from the past five elections. At 45 per cent, the NDP vote constituted a strong mandate and reflected broad public support. Furthermore the government representation was broadly based, including MLAs from all parts of the province: metropolitan Halifax, the mid-sized cities, and the small-town and rural ridings. It enjoyed a reputation with media and civil servants as an intelligent and skilful legislative opposition. Temperamentally it was seen as reformist in a calm and incremental way that contrasted with the sometimes incoherent opportunism of its Conservative predecessor led by premier Rodney MacDonald.

Within weeks of assuming office the NDP demonstrated its appreciation of the limits of office and the desirability of centralizing power in the Premier's Office. Dexter recruited key political staff into an expanded Premier's Office. In addition to the premier's deputy minister – who was retained from the prior administration – the parallel positions of chief of staff, principal secretary, and deputy minister of policy and priorities were filled by key NDP activists. To be sure, this phenomenon of expanding the policy and messaging capacity at the centre of government is not unique to the Dexter government. It has become a noticeable pattern of institutional reform among numerous neoliberal governments throughout the country (see the Ontario and Alberta chapters here).

The locus of power can be gauged in part by the character of government policy initiatives. The Throne Speech of 17 September 2009 affirmed intentions "to keep the promises we made" while "living within our means."[37] There was little place here for grand rhetoric. The strategic gamble seemed to be that modest but concrete measures marked the limits of forward programming in an uncertain environment and would match the electorate's appetite for incremental change.

However, the coordinates of power involve structural constraints as well as factors of agency. The NDP inherited a swelling budget deficit, driven by the 2008–9 recession and exacerbated by the MacDonald Conservatives' pre-election spending. The full extent was made clear only by the Deloitte external audit of provincial finances.[38] Furthermore Deloitte confirmed a bleak provincial revenue picture, as "conflicting cost and revenue pressures are creating the single largest financial management challenge for the Nova Scotia Government for the decade ahead. Nova Scotia must not only address the cost pressures all Canadian governments are facing, but it must also address the expiry of short-term revenue sources that it has become dependent on." One fiscal pressure that the report highlighted was that of offshore petroleum receipts, a significant "own-source" revenue ever since Sable gas production began at the turn of the century, had peaked, and was set to decline.

In addition to the legacy obligations and inherited challenges, there loomed the classic question of how the Nova Scotia power structure would respond to the first ever victory of a nominally social democratic movement in the province. These concerns can be described only as muted and doubtless owed much to the factors just outlined. It is also worth considering that the provincial power structure was not stable itself, in wake of the U.S. sub-prime explosion, the financial meltdown of 2008–9, and the collapse of trade. In addition, the post-2006 experience with minority government in Ottawa, including the extraordinary near-death of the Harper government in December 2008, may also have partially discounted market-sector anxieties about a centre-left government in Nova Scotia.

By the end of its first session, the government removed the HST from home electricity bills; established a new independent agency for energy efficiency; expanded the coverage of the Nova Scotia child benefit; increased the equity tax credit; placed hard caps on greenhouse gas emissions; legislated a 25 per cent renewable electricity target by 2015; took the first steps in a poverty-reduction strategy (raising the income threshold for the provincial child benefit); launched a renewable energy strategy; raised the target for protected lands to 12 per cent by 2015; appointed an advisor on emergency room services; and banned uranium mining. In addition the government began revising the employment support and income assistance program; increased in the secondary road paving allotment by 50 per cent; and authorized a home construction rebate to stimulate new building. By the close of the year, the Dexter government was able to point to a list of election commitments fulfilled.[39]

The NDP had been unequivocal in its call for the provincial budget to be balanced in year one. However significant this had been on the campaign trail, it was a highly debatable fiscal centrepiece in the midst of a recession. Almost from the moment of taking office, the balanced budget pledge was in doubt. According to the Deloitte audit, the Conservatives' spring forecast of a $256 million deficit had turned into a record shortfall more than double that size for 2009–10. In addition Deloitte reported that the deficit was on an upward trend that would push it to $1.4 billion in four years.

Dexter and his finance minister, Graham Steele, set out a late summer narrative fashioned around the advice of third-party experts. The profligacy of the prior government was manifest and Deloitte had confirmed the scale. The NDP capitalized on the perception of the "MacDonald deficit" as an unavoidable legacy. Opposition critics argued that the NDP had inflated the deficit by its 2009–10 treatment of continuing financial obligations to universities. In general, however, the Dexter government enjoyed the benefit of the doubt on its September fiscal response.

In tactical terms, the audit also established a new baseline for a multiyear budgetary transition "back to balance." The Dexter government was helped in this respect by the work of its independent four-person Economic Advisory Panel (EAP), created to suggest "priorities in light of the fiscal challenge." The EAP's advice – to close the deficit over a four-year period, in light of business cycle weakness – helped to legitimate this option.[40] The workout of this fiscal strategy during the autumn of 2009 drew either positive responses (from media outlets) or silence (from business interest groups). During this time the government's public rating swelled from 45 per cent on voting day to a record 63 per cent (August) and 57 per cent (November).[41]

Obviously a composite evaluation can be based on many measures. The NDP enjoyed a generally effective first session in the House. Federal-provincial stimulus funds were directed to support a series of infrastructural projects, and provincial grant and loan assistance seemed to be aimed at reinforcing large employers in weathering the recession. Most of these projects could be justified under the NDP commitment to workforce development. However, latent within the industrial assistance program was a political liability, since while the presence of support was locally salient, so too was its absence. Support for the Northern Pulp Company (New Glasgow), the Bluenose Schooner renovations (Lunenburg), and Irving Shipyards (Shelburne and Halifax) was duly noted.[42] So too, however, was its absence for a call centre that closed in Canso, a sawmill in rural Queen's County, or the CAT fast ferry from Yarmouth to New England (which closed when the government declined to provide a $10–12 million subsidy for the upcoming summer season).[43]

As was true of provincial NDP governments in Ontario, Manitoba, Saskatchewan, and British Columbia, differences began to emerge between government policy initiatives on resource and environmental issues and the outlooks of social advocacy groups. Given the party's traditional affinities with progressive civil society groups, this tension was telling. Certainly there was little criticism of the NDP's tougher renewable electricity targets or the hard caps on power generators for greenhouse gas emissions. But biofuel electricity-generating investments, forest clear-cutting and whole tree logging, and biosolid farm fertilizer applications were another matter. In each case ministers made concrete announcements in politically contested policy fields, sometimes with a surprising lack of context. Biofuels were justified as an essential part of the renewable electricity strategy but with no apparent awareness of the extensive history of forest policy debates in the province. It was left to the *Chronicle Herald*, of all voices, to question the long-term impact on the forest resource.[44] On the related issue of accelerated clear-cutting and whole tree extraction, the Ecology Action Centre and rural ecology groups were quick to express concern. The Department of Natural Resources tried to steer clear, and pulp and paper operators were left to defend their own sustainability credentials. The environment minister further endorsed the farm application of biosolid field treatments by invoking the force of "science." In all of these cases community groups and ENGOs found themselves on the other side of the issue. Perhaps the most symbolically charged of these announcements came in March 2010 when the energy minister indicated that a previous Conservative pledge on the remediation of Boat Harbour pulp pollution was no longer considered binding. The Pictou Landing First Nation, on whose lands Boat Harbour sits, denounced this retreat, which coincided with a provincial announcement of a $75 million loan to the pulp mill whose effluents were the cause of the pollution.[45] This prompted the premier to step in to indicate that he considered the issue still open. On the face of these issues, a number of common traits can be discerned. Most prominently, ministers seemed to be relying heavily upon departmental officials and were uneasy or unwilling to engage in public dialogue.

The politically unexpected always makes up a substantial part of a political agenda, and the NDP's single term featured a number of such cases that weakened the government. Some were highly particular, such as the lingering problem of an illegal construction union campaign donation to the NDP in 2009 that contravened election expenses law (and was quickly repaid) or a possible conflict of interest by the fisheries minister who announced appointments to the fisherman's loan board while a transaction involving his own boat was before the board. Other matters were more comprehensive. The list of emerging issues also included public-sector labour negotiations across the province. Only the teachers had settled their new contract under the Conservative regime (with a 3 per cent multi-year wage deal) while unionized workers from hospitals to public servants were still in negotiation.

As 2010 began, the momentum seemed to continue to the new government's advantage. The NDP launched public fiscal consultations in the run-up to the signature 2010–11 budget, using a "Back to Balance" discussion paper to illustrate the dimensions of the choice.[46] January also brought the settlement, after some tense eleventh-hour negotiations, of major public-sector union contracts. This was significant coup in light of the recessionary environment, and the government could expect to gain significant credit for the fact.

However, the provincial political climate was fractured dramatically on 3 February 2010, and with it went the NDP governing narrative. The trigger was the release of the auditor general's annual report and its findings on MLA expenses. It had been fifteen years since last review of the Speaker's Office budget. Few were prepared, however, for the firestorm of media and public excoriation that accompanied the report.

The expense regime is a multilayered but loosely defined list of claim categories. Some of them involved expense-free claims for matters like the member's monthly allowance, the member's travel within the constituency, and the qualifying member's Halifax apartment allowance. For non-Halifax members there was also a weekly mileage allowance to and from home. All members were eligible for a per diem while the House was in session. An annual electronic technology allowance was authorized, as was a lump-sum departure allowance for retiring or defeated members. In addition the chairpersons of committees were paid fixed annual stipends of several thousand dollars, regardless of the frequency of committee meetings.

Because the 2010 expenses scandal unfolded in a sequence of steps, the media coverage was extensive. The auditor general's initial report of 3 February stressed "serious weaknesses in the funding system for members' constituency and other expenses, which increase the risk of excessive and inappropriate expenditures by members."[47]

Beyond the dubious individual deals for cameras, computers, televisions, and a portable electrical generator, the auditor also drew attention to unreported staff salary supplements, double claims on expenses, and receipt-free reimbursements that were impossible to audit. So intense was the preoccupation with shady expenses that other powerful chapters of the report, including one on the performance of public-private partnership (P3) financing, were entirely ignored by the media.[48] What followed was a strikingly ad hoc (even chaotic) response: a confusing ten-day parade of MLAs stepping forward to claim specific items while the media fed a righteous and populist indignation.[49]

Of particular interest to the media in week one was a series of purchases amounting to some $77,000 that had been flagged without naming the MLAs involved. Since neither the auditor general nor the Speaker felt it appropriate to attach names, much of the first week was devoted to questions of "who bought what." In week two the media discussion shifted towards the details of the expense regime itself. Week two also saw the resignation of the Yarmouth Conservative MLA whose records had led the publicity parade. The auditor general then raised the stakes with the announcement of a follow-up "forensic audit" to address potential illegality not within the purview of the original "value for money audit."[50] A possible direction of this inquiry emerged in week three, with details about the income supplements to MLAs staff. Thirty MLAs had expensed $185,687 to staff members between 2006 and 2009.[51] In many (if not most) cases, tax reporting had not been done. In week five, the Glace Bay Liberal MLA announced his resignation (four MLAs were ultimately charged in 2011).[52]

The broad scope of the auditor general's findings, together with the prolonged glare of media coverage, left an indelible imprint of malfeasance on the public mind, which was captured in a banner newspaper headline for "The House of Frill Repute." The fact that all parties seemed to share equally in the blame meant that the fallout was generic as opposed to partisan-based. For the government, however, the expenses furore put a significant dent in its reformist credentials. At best, the government appeared to be slow and fragmented in its response. At worst, critics charged it was complicit with a culture of petty spoils reminiscent of Buchananism in the 1980s. As a result, the second legislative session that opened in February 2010, with a new slate of NDP bills and announcements, was pushed off the front page.[53]

Despite the political tsunami of the expenses affair, there were substantive issues in the second legislative session. The 2010–11 budget confirmed a four-year plan for balancing public accounts, with the 2010–11 deficit set at $222 million. This was far from a draconian response, suggesting that the Dexter government might be centring its fiscal tack between the Scylla of Buchanan and the Charybdis of Savage. In the end, a combination of revenue factors enabled the NDP to announce a surprising end-of-year surplus, although the budget plan for 2011–12 (year three for the Dexter government) renewed the forecast for a three-digit deficit. The 2012–13 deficit forecast stood, intractably, at $211 million.[54]

Well into year three of its only term of office, the NDP was polling at levels (41 to 45 per cent) only slightly below the June 2009 election outcome.[55] While public support inevitably varies (there was a surge into the 60 per cent range in the fall of 2009 and a plunge into the high 30s by the summer of 2010), the striking fact was the polling resilience of the government. It should be recalled, however, that the Conservatives were effectively leaderless until 2010, a time in which the Liberals gained modest traction at best. In the summer of 2011 the NDP passed into the second half of its first majority mandate.

Year three also opened with two profound shocks to the Nova Scotia political economy that might be described as "mills" and "ships." Part one involved a crisis in the forest industry. Two of the three major provincial pulp and paper mills were suddenly at risk: the New Page facility at Port Hawkesbury was closed in September 2011 and the Abitibi Bowater mill at Liverpool was declared unprofitable and set up for closure in 2012. In the eastern and western regions of rural Nova Scotia, these mills anchor far larger commercial networks, including woodlot timber suppliers, loggers, truckers, and service businesses. The Dexter government suddenly found itself dealing with a deep-seated crisis in the rural economy. For a decade or more, the profit margins for commodity grade pulp and paper have been thin to non-existent, and both parent companies were in the grips of radical restructuring. Suddenly the NDP's ability to broker transitions to new ownerships became a major new challenge to its governing prospects. In the case of the New Page mill, it required a full year for new ownership to be arranged (under bankruptcy protection) and approved.[56] During this time the provincial government committed up to $125 million in a diverse package of loans, forest land purchases, and silviculture assistance, which included maintaining the mill facilities in "hot idle" condition and maintaining wood production in the field so that new ownership, once arranged, could move directly back into production. In the case of Bowater, the government provided a similar package of loans, training funds, and land purchases late in 2011. However, in this case the corporate parent, Resolute Forest Products (formerly Abitibi Bowater) imposed a final closure in June of the following year.[57] In response, the Dexter government appointed a special economic transition office to ease the dislocation in Queen's County.

The "ships" component was a far more positive business story in the autumn of 2011. Here the Irving shipyard in Halifax was designated one of two national suppliers in the massive federal procurement program for building arctic patrol vessels for the Canadian Forces.[58] A significant share of the total $33 billion outlay over twenty to thirty years was channelled to the Irving bid, with strong support from the provincial government. Immediately the Halifax airport was festooned with banners declaring, "We build ships here." The geographic contrast between rural industry distress and greater Halifax success did not go unnoticed, presenting a regional challenge for any Nova Scotia industrial policy: in order to be successful, government must ensure that the supply and employment linkages from ship construction are not confined to the Halifax-Dartmouth waterfront. In 2012, however, the federal ships program was offset, in the public mind, by announced federal program cuts emanating from the Harper-Flaherty March budget, which included major job cuts and office closures at federal departments ranging from Parks to Fisheries to the Atlantic Canada Opportunities Agency.[59] Perhaps even more ominous was the announcement of major restructuring to the federal employment insurance program that continues to play a crucial stabilizing role in the provincial (especially rural and seasonal) workforce.[60]

As is demonstrated throughout this volume, NDP governments traditionally have a tense relationship with organized labour. This was also true of the Nova Scotia NDP as its mandate unfolded. For the organized labour movement, the NDP government offered an opportunity to move beyond the historic 30 per cent density levels in the province. Yet the NDP did little to address these issues, especially in the public sector. When public-sector labour contracts came up for renegotiation, there were questions of whether 0, 1, or 2 per cent increments would prove acceptable to the unions. For the general public, one of the more disruptive events came in the spring of 2012 when Halifax hospitals began to cancel scheduled surgeries in the run-up to a possible strike action that was averted at the eleventh hour. Also on the labour front, the Dexter government drew considerable business resistance when it legislated for third-party settlement for first contract agreements between workers and employers. Overall, the organized business segment responded pragmatically to the NDP's moderate rules, and there were few categorical denunciations. Small business condemned the 2 per cent HST increase in 2009 (compared to the events described in the BC and PEI chapters, the introduction of the HST in Nova Scotia was a non-event), and the Halifax Board of Trade called for faster action on deficit reduction. The road construction industry raised a protest in 2011 when the NDP purchased a portable asphalt mill, seeing in it the seeds of creeping nationalization, but it did not gain wider resonance. It is perhaps a mark of the restrained shape of the government's fiscal strategy (directed by finance minister Graham Steele), on which organized business advocacy was relatively muted.[61]

As the shape of the double-dip recession was confirmed, a series of further business closures were announced. This included the Imperial oil refinery in Dartmouth and the Acadian Lines bus service. The NDP had already drawn a policy line in the sand when it ruled out state ownership of the paper firms. Instead it concentrated on building provincial administrative capacity for stabilization and turnaround measures in aid of failing business. This capacity is likely to be tested further in years ahead. Such policy efforts do not come without costs, as evident in the several hundred million-dollar restructuring fund that has punched a deeper hole in the public accounts. Overall, however, the NDP government showed a definite appreciation for the role of tactical interventions to secure key corporate holdings. This could take a proactive as well as a reactive form, of which Nova Scotia Power (NSP), the privately owned electric utility, is a case in point. The NDP drew upon regulatory and expenditure tools to enlist NSP in several goals, including the promotion of renewable power and the restructuring of generating capacity from coal-fired towards hydro. Take, for example, the company's partnership with Newfoundland in the proposed Muskrat Falls hydro project and the associated undersea electric transmission line to Cape Breton. At the same time, the NSP rate structure was a lightning rod for consumer discontent that was continually exploited by the opposition parties.

The 2013 Nova Scotia Election

The New Democrats led the polls in voter preference for the first three years of the government. Then, beginning in the late spring of 2012, the tables turned with the Liberal Party switching places with the NDP. It was an advantage that carried through to the October 2013 general election. By the time the dust settled after the election, the NDP had been defeated soundly and replaced by a rejuvenated Liberal Party.

This shift seems paradoxical, since there seemed to be no sharp controversies to spur such realignment in mid-2012. Perhaps an accumulation of locally salient issues reached a tipping point. For instance, the Acadians resented the government's directive to the electoral boundary redistribution commission, that three hitherto "protected" ridings could be altered. Elsewhere, Yarmouth residents were furious when the government refused to subsidize the unprofitable ferry service to New England, and Cumberland County businesses excoriated the Dexter government when an HST increase sent shoppers across the border into New Brunswick. On the other hand, the NDP offered significant financial support to stabilize the three major pulp and paper mills in Nova Scotia, and the government could claim a share of reflected glory when the federal shipbuilding contract was awarded to Halifax.

An alternate explanation is that a large cohort of unattached voters, who parked their support with the NDP in 2009 out of disillusion with the Conservatives and the Liberals, went on the move again. In aggregate terms, eighty thousand NDP votes from 2009 went elsewhere in 2013, four-fifths of them to the Liberals, while most of the rest refrained from voting. Part of this shift was to be expected, as the NDP had reached historic heights in winning power four years earlier. But the NDP campaign strategy can also be criticized for its bland conventionality and its failure to forcefully articulate either past achievement or new reformist ideas.

Conclusion

Over the last three decades the Nova Scotia social formation has been subject to intense dislocations. The rural primary resource economy has come under mounting pressure as small producers have seen their margins cut and their processing sectors restructured. This restructuring was especially devastating to fishing, forestry, and agriculture. At the same time, long-standing pillars of the manufacturing economy have also been stressed. The Sydney heavy industrial complex experienced a long decline from the 1960s until its ultimate disappearance in the 2000s. The light industry sectors in smaller towns have also been undermined. Since the 1990s, parallel pressures have beset government sector programming and employment, which were slow, uneven, and sometimes obscure processes, and the political responses were neither obvious nor straightforward.

Several strategic responses can be discerned in the modern period, each associated with a different governing era. For the Buchanan Conservatives it was the underwriting and dispersal of inward private investment and employment throughout the province. For the Savage Liberals it entailed fiscal retrenchment and the restructuring of public programs to maintain coverage in new forms. Finally, the Hamm Conservatives looked for private-sector drivers that were compatible with fiscal probity. Each of these strategies generated a legacy that closely constrained its successors. The Buchanan debt load exacerbated the Savage era's troubles. The harshness of the Savage fiscal restructuring delivered a balanced budget but roused public-sector workers and clients to more conscious defence of their interests. The Hamm-MacDonald strategy of tilting against Ottawa proved effective during an era of capital expansion but insufficient thereafter.

One profound effect of these compound changes was the Nova Scotia party system transition to a competitive three-party form. Each of the earlier governing strategies contained internal contradictions. A public-sector spending strategy could not survive the age of continuing deficits when the underpinnings fell out. A severe neoliberal restraint and restructuring strategy implied broad-scale dislocation and raised challenges of popular legitimacy that curtailed its political half-life to a single term. A strategy based on private capital investment underwritten by private infrastructure may have suited the dynamic business cycle of the early 2000s but could not be sustained after the 2008 crisis. Not only did this sequence of experiments weaken the competency claims of the traditional parties, it also freed up significant social voting blocs that were bruised by the cumulative dislocations. There was no guarantee, of course, that the Nova Scotia NDP would benefit by default. But as seen above, the repositioning of the New Democrats under McDonough, Chisholm, and Dexter modified the opportunity structure for provincial political success. A dramatic outcome was the rise of the New Democrats, first as official opposition in 1998 and later as government in 2009.

It should be asked whether the NDP advanced a comparable strategy to those discussed above. Taking office in the depths of an epic financial crisis, the Dexter government fashioned a hybrid approach. From the 2009 campaign program to the 2013 budget, the political style was incremental rather than daring. Caught between the risks of corporate capital flight and the constraints on provincial public finance, there was little room for grand designs. Public-sector unions were asked to trade job security for wage restraint. Private capital was offered incremental tax-rate cuts. Yet the basis for a greener and more renewable energy sector was also laid. The Dexter government evidently appreciated the structural weaknesses of Nova Scotia today – an aging population, a shrinking labour force, a relentless rural-to-urban demographic shift, and a social expenditure budget of potentially limitless appetite. Given the narrowness (and openly neoliberal) policies of the NDP, the electoral danger for the province's social democrats was that the opposition parties would cobble together a coalition of transitory discontents.

In many ways, that is exactly what occurred in October 2013. The McNeil Liberals gained a decisive lead in public opinion more than a year before the 2013 election. As a result, the Liberals were able to run a cautious campaign, carving out a few differentiating issues and presenting themselves principally as a fresh alternative to the New Democrats. Yet once in office, even those few Liberal contrasts with the NDP began to dissolve. Where McNeil as opposition leader had excoriated Dexter's efforts to broker new corporate owners for failing industrial firms, McNeil as premier indicated a willingness to negotiate with anchor employers. Similarly McNeil's opposition to the Muskrat Falls hydro connection to Newfoundland dissolved within a few months into the pursuit of "better terms." Also the critique of the NDP's fiscal deficits seemed forgotten when the 2014 Liberal budget announced a four-year plan for moving to surplus.[62]

Across the province, however, there were several signs that the post-2008 economic shakeout was shifting certain structural economic features. Depopulation continued despite the national economic recovery, and the air shuttles between Nova Scotia and Fort McMurray showed no sign of slackening. The rural-urban cleavage lost none of its bite. A number of small municipalities sought to dissolve into county administrations, as accumulated fiscal shortfalls combined with emergency expenditures to render them unsustainable.

It was in this context that the final report of the Ivany Commission on building a new Nova Scotia economy was released in February 2014. Warning that the province "hovers on the brink of an extended period of decline," the report called for a *projet national* for renewed provincial development.[63] To this end Ivany set out a series of economic goals, ranging from enhanced immigration, accelerated business start-ups, and export-driven growth to municipal reform and regionalized public service delivery. The thread that seeks to hold together such disparate (and perhaps garden variety) initiatives – boosting small and medium-sized industry while rescaling provincial state structures and finances – is that of a classless and apolitical "one economy." It is too early to judge whether the Ivany formula represents an alternative to openly neo-liberal strategies on the scale of those discussed earlier in the chapter. But it does open the possibility that a new political narrative might be emerging for the provincial government to grasp.

NOTES

1 Agar Adamson and Ian Stewart, "Changing Party Politics in Atlantic Canada," in *Party Politics in Canada*, ed. Hugh G. Thorburn (Scarborough, ON: Prentice Hall Canada, 2001), 313.

2 Robert J. Brym and R. James Sacouman, eds., *Underdevelopment and Social Movements in Atlantic Canada* (Toronto: New Hogtown, 1979)

3 David Elkins and Richard Simeon, *Small Worlds: Provinces and Parties in Canadian Political Life* (Toronto: Methuen, 1980). Ian Stewart reappraised this research, in a Maritime context, in *Roasting Chestnuts: The Mythology of Maritime Political Culture* (Vancouver: UBC Press, 1994).

4 P.A. Buckner and David Frank, eds., *Atlantic Canada after Confederation* (Fredericton: Acadiensis, 1985).

5 Del Muise, "'The Great Transformation': Changing the Urban Face of Nova Scotia, 1871–1921," *Nova Scotia Historical Review* 11, no. 2 (1991): 1–29.

6 Ernest R. Forbes, *Maritime Rights: The Maritime Rights Movement 1919–1927* (Montreal and Kingston: McGill-Queen's University Press, 1979).

7 T. Stephen Henderson, *Angus L. Macdonald: A Provincial Liberal* (Toronto: University of Toronto Press, 2007).

8 Peter Clancy, "Concerted Action on the Periphery? Voluntary Economic Planning in 'The New Nova Scotia,'" *Acadiensis* 26, no. 2 (1997): 3–30; C.H.J. Gilson and A.M. Wadden, "The Windsor Gypsum Strike and the Formation of the Joint Labour/Management Study Committee: Conflict

and Accommodation in the Nova Scotia Labour Movement 1957–79," in *Workers and the State in Twentieth Century Nova Scotia*, ed. Michael Earle, 190–216 (Fredericton: Acadiensis, 1989).

9 James P. Bickerton, *Nova Scotia, Ottawa, and the Politics of Regional Development* (Toronto: University of Toronto Press, 1990).

10 Nova Scotia, Department of Finance, "Statistics," www.gov.ns.ca/finance/statistics/economy.

11 For an account of the first two terms, see Peter Kavanagh, *John Buchanan: The Art of Political Survival* (Halifax: Formac, 1988).

12 For a survey of Nova Scotia provincial policy areas in the mid-1980s, see Barbara Jamieson, ed., *Governing Nova Scotia: Policies, Priorities and the 1984–85 Budget* (Halifax: Dalhousie School of Public Administration, 1984).

13 For a discussion of the fishery, see Richard Apostle and Gene Barrett, *Emptying Their Nets: Small Capital and Rural Industrialization in the Nova Scotia Fishing Industry* (Toronto: University of Toronto Press, 1992). For the rural forestry sector, see L. Anders Sandberg and Peter Clancy, *Against the Grain: Foresters and Politics in Nova Scotia* (Vancouver: UBC Press, 2000).

14 Dean Jobb, *Calculated Risk: Greed, Politics and the Westray Tragedy* (Halifax: Nimbus, 1994).

15 Peter Clancy, Jim Bickerton, Rod Haddow, and Ian Stewart, *The Savage Years: The Perils of Re-inventing Government in Nova Scotia* (Halifax: Formac Publishing, 2000).

16 See the Ontario chapter, specifically its discussion of the policies of the McGuinty government. The Liberal government can be understood as an expression of progressive competitiveness, an important variant of neoliberalism.

17 Peter Clancy, *Offshore Petroleum Politics: Regulation and Risk in the Scotian Basin* (Vancouver: UBC Press, 2011).

18 AIMS, "Atlantica: One Region – Two Futures," Halifax: AIMS, 26 October 2003; "AIMS Talks about Atlantica with Commons Committee," 26 February 2002, http://www.aims.ca/en/home/library/details.aspx/340.

19 Halifax Gateway Council, "Building the Halifax Gateway: A New Vision of the Future" (Halifax: February 2006).

20 Nova Scotia, *Canada's East Coast Gateway via Nova Scotia* (Halifax, Department of Transportation and Public Works, 2006); CPCS Transcom, *Gateway Strategy Development Initiative, Final Report*, prepared for the Government of Nova Scotia, November 2006.

21 Canada, *National Policy Framework for Strategic Gateways and Trade Corridors* (Ottawa: Transport and Infastructure, 2009), http://www.canadasgateways.gc.ca/nationalpolicy.html.

22 Charles Cirtwell, "Follow or Get Out of the Way." Halifax: AIMS, February 2009.

23 Darrell Dexter, "State of the Province Speech," 9 December 2009.

24 This period is well reviewed by Agar Adamson, "Can the Nova Scotia NDP Stand McEwan's Strong Ale?," Atlantic Provinces Political Science Association, Papers, Antigonish, 1985.

25 For another view of the change potential for the NDP, recorded in the mid-1980s, see Patrick J. Smith and Marshall W. Conley, "'Empty Harbours, Empty Dreams': The Democratic Socialist Tradition in Atlantic Canada," in *Building the Cooperative Commonweath: Essays on the Democratic Socialist Tradition in Canada*, ed. J. William Brennan, 227–51 (Regina: Canadian Plains Research Center, 1984).

26 D. Munroe Eagles, "The 1988 Nova Scotian Election," *Canadian Political Views and Life* 1, no. 1 (October 1988): 1–4.

27 It is important to remember that public sector retrenchment was a multi-level strategy encompassing the federal Chretien-Martin Liberals as well. Indeed the first electoral reaction in Nova Scotia was in 1997 when the federal NDP elected a record six MPs from the province.

28 Jennifer Henderson, "The NDP Insiders," *CBC Online News*, 1 August 2003.

29 For 2006, see Lori Turnbull, "The 2006 Provincial Election in Nova Scotia," *Canadian Political Science Review* 1, no. 2 (December 2007): 63–8.

30 Eleanor Beaton, "Darrell Dexter: The Incrementalist," *Atlantic Business Magazine*, 5 January 2010, accessed July 12, 2011, http://www .atlanticbusinessmagazine.net/?article=darrell-dexter-the-incrementalist.

31 Corporate Research Associates, "Newsroom," data consolidated from various quarterly reports, 2006–10, accessed 20 January 2012, www.cra.ca.

32 "Better Deal 2009: The NDP Plan to Make Life Better for Today's Families."

33 Lori Turnbull, "The Nova Scotia Election of 2009," *Canadian Political Science Review* 3, no. 3 (September 2009): 69–76.

34 Matt Fodor, "The Dexter NDP: Old Wine, New Bottle?," *Bullet*, 3 January 2010, http://www.socialistproject.ca/bullet/294.php.

35 Canadian Centre for Policy Alternatives – Nova Scotia, *Nova Scotia Alternative Budget 2009*) Halifax: September 2009), https://www .policyalternatives.ca/publications/reports/nova-scotia-alternative -budget-2009.

36 See Sheldrick, this volume.

37 "Speech from the Throne: A Better Deal for Today's Families," *NS House of Assembly Debates*, 17 September 2009, 8–14.

38 Deloitte and Touche LLP, *Province of Nova Scotia Financial Review: Interim Report*, 7 August 2009.

39 "A Message from Darrell," *New Democrat Voice*, December 2009.

40 Nova Scotia Economic Advisory Panel, *Addressing Nova Scotia's Fiscal Challenge*, November 2009.

41 Corporate Research Associates, *CRA Atlantic Quarterly*, Winter 2010.

42 Judy Myrden, "Pictou County Mill Gets $28m Aid," *Chronicle Herald*, 14 October 2009; Charles W. Moore, "Blowing $14.4m on Another Bluenose Refit Irresponsible," *Chronicle Herald*, 16 December 2009; Brian Medel, "Irving Revives Shipyard with $9m N.S. Loan," *Chronicle Herald*, 6 January 2010.

43 David Jackson, "Yarmouth Loses the Cat," *Chronicle-Herald*, 19 December 2009.

44 Dan Leger, "What? Burning the Forest Creates 'Green Energy'?," *Chronicle Herald*, 16 November 2009.

45 Beverley Ware, "Boat Harbour Cleanup in Doubt," *Chronicle Herald*, 3 March 2010; Gordon Delaney, "$75m Loan to Northern Pulp Slammed," *Chronicle Herald*, 5 March 2010; John MacPhee, "Boat Harbour Fix Possible," *Chronicle Herald*, 8 March 2010.

46 Nova Scotia, *A Guide: Getting Back to Balance* (Halifax: Queen's Printer, 2009).

47 Nova Scotia, *Report of the Auditor General* (Halifax: Office Auditor General, 2010), chap. 4, "Office of the Speaker: Members' Constituency and Other Expenses," 51.

48 Ralph Surette, "Fixing Politics in N.S.: A Job Still in Progress," *Chronicle Herald*, 6 February 2010.

49 David Jackson, "House of Frill Repute," *Chronicle Herald*, 4 February 2010; Jackson, "The Frill Is Gone," *Chronicle Herald*, 5 February 2010; Jackson, "2 More Ex-MLAs Reveal Spending," *Chronicle Herald*, 6 February 2010.

50 David Jackson, "Forensic Audit Will Dig Deep into MLA Expenses, AG Says," *Chronicle Herald*, 13 February 13, 2010.

51 Clare Mellor and David Jackson, "Taxman Targets MLAs Staffers," *Chronicle Herald*, 18 February 2010.

52 Alison Auld, "MLA Wilson Resigns," *Chronicle Herald*, 13 March 2010.

53 Dan Leger, "Scandal Obscures Dexter's 'Move On' Message," *Chronicle Herald*, 15 March 2010.

54 Michael MacDonald, "Province Gains on Deficit," *Chronicle-Herald*, 3 August 2012.

55 Corporate Research Associates, *CRA Atlantic Quarterly*, Spring 2012.

56 Joann Alberstat, "New Page Gets Two More Months," *Chronicle-Herald*, 1 June 2012.

57 Beverley Ware, "Black Day at Bowater Mersey," *Chronicle-Herald*, 16 June 2012.

58 Canadian Press, "Irving Shipyard Wins $25b Shipbuilding Deal," 20 October 2011.

59 Staff, "Fisheries Offices in Province Closing," *Chronicle-Herald*, 1 June 2012; David Jackson, "ACOA to Cut Funding," *Chronicle-Herald*, 23 May 2012.

60 David Jackson, "Dexter to Ottawa: Careful with EI," *Chronicle-Herald*, 16 May 2012.

61 David Jackson, "Darrell Dexter: Economy's Friend or Foe?," *Herald Magazine*, Winter 2012.

62 Government of Nova Scotia, *Budget 2014–15 Address* (Halifax: Province of Nova Scotia), accessed April 17, 2014, http://www.novascotia.ca/finance/en/home/budget/budgetdocuments/2014-2016.aspx.

63 Nova Scotia Commission on Building Our New Economy, *One Nova Scotia: Shaping Our New Economy Together (Ivany Commission)* (Halifax: Province of Nova Scotia, 2014), http://onens.ca.

4 The Political Economy of New Brunswick: Selling New Brunswick Power

DON DESSERUD

For most of its history within the Canadian federation, New Brunswick has borne the weight of its status as a "have-not" province. This has not been a weight borne lightly, as New Brunswick has continually struggled to find the magic formula to reverse its economic fortunes. However, such a formula has eluded a succession of New Brunswick governments, regardless of whether they have been Liberal or Conservative (and they have only ever been Liberal or Conservative). Yet surely here lies the problem: New Brunswick governments have repeatedly looked for a single solution, be it a large capital project exploiting a New Brunswick natural resource, a heavily subsidized call-centre industry, or, as will be the focus of this chapter, a plan to sell the province's power utility and assets to a neighbouring province. Rather than focus on people-centric policies, such as improving the quality of its education programs, or the working conditions of labour, New Brunswick governments have invariably followed agendas set by large industries.

Such was evident in the plan constructed by Liberal government of Shawn Graham to sell New Brunswick (NB) Power to Hydro-Québec in 2009, a move that provoked considerable public protest and eventually led to that government's defeat in the 2010 provincial election. This chapter seeks to explain why the Liberal government made such a controversial and polarizing decision, and it also examines the protest that followed and assesses its impact. In so doing, this chapter seeks to provide important insights into the relationships between government, political activism, economic development, and the political economy of neoliberalism in New Brunswick.

A Fateful Decision

On 29 October 2009, the Government of New Brunswick made the star-tling announcement that it had signed a memorandum of understand-ing (MOU) to sell its utility NB Power[1] to Hydro-Québec.[2] In exchange, Hydro-Québec would guarantee fixed and lower electricity rates to both commercial and residential subscribers in the province, and absorb NB Power's debt (about $4.75 billion in 2009). The news provoked shock and outrage. NB Power, argued many, belonged to the people of the province and could not be sold without their consent.[3]

As has been demonstrated in the other chapters on Atlantic Canada, the most vocal opposition to the decision came from labour unions. Labour groups quickly united with populist protest groups under the banner "NB Power Not For Sale." Tom Mann, then executive director of the New Brunswick Public Employees Union, took a leading role in organizing the protests through the Coalition of New Brunswickers: Public Power for the Public Good. Over the next few months, these organized protests grew to unprecedented levels, eventually forcing the New Brunswick government to ask that the MOU be revised.[4] How-ever, even with a revised MOU, the protests did not abate, and on 24 March 2010, New Brunswick's Liberal premier Shawn Graham stood up in the Legislative Assembly to formally announced that "it is with much regret that ... we will no longer be proceeding with discussions to finalize the energy agreement with the province of Québec."[5]

On 27 September 2010, almost eleven months after the original announcement, the Progressive Conservatives (PCs) under David Alward soundly defeated the Graham government. The PCs, a right-of-centre party that itself had once considered privatizing NB Power, swept into office by winning forty-two of fifty-five seats.[6]

This marked the first time in New Brunswick history that a govern-ment was defeated after just one term. The deal that the Liberal govern-ment promised "would sell itself" did nothing of the kind.

New Brunswick and the Challenges of Development, 1867–2011

New Brunswick remains one of the poorer provinces in Canada. The most common explanations of New Brunswick's underdevelopment point to missed[7] or stolen[8] opportunities, and many scholars look back to 1867 as the beginning of the economic woes that have plagued the province – and the Maritimes in general – ever since. The region was prosperous in 1867, but Confederation proved overly favourable to central Canadian manufactures and financiers. The shift in economic power to central Canada weakened the conditions of Maritime prosperity, and soon systemic barriers to growth and development – many the result of Ottawa's national economic policies – took hold. As the Atlantic Provinces Economic Council (APEC) argued in 1987, "Central manufacturing developed apace behind the tariff wall to such an extent that overcapacity resulted. Surpluses were dumped on Maritime markets, and local producers were either absorbed by outside concerns, or simply went out of business. Regional banks were also absorbed by outside interests and moved, or took the initiative themselves and transferred their capital to the emerging manufacturing powerhouse of southern Ontario."[9]

Even the relative prosperity engineered by the full production of the war economy in the Second World War failed to improve conditions, and by the war's end the Maritimes had fallen considerably behind the rest of the country.[10] Subsequently, each Maritime province followed its own path towards economic recovery. In New Brunswick, this meant looking to large-scale enterprises and infrastructure projects heavily subsidized by the provincial state. The discovery of huge deposits of base-metal ores in northern New Brunswick in the 1950s convinced the governments of the day to focus their attention on developing a mining industry to parallel the province's forestry industry as two emerging pillars of what would become New Brunswick's four-pillar economy.[11] Manufacturing would be the third pillar, and eventually energy would be added as a fourth, both through the processing of oil and natural gas[12] and the generation of electricity. The latter would be accomplished through the construction of hydroelectric dams, coal and oil-fired generators, and a nuclear reactor at Point Lepreau.[13] But all four industries would be primarily export-based (at present just over 44 per cent of New Brunswick's gross domestic product is accounted for by exports).[14] The consequence is that New Brunswick's economy continues to be overly dependent on exports, which in turn are based on primary extractive and processing activities in industries notorious for their international market vagaries.

A succession of governments in New Brunswick subsidized these four industries through outright grants, tax breaks, forgivable loans, low payroll taxes, and other measures, all in hope that the industries would flourish or at least remain in the province. Some of these policies seemed to make economic sense, such as the 1960s Liberal premier

Louis Robichaud's expansion of the province's capacity to generate hydroelectricity[15] and infrastructure support for the mining industry in northern New Brunswick.[16] Others, such as PC premier Richard Hatfield's deal with Malcolm Bricklin in the mid-1970s to build sports cars in New Brunswick,[17] boarded on the outrageous.

In 1987, Frank McKenna and the Liberal Party secured an astonishing electoral victory by winning all fifty-eight seats in the New Brunswick Legislative Assembly.[18] Premier McKenna immediately set forth on an ambitious plan of economic development, which included cutting social and welfare programs, privatizing government services, and aggressively marketing New Brunswick to potential national and international investors as a province "open for business."[19] While the "McKenna Miracle"[20] did increase investor confidence, the promised economic turnaround did not take place.[21] Meanwhile, public opposition grew, fuelled by the impression that McKenna's cuts and privatization efforts were not merely attempts at running a frugal government but constituted a neoliberal rollback of the function that government was expected to play in New Brunswick: to be the protector of its citizens and trustee of the public good. Therefore, the policies that elicited the strongest emotional reaction were those that affected hospitals, youth services, welfare, and education.

Unlike those of the right-wing governments in British Columbia, Alberta, Saskatchewan, and Ontario in the 1980s and 1990s, not all of McKenna's policies were openly neoliberal, and not all of the protest came from the left. For example, the McKenna Liberals, like the Hatfield Progressive Conservatives (1970–87) and Louis Robichaud Liberals (1960–70) before him, continued to expand and entrench French-language rights in the province. This lead to the formation of a right-wing populist party, the Confederation of Regions (CoR), which held its first convention in Fredericton in 1989. Running on a platform that promised to repeal "official bilingualism," CoR managed to win eight seats in 1991 and formed the Official Opposition. Although short lived,[22] CoR's success exposed a right-wing populist protest streak in New Brunswick political culture that in 1999 was exploited by PC leader Bernard Lord.[23] More recently, this right-wing protest streak also manifested itself throughout the campaign against the sale of NB Power and became the basis for the People's Alliance of New Brunswick (PANB), a party that ran (unsuccessfully) in the 2010 election.[24]

Of all the protests against the McKenna government's reforms, none was so dramatic as what took place 2 May 1997 by a group of parents in

Saint-Sauveur, a small village in northeastern New Brunswick. Part of McKenna's cost-cutting measures included the closing of schools and the elimination of locally elected school boards, replacing them with parent committees. Although the government defended this decision as democratic, Jacques Poitras argues that the policy actually limited local democracy because it "left no outlet for those who wanted to challenge decisions." Frustrated with the government's decision to close local schools, some of the citizens of Saint-Sauveur decided to take matters into their own hands and blocked the road with a burning barricade of old tires. The McKenna government responded with force, and, writes Poitras, "there, amid a hurricane of tear gas, yapping police dogs and a roaring RCMP helicopter, the McKenna Miracle imploded."[25]

McKenna resigned in 1997 and was eventually replaced by veteran Liberal Cabinet minister Camille Theriault. Given Bernard Lord's lack of experience and low public profile, few gave the new PC leader much of a chance going into the 1999 election. However, Lord won in a landslide, winning forty-four seats to the Liberal's ten (the NDP retained its single seat). Lord's success in the 1999 election can be attributed to his ability to attract disaffected CoR supporters while capitalizing on the public's disillusionment with McKenna's economic policies, particularly his aggressive privatization agenda. Significantly, Lord also benefited from a public backlash against the Liberals' plan to allow for a privately run, tolled highway to connect the province's three major cities, Fredericton, Saint John, and Moncton. A protest group calling themselves the Tollbusters dogged the Liberal premier and ultimately knocked the Liberal campaign off its stride.[26] Again, the issue was whether a government had a right to privatize a public good, in this case a highway.

The 1999 PC campaign also adopted many of the CoR Party's promises, such as calls for referenda, recall legislation, and other mechanisms to convince MLAs to be more accountable to their constituents.[27] In addition, Lord offered to return state support to those sectors the Liberals had found too expensive and to abandon the Liberal strategy of selling New Brunswick as (merely) a good place to do business.

Nevertheless, the Lord government's popularity soon began to wane. The democratic reforms Lord promised in the 1999 campaign were slow in coming, while others were deemed impractical. Spending was increased in many sectors, but cuts were also made in others. Mimicking neoliberal governments throughout the country, Lord lowered corporate taxes, "in hopes of making the province attractive for investment."[28]

Public consultations did take place, but Lord had backed himself into a corner: when he consulted, he was criticized for procrastination; when he did not, he was accused of betraying his promises. Meanwhile, the Liberals chose a new leader, Shawn Graham, who quickly made a reputation as an aggressive, confident opposition leader.

The PCs won the 2003 election by the smallest of margins, keeping twenty-eight seats to the Liberals' twenty-six (the NDP once again held onto one seat). The next three years were difficult for the Lord government, which saw a revitalized Liberal opposition pushing the Lord government on every item, and even forcing the Speaker to cast deciding votes on the floor of the legislature. By 2006, Lord had had enough, and he called an election a year early. This time, the Liberals were victorious, winning twenty-nine seats to the PCs' twenty-six (no other party won a seat).[29] The new Liberal premier did not waste time pursuing his promise of "transformational change." However, one after another, the Graham initiatives fell short.

The Liberals' 2006 platform had three main planks: education, energy, and the economy. Immediately after winning the election, the Graham government promised that its policies would bring forth a self-sufficient New Brunswick by 2026.[30] The government also created a commission on postsecondary education to review education spending in the province (PSE). The committee recommended reorganizing the province's post-secondary education system, further integration of the community colleges with the universities, and a transformation of the Saint John campus of the University of New Brunswick into a "polytechnic."[31] Equally significant reforms were proposed for the province's French-language programs, which included scrapping both New Brunswick's early French immersion and core French programs and replacing both with an integrated program. Transformational change was also promised for the energy sector. New Brunswick would work with the federal government to refurbishment the nuclear generating station at Point Lepreau and construct a second nuclear generating station (Point Lepreau II).[32] Coupled with Irving Oil's plan to construct a second oil refinery, Saint John would also become an "energy hub" and its new polytechnic would be charged with training the technicians and workers soon to be demanded by the energy sector.[33] Economic renewal would be the consequence of the first two transformations. With a revitalized, efficient, and integrated education system coupled with a diversified energy production industry, New Brunswick's economy would grow at a steady but significant rate.

But things did not work out the way the government planned. Throughout Graham's term, public protest zeroed in on the reforms to education, attacking, first, the proposals to scrap the province's French immersion program,[34] and second, the proposal to transform New Brunswick's post-secondary education system into one that would serve primarily the industrial needs of the province.[35]

The first decision prompted protest and eventually a legal challenge. But the second issue sparked the most public protest. For perhaps the first time in New Brunswick's political history, social media revealed its potency. Facebook, YouTube, and several blogs provided robust forums for the exchange of ideas and opinions. As well, such social media allowed for efficient organization of protest events. Rallies were held across the province, and despite government assurances that these protests would die down, protestors kept up the pressure.

On 31 January 2008, Premier Graham delivered his annual "State of the Province" address and announced that a "working group" comprising the province's university and college presidents to reconsider the PSE's original report. Meanwhile, the premier promised that "the University of New Brunswick in Saint John [would] remain the University of New Brunswick in Saint John [and retain] programs like liberal arts while expanding with new program offerings to meet emerging economic opportunities."[36] The government had backed down, and most interpreted its tepid support for the Saint John Campus as a face-saving way out of the crisis.

Elsewhere, the government's other plans began to unravel. First, the refurbishment of Point Lepreau ran into lengthy and costly overruns (which became a significant factor in the decision to sell NB Power). Then Irving Oil announced that it was indefinitely postponing its plans to build a second refinery. The plans to build a second reactor also hit snags, with Atomic Energy of Canada Limited (AECL) losing interest.

Meanwhile, New Brunswick's economy continued to worsen. Exports suffered as the result of a stronger Canadian dollar, while technological innovations in key industrial sectors such as forestry[37] undermined New Brunswick's geographic advantage. New Brunswick's debt rose to unprecedented levels and was pegged at $7.4 billion (in September 2009), an increase of $0.5 billion in the 2008–9 fiscal year alone. The $19-million surplus of 2008 was now a deficit of $192.3 million.[38] With the election date "fixed" for 27 September 2010, time was running out, and the Graham government faced a short year in which to respond to these growing political and economic crises.

By 2009, the government was polling at record lows, and the Liberals knew they had to do something to prevent a defeat in the next election. Someone in the Premier's Office, possibly the premier himself, decided that selling NB Power to Hydro-Québec would reverse the government's fortunes. Explaining how the Liberal government could come to this conclusion requires us to consider the ideological context of the Graham government, its decision-making style, and its obsession with "transformational change" in the province.

NB Power and the Politics of Neoliberalism in New Brunswick

The history of New Brunswick's power utility is similar to those of power utilities across the country. Over time, respective provincial governments have consolidated their private power-generating enterprises into a single public utility. In New Brunswick, this process began in 1920 when the Liberal government under Walter E. Foster brought forward the New Brunswick Electric Power Act, which in turn created the New Brunswick Electric Power Commission. Over the next sixty years, the commission (which changed its name to NB Power in the 1970s) bought or built new generating stations, eventually consolidating most of the power generation of the province under one utility.[39]

There are currently nine hydroelectric generating stations in the province. NB Power owns seven, one is privately owned, and NB Power and a private company operate another jointly. The province also has ten thermo-generators. Two are also privately owned. Finally, New Brunswick has a Canada Deuterium Uranium (CANDU) nuclear reactor at Point Lepreau, which was completed in 1981 and began producing power in 1983 but has been offline since May 2008 as a major refurbishment takes place. By some estimates, the delays in this refurbishment cost NB Power anywhere from $0.5 to $1 million a day to replace the power not being generated by the reactor.[40]

The New Brunswick media invariably preface references to NB Power with the adjective "debt-laden." The utility has indeed suffered debt for much of its history, and a succession of New Brunswick governments has tried to find some way to deal with it. In the early 1990s, with a goal of seeing NB Power operate "more like a business," Premier McKenna moved the chairmanship of NB Power out of Cabinet and appointed "the first non-elected or non-politician chairman of the board of directors."[41] Yet still the debt load continued to increase, so much so that then-PC leader Bernard Valcourt tried, albeit unsuccessfully, to make NB Power's debt an election issue in 1995. He was convinced that if the public knew how high the debt load was, McKenna's reputation as a sound fiscal manager would be tarnished.[42] In 1998, a year after McKenna retired, the New Brunswick Government (then under interim Liberal leader Ray Frenette) produced a discussion paper titled "Electricity in New Brunswick beyond 2000," which pointed out that "NB Power currently has an inappropriately high level of debt, resulting primarily from an aggressive program over the past twenty years to construct new generation facilities, and a failure to raise rates charged for electricity by sufficient amounts during that period. In addition, current operational problems at the Point Lepreau nuclear facility are placing an added strain on NB Power's ability to pay down its debt."[43]

When Bernard Lord became premier in 1999, he also tried to find a way to alleviate the utility's economic woes.[44] Lord's solution was to break the utility into four distinct companies, all owned by a holding company (Holdco). Although not exactly privatization, the logic for splitting the companies was consistent with those advocating selling NB Power to the private sector. As Richard Wilbur explained, with the "debt-ridden facility" now owing $2.9 billion and about to accrue an additional debt of $1.6 billion, Lord wanted each of the four companies to be "responsible for any money that they would borrow and [know that] the province would not guarantee their loans. Premier Lord said that the province 'just can't afford to increase its debt by borrowing the money. We want someone else to put their money on the line.'"[45]

Problems continued. A deal to purchase Orimulsion from Venezuela, which would be used at the thermo-generator at Coleson Cove, collapsed but not before the utility spent about $750 million on refitting Coleson Cove to burn the new fuel. NP Power sued to recover damages, but was only able to settle the matter on 3 August 2007.[46]

By the time of the 2006 election campaign, NB Power's overall debt was still growing. However, the PC government did not seem to be worried. Its platform ("Getting Results, Together") dealt with NB Power in one sentence: "The cost of home heating was recently made more affordable by the decision to cap the increase on rising NB Power rates and to rebate consumers 8 percent, an amount equivalent to the Provincial portion of the Harmonized Sales Tax."[47] The Liberals, on the other hand, emphasized the importance of NB Power as a public service. Its "Charter for Change" outlined a comprehensive set of plans for NB Power and energy production in the province in general, including, among other things, a pledge to "maintain NB Power as a *publicly-owned* utility that will serve all New Brunswickers equally; Amend the *Electricity Act* to include a clear statement of purpose that puts the *public good* of New Brunswickers at the forefront; [and] Establish a no-disconnect policy between November 1 and March 31 for households in legitimate economic need."[48]

Both parties, but particularly the Liberals, claimed to understand that the public saw the provision of services by NB Power as a public good, and that the role of government was to ensure that the utility continued to provide such a role. It is hardly surprising, then, when faced with such a blatant disregard for its election promise, the public reacted strongly to the Liberal government's announcement (seemingly out of nowhere) that the power utility was to be sold to another province.

To recap, NB Power was (and continues to be) a utility burdened by debt, and this debt has been a concern to a succession of New Brunswick governments. Until the Graham Liberals, however, no government was prepared to do anything more than restructure the utility or to find some means of removing NB Power's debt from the government's books. Occasionally, the idea to privatize the utility would be floated, the latest when Bernard Lord was premier.[49] Yet such ideas were almost immediately shelved in the face of strong public opposition to such an initiative.

However, the Graham Liberals were not "most governments." Once elected in 2006, the Graham government lost no time in declaring its real attitude towards NB Power and the public service it supplied. For example, the new energy minister, Jack Keir, proposed that NB Power should charge market rates and no longer receive subsidies from the New Brunswick taxpayer. "We should not," he continued, "be using NB Power as a social program. We have social programs."[50] With this in mind, the Graham government began looking at different ways to rid itself of the NB Power "burden."

Negotiations with the Province of Quebec began in January 2009.[51] By May of 2009, the code name assigned to the negotiations – Operation Penelope – began appearing on the agenda of the monthly meetings held between the president of NB Power and the premier. How, then, did such a controversial deal negotiated over a nine-month period avoid controversy or scrutiny? The answer is simple: the negotiations were completed in private and only a few ministers were privy to the dealings.

Similar to neoliberal governments throughout Canada, decision-making in New Brunswick has become increasingly concentrated in the Office of the Premier.[52] As elsewhere, this concentration of power has led to an increasing democratic deficit in the province. Beginning with Louis Robichaud's ambitious program of Equal Opportunity in the 1960s, the Office of the Premier began acquiring more and more responsibilities for social and economic policies. Increasingly, decision-making moved out of Cabinet and into the hands of the premier, his advisors, and carefully selected senior civil servants.[53] Under PC premier Richard Hatfield, the professionalization of the civil service continued, entrenching the power of the premier's bureaucratic advisors.[54] Power was further concentrated into the Office of the Premier under Frank McKenna, who "felt quite at ease being labeled (as he was) the 'CEO of the province.'"[55]

Under Bernard Lord, McKenna's simplified Cabinet committee system – under which six committees were reduced to two, one chaired by the premier and the other by the minister of finance – was retained.[56] Graham retained the same two Cabinet committees as well, but the problem under Graham – at least as indicated by some of his Cabinet colleagues – was that Cabinet ceased to be a decision-making body at all. Savoie has famously said that over time the function of Cabinet in Ottawa has become a glorified focus group.[57] Under Graham, Cabinet did not even play that role.[58]

The centralization of power in the Premier's Office became readily apparent when Graham announced the MOU to sell NB Power. Almost immediately, rumours of dissatisfaction from within Cabinet emerged. And while it is difficult to determine exactly when members of Cabinet began to voice their opposition to the deal, it is significant that dissent emerged from the confines of Cabinet solidarity at all. By Christmas 2009, it was all but official that at least three Cabinet ministers were prepared to break ranks.[59]

It is unknown if any other dissent took place within Cabinet. However, when interviewed by this author and speaking under conditions of anonymity, one former Cabinet minister complained that, in any case, neither Cabinet dissent nor support was relevant as far as Graham's decision to sell NB Power went: "We had *zero* input. We didn't know. We were told two weeks before after nine months of secret negotiations of 'Operation Penelope' (as it was called). When we saw the MOU on the Monday night [26 October 2009] before the Thursday announcement it had little similarity to what we were told for the previous ten days. It was, like all 'special projects,' decided beforehand [and presented] to Cabinet [with] no room for refusal. We were less, at times, than even a focus group."

So instead of relying on advice from people who had a better sense of (and ear for) the public's concerns, or even from experts in the energy field who just a year before advised against selling NB Power,[60] Graham saw the proposal to sell NB Power as an opportunity to rid himself of a colossal headache and provide an instant solution to a problem that had plagued New Brunswick governments for years. At the same time, the Liberals seemed to believe that the public shared its concerns over NB Power's burgeoning debt and would therefore welcome the decision. The premier was convinced that, with this sale, the controversies dogging the Liberals over the past three years would be forgotten and the party would be propelled to victory in 2010.

The Politics of Privatization: The 2010 Election and Its Aftermath

The results of the 2010 election were not surprising, except perhaps for the magnitude of the Progressive Conservative win. David Alward's PCs won forty-two seats (48.8 per cent of the popular vote); the Liberals won just thirteen seats (34.5 per cent of the popular vote, a historic low). No other party won a seat, although the 2010 election tied a record for the most parties (five) running in a New Brunswick provincial election. Besides the Liberals and the PCs, the NDP, Greens, and PANB all fielded candidates. Of the three other parties, the NDP had the best showing, with 10.4 per cent of the popular vote.

The Liberals made two strategic errors. First, Graham expected the public to favour privatizing NB Power; second, the Liberals assumed the public would regard selling NB Power to another province's public utility as the same as privatizing it, perhaps even considering Hydro-Québec as an even more attractive owner. However, Graham was wrong on both counts.

The neoliberal defence of privatization is that government managers make political decisions, not business decisions. Political decisions, such as respecting the public's demands (reflected in their electoral behaviour) makes for "bad business." On the other hand, making decisions based on the desire for profit, even if such a desire disregards the public good, makes for "good business." Under this argument, and in the context of the decision to sell NB Power, maintaining a viable workforce with good wages and producing power at a reasonable rate would be "bad business." Making a profit, even if that meant laying off workers, cutting wages,[61] raising rates, and purchasing cheap raw materials from environmentally questionable sources constitutes "good business" decisions.

As well, privatization is supposed to provide better service (usually framed as "more economical delivery of service") and helps relieve the government's debt.[62] But the public has to be convinced that government debt is a significant problem. Once that happens, the logic of privatization invariably follows. As H.T. Wilson explains, "If the public debt is a (or the) key concept for defining the problem with mature capitalist economies for neo-conservatives, then privatization is certainly one of the major vehicles for resolving it."[63] Of course, it is true that provincial debt and its associated high service costs is a serious issue: the higher the debt load, the less money is available to pay for necessary public services. However, the use of debt as a justification for policies such as privatization is another thing altogether and is too often a means of justifying a government's abnegation of its responsibilities as stewards of the public good.[64] Furthermore, whether it is socially just to make a profit over services essential to the basic needs of the people is seldom questioned. There are, after all, other routes a government can take to reduce debt: one is to increase productivity – and therefore taxable profits – through better training programs and investments in education.[65] At the very least, governments can raise (or at least avoid lowering) corporate taxes.

Still, privatization does have an intuitive appeal, one that proponents are quick to exploit.[66] The cynicism of the public towards governments and how they operate feeds into the deceptive argument that, since governments appear to be inept, the private sector must necessarily be more efficient and productive. Therefore, it is conceivable that a bid to sell NB Power to a (say) New Brunswick company might have been accepted, albeit grudgingly, by the public. At least there would have been some comfort from the fact that any company operating in New Brunswick would still be subject to New Brunswick regulations, which in turn would be administered by a government the public had the ability to re-elect or defeat.[67]

However, the Graham government was not proposing to privatize NB Power; it was proposing to sell it to another province. The government may have thought it could justify the sale on the grounds that selling the utility to Hydro-Québec was just like privatizing it. But the public of New Brunswick thought differently. NB Power was a public utility, owned by the people, built to serve the people, and designed to provide an essential and vital service. It was and is, then, a public good. As the NB Power's own website puts it, "Here to serve the people of our province, NB Power has become part of the everyday lives of New Brunswickers. We've warmed homes, employed thousands, powered Christmas trees, and lit the way home."[68] Were the sale to go through, this service would be in the hands of a company beholden not to the people of New Brunswick but to a government of another province, a government that would put the interests of its own public first, as is the duty of any provincial government.[69] No New Brunswicker had a vote in Quebec.

Finally, and ironically, the Graham government's choice of another province as a potential buyer undermined the one argument it might have been able to sustain: that privatizing a public utility is a good idea because the private sector should do a better job of running the enterprise. But Hydro-Québec is not a private company, a point made very clear at the press conference that announced the deal on 29 October 2009. The photos and news clips of the press conference all showed, not the chairmen of NB Power and Hydro-Québec shaking hands, but premier Shawn Graham shaking hands with premier Jean Charest. Now, it is one thing for a government to say that the private sector can manage a utility better than government can; it is another to say that the Government of New Brunswick cannot manage NB Power but the Government of Quebec can. The first is based on a theory of competence that says that private managers are more efficient than government ones, because such managers respond to different incentives.[70] The second says that the New Brunswick government is incompetent but the Quebec government is not. This, then, undermined the argument that governments cannot run power utilities. Apparently governments can, because the Government of Quebec can. Meetings were held around the province in an attempt to sell the deal to the public, but the same question was asked over and over: "If the New Brunswick government can't run NB Power, why is it that Quebec can?"

The Liberal government tracked public opinion throughout the NB Power protests. The 4 November 2009 poll asked those who opposed the sale of NB Power why they were unsupportive. The single reason cited by the largest number of respondents (28 per cent) was that NB Power was a provincial asset and should remain so. Most of the other reasons that people were against the sale pointed to the same conclusion: the province should be able to solve NB Power's problems itself, and selling it to another province would mean a loss of public control. What happened in New Brunswick, then, was a collective realization that the Graham government was not only planning to sell something that provided an essential service – heat and light in a province with a long, dark winter rapidly approaching – but that it was planning to sell something it did not own: NB Power was owned by the people, and the people had not been asked whether they wanted it sold. At the same time, the government was admitting it had given up trying to solve the NB Power problem.

In summary, NB Power's growing debt, coupled with its crumbling infrastructure and questionable long-term ability to meet the future power demands of its customers, convinced the Graham government that a dramatic solution was needed. But it completely misread the New Brunswick public's understanding and expectations of the utility. NB Power might not be a social program, as the energy minister put it, but it was a public service providing a needed public good. Threatening to sell it would mean New Brunswickers would be vulnerable, subject to the decisions made by a government in a different province. Privatizing NB Power would have also been unpopular, but at least a private company would have had to accept the regulations imposed upon it by the New Brunswick government. Would another province, particularly a large and powerful province like Quebec, be so willing to accept New Brunswick regulatory oversight and authority? A majority of New Brunswickers did not think so, and a significant number knew how to take the issue to the streets in the form of sustained public protest.

Conclusion

Under the premiership of Shawn Graham, New Brunswick's Liberal government wanted to leave a lasting legacy. It hoped to have an impact similar in scale to that of Louis Robichaud's Program for Equal Opportunity in the 1960s, and Frank McKenna's "Miracle" in the 1990s. However, none of its efforts at transformational change worked, and by 2009 it was becoming somewhat desperate for a legacy item. A history of debt problems made NB Power a likely target, and Quebec's desire to expand its power monopoly made Quebec an attractive partner.

But the Graham government had already lost the trust of New Brunswickers, and this had little chance of convincing the public that selling the utility to Quebec was a good idea. Much has been made of the public's "emotional" reaction to the proposed deal, with the implication that people behaving emotionally are not thinking rationally. However, public utilities such as power companies provide essential and life-sustaining services, which are indeed regarded with an emotional attachment. It should not be surprising that in a province with long, dark, and cold winters, people might worry about being warm and being able to see at night. Meanwhile, New Brunswickers are politically patient and generally support only one of the two conventional parties: the Liberals or the PCs. However, they can react strongly when they believe their core values are being threatened, and over the years a significant number of New Brunswickers had developed considerable skill in staging effective protests under such circumstances. While the Graham government's transformational change agenda repeatedly struck a nerve in the province, the proposed sale of NB Power to Hydro-Québec hit it with a mighty blow. The Liberal government was not only abandoning its responsibilities as stewards of a public good, it was selling them to another province. And so the public responded accordingly.

In the end, the deal to sell NB Power was called off. Whether it was the Liberal or Quebec government that cancelled the deal to sell NB Power to Hydro-Québec is not known.[71] During the leadership debates, Premier Graham tried to find something positive to say about the entire debacle and suggested that by cancelling the deal, he proved that his government listened to the people. Premier Charest, however, claimed that the assets included in the revised deal did not meet the Quebec government's expectations.[72] There is something to Premier Charest's claim. In a post-election interview, Graham was asked whether he could have done a better job of selling the proposed deal to the New Brunswick public. Graham explained that he had not been in a position to reveal just how badly the province needed the deal, because he was afraid he would scare off the potential buyer: "If you're trying to dispose of an asset, you can't go out and tell everyone how bad it is. It's like, 'I want you to buy this car, but the car isn't working.' That was the conundrum we were in."[73]

NOTES

1 For a profile, see NB Power, *Serving You ... Today and Tomorrow, 2009/10, Sustainability Report*, www.nbpower.com/html/en/about/publications/annual/2009-10AR-ENG.pdf.
2 "Québec, N.B. Strike $4.8B Deal for NB Power," CBC News, 29 October 2009, accessed 3 July 2011, www.cbc.ca/canada/new-brunswick/quebec-n-b-strike-4-8b-deal-for-nb-power-1.787566.

3 John Pollack, "Hundreds of Demonstrators Protest NB Power Sale Agreement at Legislature," *Telegraph Journal,* 18 November 2009.

4 "Province Retains Control of NB Power in Revised Deal: N.B., Québec Premiers Both Praise New Agreement," CBC News, 19 January 2010.

5 Shawn McCarthy and Rheal Seguin, "N.B., Québec's Ambitions for Power Fizzle Out as Hydro Deal Falls Through," *Globe and Mail,* 25 March 2010; "Reaction from NB Power Deal Collapse," CBC News, 25 March 2010, accessed 2 May 2010, www.cbc.ca/canada/new-brunswick/story/2010/03/24/nb-nbpower-Québec-deal-reaction-308.html.

6 That the PCs, and not the NDP were the beneficiaries of the public's anger is perplexing. However, the NDP has enjoyed only the most limited success in New Brunswick. Some have argued that the lack of success of all third parties, left or right, is the result of the intense parochialism and strong partisan loyalties of New Brunswick voters to the old-line Liberals and PCs. See Donald Blake, "Electoral Democracy in the Provinces," *Choices* 7, no. 2 (2001): 1–37; R. Kenneth Carty and Munroe Eagles, "Party Activity across Electoral Cycles: The New Brunswick Party System, 1979–1994," *Canadian Journal of Political Science* 36 (2003): 381–99. Others argue that powerful industrial interests monopolize the province's traditional media, enjoy a comfortable relationship with the two traditional parties, and have thwarted the growth of strong union movements and a broader culture of social activism. On this point, see D.J. Loree and D.R. Pullman, "Sociopolitical Facets of a Plural Province: Reasons for the Failure of 'Third Parties' in New Brunswick, Canada," *Plural Societies* 10 (1979): 85–102; Erin Steuter and Geoff Martin, "The Irvings Cover Themselves: Media Representations of the Irving Oil Refinery Strike, 1994–1996," *Canadian Journal of Communication* 24 (1999): 1–18. The punishing effects of the first-past-the-post electoral system have likely also had an effect on the New Brunswick public's patience with third parties. See, for example, Rein Taagepera, "Party Size Baselines Imposed by Institutional Constraints: Theory for Simple Electoral Systems," *Journal of Theoretical Politics* 3 (2001): 331–54. Finally, see Shaun Bowler and David J. Lanoue, "Strategic and Protest Voting for Third Parties: The Case of the Canadian NDP," *Political Research Quarterly* 45 (1992): 485–99; Nicole O'Byrne and Gregory Ericson, "Is There a Future for the NDP in New Brunswick?," *Inroads: The Canadian Journal of Opinion* 28 (2011): 20–3.

7 Young argues that the province squandered post-war surpluses, while Savoie sees the region's failure to embrace Maritime Union as a major cause of its economic stagnation. R.A. Young, "'And the People Will Sink into Despair': Reconstruction Policy in New Brunswick," *Canadian*

Historical Review 69 (1988): 127–66; Donald J. Savoie, *Visiting Grandchildren: Economic Development in the Maritimes* (Toronto: University of Toronto Press, 2006), 227.

8 Labour historians such as E.R. Forbes and T.W. Acheson point to the impact that national economic policies have had on the region. E.R Forbes, "Misguided Symmetry: The Destruction of Regional Transportation Policy for the Maritimes," in *Canada and the Burden of Unity*, ed. David Jay Bercuson, 60–86 (Toronto: University of Toronto Press, 1977); Forbes, *The Maritime Rights Movement, 1919–1927: A Study in Canadian Regionalism* (Montreal and Kingston: McGill-Queen's University Press, 1979); T.W. Acheson, "The National Policy and the Industrialization of the Maritimes, 1880–1910," *Acadiensis* 1 (1971): 3–28. In general, see S.A. Saunders, *The Economic History of the Maritime Provinces* (Fredericton: Acadiensis, 1984).

9 Atlantic Provinces Economic Council, *Atlantic Canada Today* (Halifax: Formac, 1987), 8. See also David Alexander, "Economic Growth in the Atlantic Region, 1880–1940," *Acadiensis* 8 (1978): 47–76; Donald J. Savoie, "New Brunswick: Let's Not Waste a Crisis," *Journal of New Brunswick Studies* 1 (2010): 54–63.

10 B.S. Keirstead, *The Economic Effects of the War on the Maritime Provinces of Canada* (Halifax: Lattimer, 1944); E.R. Forbes, "Consolidating Disparity: The Maritimes and the Industrialization of Canada during the Second World War," in *Atlantic Canada after Confederation*, ed. P.A. Buckner and David Frank, 2nd ed., 383–407 (Fredericton: Acadiensis, 1988).

11 Margaret Conrad, "The 1950s: The Decade of Development," in *The Atlantic Provinces in Confederation*, ed. E.R. Forbes and D.A. Muise, 382–420 (Toronto: University of Toronto Press, 1993); James L. Kenny, "A New Dependency: State, Local Capital, and the Development of New Brunswick's Base Metal Industry, 1960," *Canadian Historical Review* 78 (1997): 1–39; Della Stanley, "The 1960s: The Illusions and Realities of Progress," in *The Atlantic Provinces in Confederation*, ed. Ernest Forbes and D.A. Muise, 421–59 (Fredericton: Acadiensis, 1993); A.C. Parks, "The Atlantic Provinces of Canada," *Journal of Industrial Economics* 13 (1965): 76–87.

12 Petroleum products produced at the Irving Oil refinery in Saint John account for more than half of all New Brunswick exports. See Government of New Brunswick (hereafter GNB), *The New Brunswick Reality Report: Part 2; An Export-Driven Economy* (Fredericton: Queen's Printer, 2007), 4–10.

13 Ernest R. Forbes, *Maritime Rights: The Maritime Rights Movement, 1919–27: A Study in Canadian Regionalism* (Montreal and Kingston: McGill-Queen's University Press, 1979), 6. Also see Export Development Canada, "New

Brunswick Export Growth to Lead Country in 2010, Says EDC," 28 May 2010, http://www.newswire.ca/en/story/519199/new-brunswick -export-growth-to-lead-country-in-2010-says-edc. The fishery, still an important industry, nevertheless has never been as important to the New Brunswick economy has it has been to Newfoundland, Nova Scotia, or PEI. According to Export Development Canada, New Brunswick's "third largest export sector ... is agrifood, accounting for 11 percent of the province's total."

14 GNB, Ministry of Finance, "Merchandise Domestic Exports, Customs- Based," 2014, http://www2.gnb.ca/content/dam/gnb/Departments/ fin/pdf/esi/Exports-Exportations.pdf.

15 But see Joshua John Dickison, "Making New Brunswickers Modern: Natural and Human Resource Development in Mactaquac Regional Development Plan 1965–1975" (MA thesis, University of New Brunswick, 2006); Katie Shawn Ferrar, "Power for Progress: The Mactaquac Hydroelectric Development and Regional Development Plans, 1964–1968" (MA thesis, University of New Brunswick, 2005).

16 Donald Savoie argues that such initiatives rarely produced the results expected. Donald J. Savoie, *La lutte pour le développement: Le cas du Nord-Est* (Québec: Les Presses de l'Université du Québec, 1988); Savoie, "Rural Redevelopment in Canada: The Case of Northeast New Brunswick," *Journal of Rural Studies* 5 (1989): 185–97.

17 H.A. Fredericks, with Allan Chambers, *Bricklin* (Fredericton: Brunswick, 1977).

18 Stewart Hyson, "The Horrible Example: New Brunswick's 58-to-0 Election Result Is a Clear Argument for the Advantages of Proportional Representation," *Policy Options* 9, no. 8 (1988), 25–7; Hyson, "Where's 'Her Majesty's Loyal Opposition' in the Loyalist Province?" *Canadian Parliamentary Review* 11, no. 2 (1988), 22–5; Philip Lee, *Frank: The Life and Politics of Frank McKenna* (Fredericton: Goose Lane Editions, 2001).

19 Donald J. Savoie, *Pulling against Gravity: Economic Development in New Brunswick during the McKenna Years* (Montreal: Institute for Research in Public Policy, 2001), 101.

20 John Lownsbrough, "The Energizer Premier," *Report on Business,* March 1993.

21 William J. Milne, *The McKenna Miracle: Myth or Reality?* (Toronto: Centre for Public Management, University of Toronto, 1996); Savoie, *Pulling against Gravity.*

22 See Geoffrey R. Martin, "We've Seen It All Before: The Rise and Fall of the Confederation of Regions Party of New Brunswick, 1988–1995," *Journal of*

Canadian Studies 33 (1998): 22–38. The party failed to win any seats in the subsequent election and eventually disbanded on 31 March 2002.

23 Chedly Belkhodja, "La dimension populiste de l'émergence et du succès électoral du Parti Confederation of Regions au Nouveau-Brunswick," *Canadian Journal of Political Science* 32 (1999): 293–315.

24 "People's Alliance Forms New N.B. Political Party," CBC News, 9 June 2010, www.cbc.ca/news/canada/new-brunswick/story/2010/06/09/nb -panb-official-party-status-221.html. ˙

25 Jacques Poitras, *The Right Fight: Bernard Lord and the Conservative Dilemma* (Fredericton: Goose Lane Editions, 2004), 250.

26 See William Shaffir and Steven Kleinknect, "The Trauma of Political Defeat," *Canadian Parliamentary Review* (Autumn 2002): 16–21.

27 Election platforms for New Brunswick political parties (the earliest is the Liberals' 1974 platform) can be found at Poltext, www.poltext.capp .ulaval.ca/cms/index.php?menu=16&temps=1290439249. The PC election platform called for "MLA Responsibility Act setting out the key roles and duties of MLAs, a code of conduct, and requiring that each MLA hold at least two public meetings per year" (9). According to the basic principles of the 1999 platform, "We believe that government is an extension of the will of the people; therefore, we must answer to the people for the responsibilities which we accept. We will consult with New Brunswickers on public policy matters before implementing solutions" (1). See William Cross, "Leadership Selection in New Brunswick: Balancing Language Representation and Populist Impulses," in *Political Parties, Representation, and Electoral Democracy in Canada*, ed. William Cross, 37–54 (Don Mills, ON: Oxford University Press, 2002).

28 Stewart Hyson, "Governing from the Centre in New Brunswick," in *Executive Styles in Canada: Cabinet Decision-Making Structures and Practices at the Federal and Provincial Levels*, ed. Luc Bernier, Keith Brownsey, and Michael Howlett (Toronto: University of Toronto Press, 2005), 88.

29 See Don Desserud, "The 2006 Provincial Election in New Brunswick," *Canadian Political Science Review* 2 (2008): 51–63.

30 GNB, *The Road to Self-Sufficiency: A Common Cause* (Fredericton: Queen's Printer, 2007), 2. For discussion, see Michael Boudreau, Peter G. Toner, and Tony Tremblay, eds., *Exploring the Dimensions of Self-Sufficiency for New Brunswick* (Fredericton: New Brunswick and Atlantic Studies Research and Development Centre, 2009).

31 See Rick Miner and Jacques L'Ecuyer, *Advantage New Brunswick: A Province Reaches to Fulfill Its Destiny* (Fredericton: Commission on Post-Secondary Education in New Brunswick, 2007), www.gnb.ca/cpse-ceps/EN/docs/

CEPNB_cahier_ang_LR.pdf. See as well Association of University of New Brunswick Teachers, "AUNBT & the New Brunswick Post-Secondary Education Crisis," 2008, http://aunbt.caut.ca/psecrisis.html.

32 A promise that had also been made by Richard Hatfield in 1982. See Lee, *Frank*, 109.

33 GNB, *Our Action Plan to Be Self-Sufficient in New Brunswick* (Fredericton: Queen's Printer, 2007), 19.

34 New Brunswick Court of Queen's Bench, *Small & Ryan v New Brunswick (Minister of Education)*, NBQB 201 (2008), 7. Tom Bateman, "The Law and Politics of Public Consultation in New Brunswick," presented to the Annual Meeting of the Atlantic Provinces Political Science Association, 3–5 October 2008, Halifax.

35 See E.J. Hyslop-Margison and A. Sears, "The Neoliberal Assault on Democratic Learning," *UCFV Research* 2, no. 1 (2008): 28–38.

36 See GNB, "State of the Province Address: 2008 to Be Turning Point for Province," news release, http://www2.gnb.ca/content/gnb/en/news/news_release.2008.01.0119.html.

37 According to the New Brunswick Forestry Products Association, as of 2010 the forest sector directly contributed just over 5 per cent to the provincial GDP. At 5.1 per cent, that makes the forest products industry in New Brunswick more important to the provincial economy than in all other provinces in Canada. See New Brunswick Forestry Products Association, *Economic Value*, www.nbforestry.com/economy/economic-value. See also APEC, "Building Competitiveness in Atlantic Canada's Forest Industries: A Strategy for Future Prosperity," *APEC Forum on Competitiveness, 2005–2010*, August 2008, https://www.apec-econ.ca/publications/view/?do-load=1&publication.id=167&site.page.id=103004&search-form.theme=Industry%20Specific%20Reports. See also Lyndhurst Collins, "Environmental Performance and Technological Innovation: The Pulp and Paper Industry as a Case in Point," *Technology in Society* 16 (1994): 427–46. For the 2010 exports by commodity, see GNB, Department of Finance, "Provincial Profile: New Brunswick, Canada," http://www2.gnb.ca/content/dam/gnb/Departments/ed-de/PDF/ExportTrade-Commerce/NBProfile2014.pdf.

38 Quentin Casey, "Provincial Deficit $192M, Figures Show," *Telegraph Journal*, 29 September 2009. Nevertheless, when calculated as debt per capita, New Brunswick's is $11,149, while Ontario's is $14,790, Quebec's is $18,247, and Nova Scotia's is $14,183. The national debt per person is $15,765, and the Atlantic average is $12,488. See Gouvernement de la province de Québec (GPQ), *Dette nette des gouvernements par habitant au 31 mars, 1987–2011*,

Institute de la statistique du Québec, *Interprovincial Comparisons* (2010), table 13.11, www.stat.gouv.qc.ca/donstat/econm_finnc/conjn_econm/ TSC/pdf/chap13.pdf.

39 James L. Kenny and Andrew Secord, "Public Power for Industry: A Re-examination of the New Brunswick Case, 1940–1960," *Acadiensis* 30 (2001): 84–108.

40 "N.B. Nuclear Plant Faces Delay over Fuel Tubes," CBC News, 9 October 2010; Greg Weston, "Power Doesn't Cost $1m per Day," *Telegraph Journal*, 19 January 2010.

41 Savoie, *Pulling against Gravity*, 133.

42 Poitras, *The Right Fight*, 224.

43 GNB, "Electricity in New Brunswick beyond 2000: Discussion Paper" (Fredericton: Queen's Printer, 1998), 2.

44 "Electricity in New Brunswick and Options for Its Future, Special Task Force," co-chaired by David D. Hay and Donald J. Savoie (1998), www .gnb.ca/legis/business/committees/previous/reports-e/electricityfuture/ index-e.asp; Chris Borden, "Electricity in New Brunswick and Options for Its Future: Summary of the New Brunswick Government's Task Force Findings," *Utilities Law Review* 10 (1999): 30–1.

45 Richard Wilbur, "New Brunswick," *Canadian Annual Review of Politics and Public Affairs 2002*, ed. David Muttimer (Toronto: University of Toronto Press), 218. See also Kathy Kaufield, "Province Divides NB Power: Four Companies Expected to Operate like Commercial Businesses," *Telegraph-Journal*, 31 May 2002. For criticism, see CUPE, *Deregulation, Privatization and the Ontario Power Failure*, 24 September 2003. Ironically, the Alward Conservative government announced in May 2013 that it was recombining these companies. The energy and mines minister, Craig Leonard, is quoted as saying, "Not only does it make good business sense, but other changes we are bringing forward will help to strengthen the utility's management and board of directors, require greater transparency at the utility and allow NB Power to pay down debt and operate like a business." See GNB, Energy and Mines, "New Electricity Act Introduced," news release, http://www2.gnb.ca/content/gnb/en/departments/energy/news/ news_release.2013.05.0408.html.

46 The settlement provided NB Power with $115 million cash and "an in-kind portion representing a commitment to deliver a specified quantity of fuel which is expected to be fulfilled by March 2010." NB Power, *2007/08 Annual Report*, n27, www.nbpower.com/html/en/about/publications/ annual/AnnualReport0708.pdf.

47 New Brunswick Liberal Party, *Getting Results, Together*, 2006, 19.

48 Ibid., 16 (emphasis added).
49 "Cabinet Minister Clarifies His NB Power View," CBC News, 19 November 2009, www.cbc.ca/politics/story/2009/11/18/nb-lamrock-nbpower-530. html.
50 Mary Moszynski, "N.B. Government Preparing to Shake Up Structure of Provincial Utility," Canadian Press NewsWire, 18 December 2006, quoted in *CBCA Reference and Current Events*, document 1182840001, http:// rlproxy.upei.ca/login?url=http://search.proquest.com.proxy.library.upei .ca/docview/359787524?accountid=14670.
51 Quentin Casey, "How Accord Was Reached," *Telegraph Journal*, 30 October 2009.
52 Donald J. Savoie, *Governing from the Centre: The Concentration of Power in Canadian Politics* (Toronto: University of Toronto Press, 1999); Luc Bernier, Keith Brownsey, and Michael Howlett, eds., *Executive Styles in Canada: Cabinet Structures and Leadership Practices in Canadian Government* (Toronto: University of Toronto Press, 2005).
53 Stephen Tomblin, *Ottawa and the Outer Provinces: The Challenge of Regional Integration in Canada* (Toronto: James Lorimer, 1995), 75; Pier Bouchard and Sylvain Vézina, "Modernizing New Brunswick's Public Administration: The Robichaud Model," in *The Robichaud Era, 1960–70: Colloquium Proceedings*, 53–66 (Moncton: Canadian Institute for Research on Regional Development, 2001); Lisa Pasolli, "Bureaucratizing the Atlantic Revolution: The Saskatchewan Mafia and the Modernization of the New Brunswick Civil Service, 1960–1970" (MA thesis, University of New Brunswick, 2007).
54 Donald J. Savoie, "Governing a 'Have-Less' Province: Unravelling the New Brunswick Budget Process in the Hatfield Era," in *Budgeting in the Provinces: Leadership and the Provinces*, Monographs on Canadian Public Administration no. 11, ed. Allan M. Maslove, 31–54 (Toronto: Institute of Public Administration of Canada, 1989); Hugh P. Mellon, "Political Communications and Government Reform: New Brunswick under Richard Hatfield" (PhD diss., Queen's University, 1990).
55 Savoie, *Pulling against Gravity*, 85.
56 Hyson, "Governing from the Centre in NB," 87.
57 Savoie, *Governing from the Centre*, 261.
58 The executives of NB Power, although apparently supportive, were also left out of the discussions. Furthermore, the executives saw the negotiations as between the New Brunswick and Quebec governments, and not between NB Power and Hydro-Québec. See Greg Weston, "NB Power CEO Says Proposed Sale 'Made Sense,'" *Times and Transcript*, 2 March 2011.

59 "3 Liberal Ministers Won't Vote for NB Power Deal: N.B. Premier Denies
    Caucus Revolt over NB Power sale," CBC News, 18 January 2010, http://
    www.cbc.ca/m/touch/canada/new-brunswick/story/1.875415.

60 "Government Was Counselled Not to Sell NB Power," CBC News, 16 April
    2010, http://www.cbc.ca/news/canada/new-brunswick/government
    -was-counselled-not-to-sell-nb-power-1.974585.

61 "NB Power Union Slams Hydro-Québec deal," CBC News, 13 November
    2009, http://www.cbc.ca/news/canada/new-brunswick/nb-power
    -union-slams-hydro-qu%C3%A9bec-deal-1.812001. Consider as well
    the concerns expressed by Local 37 of the International Brotherhood
    of Electrical Workers, the union representing 2,200 NB Power workers.
    Under the proposed deal, union members risked losing their pensions.
    The MOU stated that the current union contracts would "be respected,"
    but according to a union lawyer, "the word 'respected' has no legal
    standing."

62 However, the provincial auditor general claimed the sale would do nothing
    to alleviate the provincial debt. See "Power Sale Won't Help Debt: Auditor
    General," CBC News, 14 November 2009.

63 H.T. Wilson, *Capitalism after Postmodernism: Neo-Conservatism, Legitimacy
    and the Theory of Public Capital* (Leiden: Brill, 2002), 195.

64 For discussion, see Steve McBride, *Dismantling a Nation: The Transition to
    Corporate Rule in Canada* (Winnipeg: Fernwood, 1997); Jeanne Kirk Laux,
    "How Private Is Privatization?," *Canadian Public Policy* 19 (1983): 398–411;
    Thom Workman, *Banking on Deception: The Discourse of Fiscal Crisis*
    (Winnipeg: Fernwood, 1996); and Robert Chernomas and Ian Hudson,
    Social Murder: And Other Shortcomings of Conservative Economics (Winnipeg:
    Arbeiter Ring, 2007).

65 Todd Hirsch, "Businesses, Invest in Literacy," *Telegraph Journal*, 4
    November 2010. Hirsch argues, "One recent report on the subject
    shows that improving literacy scores by one percent would increase
    labour productivity by 2.5 percent." On the importance of education
    for economic and civic development, and the dangers to both posed
    by privatization, see Martha Minow, "Public and Private Partnerships:
    Accounting for the New Religion," *Harvard Law Review* 116 (2003): 2–42.

66 But see Marc Zwelling, "Privatization: A Reality Check; Canadians Really
    Do Not Want to Privatize the Public Services That Are Most Important to
    Them," 2007, www.publicvalues.ca/ViewArticle.cfm?Ref=002.

67 Even this argument was regarded with suspicion in New Brunswick,
    where the effectiveness of government regulation of its dominant
    industries is often questioned.

68 NB Power, "History," 2010, www.nbpower.com/html/en/about/publications/history.html. Such sentiment is not unique to New Brunswick; note the title of Merrill Denison's history of Ontario Hydro: *The People's Power: The History of Ontario Hydro* (Toronto: McClelland and Stewart, 1960).

69 Several reports have argued that the rise in power rates was one of several factors affecting the viability of New Brunswick's forestry industry. But this is a problem that affects the forestry industry across the country (in Quebec and Ontario, as well as in Atlantic Canada). See Rob Linke, "Québec's Forestry Industry Is at a Crossroads," *Telegraph Journal*, 11 December 2009. See also "Pulp and Paper Woes Reach Far and Wide," CBC News, 1 September 2009, http://www.cbc.ca/news/business/pulp-and-paper-woes-reach-far-and-wide-1.830189.

70 David Hall, Emanuele Lobina, and Robin de la Motte, "Public Resistance to Privatisation in Water and Energy," *Development in Practice* 15 (2005): 292; Massimo Florio, *The Great Divestiture: Evaluating the Welfare Impact of the British Privatizations 1979–1997* (Cambridge, MA: MIT Press, 2004). Hall, Lobina, and de la Motte, referencing Florio, claim that "an exhaustive review of the economic aspects of the mass privatisations in the UK has concluded that there was no significant efficiency gain, while there is clear evidence of a regressive effect on the distribution of income and wealth."

71 Note that in the government's poll taken just after the deal's cancellation was announced, respondents were asked, "Do you agree or disagree with the following statements: 'It makes me angry to think the government took New Brunswick through all the controversy associated with the power deal with Québec only to walk away from the negotiations so late in the game.'" Fifty-one per cent agreed; 29 per cent "strongly."

72 Marianne White, "N.B., Québec Scrap Power Deal," *National Post*, 25 March 2010.

73 Chris Morris, "Relaxed Graham Says He Has No Regrets," *Telegraph Journal*, 15 November 2010.

PART TWO

Neoliberalism and the Decline
of Central Canada

5 Quebec Nationalism and Quebec Politics, from Left to Right

PETER GRAEFE

Quebec politics is often understood in terms of the relationship of Quebec to Canada. Within that dynamic, there is an ongoing competition between the autonomist nationalism of the Quebec Liberal Party, which believes Canadian federalism can be reformed in depth to become consistent with Quebecers' prime loyalty to Quebec, and the sovereigntist nationalism of the Parti Québécois (PQ), which argues that Quebec needs to take on the main accoutrements of nation-state sovereignty if it is to flourish fully. But looking at Quebec politics as a battle of the "federalists" and the "sovereigntists" reduces it to a single dimension of conflict and ignores the importance of questions of social and economic development, to say nothing of other forms of identity politics, to the warp and woof of Quebec political life.[1] Just like in the other provinces, debates about the role of the state under neoliberal globalization have been key terms of political division. Indeed, this debate has been held more openly than in other provinces, such as through the convocation of socio-economic summits. Another unique site for discussing development models has come from high-profile personalities publishing and defending manifestos that set out programs for change.

Given the primacy of the national question in organizing partisan political competition, the mobilization of actors around these questions has been affected by strategic choices taken by the nationalist camps. The manner in which the mainstream federalist and sovereigntist forces define their nationalism provides an opportunity structure that favours certain kinds of claims and actors over others. Thus, the Parti Québécois' referendum strategy in the early 1990s provided an unparalleled opening for progressive actors to propose social democratic development strategies and to root them within the margins of the state. With the loss of the referendum, this opening was worn down, both from the PQ's concessions to neoliberal statecraft, which alienated its base on the left, and from the ongoing neoliberal critique channelled by the two main opposition parties, which chipped off support on the right. The subsequent Liberal government, while elected largely on a "good government" platform, adopted a neoliberal program seeking an in-depth transformation of politics and society. Yet this strategy has been contained by the need to maintain a sufficient appeal to nationalists, particularly as the upstart Action Démocratique du Québec (ADQ) politicized questions of identity and inclusion. The by-product of these debates has likewise pushed the PQ to embrace a more exclusionary and conservative form of nationalism. Even as the Liberal government imploded over repeated revelations of corruption and shady dealing, the successor PQ government, elected in September 2012, adds to a morose political outlook, as it stumbled to deliver changes of any stature. While its program showed signs of ecological and social democratic leanings, and it remained committed to sovereignty, its actions for either socio-economic change or national self-determination were so thin as to inspire cynicism more than engagement. That cynicism was clearly evident in the PQ's stunning electoral defeat in 2014. In fact, the PQ's transformation from social democratic to moderate nationalist party was a defining characteristic of the 2014 campaign. During the election the party embraced a conservative form of nationalism in its "Charter of Quebec Values" and tried to solidify its economic bona fides with star candidate Pierre Karl Péladeau, owner of Quebecor and Sun Media. Neither strategy proved successful in prying voters away from the Liberals or the Coalition, but they did convince a part of the PQ electorate to stay home.

Thinking about Quebec

As with many political communities, Quebec is often grasped by both Quebecers and non-Quebecers in monolithic terms. This is variously seen in the complaint of "what does Quebec want," in the claims of what Quebec nationalism *is* (be it civic, ethnic, conservative, or whatever), in an English-Canadian left, which looks to Quebec as a bastion of progress, or in the arguments of Quebec social democrats who proclaim to hold a more modern take on social justice (a "Quebec model"). While this monolithic view makes life easier for journalists and media commentators, it hobbles political analysis. In the latter case, attention must be paid precisely to the diversity of interests within Quebec and the manner in which they organize competing claims around such questions as how to define Quebec's national community and its place in Canada, or how to use state power to regulate economic and social development. This sort of analysis *may* arrive at similar conclusions about the nature of Quebec politics and society, but rather than seeing these outcomes as inhering in some essentialist *québécitude*, it understands them as a series of power-laden compromises between social actors. It remains attentive to those actors excluded from the compromises as well as those within the compromise who may seek to change them in order to better attain their interests.

As linkages between state and society, political parties are essential sites for mediating and brokering compromises between social actors. Given how important nationalism has been as the principal cleavage of Quebec politics, other social divisions and debates have had to work through a language of nationalism and to demonstrate how their claims align with particular understandings of national progress. This does not mean that the influence of economic restructuring or the social actors championing (and resisting) neoliberalism are absent or secondary to Quebec politics, but only that we need to be aware of how these forces work on and through questions of nationalism, redefining it in the process.

The Two-Headed Recession, 1980 to the Early 1990s

Quebec entered the 1990s amidst great turmoil. The political headlines focused on the province's place in Canada as a new constitutional order was imposed on Quebec without its consent by the federal government and the other nine provincial premiers in 1982. The attempt to repair this exclusion by incorporating elements of the vision of federalist nationalists, namely the idea that Quebec existed as a distinct society within Canada, and that certain federal practices be curtailed (such as the federal spending power, or the federal government's monopoly of the power to appoint senators and Supreme Court justices), failed as a result of its wild unpopularity in the rest of Canada.

The turmoil, however, was not solely constitutional. The recessions of the early 1980s and early 1990s hit Quebec hard and opened the question of the appropriate role of the state in social and economic development. In response to the rapid rise of interest rates orchestrated by the U.S. Treasury in 1979–80, followed closely by the Bank of Canada,

Quebec's debt burden grew quickly (see the introduction). The budgetary situation was further aggravated by a harsh recession that shook out Quebec's manufacturing sector, as the interest rate hike shook inflation out of the economy at the cost of jobs. With unemployment rates briefly surpassing 15 per cent in 1982–3 and deficits soaring, given the reduced tax revenues and increased expenses associated with an economic downturn, there was an opening for questioning the existing Keynesian state. Employers' associations stepped into the breech to call for a complete overhaul of the state in a neoliberal direction. Their prescription was an in-depth revision of the state–economy relationship in the direction of lower taxation, less regulation, and a retreat of the state from economic intervention.[2]

The Liberals, then in opposition, took up this view and started to implement it following their landslide election in 1985. The Liberals' early enthusiasm for these ideas dissipated in the face of public opposition, as well as some tough and violent strikes when the government was seeking to privatize state assets and decertify the public employees' union in the process.[3] Indeed, to carry out the radical forms of privatization, deregulation, and state retrenchment that were touted in the early months of the Liberal government would have required a divisive, "two nations" strategy. This was not a natural politics for Premier Bourassa, who was more the cautious strategist than an ideologically driven politician. Nor did it fit well with the government's attempt to entrench the legitimacy of a more federalist nationalism through changes to the Canadian constitution. Let us be clear that the Liberal's embrace of neoliberalism was not devoid of nationalism: it celebrated the entrepreneurialism of Quebecers and argued that the nation would prosper fully once the yoke of state regulation and taxation was lifted. However, it was too radical for its time: many Quebecers might ask whether the nationalism of the preceding period, which strongly emphasized state-building as a form of national progress, was still the way forward as they saw merits in it for both material progress (social security and protection, upward economic mobility for francophones) and for national pride.

In addition, while the neoliberal turn coincided with the late 1980s economic uptick and Montreal real estate boom, economic prospects remained grim. Unemployment dipped under 10 per cent only in the peak year of 1989, while urban poverty rates remained among the highest in Canada (although the lower rental costs in Quebec do overstate Quebec's comparative poverty). In this context, the business

Table 5.1. Quebec Economic Background

While this chapter refers to conjunctural economic factors, this table fills in the broader sweep of economic transformation over the past quarter century.

Economic growth: From 1981 to 2007, real gross domestic product per capita grew 45.7 per cent, compared to 46.8 per cent in Ontario and 53.4 per cent for Canada as a whole. Annual real GDP growth was uneven, with slow growth in the 1980 recessions (0.8 per cent a year for 1981–4), a late 1980s boom (2.9 per cent from 1985 to 1989), more slow growth in the early 1990s (1 per cent from 1990 to 1994), followed by the late 1990s boom (3.4 per cent from 1995 to 1999) and a slowing in the 2000s ahead of the 2008 financial crisis (1.9 per cent 2000–4 and 2.9 per cent for 2005–7).

Sectoral change: These economic cycles led to some sectoral change. Financial products, activities, and industries grew to occupy 17 per cent of GDP in 2007 (growing $12.1 billion from 2001 to 2007), more or less equal to manufacturing (whose contribution to GDP dropped $15 billion over the same period). In employment, manufacturing bounced back after the 1990s recession and then declined by 20 per cent after 2004, while financial services struggled in the 1990s but have increased by 16 per cent in finance, 30 per cent in insurance and real estate, and 28 per cent in professional services.

Labour markets: Unemployment swung from a peak of 15.8 per cent in 1983 to just below 10 per cent at the end of the 1980s, and then back up to 14.2 per cent in 1993. This rate then declined over the 1990s to bottom out at 6.8 per cent at the onset of the 2008 recession (which has pushed it up closer to 9 per cent). Employment rates have also moved with economic cycles but have shown a secular increase from about 58 per cent at the peak of the 1980s boom, to over 61 per cent in 2007. Part of this is driven by an increase in employment rates for twenty-five- to forty-four-year-old women, which has gone from being 10 percentage points lower than Ontario to being 1.5 percentage points higher.

Job quality: Most of the increase in part-time and atypical work took place in the 1970s and 1980s, but since then, the share of non-standard jobs has been steady at about one-third of total employment. Despite economic growth, median family earnings fell from $53,900 in 1976 to $51,900 in 2007. While earning inequality as measured by the Gini coefficient has remained lower than for Canada as a whole, it did track up from .33 in 1992 to .36 in the early 2000s.

Poverty and the social wage: Relative poverty has been below the Canadian average for at least two decades and fell by 2.5 percentage points (to 9 per cent) between 1996 and 2006, as compared to a 1-percentage point fall (to 11.4 per cent) in Canada as a whole. Inequality post-tax and transfer is lower than in the rest of Canada and has been growing more slowly than in the rest of Canada since the 1990s recession.

community's push for neoliberal reform was paired with interest in exploring more coordinative forms of social and economic governance. This could be seen, for instance, in a willingness to join the Forum pour l'emploi (Forum for jobs), a grouping of non-governmental actors (community groups, unions, employers) searching for ways to create more paid jobs, or in the willingness of employers to participate on sectoral boards in order to find joint solutions to common problems such as training, research and development, and export promotion.[4]

In sum, when the recession of the early 1990s hit, neoliberalism in Quebec remained shaky and tentative. The recession further raised the question of appropriate development strategies for Quebec, as unemployment rates rose to 14.2 per cent in early 1992 and remained above 10 per cent into 1998. Poverty also grew, from 19.4 per cent in 1990 to 23.4 per cent in 1995, while average household incomes fell 7.4 per cent over the same period.[5]

In this context, a variety of development strategies entered into debate. Certainly for the employers' federations, the problem was not one of too much neoliberalism, but in fact of insufficient neoliberalism, and so they continued to push for state retrenchment and market liberalization.[6] The union federations nevertheless looked to build on the experience of the Forum pour l'emploi and the Bélanger-Campeau commission (see below) by proposing a more partnership-based or *concertational* approach to development. This was based on the idea that competitive economies could be built not only through market-based reforms, but also through ongoing dialogue between all economic actors. Indeed, the latter type of progressive competitiveness was preferable (and was borrowed by the McGuinty Liberals in Ontario a decade later), because it allowed a wider number of agendas to be served, including the unions' agenda of maintaining high-quality, well-paid jobs. Concertation could produce this result because it allowed employers, workers, and their communities to find positive-sum compromises as well as to provide competitiveness-enhancing public goods that a free market could not. For instance, sectoral concertation could allow employers and unions to develop training strategies and thus create a better skilled workforce, whereas employers left on their own would not invest in training for fear their competitors would poach their skilled workers. Similarly, firm-level worker-management partnerships might make unions look more favourably at the adoption of new technologies or types of work organization, in return for ensuring that jobs would not be lost.[7] This approach could also be extended to the community, where bringing together all actors might lead to a fuller and more coordinated use of community resources to create jobs and wealth, and to Quebec as a whole, where summits of the major social actors could make mutually binding commitments in order to meet shared goals such as economic growth and increased employment.[8]

Two other progressive visions joined the unions' alternative development model. The first, closer to the unions' position, was a vision of community economic development that came to take on the label of *économie sociale* or social economy. While this came in more and less radical versions, it represented a distillation of a decade of community experiences in coping with high unemployment and growing poverty rates. There was recognition that investment in community entrepreneurship could yield jobs as well as goods and services aiding those in poverty. A typical example might be a community restaurant that served inexpensive meals in a poor neighbourhood. The poverty-fighting good, namely providing people living in poverty with the opportunity to socialize with others and eat at low cost, comes with other assorted goods, such as jobs in running the restaurant and training opportunities in cooking and food service. The case for state involvement in supporting social entrepreneurship thus rested in part on an economic argument, that community resources could be put to productive use in this manner. But it was also argued that such support allowed the state to meet social needs more efficiently and flexibly than through traditional state-delivered programs. Finally, a case could be made that such policies furthered the democratization of the state and the economy, as social economy organizations remained answerable and accountable to their employees and the users of their services.[9]

The other alternative development model came out of a reinvigorated women's movement. Strongly informed by the experiences of women living with violence and with poverty, it brought forward alternative ways of thinking about the economy and organizing economic activity that had been incubated in Quebec's network of women's centres. This vision was placed most squarely on the agenda by the 1995 Bread and Roses March against poverty and violence. The March from Montreal to Quebec City drew a great deal of attention in the smaller centres that it passed through and in the Quebec press. Behind the march was a set of demands for organizing the economy around the principles of need and social utility rather than principles of profit. The first demand was for the state to fund "social infrastructures" to recognize women's existing unpaid and underpaid labour. It argued that the state was already funding jobs in the community sector in the guise of work placements in the province's social assistance system, and that that money could be put to better use in consolidating those positions. Such spending would increase the capacity of organizations to meet the needs of people living in poverty, even while creating and sustaining high-quality jobs. The march also argued for the re-regulation of labour markets through measures to increase the minimum wage, to strengthen labour standards, and to apply labour standards legislation to job sectors that were outside its remit.[10]

In sum, where the labour movement embraced the idea of competitiveness but argued that it could be made more inclusive through social partnership, and where actors in the social economy called for support for social entrepreneurship in order to carve out space for an alternative economy within the existing one, the women's movement called for state investment and labour market re-regulation that would de-centre competitiveness and profit in favour of need. All three alternatives had their strengths and weaknesses. The union position fit with social democratic thinking in Europe and Australia, but the experience with such strategies in practice regularly proved disappointing, as the needs for competitiveness regularly diluted any progressive gains. The program of social economy had the benefit of fitting with existing practices of small business development and of greater use of non-profits for delivering public services, but the ability of such interventions to reach a sufficient scale to reorient dominant market-based development strategies was and remains unclear. Finally, while the women's movement laid out a program that most clearly looked beyond the neoliberal status quo, it was not clear what political forces would mobilize the power necessary to challenge that status quo, particularly in the tax and regulatory increases that such a program would necessitate.[11]

All Aboard the Sovereigntist Train: An Open Nationalism

In light of this constitutional and economic turbulence, the Liberal Party crumbled. The opposition Parti Québécois had plenty of opportunity to plan a strategy to not only win government but also potentially win a referendum on sovereignty and thus ultimately start the process of gaining independence. The failure of the Meech Lake Accord in 1990, and the virulent rejection by the rest of Canada of the Liberals' federalist nationalism, forced the government to seek a new basis of nationalist legitimacy. The Liberals needed legitimacy both in the face of the

Parti Québécois and as bargaining leverage with its Canadian partners. In 1990, Premier Bourassa created the Bélanger-Campeau commission, which brought together representatives of all parties as well as of major social sectors such as business, labour, school boards, and the cooperative movement. The co-presidents were both well known in the business community, with Bélanger associated with the Liberal Party and Campeau with the PQ. Their selection was an attempt to show that whatever plan for Quebec's future the commission came up with would be consistent with a pro-business nationalism. The commission reported that the Canadian experience was blocked, and that Quebec should have a referendum on sovereignty in 1992, unless an acceptable offer was forthcoming from the rest of Canada. An offer did materialize (the Charlottetown Accord), but it was soundly rejected in Quebec in October 1992. Unwilling to support sovereignty, the Liberals had nowhere to go.

It became obvious that the Parti Québécois was most likely to win the next provincial election and then embark on a referendum. That still left open a series of questions about how it would define a *projet de pays* and its associated *projet de société*. A nationalist party like the PQ needs to set out a vision of a new, sovereign society in order to compete for votes in a referendum. To simply promise that the flags would change from the maple leaf to the fleur-de-lys may be enough to win some votes, but certainly half the population is unlikely to run the risks of such a momentous change for such thin benefits. A nationalist party thus needs also to promise that sovereignty will transform social relations of domination and inequality, at the same time hemming in such promises so that those on the more dominant end of those relations do not mobilize too strongly against the project.

Faced with the need to get to 50 per cent plus one on referendum day, and where the traditional baseline support for the party's option was probably closer to 40 per cent, the opposition Parti Québécois adopted an open definition of the nation in an effort to expand its base. This included taking a very wide definition of the national community. While the PQ saw sovereignty as the project of a historic community that originated in New France, it argued that belonging as a Quebecer rested on a much thinner sense of community rooted in geography and language. In other words, living within the borders of Quebec and using French as the public language were essential elements of the Québécois "community." To these were sometimes added respect for the Quebec Charter of Rights, and particularly respecting gender equality, as well as the duty to participate in the life of the nation. This view of the nation had much in common with Canadian multiculturalism, including the tension between a surface acceptance of diversity and a deep concern that newcomers adopt a primary loyalty to the correct national community and national values.[12]

In a similar fashion, the PQ set out to define a political economy for the nation-to-be that might secure its base among the labour and progressive social movements. In its "action plan" for sovereignty, *Québec in a New World*, the PQ took up a good deal of the labour movement's thinking about social partnerships and competitiveness.[13] There is an obvious synergy between nationalist thought and social partnership, as nationalist thought will often seek to define a united national community that is not riven with class inequalities. Yet the PQ pushed their argumentation further. In their view, the pressures of global competition required societies to throw all of their energies and resources into competitiveness. No society could afford to exclude a large number of citizens in poverty and still succeed. Nationalism, however, could provide a series of shared codes and feelings of solidarity to enable Quebec to maximize the mobilization of citizens and ensure that positive-sum compromises were made. Once in power, the PQ responded positively to the union demand for a targeted 1 per cent corporate tax dedicated to training and directed by the social partners.

Similarly, when the community and women's movements made claims for support for the social economy or social infrastructures in the PQ government's first year, they received a positive hearing. For instance, the PQ government responded to the Bread and Roses March of 1995 by appointing a consultative committee to study the potential of developing the sort of social infrastructures set out in the march's demands and tried to give greater space for women's representation on regional development bodies. Demands by rights and advocacy organizations also put into motion a long process of finding a means to provide core funding for "autonomous community action." This again was a strategy of inclusion, whose importance was reinforced by the 1994 election results: the PQ won handily with seventy-seven seats to forty-four for the Liberals and one to the upstart Action Démocratique (ADQ) Party, but the popular vote was nearly tied (44.75 per cent for the PQ vs 44.40 per cent for the Liberals).

The PQ's first year in power was spent preparing a referendum for 1995. The sovereigntist side lost the October 1995 referendum, garnering 49.4 per cent of the vote, but the sense of coming so close had the effect of making it feel as if a win was just a few years away. The razor-thin defeat encouraged the PQ to continue with their "big tent" strategy of inclusion, but in a more difficult situation. After all, when in opposition or even in the year leading up to the referendum, the actualization of inclusion and of reconfigured relations of domination could be suspended into the future. The process of governing in a difficult economic situation, with unemployment stubbornly above 10 per cent and with a growing load of public debt, however, meant the PQ had to start defining what its priorities truly were. In addition, the referendum-night comments by then premier Parizeau, which some took as defining a more exclusivist definition of the nation and of scapegoating those outside it for the loss,[14] also meant the PQ had difficult work ahead to convince voters that its inclusive definition of the nation was sincere.

On the latter front, this led the PQ government to continue to define ways of belonging to Quebec that did not pass solely through identification with the historic French-Canadian community. This included the definition of a policy of interculturalism, which was sold as a better alternative to Canadian multiculturalism,[15] and some mooting of the idea of a Quebec citizenship.[16] It was, however, on the socio-economic front where the road was harder for the PQ. The business community made it clear to Lucien Bouchard, when he replaced Parizeau as premier in the aftermath of the referendum, that they would not continue to invest in Quebec if the government did not see to controlling the deficit by cutting public expenditures. This placed Bouchard in a tough spot: while he was close to the business community in economic vision, his nationalism had brought him to lead a centre-left party, which saw in him their best hope for achieving sovereignty. Much as the PQ itself tried to reconcile these tensions in *Québec in a New World*, Bouchard looked to new socio-economic partnerships as a possible solution to these underlying political tensions.

Bouchard tried to square the circle of reconciling business demands with the cultivation of alliances with progressive social movements by convoking two socio-economic summits in early 1996. These summits, held on the premise that Quebec's model of social and economic development was broken and needed to be reinvented, brought together representatives of business and labour, but also of numerous other sectors such as students' groups, women's groups, and community development leaders. The main trade-off engineered was a commitment to eliminating the deficit in two years without increasing taxes, in return for concerted efforts to reduce unemployment. The summits also served as the place where the demands of community actors about the social economy were more fully developed and given some institutional expression in the creation of a Chantier de l'économie sociale, which would monitor the creation of new jobs in the sector in the wake of the summits' commitments. While the women's and students' groups left the second summit when they could not get commitment to a poverty elimination strategy, their opposition was somewhat contained by the commitment to move forward on a family policy that would include a universal and affordable childcare program.

It was not that Quebec stood outside of the ambient neoliberalism of these years. Rather, it is that social forces managed to punch out spaces (both discursive and institutional) within the neoliberal state for alternatives. Their success in the Quebec case owes something to their organization, but the argument here is also that the nationalism advanced by the PQ in the early 1990s made the state more porous to these demands than in other provinces, or indeed than in a later period. Having found a place in the state nevertheless did not mean they were leading the state. Rather, ongoing mobilization and strategizing were required to ensure that these spaces were not co-opted or closed down by more dominant centres of power such as the Ministry of Finance or Treasury Board.

For instance, while the women's movement put the question of the social economy on the agenda, the institutions created to study this area and ultimately to implement policies, moved from the women's movement's vision of social infrastructures towards a set of policies not very different from traditional small business development policies, such as assistance with start-up capital and developing business plans. Its attempts to renew its claims for an alternative form of development around the World March of Women in 2000 likewise could not find much traction in the state, to the point that a number of leading feminists started to explore founding an alternative political party. The labour movement likewise could vaunt its recognition as a social partner in the 1996 summits, but that representation did little to affect the government's budgetary policies needed to implement the summits' zero deficit commitment, which involved significant downsizing of public sector workplaces and cuts to programs. Indeed, as the PQ's term in power continued, social partnership became less a means of leverage for the unions and more like a pair of handcuffs, as business used the need for "consensus" to opt out of budgetary or labour market policies that might impose costs on them or reduce their freedom to manage.[17]

By the end of the PQ's time in power in 2003, the openings for progressive projects had narrowed. Support for sovereignty trended down only slightly but the salience of the issue declined greatly, making it clear that there was no appetite for another referendum. While the PQ remained insistent that a referendum would be held following its re-election, the waning of popular enthusiasm raised questions about how likely this would be, and as such took pressure off the PQ to maintain its coalition. Indeed, inside the party, certain influential ministers such as François Legault and Joseph Facal were critical of responding to such interests on the grounds that they always demanded more from the government in return for little political credit. Of course, the same could be said of the employers federations: the PQ eliminated the deficit, cut taxes, reduced regulation, and started to experiment with public-private partnerships in delivering state services, yet the business community remained very impatient with the government and created new institutions like the pro-free-market Montreal Economic Institute in an attempt to shift the political terms of debate.[18]

As the need for inclusion for the short-term success of the sovereigntist project fell, the PQ also became more receptive to alternative political economy strategies to frame their policies. Whereas the first term (1994–8) of the PQ showed some commitment to the idea of social partnerships, by the end of its second term, it adopted what might be called a "knowledge-based economy" or what elsewhere has been called "progressive competitiveness" (see Ontario chapter).[19] In this view, superior economic performance requires a relatively liberalized economy coupled with strategic state investments in poverty prevention, life-long learning and early childhood development, to prevent forms of social exclusion that undermine human capital or increase costs for the state (such as in policing, incarceration, or reparative social services).[20]

There are clear continuities with the PQ's earlier thinking, laid out in *Québec in a New World*, about globalization requiring all hands on deck. However, while earlier views made a virtue of concertation by social actors and by state action to ensure that such partnerships informed economic decision-making, this later view placed decision-making in the hands of the state (which could technocratically decide on where to intervene, independent of other social actors), and sought to insulate private enterprise from too much oversight or control. This new thinking was seen in the government's 1998 industrial policy, which emphasized private economic decision-making, leaving a place for the state to ensure social cohesion.[21] In other words, the state's role was to ensure that the inequality and exclusion produced by a relatively unfettered capitalism did not come to undermine continued capital accumulation. This could take the form of targeted interventions for certain at-risk populations, such as children living in poverty, but also of broader strategies to ensure the reproduction of a relatively healthy and educated labour force.

The decision to reduce stakeholder participation on regional health boards and to diminish the power of the social partners in labour-market training was another sign of the PQ's transformation. The quiet launch of bureaucratic rationalization and public-private partnerships in the latter years of the Bouchard and Landry governments further testified to a reorientation of the state away from representing group demands, towards creating a lean, entrepreneurial state that might intervene strategically to support a dynamic, private enterprise–led economy. In this context, progressive actors were also less able to sustain productive forms of insider-outsider links with the state as exclusion led to experimentation with political alternatives, and as groups on the left of the PQ, still relatively disorganized when the PQ was re-elected in 1998, started to coalesce into a viable (if marginal) party. This movement gathered the remnants of small far-left parties with anti-globalization activists to form the Union des forces progressistes (UFP) in 2002, which then merged with the community and feminist movement activists in Option Citoyenne to form Québec Solidaire (QS) in 2006.

To say the openings grew narrower after 1998 is not to say that they closed. A large campaign by anti-poverty organizations could still get the government to adopt an anti-poverty strategy with the goal of eliminating poverty.[22] Similarly, a mobilization led by the group Au bas de l'échelle pushed changes to labour standards legislation that increased the coverage and protection to those at the bottom of the labour market. Advocacy organizations also prodded the PQ to recognize the citizenship-building contribution of "autonomous community action" and thus to commit to formal institutional arrangements to provide stable, core funding to these groups. With the benefit of hindsight, the influence of these social actors in pushing for child and family benefits as well as better services can be seen in Quebec as bucking the Canadian trend towards greater inequality.[23]

Despite these gains, the view from labour and the progressive social movements going into the 2003 elections was that the PQ had made too many accommodations with neoliberalism and had exhausted much of the progressive energy that had surrounded its societal project a decade earlier. A senior advisor to one of the major union federations was very candid: while they generally preferred a PQ government, sometimes it was time for a change, so why not let the Liberals have a try?[24] Many other social movement activists instead looked left, leaving the PQ for the fledgling UFP.

The Quebec Liberal Government and a More Conservative Nationalism

This relatively benign sense of what a Liberal government might bring perhaps reflected a middle-of-the-road Liberal campaign, based on promises of providing good government. The Liberals had run in 1998 on a strongly neoliberal platform of transforming Quebec's development strategies, but some thought that cost them support by being too radical. The small Action Démocratique du Québec Party took up that platform with gusto, with much success in by-elections, which increased their representation from one seat (in the 1998 general election) to five in 2003. While there was substantial mobilization by the left to criticize the ADQ's neoliberalism, it allowed the Liberals under former federal Conservative leader Jean Charest to appear as the champions of a reasonable neoliberal statecraft by comparison. They also looked fresher than a PQ government that had spent nearly a decade in office.

This Liberal reading proved illusory. The new government moved quickly to dismantle or reconfigure a series of institutions of concertation such as local and regional health and social service boards and local development boards, so as to diminish stakeholder involvement. The official explanation from the premier was that concertation did not enrich decision-making but simply created a "corporatism" that prevented necessary changes by allowing groups to protect their narrow self-interest. Yet this change also had the twin effects of removing representation within the state from less powerful groups and of removing potential points of resistance to the Liberals' reform agenda.[25] In industrial relations, the government changed the labour code to make it easier for firms to get rid of a union in cases where work was subcontracted, and it unilaterally rearranged union representation in the health sector. The Liberals also tried to roll back the highly popular five-dollar-per-day day-care program, by proposing to significantly increase the daily rate for those with higher incomes. This was beaten back by a wave of protests (although the daily rate increased to seven dollars), but the government allowed the private sector to increase its share of the care market relative to non-profit providers, and it reduced the amount of community involvement in service planning and delivery.[26] Another controversial aspect of the government's agenda was to make wider recourse to public-private partnerships in delivering public services, despite concerns about the cost effectiveness of such partnerships for the sorts of projects envisaged.

This program was met by large-scale mobilizations led by the labour movement, as well as through a student strike over changes to the student loans and bursaries policy that shut down parts of several universities in February and March 2005. Leaders of these mobilizations argued that the Liberals had run on an innocuous platform so they lacked a mandate for such controversial reforms.[27] The popularity of the government was damaged in the process, indicating a limited popular appetite for major changes in economic and social institutions. These protests pushed the government towards incremental changes, such as increasing the role of the private sector in the development and management of public infrastructure (the famed "public-private partnerships"), and slowly opening the door to for-profit providers of medical services. Talk of uprooting the corporatist interests inhibiting change largely disappeared. This loss of momentum raised new frustrations for the business community and led to the highly publicized release of the "Clear-Eyed Manifesto," which criticized the inability of the government to uproot "corporatism," and the capacity of groups to prevent a more substantial adoption of market liberalism.[28]

This neoliberal program sat uncomfortably with the national question. While it remained true to Quebec's long-term criticisms of the federation, as well as to the autonomist nationalism of the Liberal Party, it was seemingly content to accept the status quo. The government did innovate in better institutionalizing interprovincial coordination by enjoining the other provinces to create a Council of the Federation, and it obtained a formalized procedure of input into the Canadian delegation at UNESCO, providing some recognition that Quebec's constitutional power over culture and education had international application. But these moves were negated by the sense that the government's anti-statism was reducing the Quebec state from that of a nation to that of a province.[29] The Liberals also had a tough time selling the vision of the nation (the sum of the individual achievements of its members in a liberalized capitalist framework) as an adequate replacement for aspects of the nation's social and economic culture (such as concertational governance) that they were dismantling. The government was also hurt by studies showing that the place of the French language was slipping in Montreal, and by its timidity in responding or in even ensuring its own bureaucrats rigorously protected French as the language of public service.

Despite the government's vulnerability on this front, the PQ was unable to capitalize. It was hurt by the ADQ's aggressive appeals to a more conservative nationalism, which was predicated in terms of the nation's progress passing through private endeavours and not the state, and in terms of defining the nation around the markers of the historic French-Canadian community. The ADQ was particularly effective in mobilizing a sense of regional grievance against Montreal. In this framing, the ADQ argued that the PQ had embraced the multicultural social democracy of Montreal, alternatively showing shame and indifference to the struggles and ways of living of the rest of the province.

In this context, the PQ was badly caught. As long as its main opposition was the Liberals, who heavily courted ethnic and immigrant voters and held their overwhelming support, the PQ could continue to open their definition of the nation without fearing much conservative backlash. Against the Liberals' nationalism that claimed to be consistent with the recognition of multiculturalism and that would not cut the communities off from their Canadian linkages, the PQ could offer a nationalism based on interculturalism, which would include newcomers in the building of a new sovereign state. Indeed, the first reaction of then PQ leader André Boisclair when the ADQ began to play up conservative notions of the political community was to continue to push an open definition of "the people," albeit somewhat Jacobin in inspiration. The Liberals were also badly caught, as the ADQ could sever the Liberal coalition of conservative francophones outside Montreal and anglophones and cultural communities in Montreal by marrying free enterprise to a more exclusivist definition of "the people."

The net result was to transform the 2007 general election from a referendum on Charest's reengineering of the state into a more complex competition about identity and economy. The ADQ was able to split the other parties and come up the middle, gaining status as the official opposition and nearly upsetting the Liberal government. In giving forty-eight seats to the Liberals, forty-one to the ADQ, and thirty-six to the PQ, Quebec was governed by a minority government for the first time since 1878. One result was a very cautious and centrist Liberal government, aided by a very undisciplined and unfocused ADQ opposition. A more significant result was that the national project was pulled to the right, as the PQ also moved to tighten and narrow its definition of the Quebec nation. Indeed, the ADQ itself was caught between its appeals to a conservative nationalism on questions of identity and a poorly defined and articulated "autonomist" position, and could never really connect them: how the ADQ was going to carve out a far more autonomous space for Quebec within Canada than the Quebec Liberals had done, without developing a strong bargaining position through sovereignty (sometimes the PQ strategy) or through cultivating alliances with other Canadian actors (sometimes the Liberal strategy) was never clear. While the ADQ brought questions of national identity to the fore, it could not master them. This dilemma, coupled with its tawdry grandstanding style of opposition, led the ADQ to collapse to seven seats in the 2008 election in which the PQ was returned to official opposition (fifty-one seats), and the Liberals re-elected as government (sixty-six seats).

The ADQ was subsequently eclipsed by and then joined the Coalition Avenir Québec (CAQ), a party formed by former PQ Cabinet minister François Legault, backed by the telecommunications and banking mogul Charles Sirois. He repeated parts of the "Clear-Eyed" manifesto around increased tuition fees and public sector rationalization, but toned down the rhetoric on health privatization. The CAQ also campaigned to strengthen provisions of the language law and to ensure higher levels of domestic economic control, which differs from other recent right-wing projects. Given that a core aspect of the party's positioning is to not deal with the national question for a decade, its program can be read as a conservative attempt to strengthen the nation through emphasis on culture and economy. Given the blockage on Quebec's political status, the right has regrouped around the promise of national progress through renewed market liberalism.[30]

The PQ, on the other hand, reframed itself for a short time around a more conservative definition of the nation. Following its relegation to third-party status in the 2007 election, it turned to long-time stalwart Pauline Marois as leader and accepted her argument to not move immediately to adopt a timetable for a referendum. In pushing a referendum into the future, the PQ no longer had to aim to federate 50 per cent of the population, but could instead focus on its core vote of 35–40 per cent of the population. On the front of identity, this allowed the party to come forward with proposals to limit citizenship rights, such as voting or standing as a candidate in provincial and municipal elections to those with sufficient knowledge of French. While the English-Canadian press treated this as a further sign of Quebec nationalism's intolerance for diversity, sovereigntist intellectual (and now PQ Cabinet minister) Jean-François Lisée noted that this kind of demand is liberal when compared internationally.[31] Indeed, the current federal Conservative government has floated similar ideas about tying language to citizenship rights, without a similar critical media response.

The re-centring of the PQ on a slightly more conservative view of the nation and the lack of a clear referendum timetable also loosened ties with the social movements. The left political club within the PQ, the SPQLibre, was closed by the party leadership in March 2010, even as Marois claimed the PQ should modernize its vision of social democracy by putting greater emphasis on creating individual wealth! Paradoxically, the botched attempt by former Bloc Québécois leader Gilles Duceppe to replace Marois in January 2012, which was backed by several labour notables in the party, resulted in Marois returning to a more traditional centre-left posture.

Relations with the labour movement have also been strained, as on the PQ's decision to demand a faster return to balanced budgets following the 2008–10 financial crisis, even if this necessarily would mean significant cuts to state programs and services. With time, the seemingly opportunistic positioning of the PQ on the national and social questions nevertheless seems to have backfired, as voters turned away from the corruption-tainted Liberals, only to find the PQ willing to trade away principles for short-term electoral advantage. For example, during the student strike in the spring of 2012, while the PQ opposed fee increases and called on the government to negotiate, strong mutual suspicions between the party and the student leaders prevented the party from being the natural and obvious political relay for the strikers. While sympathetic to the students, the party made sure to remain above the fray, ready to broker a freeze in tuition fees but not to open the door to more radical changes such as reducing or abolishing fees, or changing the social vocation of the university.

This opened the space for the left party, Québec Solidaire (QS). As mentioned above, it federated a sizeable core of socialist and social democratic activists on a robust social democratic platform of expanding public services and public ownership and regulating private enterprise. It remains a nationalist party in favour of sovereignty but is also the true heir of the PQ's open nationalism of the 1990s, rejecting the latter's conservative turn as detrimental to a project of social reform that must necessarily include and mobilize across ethnic and national divisions. While the QS polled around 4 per cent in both the 2007 and 2008 elections, it did elect its charismatic co-spokesperson, Amir Khadir, to the National Assembly in 2008. Khadir regularly ranks among Quebec's most popular politicians and was joined by Françoise David in 2012 and Manon Massé in 2014.

Looking Forward

During and following the 2007 minority government period, it appeared that the Liberal government was prepared to mellow its neoliberalism further to the point of largely managing the status quo. The Public-Private Partnership Agency was shut down with little fanfare, while the language of re-engineering the state elicited embarrassment more than commitment. When the Task Force on Fees for Public Services called for much greater use of service fees for water, electricity, roads, and childcare, it was received coolly by Charest and largely shelved. Much the same could be said of the Task Force on the Funding of the Health System, which proposed creating more space for private insurance and raising money through a health levy that would be calculated in part on the basis of how much one used the health system. The global economic crisis, in addition, provided suitable cover to move to a more centrist position, as it relaxed the mantras of balanced budgets.

Yet, in the 2010 budget, the Liberals returned to a more aggressive posture, both in attempting to eliminate the deficit by 2013–14, necessitating public-sector cutbacks, and in bringing in university tuition hikes and a health surcharge, as well as promising a usage-based tax for health services in the near future. While the health and education budgets are slated to increase over these years (albeit at growth rates below the previous trend), this will require all other departments to slightly shrink their spending annually. The 2010 budget gave rise to significant demonstrations against austerity, including a very large demonstration on May Day. The labour federations did not feed and sustain this movement, engaged as they were in renegotiating public-sector contracts. Given a relatively unreceptive PQ and the lack of high-profile labour support, this mobilization has largely receded without having shaken the austerity agenda.

The Liberals' return to an aggressive stance reflected their lack of legitimacy, given persistent allegations of corruption and kickbacks in the awarding of construction contracts, day-care centre licences, and even judicial appointments. Having lost the public's trust, and having the PQ offering a set of social and economic policies similar to its own, the Liberals sharpened their ideological position as a gamble to shift political debate. Given the relatively negative reception of the budget's health proposals, and seemingly endless new allegations of shady dealings with large donors, this had little traction. Charest instead tried to make a conservative appeal to social order in response to the disruptions of the 2012 student strike in order to mobilize a bloc of Conservative and anglophone votes.

This appeal formed the basis of Charest's strategy in calling the provincial election in 2012. He was quickly derailed by the CAQ's success in making corruption a core theme of the campaign and ended with fifty seats and 31 per cent of the vote (the lowest percentage for the Liberals since Confederation). In the end, the CAQ ate into the Liberal vote, but not enough to win a large number of seats (nineteen, with 27 per cent of the vote). Marois, meanwhile, played on the conservative definition of identity, on the one hand, and on a somewhat pro-environment and left-leaning platform, on the other, to hold onto the PQ's traditional supporters and keep them from the QS (whose co-spokesperson, Francoise David, won the party a second seat) or from small sovereigntist parties like Option Nationale. Her fifty-four seats gave her a thin minority government, with 32 per cent of the vote.

The PQ government brought little change, despite its more moderate and socially conscious platform. In its first days, it cancelled the tuition hikes that were at the base of the spring 2012 student strike and boasted respected environmentalists as ministers for the environment and for natural resources, respectively. It was also quick to announce its intention to replace the health premium with new tax brackets for higher-income earners. The business community was quick to denounce this "radicalism" in terms of taxation, and the possibility that resource development in the north will be slowed by environmental concerns. Less than a year into its mandate, the government's green tinge faded: it only lightly changed its mining royalties scheme, while the 2013 budget emphasized the easing of barriers to private investment, including those in the resource sector.

The budgetary stance reflected further austerity on the grounds of the need to reduce provincial debt. This position disappointed some PQ constituencies, such as older social assistance recipients who saw benefits potentially reduced, and students who found that the PQ's idea of a tuition freeze included increases for inflation. Smaller cuts to the childcare system were somewhat hidden by the PQ's decision to continue to fund the creation of new spaces and to encourage public-sector care provision. This trend might surprise a few observers, but the PQ is not the relay of social movement demands for social trans-formation in the way that it was in the early 1990s, and indeed also in the early 1970s. The quick exhaustion of its reformist ambitions makes sense, given the lack of social movement accountabilities to propel it.

The PQ government also floated measures to move the definition of the national community slightly more towards the markers of the his-toric French-Canadian community, and to challenge some of the rheto-ric of the Quebec model of inter-culturalism. The fusion of the ADQ into the CAQ had taken the conservative nationalist pole out of the political equation, allowing the PQ (and the PLQ) to return to more open nationalist projects with less fear of electoral consequences. The PQ instead saw this as an opening to replace the ADQ on the terrain of a more conservative and republican stance on identity. This strategy lay behind the introduction of the so-called Charter of Quebec Values in the spring of 2013, which allowed the PQ to play to conservative nationalists in the 2014 election campaign.

In this context, the strategic choices made by the PQ in defining nationalism and their strategy for sovereignty have significantly changed the terrain of the state over the past two decades. During the 2014 election campaign, the narrowness of the PQ's sovereignty project was certainly on display. The party embraced a conservative form of nationalism while attempting to appeal to the province's busi-ness classes in the candidacy of Pierre Karl Péladeau. As it turned out, neither strategy was successful and the PQ's vote total fell to its lowest since 1970. What this means for the future of the PQ or for the sover-eignty project more generally remains an open-ended question. Yet, while the progressive social movements can still count on receiving more sympathetic hearings and making greater inroads with the PQ, the decline of the open nationalism of the early 1990s, of the "Spirit of '95," has greatly narrowed the channels for carving out alternatives to neoliberal statecraft.

NOTES

1 Daniel Salée, "Transformative Politics, the State, and the Politics of Social Change in Québec," in *Changing Canada*, ed. Wallace Clement and Leah Vosko, 25–50 (Montreal and Kingston: McGill-Queen's University Press, 2003).

2 Peter Graefe, "The Québec *Patronat*: Proposing a Neoliberal Political Economy after All," *Canadian Review of Sociology and Anthropology* 41 (2004): 181–5.

3 Gilles L. Bourque, *Le modèle québécois de développement* (Sainte-Foy: Presses de l'Université du Québec, 2000), 83–9.

4 Ibid., 112, 128.

5 Salée, "Transformative Politics," 36.

6 Graefe, "Québec *Patronat*," 185–6.

7 Confédération des Syndicats Nationaux, *Prendre les devants dans l'organisation du travail* (Montreal: CSN, 1991); Fédération des travailleurs et travailleuses du Québec, *Face aux changements, de nouvelles solidarités* (Montreal: FTQ, 1993).

8 For a fuller discussion, see Peter Graefe, "State Restructuring and the Failure of Competitive Nationalism: Trying Times for Québec Labour," in *Canada: The State of the Federation 2005*, ed. Michael Murphy (Kingston: Institute of Intergovernmental Relations, 2007), 156–9.

9 Groupe de travail sur l'économie sociale, *Osons la solidarité* (Quebec: Groupe de travail, 1996).

10 Françoise David and Louise Marcoux, *Du pain et des roses* (Montreal: Marche des femmes contre la pauvreté, 1995).

11 For fuller discussions, see Peter Graefe, "The Social Economy and the American Model: Relating New Social Policy Directions to the Old," *Global Social Policy* 6 (2006): 197–219; and Graefe, "State Restructuring and the Failure of Competitive Nationalism," in *Canada: The State of the Federation 2005*, ed. Michael Murphy, 153–76 (Kingston: Institute for Intergovernmental Relations, 2007).

12 Daniel Salée, "The Québec State and the Management of Ethnocultural Diversity," in *Belonging? Diversity, Recognition and Shared Citizenship in Canada*, ed. Keith Banting, Thomas Courchene, and F. Leslie Seidle, 105–42 (Montreal: IRPP, 2007).

13 See their action plan for sovereignty: Parti Québécois, *Québec in a New World* (Toronto: Lorimer, 1994).

14 Parizeau has long rejected this interpretation. See Jacques Parizeau, *An Independent Québec* (Montreal: Baraka Books, 2010).

15 For a discussion, see Alain-G. Gagnon and Rafaele Iacovino, *Federalism, Citizenship and Québec: Debating Multinationalism* (Toronto: University of Toronto Press, 2007).

16 Danielle Juteau, "The Citizen Makes an Entrée: Redefining the National Community in Québec," *Citizenship Studies* 6 (2002): 441–58.

17 Jean-Marc Piotte, *Du Combat au Partenariat* (Montreal: Nota Bene, 1998); Peter Graefe, "State Restructuring," 156.

18 Peter Graefe, "The Québec *Patronat*: Proposing a Neoliberal Political Economy after All," *Canadian Review of Sociology and Anthropology* 41 (2004): 171–93.

19 For more detail, see also Greg Albo, "Competitive Austerity and the Impasse of Capitalist Employment Policy," in *Between Globalism and Nationalism: The Socialist Register 1994*, ed. R. Milband and L. Panitch (London: Merlin, 1994), 146–8.

20 For example, Quebec, *Prioriser l'emploi et la solidarité: Plan d'action pour le développement des entreprises d'économie sociale* (Quebec: Ministère des finances, 2003).

21 Quebec, *Québec Objectif Emploi, Vers une Économie d'avant-garde: Une stratégie de développement économique créatrice d'emplois* (Quebec: Ministère des finances, 1998).

22 Pascale Dufour, "L'adoption du projet de loi 112 au Québec: Le produit d'une mobilisation ou une simple question de conjoncture politique," *Politique et sociétés* 23 (2004): 159–82.

23 Alain Noël, "Québec's New Politics of Redistribution," in *The Fading of Redistributive Politics*, ed. Keith Banting and John Myles, 256–84 (Vancouver: UBC Press, 2013).

24 Interview with a senior strategist, FTQ, Montreal 2005.

25 Rachel Laforest, "The Politics of State / Civil Society Relations in Québec," in *Canada: The State of the Federation 2005*, ed. Michael Murphy, 177–98 (Kingston: Institute for Intergovernmental Relations, 2007).

26 Jane Jenson, "Rolling Out or Backtracking on Québec's Child Care System? Ideology Matters," in *Public Policy for Women: The State, Income Security and Labour Market Issues*, ed. Marjorie Griffin Cohen and Jane Pulkingham, 50–70 (Toronto: University of Toronto Press, 2009).

27 Gérard Boismenu, Pascale Dufour, and Denis Saint-Martin, *Ambitions libérales et écueils politiques* (Outremont: Athéna Editions, 2004).

28 The preceding paragraphs owe a great deal to Boismenu, Dufour, and Saint-Martin, *Ambitions libérales*. See Christian Rouillard, Éric Montpetit, Isabelle Fortier, and Alain-G. Gagnon, *Reengineering the State: Towards an Impoverishment of Quebec Governance* (Ottawa: University of Ottawa Press,

2006). Also see, "Clear-Eyed Vision of Quebec," 19 October 2005, http://www.pourunquebeclucide.info/cgi-cs/cs.waframe00a8.html.

29 Rouillard et al., *Reengineering the State.*

30 Coalition pour l'avenir du Québec, *Taking Action for the Future: Action Plan* (Montreal: CAQ, November 2011); and Coalition, "An Economy of Owners, Not of Branches," position paper on the economy (Montreal: CAQ, 2011).

31 Jean-François Lisée, *Nous* (Montreal: Boréal, 2007).

6 The Transformation of Ontario Politics: The Long Ascent of Neoliberalism

BRYAN M. EVANS AND CHARLES W. SMITH

Ontario's place within Canada has been historically defined by its dominance within the pan-Canadian political economy. An important component of this power has been the strength of Ontario's ruling classes, many of whom pushed for and directly benefited from national policies designed to strengthen the province's commercial empire from the St Lawrence Seaway westward to the Pacific Ocean.[1] In the post–Second World War period, the province's high levels of industrialization and its near monopoly of the commanding heights of the service economy reinforced Ontario's political and economic power. Over four uninterrupted decades, the Progressive Conservative Party of Ontario ruled through business-friendly approaches to managing the economy while appealing to the growing middle classes through construction of a modest welfare state.[2] Over the last thirty-five years, however, both the Ontario economy and the Ontario state have been transformed through the political and economic realignments associated with neoliberalism and the restructuring of the North American trade and investment bloc. While this restructuring began in the late 1980s, the Conservative governments of Mike Harris and Ernie Eves (1995–2003) solidified the transformation by weakening institutions promoting modest wage redistribution, workplace rights, and progressive social programs.

Some have argued that the 2003 election victory of the Ontario Liberals represents a return to "political moderation" and "the pre-1985 status quo."[3] We contend, however, that the Liberal governments have reinforced and deepened neoliberalism in the province. This trend has manifested itself in Ontario, as elsewhere, through three broad phases of neoliberalization. First, a quiet rolling back of the economic and political relations that characterized the post-war period marked the 1980s and early 1990s. In this stage, Ontario underwent a steady economic realignment that was managed somewhat ironically by the centre-left Liberals and New Democratic Party (NDP). Although both parties attempted to maintain the welfare state without dramatically altering the post-war regime of accumulation, neither was successful.

Second, the 1990s saw a shift in the implementation of neoliberal policies towards "roll-out" strategies, where the capacities of the provincial state were actively employed in implementing neoliberal policies, and the emphasis centred on creating quasi-markets in public services, competition, and commercialization of, within, and between public-sector organizations. At the same time, Ontario underwent a dramatic restructuring of the class alliances that were cemented to the North-South trading flow as a consequence of Canadian trade liberalization with the United States and Mexico. The Conservative government solidified many of these economic changes through a sustained assault on the capacity of working people to resist neoliberal transformation. Finally, the third stage of neoliberalization in the first decade of the twenty-first century has witnessed the Liberal governments of Dalton McGuinty and Kathleen Wynne, with a few notable exceptions, normalize the marketization of public services, continue the incursions on the rights of working people, while doing little to substantively strengthen programs that assist the poor and marginalized.[4]

In this chapter, we argue that the process of neoliberalization in the 1990s transformed politics in Ontario. Although the organization of the state itself has remained remarkably stable since the early 1970s, the patina of stability hides a significant reordering of power and the reprioritization of economic and state functions within and between social forces and institutions at the heart of the province. Ultimately, we maintain that this reordering of power reflects the shifting terrain of class power within Ontario's broader political economy.

The Decline of Post-war Ontario, 1970–85

The material foundation for Ontario's post-war dominance was the economic growth that characterized the "golden age" of capitalism in North America. In this period, Ontario's economy was transformed from an agrarian-resource base to a centre for branch-plant manufacturing employing a large labour force of skilled and semi-skilled workers.[5] This growth was precipitated by federal economic policies that prioritized central Canadian manufacturing and finance through managed trade. Perhaps the most notable agreement in this area was the 1965 Canada–United States Auto Pact, which accelerated trade between the two countries and provided stable levels of accumulation for branch plant auto companies in southern Ontario.[6] As the unions in these industries had consented to the post-war legal framework regulating labour relations, there was little need for employers or the state to challenge the labour relations model that emerged after the war. This level of class compromise led to average real growth of nearly 5 per cent per year, while real per capita incomes tripled between 1939 and 1975.

Provincial government expenditures, expressed as a percentage of gross domestic product (GDP) grew from 3.08 per cent in 1947 to 16.30 per cent in 1985.[7] A more generalized expansion of activities is indicated by the growth of functional departments, that is departments responsible for discrete areas of policy such as transportation, health, labour, etc., rising from twenty in 1950 to twenty-seven by 1973.[8] Employment in the Ontario public service (OPS) also expanded dramatically from 11,368 persons in 1947 to 75,770 in 1970 and 80,885 in 1985.[9] Notwithstanding the growth in the public service, the post-war Conservative governments maintained poorly coordinated plans to address public service expansion. The influence of department-based public servants in framing post-war policy was derived from the organization within the state that stemmed from pre-Confederation state organization.[10] The practice of political brokerage runs deep in Ontario politics, as it does elsewhere. Elements of patronage – that is, rewarding and consolidating the support of various class and sectoral interests in order to mitigate inter- and intra-class conflict, thus sustaining political legitimacy – were all present throughout the long Conservative rule.

The organization of the state along economic, political, and service-delivery sectoral divisions facilitated what we call the "Ontario model" of brokerage politics. For example, economic sectoral interests in agriculture, industry, energy, natural resources, tourism, and transportation were all represented within the state through their own departments. Similarly, the management of political relations is illustrated though offices/departments with ministerial rank representing labour, women's issues, Aboriginal, and Northern Ontario interests. What are identified here as service-delivery sectoral divisions are much more complex, spanning both political and economic interests. Health care, education (including post-secondary), and social services, especially since the 1960s, shaped province building and cut across these class and sectoral boundaries as interventions serving capital accumulation, competitiveness, and legitimacy objectives. Over time, these policy fields soon represented two-thirds of all provincial spending. As a result, the new political importance of these programs substantially expanded the importance of the public sector in political and economic terms and created new and influential actors such as institutional managers, for-profit suppliers, public-sector unions, and professional associations.[11]

Given the expansion of state functions, the challenge confronting the post-war governments was how to employ the resources of the provincial state to consolidate and expand industrialization. For the governments of Leslie Frost, John Robarts, and William G. (Bill) Davis, spanning 1949 to 1984, the most effective way to achieve these dual goals was to encourage "the exploitation of provincial resources and promote energy and highway construction in order to create a favourable investment climate."[12] The underlying criterion for any moderately progressive social or labour policy was that such measures be "economically practicable."[13] This overarching strategy ensured that state interventions did not compromise the primary objective of facilitating capital accumulation. In the area of social policy reform, for instance, it was the cost-sharing programs initiated by the federal government in the late 1960s that drove expansion of these fields. at the provincial level. Even within these areas, the Conservatives' traditional alliance with business led the government to oppose the extension of the Canada Pension Plan in 1966 and national medicare in 1968.[14] Yet the approach to social reform combined with a becalmed and institutionalized labour movement ensured that Ontario's post-war compromise was both moderate and accepting of a political-economic system that delivered the goods to a large part of the industrial and unionized working class.

As the inflationary crisis of the 1970s unfolded into a general recession in the early 1980s, the Conservatives were faced with a series of dilemmas. The general decline in the economy brought increasing hardship to Ontario workers as high unemployment, combined with double-digit inflation, took its toll on working-class living standards.[15] Pressure from international trade regimes also brought with it a series of plant closures that intensified the jobs crisis in the province. In dealing with the crisis, Davis used a combination of temporary measures to limit wage increases in the public sector while also using the state to address some of the most devastating consequences of the recession.[16]

This balancing act saw the government adopt a 5 per cent ceiling for public-sector workers in its 1982 Inflation Restraint Act. The new act, which mimicked the federal government's "6 and 5" anti-inflation program (referring to the legislated ceiling for wage increases – 6 per cent in the first year and 5 per cent in the second), virtually eliminated collective bargaining in the provincial public service and denied public-sector workers the right to strike. While the government showed that it was willing to use coercive means to constrain collective bargaining, it also created the Employment Development Fund to provide a series of grants to large corporations in order to maintain competitiveness and retain jobs.[17] In 1981, the government also surprised many of its supporters by spending $650 million in order to purchase a 25 per cent share of ownership in Sun Oil Co., reinforcing Ontario's support for the National Energy Program and the Trudeau economic plan. These initiatives alienated right-wing members of Davis's Cabinet who opposed public ownership on principle. Davis responded with a series of business tax cuts in the 1983 and 1984 budgets. To be sure, this was not an aggressive austerity program, as the government also provided limited protection for laid-off workers, although program and capital spending fell below 15 per cent of total GDP during the recession, well below post-war levels.[18]

The Liberal/NDP Transition, 1985–90

Within this climate, the break in Conservative Party rule in 1985 led to a historic shift in the governing coalition of the province. Having selected an openly neoliberal reformer in Frank Miller to replace Bill Davis, the Conservatives entered the 1985 campaign with an ambiguous platform and far more rigid and less popular candidate than any time since the party's electoral victory in 1943.[19] In the subsequent election, Miller was able to squeeze out a thin minority government, despite losing the popular vote to the Liberals. Although Miller attempted to form a government, years of shared experience in opposition and a number of common platform commitments led to a formal agreement between the Liberals and NDP (the "accord") that ensured political stability for two years.

The political transition at Queen's Park occurred under the auspices of a significant economic boom. Between 1983 and 1989, the provincial economy outpaced most other regions with growth levels averaging 5.6 per cent.[20] Yet underlying this growth were forces that were repositioning the region's economy within North America while also transforming how people worked.[21] By the time the federal government implemented the Canada–United States Free Trade Agreement in 1988, international financial forces were pulling branch plant auto producers into tighter integration networks in the United States. Yet Ontario's growth model was not based on innovation or increased productivity in the manufacturing sector.[22] Rather, producers maintained a competitive advantage that depended on a low Canadian dollar and low interest rates.[23] Further underlying the social conditions of Ontario's boom were subtle shifts in employment patterns that further pointed to weakness. During the boom, the percentage of workers in well-paid unionized manufacturing jobs fell while employment in services exploded. At the same time, part-time employment showed a slow but steady rise, while total hours worked per week increased sharply.[24] Meanwhile, measured against inflation, average weekly earnings grew only by a meagre 0.15 per cent over the entire boom.[25] In other words, workers were working longer and harder while the benefits of the boom were disproportionately going to the affluent.

In order to respond to these new economic realities, the Liberal government of David Peterson began a centralization of political power over the policy process. At the apex of the administrative state were the Premier's Office and the Cabinet Office. For most of Ontario's history, both institutions were rather sleepy administrative backwaters, but this began to change under the Peterson Liberals. Between 1985 and 1990, the Cabinet Office grew from forty to eighty-two staff while the Premier's Office remained a constant thirty. During these years, the Ontario public sector also continued to expand. Through the post-war period, the matrix of government departments responsible for policy development, regulation, direct program delivery, and program financing remained numerically stable between nineteen and twenty-seven.[26] The more interventionist Liberal and NDP governments between 1985 and 1995 saw the number of ministries expand to thirty-four. New discrete centres for policy development and political integration were established, including those responsible for women's issues, Aboriginals, seniors, skills development, persons with disabilities, financial regulation, and francophone affairs. The mini-boom also generated annual increases in government revenues in the range of 9 to 15 per cent, enabling the government to create new structures representing important socio-economic constituencies within the state. These changes were modest efforts to democratize access and representativeness to and within the state itself, which made a contribution to establishing a relatively more robust form to liberal democratic representative institutions.[27]

While the Liberals did bring in an agenda of modernization after the years of "backwardness into which Queen's Park had fallen under the long Tory reign,"[28] the government maintained a cautious approach to the economy. The caution was surprising, given the ambitious project for reform recommended by the Premier's Council, which identified structural competitiveness problems in Ontario manufacturing sectors, augmented by the transition to free trade in 1988.[29] Contrary to the blunt restructuring occurring in jurisdictions like Saskatchewan (chapter 8) and British Columbia (chapter 10), the council advocated for greater political and economic cooperation between business, labour, and the provincial state. In this spirit, the council recommended ambitious recapitalization incentive plans; new worker training centres; worker ownership programs; new organizations to improve research and development; strategies to address industrial restructuring; and aggressive plans to address Ontario's productivity gap. When the boom conditions weakened and pressure from the forces promoting free trade intensified, however, the Liberals dropped or abandoned most of these proposals, along with promises to extend medical care and building more affordable housing.[30]

The Peterson Liberal government existed in the context of the historic, and ultimately transformative, Canada–United States Free Trade debate. While Peterson's government opposed free trade, it was fated to be the last government of what had been Canada's "heartland" province. Indeed, Peterson's opposition to free trade was not strong enough to shift the opinion of the largest business groups that had long coveted it. Within Ontario, Peterson had to contend with the transition within the industrial classes (represented most prominently by the Canadian Manufacturers Association) who had moved away from state protectionism and, at the strong urging of the Business Council on National Issues (BCNI), tepidly endorsed free trade.[31] By moving away from tariff protection, the manufacturers signalled that they were willing to forgo any social contract within a single state. Almost overnight, this shifting class position began to transform Ontario's economic reality. Between 1988 and 1990, the number of plant closures more than doubled, jumping from 9,256 to 20,554.[32] Over the next decade, the number of auto parts plants fell by 14 per cent and that of electronic parts plants by 19 per cent. And this destruction of work and workplaces took place in the context of a 63 per cent growth in exports.[33] Consequently, Ontario's economy contracted by 5 per cent and unemployment doubled to 10.9 per cent.[34] While Ontario's unemployment rate began to ease in 1994, it has never returned to the pre-CUFTA rate of 5 per cent.

Faced with these challenges, Peterson's government did not survive to weather the full effect of the profound economic restructuring that was underway. During the years of minority government, Peterson's pragmatic approach to policymaking and economic reform contributed to his crushing majority in 1987. Yet in other areas the Liberals proved just as willing as Conservatives to end legal strikes, legislating striking teachers and Toronto Wheel Trans workers back to work (in alliance with the NDP) and ending a construction strike and a Toronto Transit strike during the majority years.[35] Petty scandals combined with popular frustration with endless constitutional negotiations and a growing sense of economic insecurity in the wake of free trade fuelled Liberal unpopularity by the end of 1989. In the ensuing election, almost all observers of provincial politics, including the political parties themselves, were taken by surprise. For the first time in Ontario history, the social democratic NDP formed a majority government.

The NDP in Power, 1990–5

The NDP entered government in 1990 and faced two immediate economic crises. The first was a significant retrenchment of the federal government's commitment to fund the post-war welfare state. The Mulroney government had made several changes to the Unemployment Insurance system that pushed the unemployed onto provincial welfare systems. At the same time, the federal government capped major portions of the Canadian Assistant Plan to "have provinces." According to one government study, this change, combined with the Chrétien cuts to provincial transfers in 1993 and 1994, resulted in a loss of $7 billion by 1995.[36] The second crisis was the world recession that began in 1990.[37] For Ontario, the recession reflected a period of significant economic and social restructuring. Although total GDP remained high, it declined 3 per cent in 1990 and 2.9 per cent in 1991 as plant closures continued displacing thousands of industrial workers.[38] Unlike in previous recessions, these job losses were permanent, as the percentage of all workers participating in the manufacturing sector dropped to 18 per cent of the total workforce by 1999, far below levels in the 1970s and 1980s.[39]

The economic dislocation of the Ontario workforce was reflected in the high unemployment of the period. In 1990, unemployment hovered at 6.3 per cent. By the end of 1991, it was 9.6 per cent, representing a loss of 250,000 jobs. In the following four years unemployment averaged 10.2 per cent.[40] What is more, even as the economy began to recover in the spring of 1993, workers continued to report difficulty in finding permanent employment. By 1999, the average rate of long-term unemployment (unemployed for more than twenty-seven weeks) was 29 per cent of all unemployed workers.[41] The jobs crisis also weakened long-term income levels in the province. Average annual household income in the early 1990s hovered near $64,000 while individual income was in the $33,000 range.[42] As the decade progressed, average annual Ontario household and individual incomes dropped to a decade-low of $60,100 in 1997, marking a drop of 3.84 per cent from the previous year, and down 7.40 per cent from the high of $64,900 in 1991. Throughout the decade, average individual income showed similar trends, dropping to $30,360 in 1997, a decline of 8 per cent.[43]

In order to address the crisis, the NDP's first budget was a classic Keynesian stimulus package.[44] The government's $10 billion deficit was designed to stimulate job creation through direct spending while also increasing social transfers to the unemployed.[45] In that budget, spending on social services increased from 13.5 per cent in the last Liberal budget to 17.0 per cent in 1991. Despite choosing job creation and the protection of the poor over austerity, the budget was opposed by the largest businesses in Ontario. Businesses maintained that the deficit was contributing to (and in some cases causing) the crisis gripping the provincial economy. These same businesses warned of impending bankruptcy if drastic measures were not taken to address the provincial debt.[46] This pressure played an important role in changing the position of the premier and Cabinet. After 1991, the government began to view the province's deficit and debt (and its subsequent credit rating from foreign bond traders) as the cause of the recession rather than observing it as a symptom of the larger economic crisis gripping the capitalist world.[47]

The premier's abrupt turn away from Keynesian policies was a defining moment in modern Ontario politics. Whereas the NDP was historically committed to manage capitalism in alliance with organized labour, the "new" NDP's response to its business critics was to embrace austerity. Part of this new agenda was exemplified in the government's industrial policy that spoke of new public-private partnerships and skills training to address worker displacements,[48] but included a campaign to eradicate welfare fraud, failing to pass benefits for same-sex couples, and retreating from public auto-insurance which had been a long-standing NDP commitment. The party also retreated on its labour law agenda, mostly because of a coordinated effort by business to oppose any legislative attempt to expand workers' rights. The NDP's eventual amendments to the Ontario Labour Relations Act (OLRA) – while advancing issues such as anti-scab provisions – also stopped short of freedoms provided in other provinces such as extending the ability of unions to organize in new sectors.

The NDP further alienated its own supporters in the spring of 1993 when it promised businesses that it would hold the line on the $10 billion deficit. In so doing, the government introduced a three-pronged austerity strategy to rein in public spending. First, the party promised to implement a series of new tax increases that would raise $2 billion in revenue. Second, the government introduced an expenditure control plan designed to find "efficiencies" in the public service, cutting back on service and eliminating 11,000 public-sector jobs, for a savings of $4 billion. Finally, the plan promised to save an additional $2 billion by entering into a "social contract" with public-sector workers. The social contract reflected an unusually nefarious action by the social democratic party, as the government unilaterally opened existing collective agreements and rolled back wages and benefits. Public-sector workers were also given mandatory unpaid days off (dubbed "Rae Days" by critics) in order to cut costs. The resulting Social Contract Act shattered the New Democrats' political base and further dimmed its already bleak electoral prospects. In the subsequent election, the "Common Sense Revolutionaries" in the Ontario Progressive Conservative Party took back Queen's Park and in so doing introduced a new style of governing to Ontario.

The Common Sense (Counter-) Revolution, 1995–2003

The election of the Mike Harris government marked an end to the loose post-war compromise between business, labour, and the state. The Conservatives were able to accomplish this structural change for two reasons. First, the party had the good fortune to be elected when Ontario was moving out of a recession. In fact, recovery had begun late in 1993 as the unemployment rates had fallen below 9.0 per cent by October of that year. By 1995, unemployment had fallen to 8.7 per cent and economic growth rates had risen 4.1 per cent since 1994.[49] Although the improved economic climate was added relief for thousands of workers, the rate of recovery was far below that of the 1980s. The forces behind this slower recovery were, in part, the result of the continued expansion of Ontario's integration into the new North American trading bloc.

Second, the Conservatives' "Common Sense" revolution borrowed heavily from neoconservative movements in the United Kingdom and the United States, which sought to impose market-oriented policies with an authoritarian populism in order to divide the electorate between the "haves" and the "have-nots."[50] Reflecting this ideology, the Conservative platform promised to reward "individual initiative" by promising an abundance of tax cuts for the affluent and middle class while also reducing red tape and eliminating "bureaucratic barriers to jobs, growth and investment."[51] Savings would be squeezed from the poor and unemployed through cuts to welfare services; the introduction of "workfare"; cracking down on welfare fraud; repealing NDP labour reforms; ending subsidies for childcare; and cutting premiums to the Workers' Compensation Board. In sum, despite an improving economy, a sense of insecurity was widespread, and the politics of blaming the poor and public employees had traction.

At the centre of this agenda was a motivation to shrink public expenditures in order to alter the redistributive role of the state. After their election, the Conservatives merged and reorganized numerous ministries, reducing the number of public servants from 90,000 in 1990 to 60,000 in 2000.[52] But the rearranging of the deck chairs masked a significant shift of power to the Finance Ministry, the Premier's Office, and the Cabinet Office. More dramatically, the Cabinet Office grew from 82 positions in 1990 to 133 in 1995. Paradoxically, the anti-statism of the Common Sense Revolution required the capacity at the centre to drive the revolution forward. As was occurring in Alberta under the Klein revolution (chapter 9), the Harris Cabinet Office reached beyond the 200-person mark between 1995 and 2003.[53] This consideration of and eventual construction of a robust "centre of government" at the heart of the Ontario state was a necessary institutional innovation intended to exercise greater control over policy and communications. Indeed two new senior-ranking positions were created in the Cabinet: a deputy minister responsible for policy and one for communications were appointed. The purpose was to impose greater central control and coherence over all policy initiatives and communications emanating from the ministries and agencies.

Given that rolling back public expenditures and reducing taxes was central to the politics of the Common Sense Revolution, the Finance

Ministry provided a strategically central role. One of the first priorities of the new finance minister, Ernie Eves, was to drastically cut public spending, which Eves accomplished in his first budget by slashing social assistance rates 21.6 per cent; tightening eligibility for social assistance and welfare; capping pay equity settlements; reducing transfers to municipalities with high welfare caseloads; cancelling numerous job training programs; repealing the Advocacy Act (thus abolishing the Advocacy Commission); and eliminating the Royal Commission on Workers' Compensation.[54] These cuts coincided with the introduction of Bill 7, which repealed all of the NDP's additions to the OLRA but also included several amendments making it more difficult for workers to unionize and strike. The government also promised to restore "workplace democracy" through a new purposive clause in the OLRA emphasizing neoliberal values of flexibility, productivity, and communication in the workplace. Bill 7 also eliminated annual increases to the minimum wage.[55]

The Harris government's assault on the public sector continued throughout the first and second terms. In particular the government introduced a draconian "omnibus" bill that sought a sweeping restructuring of municipalities, school boards, hospitals, and environmental regulations, while also introducing new service fees and road tolls.[56] The Conservatives also proceeded with several privatizations (including selling Highway 407) and made changes to the Employment Standards Act (ESA), making it more difficult for workers to file complaints to the Ministry of Labour and privatized the collection of monies for employer violations of the act.[57] Although workers and community activists staged impressive acts of resistance to these changes during the Days of Action between 1995 and 1998, Harris's government continued to benefit from a stronger job market and steady economic growth after 1995. In the subsequent election, the Tories also gained from their regressive changes to election laws in Ontario. Having already altered the election boundaries, the Tories shortened the campaign period (from forty to twenty-eight days) and used their considerable advantage in corporate fundraising to mount an aggressive advertising campaign, which contributed to the government winning a second majority in 1999.[58]

Between 1999 and 2003, their second term in government, the Conservatives continued to promote flexible labour markets, shrinking the state, and lowering personal and corporate taxes. Under Harris, there was a general increase in part-time employment, averaging 18.4 per cent over the Conservative rule.[59] This number far outpaced the post-war average, expressing the Conservatives' objective to promote flexible and competitive labour markets by making it easier for employers to turn to part-time work strategies. In early 2000, the government responded to employer demands by amending the ESA, making it easier for employers to extend the hours of work before paying overtime while also weakening vacation and holiday pay benefits.[60] The overall result of the Common Sense Revolution's restructuring of the Ontario regulatory state and its role in managing the political economy (especially the labour market) was a growing wage gap. Throughout the period, average economic growth stood at 3.7 per cent while average weekly wages (less inflation) declined 0.4 per cent.[61] From this perspective, the Common Sense Revolution should be best remembered as an economic and political realignment that shifted the benefits of economic growth overwhelmingly away from the working and middle classes to the most affluent.

One of the goals of the Common Sense Revolution was to privatize Crown assets. Similar to issues in New Brunswick (chapter 4), the Ontario Conservatives targeted the provincial hydro utility. For the Harris government, a policy of opening electricity production and distribution to the market was consistent with its ideology, and the idea had the support of the province's largest industries and CEOs.[62] The objective was that at some point market forces of supply and demand should determine the price for electricity.[63] The 1998 Electricity Competition Act disaggregated Ontario Hydro into three new entities – Hydro One, Ontario Power Generation, and the Independent Electricity System Operator. The new legislation re-founded the newly created entities, and indeed all entities within the electricity production and distribution sector, as corporations under the Ontario Business Corporations Act. The net effect was the commercialization of Ontario's energy sector.

In December 2001, in his last major act as premier of Ontario, Mike Harris announced that the market for electricity supply would open on 1 May 2002 with the selling of Hydro One. Harris's successor, Ernie Eves announced that he was committed to the principle that Hydro One would become "a private sector disciplined operation."[64] Faced with internal opposition and a frustrated public, Eves announced a policy volte-face like few in Ontario's history on 11 November 2002. The key elements of the new policy included re-establishing the price of electricity at 4.3 cents per kilowatt-hour, the price that existed prior to market opening, and freezing it there over four years.[65] In the course of nine months, Eves had traversed electricity policy spectrum ranging from open-market enthusiast to abandonment of the Hydro One sell-off, closing down the retail electricity supply market, and complete abdication of any pretence to even partial privatization.[66]

In contrast to the focused policy agenda of the first term, the final years of the Harris-Eves governments were characterized as "direction-less, disorganized and at times almost out of control," and a leading Conservative complained, "There was no discipline on spending."[67] But there was a political context to these episodes that went beyond any personal qualities. This was the neoliberal impasse as the limits of the Common Sense Revolution had been reached. The unarticulated but very real question was how to successfully continue to pursue the project of embedding neoliberalism in Ontario. A partial response to this question came with the party's election platform, released 16 May 2003. It was in tone and content a return to the roots of the Common Sense Revolution manifesto, but public opinion had clearly tired of the hostility. It contained proposals for "new rights for taxpayers," a ban on teachers' strikes during the school year, the hiring of more police, a not-so-veiled racist proposal for "skilled immigrants in, criminals out," as well as a promise to "prevent illegal immigrants and deportees from using OHIP" and legal aid, the incarceration of the homeless, a "crack-down" on welfare fraud, and, of course, further tax cuts.[68] The Liberals, in contrast, presented a Third Way–influenced platform encompassing five policy booklets. For the first time since the social contract, the pro-tection of public services was a stated priority.[69] However, a turning point in the campaign came when Eves was out-manoeuvred by Lib-eral leader Dalton McGuinty when he signed a pledge not to increase taxes.[70] On 2 October 2003, the McGuinty Liberals ended eight years of Conservative rule. The electoral demise of the Conservatives, however, cannot be conflated with the defeat of neoliberalism in Ontario.

Consolidating the "Revolution": Dalton McGuinty and the Ontario Liberals, 2003–13

During the election, McGuinty differentiated his party from the Com-mon Sense Revolution by centring on the necessity to reinvest in public health and education. Yet the Liberals expressed little interest in roll-ing back the fiscal legacy of the Conservatives. In fact, the Liberal elec-tion platform committed to "keeping taxes down" and emphasized the point, claiming that "Ontario workers and their families already pay enough."[71] By appealing to the populist anti-tax legacy of the Conservatives, the Liberals embraced a Third Way progressive competitiveness variant of neoliberal policy.[72] The objective was not to roll back neoliberal restructuring but rather to consolidate and normalize it by dulling the destabilizing polarization of the Harris-Eves era. The privileging of private business interests as observed in signature policy initiatives such as the Green Energy Act, and infrastructure renewal in particular, demonstrate this. Even the welcomed reinvestment in social programs such as education, health care, and poverty reduction were contextualized in terms of their contribution to Ontario's competitiveness. In short, the Liberals' policy agenda created a more rational and legitimate variant of neoliberalism that sought to broaden the political base for this project.

The Ontario Liberals' most obvious acceptance of neoliberalism was their unwillingness to reverse the economic trajectory of the Common Sense Revolution. Between 2003 and 2009 Ontario's GDP grew by a relatively flat average of 0.9 per cent. This slow level of growth combined with years of declining state revenue made Ontario particularly vulnerable to the Great Recession, which saw the economy shrink 0.9 per cent in 2008 and 3.6 per cent in 2009, resulting in a loss of 161,000 jobs. The failing economic fortunes of Ontario in 2008 and 2009 exposed a general stagnation in provincial wages, which averaged only 0.88 per cent between 2003 and 2009.[73] The divergent trends in income and economic expansion, at least until 2013, indicate tectonic shifts in the traditional methods for redistributing wealth – progressive taxation and substantial labour union density – over the past two decades. Although the Harris Conservatives did the heavy lifting, the Liberals have not fundamentally altered the decline or stagnation in these areas. Under McGuinty, fighting the Conservative deficit took priority over improving public finances through new or progressive taxation. Although the government introduced an income-geared health tax in 2004,[74] forgone revenue from the Conservative tax cuts in 1995 had grown to $18 billion by 2009.[75] Added to this decline in provincial fiscal capacity was the Liberals' decision to cut corporate taxes in their 2008–9 budget (alongside harmonizing provincial sales taxes with the federal Goods and Services tax), which further weakened the remaining social safety net.

The Liberals have shown little interest in reversing the most regressive changes to Ontario's labour laws. The de facto acceptance of the Conservatives' labour policies has had significant implications for workers and unions in Ontario. Union density in the province achieved a post-war high in 1991 in which 32.5 per cent of employees belonged to a labour union. By 2012, this figure declined to 28.2 per cent.[76] These aggregate numbers hide the evisceration of private sector unions that took place through the 1980s and 1990s. In 1981, the union density rate in Ontario's private sector was 27.8 per cent but had fallen to 15.2 per cent in 2012.[77] In the manufacturing sector, the very heart of Ontario's post-war model of prosperity, the decline of unionization was yet more dramatic, where union density fell from a high of 46.8 per cent in 1976 to 21.0 per cent in 2012.[78] In contrast, union density in Ontario's public sector has remained consistently high, ranging from 65 to 75 per cent through the 1990s and into the first decade of the twenty-first century.

Of course, the material basis underlying these trends in Ontario's "new economy" is the increasing proportion of the workforce, in both relative and absolute terms, employed in the service sector. In 1981, 65.1 per cent of Ontario workers were employed in services. By 2011, this figure had grown to 78.9 per cent of all employees.[79] In contrast, employment in manufacturing has declined consistently from 24.8 per cent in 1981 to 11.8 per cent of the labour force in 2011.[80] This transformation has had a significant and negative effect on income redistribution, given that the service sector, with the notable exception of the public sector, is characterized by very low rates of unionization.

The expansion of service-sector employment appears to have engendered an expansion in precarious employment, defined here as including a variety of employment relationships such as temporary, short-term contract, and casual employment. In a 2013 study, precarious work in Southern Ontario was measured at a shocking 50 per cent of the labour market.[81] Notwithstanding the Liberal government's introduction of an ill-defined anti-poverty strategy in 2008 and its increase in the minimum wage to $10.25 per hour in 2010,[82] expanding precarity in the labour market has resulted in downward pressure on the incomes of all workers. To illustrate, in 2010, the median weekly earnings of a temporary worker were $427, in contrast to the $800 earned by a permanent worker. Although the government introduced two amendments to the ESA in 2009 in order to address abuse of precarious workers employed by temporary agencies and in-home (foreign) caregivers, this did not addresses the wage gaps or lack of protection for these workers. Precarious work relationships have also grown in the public service. The broader public sector has historically been a bastion of "good jobs," but incremental neoliberalization has affected the employment relationship between public-sector workers and the state as employer. Of course, it could not be otherwise, given that 60 to 80 per cent of the Ontario government's expenditures go to the wages and salaries of public-sector workers.

The changes within the state have eroded trust in the permanent public service. This trend is most notable in the appointment of an increasing number of persons from outside of the OPS to the most senior ranking position of deputy minister. Through the premiership of Bill Davis, only 10.6 per cent of new deputy ministers were appointed from outside the public service. These numbers spiked under the Peterson Liberals, who appointed 32.0 per cent of new deputy ministers from outside of the OPS. Under the NDP, external appointees dropped to 20.8 per cent. Through the Common Sense Revolution years, 27.6 per cent of new deputies were external appointments. But the first term of the McGuinty premiership (2003–7) saw 42.0 per cent of all new deputies appointed from external positions.[83] This tendency towards appointing external candidates to the most senior management positions within the public service, and particularly so under McGuinty, can be understood as an expression of both politicization of the senior ranks of state executive managers and of the ascent of a more explicitly managerialist role for the senior public service as opposed to policy development.

A proliferation of ministries responsible for business, and more broadly, competitiveness policy development has also intensified. Small policy ministries dedicated to innovation, science and technology, small business and entrepreneurship, and infrastructure came to dot the public administrative landscape. And perhaps most significant is the ascent of the post-secondary education ministry as a key competitiveness policy ministry under the Liberals. In McGuinty's first term from 2003 to 2007, spending on post-secondary education grew by 45 per cent, more than for any other area of expenditure.[84] This relative growth in new investments still left Ontario students with the highest tuition in the country and among the lowest number of student-to-faculty ratios. And still, the level of operating funds per student is 12 per cent below what it was in 1995-6, the year that the Common Sense Revolution began.[85] Nonetheless, the Ontario Liberals have framed their economic competitiveness policy in human capital terms, entailing the commercialization of research and development on the one hand and creating a workforce characterized by high levels of skills and knowledge on the other. The Ministry of Research and Innovation, the mandate of which is closely linked to the expanded and strategic role of post-secondary education, employs public resources as a catalyst for research and development leading to market-driven policy solutions. In particular it has the role of identifying potential "winners" in fields where Ontario has a global competitive advantage and directing resources towards these sectors.[86] Not as interventionist as the recommendations of the Premier's Council in the late 1980s, the Research and Innovation Ministry clearly expresses an understanding of the role of the state in enhancing business-led competitiveness and accumulation.

In 2003 the Liberals created a powerful new ministry for public infrastructure. This ministry signalled the government's efforts to employ the Ontario state to blur the distinctions between public and private sectors. This new ministry was to be "the repository of the government's expertise in the area of infrastructure financing, capital procurement, initiative management, related financial analysis and asset management."[87] For the Liberals, this was not some minor agency, as the 2005 budget announced a five-year, $30 billion public infrastructure development plan as part of a more comprehensive economic growth strategy.[88] In addition, the new ministry brought together under the political leadership of a single Cabinet minister a number of large Crown corporations and agencies including the LCBO, Hydro One, and Ontario Power Generation. This consolidation of public agencies was recommended through a review of public assets that the government announced in its first budget. The objective of the review was to identify government-owned entities for possible privatization and then to reallocate any proceeds from sales to infrastructure development.[89] In doing so, the centralized political direction enabled by the new ministry would ensure more direct and strategic decision-making over the future ownership of these assets and would provide the institutional foundation to pursue a more comprehensive infrastructure renewal-planning and roll-out implementation.

The potential for private-sector involvement in a broad range of activities related to infrastructure renewal was acknowledged as one where "significant opportunities exist for private sector innovation in design, construction, service delivery and/or asset use."[90] In other words, there was no aspect of infrastructure development that prohibited for-profit involvement.[91] Concretely this meant the government believed that the private sector should lead in procurement, management of projects, financing, asset management, and service provision.[92] Despite having vigorously opposed the previous Conservative government's public-private partnership (P3s) strategies, the Liberals now embrace them.[93]

The great recessions in 2008 and 2009 reinforced the political and economic restructuring that occurred under the NDP, Conservative, and Liberal governments in the 1990s and 2000s. Although the Liberals responded to the recessionary crisis with a large stimulus plan, their actions since then have concentrated on its "Open for Business" plan, introduced in 2010. Under its "Open for Business" plan, the Liberal government embraced a more aggressive tax cut agenda catering to new foreign direct investment, restructuring and downsizing the OPS, and opening the north for new mining projects, specifically in the environmentally volatile and contested land claims with First Nations groups in the Northern "Ring of Fire" region.[94] The core of McGuinty's "Open for Business" strategy has very much consolidated the aggressive neoliberal restructuring of the NDP and Conservative years. While the McGuinty government entered the 2011 campaign concentrating on "moving forward together," the reality is that Ontario is less inclusive and more unequal than at any point since the Great Depression. Although the Liberals replaced the polarizing rhetoric of the Harris years with the language of partnership and "One Ontario," that language has masked the consolidation of the neoliberal project, which began in the early 1990s.

The 2011 Election: Ontario's Third Way and the Politics of Insecurity

The Liberals' genuine embrace of neoliberal fiscal policies, combined with an increasingly unpopular leader in Dalton McGuinty, contributed to a relative decline in their political support through the summer of 2011. Indeed, a number of opinion polls, nearly consistently, showed the Liberal government trailing the Progressive Conservatives by five to eight percentage points leading up to the fall 2011 election. The post-Tory dynasty political lore was that a "three-peat" was unlikely, as no government had secured a third mandate since Bill Davis in the 1970s. Moreover, this was a Liberal government seeking a third term, which had not happened since the late nineteenth century. When the votes were tallied, however, the McGuinty Liberals won a third straight government, though the party failed to win an outright majority (by a single seat). Eighteen Liberal seats were lost, and their share of the popular vote fell 4.6 per cent to 37.6 per cent. For the Conservatives, it was their election to lose. While gaining eleven seats and increasing their share of the popular vote by 3.8 per cent for a total of 35.4 per cent, it was far from what polls were suggesting only a few weeks prior. The NDP was the biggest beneficiary of Liberal losses, gaining 6.0 per cent in the popular vote to just shy of 23.0 per cent and gaining seven seats, for a total of seventeen. After sixteen years of wallowing in the wake of the Rae government, the NDP seemed to have regained some of its traditional support. Yet the opposition gains were modest, given the weakness of Ontario's economy, the poor state of public finances, the introduction of an unpopular Harmonized Sales Tax, and a series of high-profile scandals. Also noteworthy was that the public participation rate in the 2011 provincial election fell to a historic low of 49.2 per cent. In many ways, the falling voter turnout is a clear signal that disengagement with the political system is an ongoing symptom of neoliberal convergence in almost all jurisdictions.

A number of factors caused the tide to turn and deliver a historic win for McGuinty's Liberals. In particular, a number of Conservative blunders seemed to confirm the fear that under Conservative leader Tim Hudak, Ontario would return to the politics of conflict that so marked the years of the Common Sense Revolution. Specifically, Hudak's attack on "foreign workers," in response to a Liberal proposal to provide tax-credit assistance to businesses hiring skilled immigrants, did little to help his party win votes among Ontario's large immigrant population. A second public relations fiasco arrived with Hudak's defence of a candidate whose campaign pamphlet contained homophobic messages. Third, the PC platform's commitment to cut public spending, dismantle regulations, and close government agencies sounded eerily similar to the divisive years of Mike Harris.

As for the NDP, under new leader Andrea Horwath, the campaign and platform failed to reflect traditional social democratic themes and issues. Like in NDP platforms in British Columbia, Saskatchewan, Manitoba, and Nova Scotia, the NDP was not able to offer an economic alternative to the other parties. Despite the economic downturn and deepening inequality, the NDP refused to use the election as a vehicle to inject a more substantive debate around poverty, the need to expand labour union rights, improve progressive taxation, or broaden public services. On the basis of its performance in the 2011 election, the Ontario NDP was now an openly neoliberal party that rejected the best of Keynesianism and was farther to the right than the Bob Rae era.[95] The Liberals ran a tightly focused campaign that continued on the progressive competitiveness themes that characterized the McGuinty government since 2003: building a healthy, highly skilled, and high-wage workforce; a de facto industrial policy seeking to attract investment in building a green economy and cleaner, renewable sources of energy; and infrastructure renewal. In the end, the Liberals presented a more substantive, albeit clear neoliberal vision of Ontario's future.

The first Throne Speech and economic statement of the third mandate delivered in 2011 stated the obvious: that Ontarians are living in "a time of significant global change, upheaval and uncertainty. Many fear that the world's largest trading bloc – the European Union – is on the verge of recession as it struggles to deal with its ongoing debt crisis. For the world's largest economy and our biggest trading partner, the United States, overcoming their economic challenges will also take many years and great effort. We don't fully know what the global economic uncertainty means for Ontario."[96] The following day, the finance minister signalled that an era of austerity was dawning in Ontario. Economic growth was forecast to be tepid for 2.5 per cent in 2013 and 2.6 in 2014.[97] While explicitly rejecting cuts across the board, McGuinty instead proposed a fundamental restructuring of the means by which public services are delivered. The 2012 Commission on the Reform of Ontario's Public Services, led by Toronto Dominion Bank economist Don Drummond, presented a program for drastically reducing the size of the provincial state.[98] Recommendations, delivered in early 2012, provided a wide range of market-driven prescriptions, including massive privatization and significant expansion of contracting out public services.[99] However, the Liberals shifted their deficit-reduction strategy to more clearly focus on wage controls and the suspension of collective bargaining. In the autumn of 2012, the Liberals intervened directly to seize control of bargaining throughout the Ontario broader public sector. Bill 115, the Putting Students First Act 2012, froze compensation and centralized decision-making over the terms and conditions of employment in Ontario's primary and secondary education systems. The Protecting Public Services Act extended the pay freeze to unionized public-sector workers, which would terminate only when the deficit is eliminated.[100] In both instances, ministers were empowered to act unilaterally on labour relations matters, including issuing back-to-work orders.

Although the Ontario public seems to be at odds with such a narrow vision of government (McGuinty was denied a majority government in late 2012 with a by-election loss to the NDP in Kitchener-Waterloo – a traditional Conservative stronghold), the Liberals have not abandoned the austerity measures that are accompanying the most recent stages of neoliberalization in the province. McGuinty's ill-planned and badly executed resignation in the fall of 2012 suggested that the Liberal string of electoral victories might be coming to an end. Yet none of the opposition parties signalled that they would offer an alternative to the neoliberal vision of the province.

Kathleen Wynne: Change or Continuity with Neoliberalism?

Kathleen Wynne was elected leader of the Liberal Party on 26 January 2013. Prior to being elected in 2003, Wynne was a Toronto school trustee who had risen to prominence as an activist opposing the education cuts during the Harris years. Her community activism and advocacy for public education marked her as a left-leaning Liberal, and her successful leadership bid suggested that the party was repositioning itself to address the loss of support to the NDP and win back support from the teachers. During the leadership race Wynne stated she wanted to be known and remembered as the social justice premier.[101] The question, however, remains: will the Wynne premiership constitute a substantive transformation of Ontario politics and policy in a more progressive direction, or is the purpose of her government a combination of electoral strategy and an effort to provide greater legitimacy to the ongoing norming of neoliberalism into the fabric of the Ontario state and society? A review of several key signature initiatives of the Wynne government in the first four months suggests that the latter is a more accurate depiction.

The Commission for the Review of Social Assistance in Ontario released its final report on 24 October 2012. Many social justice and poverty-reduction activists were confident that Ontario was entering into a "once-in-a-generation" chance to make substantial changes to the welfare system.[102] However, the 2013 budget made minimal changes. As one journalist wrote, "Premier Kathleen Wynne wanted to do the right thing. She was prepared to take a political risk for the 850,000 Ontarians struggling to get by on subsistence-level welfare payments. But three months into the job, she realized there was no realistic prospect of 'charting a new course on social assistance' as a far-sighted provincial commission proposed."[103]

One of the first decisions made by Premier Wynne was to repeal Bill 115, the Putting Students First Act. However, it had survived long enough to structure several contracts and, most importantly, contributed to destroying the trust and cooperation that had previously existed between the teachers' unions and government.[104] Furthermore, the government made it clear that all contracts signed under Bill 115 were valid and enforceable until they expired in late 2014. Under the shadow of Bill 115, a deal was struck between the government and the Ontario Secondary School Teacher's Federation (OSSTF), which saw concessions from both sides as the OSSTF agreed to wage freezes and unpaid professional development days, but also won on the issue of sick days and maternity-leave benefits.[105] A deal between the government and the Elementary Teachers' Federation of Ontario (ETFO) was also struck; however, in this case, ETFO employed militant tactics (threatening to strike) to force the government to cede to many of the union's demands. The main part of the deal was a 2 per cent raise in 2014.[106] Notwithstanding the ETFO's gains, the Ontario government claims that it saved $1.8 billion through the Bill 115 framework.[107]

Despite Wynne's rhetoric of a "fair society" in the 2013 budget, the enduring theme is one of fiscal restraint in order to eliminate the deficit by 2017–18. The path to balance plan includes driving per capita program expenditures to the lowest in the country. In 2012, Ontario had the second-lowest program spending per capita at $8,726.[108] Wynne's budget states, "Managing the growth in program spending will continue to be a key component of the Province's fiscal plan." The expenditure forecast through to 2017–18 projects an average annual rate of increase of less than 1 per cent.[109] And the attack, though more muted, on public-sector workers continues with controls on public sector compensation with both salary freezes and low public-sector settlements.[110] With respect to corporate taxes, the budget cuts corporate tax rate to below U.S. and G8 averages, which the government believes will make Ontario internationally competitive. The corporate tax rate remains frozen at 11.5 per cent, but this was the result of NDP pressure not to cut the rate further. To be sure, Wynne's government marks a shift in style. Yet there is no substantive change from the McGuinty era. Indeed, while it is speculative, if it were not for the minority status of the Wynne Liberals, until the election of June 2014 when a majority was achieved, and the need for NDP support in the legislature, would even the stylistic differences be that significant?

Conclusions: Ontario's Neoliberal State

Over the past three decades, Ontario's political and economic trajectory has been similar to that of most other provinces in Canada. As the national post-war Keynesian consensus began to wobble in the 1970s, Ontario could not escape. Yet there are several unique characteristics of Ontario's process of neoliberalization that differentiate it from other provinces. While the shift began in the 1970s, neoliberalism had its most obvious beginning with the NDP's turn to rollback policies associated with the Social Contract Act. This was preceded by the neoliberal revolution unleashed during the Common Sense Revolution. At the centre of this transformation were not simply changes in government policy. Rather, Ontario underwent a class shift that witnessed the ruling classes radically reorientate within the new North American trading bloc. The implications of this shift were a restructuring of the labour market towards non-union, precarious work that has lowered the living standards for most working-class people in the province.

During the McGuinty-Wynne years, there has been an acceleration of these labour market changes. In fact, one characteristic of McGuinty's last year as premier (and Wynne's first) was a direct assault on the OPS, and specifically middle-class teachers and government workers. Notwithstanding these attacks, what has been most astonishing through two full decades of neoliberal restructuring with its consequent deepening of inequality and declining public services is the near non-existent resistance from social movements and labour unions. Other than the Days of Action in response to the early days of the Common Sense Revolution, there has been what can only be described as a collective resignation to Thatcher's refrain that "there is no alternative" in Ontario.

So thorough and complete has the neoliberalization of Ontario been that a progressive alternative is difficult to contemplate. Considering the economic turmoil unleashed in the wake of the Great Recession, the lack of real political alternatives is startling. The labour movement, while raising important issues about poverty and income inequality, continues to see the NDP as a political alternative to neoliberalism. Nothing in the Ontario NDP, however, suggests this is true. Indeed, the politics of resistance have been so emaciated that social movements and labour unions seem willing only to wage campaigns protecting historic victories won by a past generation. Yet Ontario's Conservatives under Tim Hudak have been very clear that if given the mandate, he fully intended to take aim at what remains. If Ontario teaches us anything, it is that the strategy of choosing the lesser of evils is bankrupt and is no longer sufficiently compelling to forge electoral victories in the era of neoliberalism.

NOTES

1 David Cameron and Richard Simeon, "Ontario in Confederation: The Not-so-Friendly Giant," in *The Government and Politics of Ontario*, 5th ed., ed. G. White (Toronto: University of Toronto Press, 1997), 162.

2 See John Wilson and David Hoffman, "Ontario: A Three-Party System," in *Canadian Provincial Politics: The Party Systems of the Ten Provinces*, ed. M. Robin, 198–239 (Scarborough, ON: Prentice Hall, 1972).

3 Rodney Haddow and Thomas Klassen, *Partisanship, Globalization, and Canadian Labour Market Policy: Four Provinces in Comparative Perspective* (Toronto: University of Toronto Press, 2006), 93–4.

4 Dexter Whitfield, *New Labour's Attack on Public Services* (Spokesman: Nottingham, 2006), 7. In Ontario, we build on the excellent analysis provided by Robert Macdermid and Greg Albo, "Divided Province, Growing Protests: Ontario Moves Right," in *The Provincial State in Canada: Politics in the Provinces and Territories*, ed. Keith Brownsey and Michael Howlett, 163–202 (Toronto: Broadview, 2001).

5 Macdermid and Albo, "Divided Province," 166.

6 Dimitry Anastakis, *Auto Pact: Creating a Borderless North American Auto Industry, 1960–1971* (Toronto: University of Toronto Press, 2005).

7 Ontario Ministry of Treasury and Economics, *Ontario Budget 1987* (Toronto: Queen's Printer, 1987), 67.

8 David Foot, *Provincial Public Finance in Ontario* (Toronto: Ontario Economic Council / University of Toronto Press, 1977), 20–1.

9 Ontario Civil Service Commission, *Annual Reports* (various years) (Toronto: Queen's Printer, 1947–2005); Ontario Ministry of Treasury and Economics, Sectoral and Regional Policy Branch, Statistics Section, *Ontario Statistics 1986* (Toronto: Queen's Printer, 1986), 660.

10 Bryan Evans, "From Pragmatism to Neoliberalism: The Remaking of Ontario's Politics and Administrative State 1970 to 2011" (PhD diss., York University, Toronto, 2008).

11 Ontario Management Board Secretariat, *Ideas for Organization Renewal: Organizational Renewal of the Ontario Management Board* (Ontario: Queen's Printer, 1991).

12 Keith Brownsey and Michael Howlett, "Class Structure and Political Alliances in an Industrialized Society," in *The Provincial State: Politics in Canada's Provinces and Territories*, ed. Keith Brownsey and Michael Howlett (Mississauga, ON: Copp Clark Pitman, 1992), 154–63.

13 Mark Thomas, *Regulating Flexibility: The Political Economy of Employment Standards* (Montreal and Kingston: McGill-Queen's University Press, 2009), 71.

14 Cameron and Simeon, "Ontario in Confederation," 165.

15 Robert J. Drummond, "Ontario 1980," in *The Canadian Annual Review of Politics and Public Affairs*, ed. R.B. Byers (Toronto: University of Toronto Press, 1983), 243.

16 Claire Hoy, *Bill Davis* (Toronto: Methuen, 1985), 146.

17 Drummond, "Ontario 1980," 243.

18 Canadian Centre for Policy Alternatives, *The Ontario Alternative Budget, 2002* (Toronto: CCPA, 2002), http://www.policyalternatives.ca/sites/default/files/uploads/publications/Ontario_Office_Pubs/oab2002.pdf, 4–5.

19 Rosemary Speirs, *Out of the Blue: The Fall of the Tory Dynasty in Ontario* (Toronto: Macmillan, 1986), 32.

20 Ontario Ministry of Finance, *Ontario Economic Outlook, 1994–1998* (Toronto: Queen's Printer for Ontario, 1994), tables 4 and 16. In 1984, Ontario's economy grew 9.2 per cent.

21 Macdermid and Albo, "Divided Province," 168.

22 Thomas J. Courchene and Colin R. Telmer, *From Heartland to North American Region State: The Social, Fiscal and Federal Evolution of Ontario* (Toronto: University of Toronto Faculty of Management, 1998), 33–5.

23 Ibid., 168–9.

24 Ontario Ministry of Finance, *Ontario Economic Outlook, 1994–1998*, table 31.

25 Ibid., table 35.

26 Foot, *Provincial Public Finance*, 20–1; Ontario Ministry of Treasury and Economics, *Public Accounts of Ontario, 1970–1985* (Toronto: Queen's Printer for Ontario, various years).

27 Brownsey and Howlett, "Class Structure and Political Alliances," 164.

28 Macdermid and Albo, "Divided Province," 179.

29 Ontario, *Report of the Premier's Council on Economic Issues: Competing in the New Economy*, vol. 1 (Toronto: Queen's Printer, 1989).

30 Ibid., 169.

31 David Langille, "The Business Council on National Issues and the Canadian State," *Studies in Political Economy* 24 (1987): 67–8.

32 Brian Langille, "Canadian Labour Law Reform and Free Trade," *Ottawa Law Review* 22 (1991): 598.

33 David Wolfe and Meric Gertler, "Globalization and Economic Restructuring in Ontario: From Industrial Heartland to Learning Region?," *European Planning Studies* 9 (2001): 575–92.

34 Ibid., 579.

35 Leo Panitch and Donald Swartz, *From Consent to Coercion: The Assault on Trade Union Freedoms*, 3rd ed. (Toronto: Garamond, 2003), 133.

36 Reproduced in Courchene and Telmer, *From Heartland to North American Region State*, 165–8.

37 Randall White, *Ontario since 1985* (Toronto: Eastend Books, 1998), 85–91.

38 Ontario Ministry of Finance, "Ontario Economic Outlook, 1994–1998," table 4.

39 Ontario Ministry of Finance, *Ontario Economic Outlook and Fiscal Review, 1999* (Toronto: Queen's Printer, 1999), table 20.

40 Ontario Ministry of Finance, "Ontario Economic Outlook, 1994–1998," table 32.

41 Meric S. Gertler, "Grouping towards Reflexivity: Responding to Industrial Change in Ontario," in *The Rise of the Rustbelt*, ed. P. Cooke (London: University College London Press, 1995), 105.

42 All figures from Statistics Canada, table 20204009, "Average Total Income, by Census Family Type and Living Arrangement (2007 Constant Dollars) Annual"; and table 2020701, "Market, Total and After-Tax Income, by Economic Family Type and Income Quintiles, 2007 Constant Dollars, Annual."

43 Ibid.

44 Thomas Walkom, *Rae Days: The Rise and Follies of the NDP* (Toronto: Key Porter Books, 1994), 98–106.

45 Ontario, *Ministry of Finance Budget Speech 1991* (Toronto: Queen's Printer, 1991).

46 Walkom, *Rae Days*, 114–20.

47 Panitch and Swartz, *From Consent to Coercion*, 172.

48 Ontario Ministry of Industry, Trade and Technology, *An Industrial Policy Framework for Ontario* (Toronto: Queen's Printer, 1992).

49 Ontario Ministry of Finance, *Ontario Economic Outlook and Fiscal Review*, 1999.

50 Paul Leduc Brown, "Déjà Vu: Thatcherism in Ontario," in *Open for Business, Closed to People: Mike Harris's Ontario*, ed. D.S. Ralph, A. Régimbald, and N. St-Amand (Halifax: Fernwood, 1997), 38–9.

51 Ontario Progressive Conservative Party, *The Common Sense Revolution* (Toronto: Ontario Progressive Conservative Party, 1995).

52 Ontario Civil Service Commission, *Annual Reports* (various years) (Toronto: Queen's Printer, 1990/1–2000/1).

53 Bryan Evans, "Capacity, Complexity and Leadership: Secretaries to Cabinet and Ontario's Project of Modernization at the Centre," in *Searching for Leadership: Secretaries to Cabinet in Canada*, ed. P. Dutil, 121–60 (Toronto: University of Toronto Press, 2008). Notwithstanding the Liberals' campaign against the changes, the staffing levels remained constant after 2003.

54 Ontario Ministry of Finance, *Ontario Fiscal Overview and Spending Cuts* (Toronto: Queen's Printer, 1995), 2–6.

55 James Rusk, "Tories Moving Fast on Labour Law: Repeal of NDP's Bill 40 to Be Followed by New Rules on Workplace Democratization," *Globe and Mail*, 29 July 1995.

56 Sid Noel, "Ontario's Tory Revolution," in *Revolution at Queen's Park*, ed. S. Noel, 1–17 (Toronto: Lorimer, 1997).

57 Thomas, *Regulating Flexibility*, 115–16.

58 Robert Macdermid, *Funding the Common Sense Revolutionaries: Contributions to the Progressive Conservative Party of Ontario* (Toronto: Centre for Social Justice, 1999).

59 Ontario Ministry of Finance, *Ontario Outlook and Fiscal Review 2004* (Toronto: Queen's Printer, 2004), table 24.

60 Thomas, *Regulating Flexibility*, 122.

61 Ontario Ministry of Finance, *Ontario Outlook and Fiscal Review*, tables 2 and 27.

62 Kevin Restivo, "Keep Ontario's Energy Utility Public: CEOs: Crown or Non-Profit: 30% of Respondents Still Support Privatization," *National Post*, 18 November 2002. When the plan was first floated in 2002, over half of all corporate CEOs in Ontario supported privatization, non-profit, or income trusts for Ontario Hydro.

63 "Tory Electricity Plan Makes No Sense," *Toronto Star*, 15 June 2002.

64 Ian Urquhart, "Many Hydro One Privatization Options on the Table," *Toronto Star*, 6 May 2002.

65 Office of the Premier, "Eves Takes Action to Lower Hydro Bills," news release, 11 November 2002.

66 Ian Urquhart, "Series of U-turns Leaves Eves Open to Accusations of Flip-flopping," *Toronto Star*, 21 January 2003.

67 Thomas Walkom, "How Eves' Empire Collapsed," *Toronto Star*, 3 November 2003.

68 Ontario Progressive Conservative Party, *The Road Ahead*, 2003, 6–8.

69 Liberal Party of Ontario, *Choose Change*, 2003.

70 John Ivison, "No Consent, No Tax Hike," *National Post*, 12 September 2003.

71 Ontario Liberal Party, *Achieving Our Potential: The Ontario Liberal Plan for Economic Growth*, book 3 (Toronto: Ontario Liberal Party, 2003), 5.

72 See discussion on the Third Way in Byron Sheldrick, "The Manitoba NDP and the Politics of Inoculation: Sustaining Electoral Success through the Third Way," this volume.

73 Ontario Ministry of Finance, *Ontario Economic Outlook and Economic Review 2010* (Toronto: Queen's Printer, 2010), tables 2 and 26.

74 Ontario Ministry of Finance, *Ontario Budget 2004: The Plan for Change* (Toronto: Queen's Printer, 2004), 8–9. The Liberal plan also delisted several critical areas of health care, including eye examinations and chiropractic and physiotherapy services.

75 Canadian Centre for Policy Alternatives, *No Time to Lose: An Action Blueprint for Ontario* (Toronto: CCPA, 2007), 6–7; Hugh Mackenzie, *Deficit Mania in Perspective, Ontario Budget 2010* (Toronto: CCPA, 2010), 4–5.
76 Statistics Canada, tables 2820078 and 2790078, *Labour Force Survey Estimates (LFS)*, employees by union coverage, North American Industry Classification System (NAICS), sex and age group, annually (Persons).
77 Ibid. See also, René Morissette, Grant Schellenberg, and Anick Johnson, "Diverging Trends in Unionization," *Perspectives on Labour and Income* 6 (April 2005): 5–12.
78 Statistics Canada, table 2790028, "Union Density, by Province and Industry," based on the Standard Industrial Classification, 1980 (SIC), annually and table 2820078.
79 Ontario Ministry of Finance, *Ontario Economic Outlook, 1994–1998,* table 31; Ontario Ministry of Finance, *Ontario Economic Outlook and Economic Review 2012,* table 23.
80 Ibid.
81 Poverty and Employment Precarity in Southern Ontario, *It's More Than Poverty: Employment Precarity and Household Well-being*, February 2013, http://www.unitedwaytoronto.com/document.doc?id=91.
82 Ontario, *Breaking the Cycle: Ontario's Poverty Reduction Strategy* (Toronto: Queen's Printer, 2008), 22.
83 Bryan Evans, Janet Lum, and Duncan MacLellan, "From 'Gurus' to Chief Executives? The Contestable Transformation of Ontario's Deputy Ministers, 1971 to 2007," in *Deputy Ministers: Comparative and Jurisdictional Perspectives,* ed. C. Dunn and J. Bourgault (Toronto: IPAC / University of Toronto Press, 2013).
84 Ontario Ministry of Finance, *Expenditure Estimates of the Province of Ontario* (various years) (Toronto: Queen's Printer, 2001–8).
85 Ontario Confederation of Faculty Associations, "Ontario Budget 2009 Backgrounder: Ontario's Post-Secondary Spending Plans," Working Paper Series 3 (Toronto: OCUFA, 2009), 3.
86 Ontario Ministry of Research and Innovation, *Results-Based Plan Briefing Book 2009–10* (Toronto: Queen's Printer, 2010), 2.
87 Ontario Ministry of Public Infrastructure Renewal, *Building a Better Tomorrow: An Infrastructure Planning, Financing and Procurement Framework for Ontario's Public Sector* (Toronto: Queen's Printer, 2004), 40.
88 Ontario Ministry of Finance, *Ontario Budget Speech 2005* (Toronto: Queen's Printer, 2005), 9.
89 Ibid., 11.
90 Ontario Ministry of Public Infrastructure Renewal, *Building a Better Tomorrow,* 22.

91 Ibid., 38.

92 Ibid., 42.

93 See the P3 initiatives in the Ontario Ministry of Finance, *Turning the Corner to a Better Tomorrow: 2011 Ontario Budget* (Toronto: Queen's Printer, 2011), 79–83.

94 Ontario Ministry of Finance, *Open Ontario: Ontario's Plan for Jobs and Growth 2010 Ontario Budget* (Toronto: Queen's Printer, 2010).

95 Matt Fodor, "Ontario Election 2011: Hard-Right Rejected, but Neoliberalism Still on the Agenda," *Bullet*, 14 October 2011, http://www.socialistproject.ca/bullet/555.php.

96 Government of Ontario, *Ontario Speech from the Throne* (Toronto: Queen's Printer, 2011).

97 Ontario Ministry of Finance, *Ontario Economic Outlook and Fiscal Review 2011* (Toronto: Queen's Printer, 2011), 45.

98 Ontario Ministry of Finance, *Commission on the Reform of Ontario's Public Services* (Toronto: Queen's Printer for Ontario, 2012), http://www.fin.gov.on.ca/en/reformcommission/.

99 Doug Nesbitt and Andrew Stevens, "Waiting for a Walkout: The End of McGuinty?," *Bullet*, 8 October 2012, http://www.socialistproject.ca/bullet/709.php.

100 When Premier Dalton McGuinty prorogued the legislature, the act died on the order paper.

101 Editorial, *Toronto Star*, 15 January 2013.

102 Carol Goar, "Once-in-a-Generation Chance to Modernize Welfare Lost," *Toronto Star*, 6 May 2013.

103 Ibid. However, it does represent a $400 million investment in welfare programs over three years.

104 Kristin Rushowy, "Bill 115: Ontario Government Repealing Despised Teacher Anti-Strike Law but Critics Say Problems Remain," *Toronto Star*, 21 January 2013.

105 "OSSTF Members Approve Deal with Government," CBC News, 18 April 2013, http://www.cbc.ca/news/canada/toronto/story/2013/04/18/ontario-secondary-school-teachers-federation-approves-contract-changes.html.

106 Rob Ferguson, "Ontario Teachers and Province Reach Tentative Contract Deal," *Toronto Star*, 13 June 2013.

107 Ibid.

108 Ontario Ministry of Finance, *A Prosperous and Fair Ontario 2013, Ontario Budget* (Toronto: Queen's Printer, 2013).

109 Ibid., 107.

110 Ibid., 126.

PART THREE

Neoliberalism and the "New West"

7 The Manitoba NDP and the Politics of Inoculation: Sustaining Electoral Success through the Third Way[1]

BYRON M. SHELDRICK

Manitoba is often overlooked in the study of Canadian provincial politics. Perceived as a land of bitter cold, floods, and mosquitoes, its location in the geographic centre of the country has been extended to a perception of Manitoba politics as bland, centrist, and pragmatic. Indeed, this perception of Manitoba as dominated by a "middle of the road" politics and political culture was the organizing theme of a recent volume of essays on the province.[2] Just as the stereotypes of Manitoba's climate and geography are both accurate and exaggerated, this characterization of Manitoba politics also requires a corrective. Certainly, it is undoubtedly true that Manitobans have historically voted for premiers and parties that effectively straddle the centre of the political spectrum.[3] The radicalism of provincial premiers like Ralph Klein in Alberta (see chapter 9) or Mike Harris in Ontario (see chapter 6) has been largely absent from Manitoban politics. Underpinning Manitoban politics, however, are deep political divisions, particularly between the rural south of the province and the north. Urban issues, particularly crime, poverty, and economic development are particularly salient. At the same time, Manitoba has one of the largest and fastest growing Aboriginal populations of any province, and Winnipeg has a large and growing urban Aboriginal population. The exclusion of Aboriginal people from the political and economic life of the Winnipeg, however, remains a persistent and troubling aspect of Manitoban politics.[4]

These issues, however, can easily be glossed over in a survey of Manitoban electoral politics. The moderate, centrist, and pragmatic view can obscure deep political divisions and the radicalism of politics as it is often practised in Manitoba, where there is a rich tradition of radical political organizing dating back to the Winnipeg General

Strike of 1919. There is, then, especially in Winnipeg, a dichotomy between a radical political tradition and an electoral politics that has been characterized by brokerage political parties and an absence of radical positions.

This has certainly been evident in the practice of the Manitoba New Democratic Party (NDP). The NDP has largely dominated the political landscape in Manitoba since its first election to office in 1969 under Ed Schreyer. More recently, under the leadership of Gary Doer, the party won three unprecedented majority governments. In doing so it set in place a framework for electoral success that balanced a focus on business-led private-sector growth with a careful policy of appeasement towards its core social movement constituencies. Greg Selinger, who replaced Gary Doer upon his retirement, led the NDP to a fourth majority government in October 2011 and largely contin-ued the approach established by his predecessor. Selinger's victory, however, witnessed the party's share of the vote greatly reduced from previous elections. Moreover, continued weakness in the party's elec-toral support underscores the limits of the strategy that has brought the NDP its success.

The NDP's majority governments were achieved by the govern-ment's very cautious yet strategic and tactical approach to politics. Reminiscent of the Third Way style of politics pioneered by the British Labour Party under Tony Blair, the NDP under Doer was able to secure the continued support of core groups within its constituency, while becoming increasingly seen as the "party of choice" by middle- and upper-income Manitobans.[5] The success of this strategy, particularly in Winnipeg, has been critical, given the limited possibilities for electoral growth for either party outside of the city. The NDP under Doer man-aged to square the political circle, retaining many of the neoliberal fis-cal and economic policies pioneered by the Conservative government of Gary Filmon (1988–99), while cautiously moving forward on social policy. It has thereby been able to avoid alienating the party's tradi-tional supporters.

Donne Flanagan, a long-time party activist and Doer advisor, described politics under Doer as being one of inoculation.[6] The theory was that the party needed to protect itself against both traditional areas of NDP weakness and traditional NDP opponents. In this way it could reduce the opportunities for its opponents to attack the party, and might even gain their support. In effect, this meant taking policy choices that, particularly on taxation and economic policy, would address the interests of the business community, thereby allowing the party to pursue its agenda for social justice and fairness in other areas. As Jim Silver points out, the political implications of this strategy have, in fact, been somewhat different. Continued immunization against business criticisms has meant ensuring that the demands of the party's traditional opponents are met first and continually.[7] In truth, the logic of inoculation demands this approach. The identification of policy weakness that Flanagan refers to cannot be carried out by the party on its own terms, but rather is done in reference to the views of its opponents. Consequently, only after these policy items are addressed can the needs of the party's traditional supporters be considered. In effect, the party's social justice agenda has become the tool of inoculation, not against the party's opponents, but rather against the demands and pressures of the party's core constituencies.

The success of this variant on Third Way strategy rested, in part, on the particular dynamics of Manitoban electoral politics and the nature of the political economy of the province. Manitoba's slow-growth economy has insulated it from many economic and social pressures experienced by other provinces. At the same time, it has reinforced historical electoral divisions and emphasized the political importance of Winnipeg within the province.

The sustainability of the strategy, particularly given the current economic climate, remains in question. The renewed strength of the Progressive Conservative Party in Manitoba underlines this point. While the Conservatives were able to increase their share of the popular vote dramatically in the 2011 provincial election, the party was unable to translate that support into seats. The dynamics of the first-past-the-post electoral system operated to paper over potential cracks in the NDP electoral strategy. Whether the party will change direction and reorient its strategic outlook in order to win back support remains to be seen.

This chapter is divided into four sections. The first examines the political economy of Manitoba and its relationship to electoral politics of the province. In particular, it explores how the economy of the province has reinforced deep-seated electoral divisions and contributed to the emergence of a regionally divided two-party system. This phenomenon has laid the groundwork for an effective Third Way politics in Manitoba. The second and third sections examine how the NDP in power has organized and developed public policy that builds on these political dynamics and permits the structuring of an effective "politics of inoculation." The first of these looks at the NDP's position on economic and fiscal matters, and it reveals the fundamental neoliberal orientation of the government. The next section looks at the inoculation strategy that is evident in the NDP government's labour and social policy initiatives. Finally, in the concluding section, the implications of the 2011 election result and the prospects for the party in the future will be assessed.

The Political Economy of Manitoba and the Manitoban Electoral Context

Manitoba has long been characterized as a "slow-growth" economy. Historically, the economic well-being of the province was rooted in the agricultural sector. The wheat economy dominated Manitoba prospects, creating forward and backward linkages into manufacturing, transportation, and services required to move agricultural products to market.[8] Manitoba's historic rate of economic growth hovers just around 2 per cent, significantly lower than national averages, and has demonstrated relatively little variation over time.[9] Nevertheless, the emphasis in the economy has shifted. Today, agriculture accounts for only 5 per cent of GDP, manufacturing accounts for roughly 12 per cent, construction another 5 per cent, and mining, including oil and gas, for approximately 3 per cent. The Manitoban economy is now dominated by a very diverse service sector, which accounts for roughly 72 per cent of GDP.[10] The service sector includes everything from retail and distribution, to knowledge-intensive "new economy" industries in computing, scientific research, and biotechnology.

These economic activities are far from evenly distributed across the province. Agriculture continues to dominate in the southern half of the province, even though other agricultural commodities such as canola have long supplanted wheat. Mining and resource extraction, including hydroelectric development, overwhelmingly dominates the northern portions of the province, including regional centres such as Lynn Lake and Thompson. The new service-based knowledge economy, on the other hand, is predominantly centred in urban Winnipeg, where approximately 60 per cent of the province's total population is located.

This regional economic division has a clear relationship to the electoral history of the north. Dominated by miners and resource workers, the north has tended to support the NDP overwhelmingly, while the southern agrarian regions of the province, dominated by independent family farms, have supported the Conservative Party. While family farms have given way to agribusiness, the historically established voting patterns have remained largely unchanged.

It is within this context that electoral politics have played out. Chris Adams has argued that electoral politics in Manitoba since the Second World War can be divided roughly into four periods.[11] First, from 1958 to 1969 the Progressive Conservative Party dominated under the premiership of Duff Roblin. In 1969, the New Democrats under the leadership of Ed Schreyer were victorious, ushering in a period of NDP predominance that lasted until their defeat in 1977 by the Progressive Conservatives under Sterling Lyon. Howard Pawley and the NDP, however, defeated the Progressive Conservatives after only one term in office. Pawley led the NDP to successive victories in 1981 and 1986. By the end of its first term in office, and despite a progressive record, the Pawley government was increasingly unpopular with members of the public. Proposals to expand French-language rights, combined with increases to auto insurance premiums in its second term in office, led to considerable public dissatisfaction, and high budget deficits and tax increases were a source of pointed opposition criticism and attack. During a period when governments in British Columbia (chapter 10) and Saskatchewan (chapter 8) were experimenting with rollback and roll-out variations of neoliberalism, the Pawley government was moving left. In 1986 the NDP was returned with a considerably reduced majority. Yet, in a series of missteps in 1988, the government was defeated when one of its own members voted against the budget. Pawley resigned the leadership and did not run in the next election campaign and was replaced by Gary Doer as leader.

The third period, according to Adams, is marked by the 1988 victory of the Progressive Conservatives under Gary Filmon. This election began a phase of eleven years of Tory government. Filmon was able to build on the public dissatisfaction with the Pawley government and capitalize on the growing right-wing discourse throughout the country to form a minority government. What was particularly telling, however, was that the loss of NDP support benefited the Liberals more than the Tories. The Liberals under Sharon Carstairs won twenty seats in 1988, compared to only twelve for the NDP. In 1990 the Progressive Conservatives formed a majority government and remained in office for most of the decade. Filmon's government ushered in a neoliberal turn in the province, implementing a series of rollback policies, including balanced budget legislation, downsizing public services, spending cuts, privatization, and tax reductions that were similar to measures introduced by neoliberal governments in other provinces in the 1990s and 2000s.

In 1999, the NDP under Gary Doer returned to power and have dominated the electoral scene since, ushering in the fourth electoral period. Overall, since 1969 the NDP has dominated the political scene in Manitoba in a way that few other provincial parties have been able to. During that period they have governed for twenty-seven of forty-two years. Moreover, during their periods in office they have exclusively held majority governments. This has led Nelson Wiseman to speculate that the NDP has become the natural governing party of Manitoba.[12]

The NDP's victory in 1999 was the product of both a series of failed PC policies and scandals and a careful repositioning of the party under Doer's leadership. Just as the British Labour Party had rebranded itself "New Labour," the NDP under Doer rebranded itself as "Today's NDP." As the Filmon Conservatives moved further to the right, the NDP was able to position itself as fiscally responsible and pragmatic. Filmon's difficulties stemmed from a constellation of factors. First, in March 1999 an inquiry led by retired Manitoba chief justice Alfred Monnin found that Filmon's chief of staff, along with several other senior PC operatives, had been involved in vote rigging during the 1995 election.[13] An ongoing crisis in health care, involving "hallway medicine," was also drawing considerable public attention.[14] The Tories were increasingly viewed as unreliable and unbelievable. The Conservatives had always endorsed and supported privatization. However, when Filmon assured that the Manitoba Telephone System (MTS) was an essential service and would not be privatized, then broke his promise, there was considerable public outrage. One poll indicated that 67 per cent of Manitobans were opposed to the privatization of MTS.[15] In the 1999 election campaign, however, Filmon's pledge that Manitoba Hydro would not be privatized was met with considerable public suspicion.

In light of these developments, the NDP gained considerable ground in the run-up to the 1999 election. Doer had built a reputation for reflecting a new "moderate" NDP, and he was intent to prove that "I'm not Howard Pawley."[16] This new direction was clearly in evidence when Doer and the NDP chose to support Filmon's 1999 budget. Liberal MLA

Kevin Lamoureaux, that party's only representative in the legislature, brought a non-confidence motion on the budget. It was supported by no members of the NDP, with Lamoureaux himself casting the sole vote in favour. This move may have proved shocking to some NDP core supporters, but it was a clear demonstration of Doer's intention to distance the party from its predecessors and move to the centre of the political spectrum. Of course, this was not unique to Manitoba. In British Columbia (chapter 10), Saskatchewan (chapter 8), and Nova Scotia (chapter 3) the NDP strategically moved to the political centre in order to compete for moderate votes and appeal to larger segments of the business classes.

In the 1999 election campaign, when Filmon proposed a billion dollar "50-50 pledge" that involved $500 million in new spending for education and health care, combined with $500 million in tax cuts, the plan was ridiculed by the NDP as foolish and irresponsible. The NDP's claim that the Tories' numbers did not add up, and that the NDP would be a better custodian of the province's finances, suddenly rang true for many voters: Filmon had drifted so far to the right that he had polarized the electorate and ultimately lost control of government.[17]

Table 7.1 shows the electoral results for the province since 1969 and clearly demonstrates the NDP dominance. The data, however, also demonstrate the tightness of electoral races in Manitoba. Of the twelve elections held since 1969, only one produced a minority government in 1988, and every other election has produced a majority. Nevertheless, in every campaign but two, the margin of difference between first and second place has been less than 10 percentage points, and in seven of twelve campaigns the margin of difference was 5 per cent or less. Moreover, in significant electoral campaigns that produced a change in government, the results were particularly tight. In 1969 the NDP won by only 2.8 per cent of the popular vote. In 1981 Howard Pawley defeated Sterling Lyon's Conservatives by only 3.6 per cent, and in 1986 the NDP retained government by a margin of only 0.9 per cent in the popular vote. However, the 1986 result still produced an NDP majority government. In 1988, the Filmon Conservatives defeated the NDP by nearly 15 percentage points, but surpassed the second-place Liberals by only 2.9 per cent. The beginning of the Gary Doer era saw the NDP returned to a majority government by a margin of eight seats, but only 3.7 per cent of popular vote.

Table 7.1. Electoral Results since 1969

Year	NDP(seats / % of vote)	PC(seats / % of vote)	Liberals(seats / % of vote)	Difference in popular vote between first and second place (%)
1969	28 / 38.3	22 / 35.6	5 / 24.0	2.8
1973	31 / 42.3	21 / 36.7	5 / 19.0	5.6
1977	23 / 38.6	33 / 48.8	1 / 12.3	10.2
1981	34 / 47.4	23 / 43.8	0 / 6.7	3.6
1986	30 / 41.5	26 / 40.6	1 / 13.9	0.9
1988	12 / 23.6	25 / 38.4	20 / 35.5	2.9
1990	20 / 28.8	30 / 42.0	7 / 28.2	13.2
1995	23 / 32.8	31 / 42.9	3 / 23.7	10.1
1999	32 / 44.5	24 / 40.8	1 / 13.4	3.7
2003	35 / 49.5	20 / 36.2	2 / 13.2	13.3
2007	36 / 47.9	19 / 38.0	2 / 12.4	9.9
2011	37 / 46.0	19 / 43.9	1 / 7.5	2.1

Source: Elections Manitoba

These data clearly demonstrate that majority governments in Manitoba can be generated by very slim differences in the popular vote, which can be explained by the fact that Manitoba politics is highly divided region-ally and economically. Traditionally the Progressive Conservative Party relied on the support of rural Manitoba, particularly in the southern agri-cultural belts of the province. This, in combination with the support of the Winnipeg business elite and wealthier segments of Winnipeg (primarily in the south of the city), had been sufficient to secure electoral victory. This had been the basis on which Duff Roblin had been able to build his electoral dynasty. The NDP, by contrast, has been able to reliably count on the support of the northern regions of the province, with solid support from Aboriginal communities and workers in the mining and resource-extraction industries. As a result, one can effectively draw a line across the province, with the northern half of the province being solidly NDP orange, and the south Tory blue. Since 1969 the Liberal Party, despite its brief resurgence under the leadership of Sharon Carstairs, has been rel-egated to the status of a minor, and increasingly irrelevant, third party.[18]

Effectively, then, Manitoba has become a two-party political system, with each party able to count on very clear bases for support rooted

Figure 7.1. 2011 Electoral Outcomes by Party: Manitoba, Brandon, Winnipeg

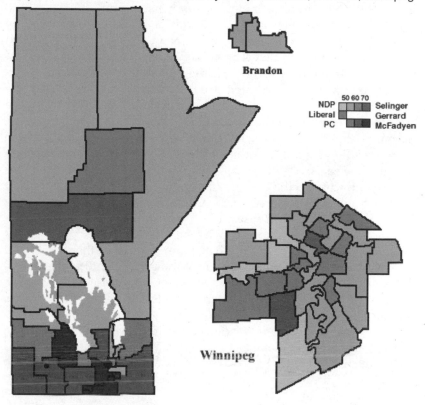

Source: Wikimedia Commons, http://commons.wikimedia.org/wiki/File:Manitoba2011
results.jpg

in regional economic divisions. The electoral map in figure 7.1 shows
clearly the regional distribution of support for the NDP and the PCs,
with the urban seats of Winnipeg forming the battleground on which
Manitoba elections are decided.[19] There are currently fifty-seven seats in
the Manitoba Legislature. Northern Manitoba and the Interlake region,
traditional NDP strongholds, represent approximately ten seats, while
southern Manitoba represents about fourteen seats that the Progressive Conservatives can reasonably count on. Brandon, Manitoba's sec-
ond-largest city, has two seats, which the NDP and the Conservatives
have historically split. This leaves the thirty-one seats of Winnipeg as

critical for a majority victory. As the electoral map demonstrates, it is here that the NDP has become increasingly successful.

In the NDP's 1999 victory, the PCs and the NDP were separated by only 3.7 per cent in overall popular vote. Nevertheless, the NDP picked up nine seats in total and six seats in Winnipeg to form a majority government. Overall the NDP won twenty-one of thirty-one possible seats in Winnipeg, which represented a tremendous breakthrough for the party. Traditionally the NDP had its greatest success in the northern sections of the city, reflecting its working-class base. In 1999, however, the party began extending its support beyond its traditional base to the more affluent ridings in the south of the city. It was increasingly clear that the party was positioning itself in a manner that made it particularly attractive to the growing urban and professional residents of Winnipeg, while the Progressive Conservatives' appeal was increasing limited to its historic rural base.

In the 2003 election campaign five seats changed hands provincially, four of them in Winnipeg. The NDP claimed three of these seats and continued to build on their success in Winnipeg, extending their overall majority. All new seats came at the expense of Conservative incumbents. In 2007, only three seats changed hands throughout the province, with the NDP again winning two additional seats in Winnipeg. In 2011, the Progressive Conservatives believed that they were poised to retake portions of Winnipeg's south. However, Winnipeg seats remained largely unchanged from the 2007 election, and the Tories' hope for a breakthrough, despite an increase in their share of the popular vote, did not materialize.

What is particularly significant about the overall electoral trajectory since 1999 is that the number of seats changing hands has consistently decreased. This trend suggests that the pattern of seat allocation between the parties has become increasingly crystallized. The political landscape in Manitoba, then, reflects a province with very clear political divisions. The first division is north-south, but increasingly, as in other parts of the country, a second and more important division is the urban-rural split. The result is that a handful of changes in ridings can lead to a change in government, and relatively small changes in overall popular vote can have tremendous impacts on the fortunes of political parties. Between 1995 and 1999, for example, the Progressive Conservatives dropped only 2 percentage points in the popular vote but lost seven seats and moved from a healthy majority government to official opposition.

This reality makes Manitoba politics well suited to a careful and tactical approach to electoral politics. The parties try to avoid positions that will polarize voters or that might lead to large shifts in popular vote. In effect, the parties do not have to think about broad platforms that will appeal across the province, for they can take those core constituencies more or less for granted. Rather, they need to structure their appeals in a fashion that will be successful in the handful of ridings that have the potential to switch hands.

Of course, it is never advisable for any political party to take their core supporters completely for granted. For the NDP in Manitoba, this is where the politics of inoculation has become so important. It has operated as a vehicle by which the core supporters of the party can be offered limited policy change that sustains their loyalty and support, while permitting the party to secure the support of new constituencies who might typically vote for opposition parties, including members of the business community. This strategy has allowed the party to balance the demands of workers, organized labour, and social movement activists with the interest of business and urban professionals. The NDP's practice of "inoculation" has resulted in the party fully embracing the neoliberal rollback strategies began by Filmon while introducing several roll-out strategies of its own.

The Inoculation Strategy: The Predominance of a Business-First Agenda

The success of the NDP under both Gary Doer and Greg Selinger has been rooted in the adoption of a Blairite Third Way strategy, which has allowed them to strategically move in different directions as necessary to broker the support of different groups. The success of the strategy, facilitated by the dynamics of the electoral system, has also been aided by the relative economic prosperity that Manitoba enjoyed throughout the 2000s. As discussed, this strategy was facilitated by Manitoba's "slow-growth" economy that has spared the province the boom-and-bust cycles experienced by other provincial economies. Consequently, during his tenure in office Doer was able to avoid some of the hard choices that other Canadian premiers had to face.

As a political strategy, the Third Way is most clearly articulated in the work of Anthony Giddens and was implemented as an electoral strategy and policy direction by Tony Blair and the British Labour Party in the late 1990s and 2000s.[20] Third Way politics has been described as a particular form of brokerage politics, in which a social democratic party attempts to stitch together support for social justice initiatives, along with a strong support for business and neoliberal capitalism. As several chapters in this volume also observe, Third Way politics also represents the neoliberalization of social democratic ideology.[21] In Britain and elsewhere it has resulted in social democratic parties distancing themselves from traditional allies in the labour movement and becoming more business friendly. It has also meant a fairly wholesale adoption, at a policy level, of many of the precepts of neoliberalism, including the paramount importance of deficit and tax reduction.

It would, of course, be incorrect to view the turn to neoliberalism by social democratic parties as solely an electoral strategy. The brief discussion of the electoral history of Manitoba in the previous section demonstrates the importance of a number of factors, including the fiscal crisis of the state, budget deficits, and economic performance more generally as factors that help explain the turn to the right by the NDP. Indeed, the adoption of neoliberalism as a policy paradigm by the Manitoba NDP is part of a broader turn to the right within social democracy.[22] The predominance of neoliberalism as a global ideology means that it is very difficult for parties of the left to resist this tendency. Social democratic parties are committed to a strategy of social change that depends on electoral success. Finding ways to win in a context of growing ideological uniformity often leaves little capacity to avoid the pressure to move to the right. Of course, as the chapters in this volume also demonstrate, different social democratic parties have embraced different strategies and approaches to achieving this goal. The inoculation strategy of the Manitoba NDP is one variant on a tendency that is very strong within Third Way politics.[23]

One hallmark of Third Way politics has been an ability to move simultaneously in different directions. Social justice initiatives supporting core constituencies are coupled with – or framed in terms that will also appeal to (or at least reassure) – those who might be otherwise be opposed to such initiatives. Increased welfare spending, as an example, might be coupled with workfare initiatives or framed in terms that emphasize individual responsibility for unemployment.[24] While in theory the politics of the Third Way could be structured in the way Donne Flanagan and Gary Doer have suggested, to inoculate a social democratic program from attack by the right, this is rarely the case. Rather, given the predominant importance of capital and

Table 7.2. Changes to Business Tax Rates in Manitoba, 2002 to 2011

	2002	2003	2004	2005	2006	2007	2008	2009	2010	2011
General rate	16.5	16.0	15.5	15.0	14.5	14.0	13.0	12.0	12.0	12.0
Small business rate	5.0	5.0	5.0	5.0	4.5	3.0	2.0	1.0	0.0	0.0

Source: Manitoba Government: Corporate income Tax Rate Reductions, http://www.gov
.mb.ca/ctt/invest/busfacts/govt/corp_reduc.html

business within the political and economic realm, coupled with the general antagonism of the mainstream press to left-wing political parties, the actual practice of Third Way politics has been the reverse. The primary accommodation is to the interests of business elites, while the demands of core supporters are satisfied, to a limited fashion, as an afterthought.

In economic and fiscal policy the accommodation of business interests was particularly evident in the policies of the NDP government. They were generally unwilling to deviate from a fairly conventional, albeit moderate neoliberal approach. In particular, the Doer government sought to distance itself from previous NDP governments and convince people that it was not going to follow a "tax and spend" policy orientation. To that end, the government quickly announced that it would live by the balanced budget legislation introduced by the previous government. Over its tenure, the Doer government brought in five balanced budgets. Significantly, the finance minister who managed this task was Doer's successor, Greg Selinger. Not surprisingly, Selinger has continued the pragmatic fiscal conservatism that was characteristic of Doer's years in office.

If the government was not going to permit deficits, it was also not going to consider tax increases. To be sure, the government did not implement radical and massive tax cuts as occurred in other provinces. However, both personal income tax rates and business and corporate taxes steadily declined over Gary Doer's three terms in office. Table 7.2 illustrates the slow but steady decrease in business tax rates.

As can be seen, small reductions in the general rate of corporate tax were effected gradually over a seven-year pertiod. In 1999, when the NDP came to power, the small business rate of taxation was 8 per cent, the second highest in the country. This was reduced to 5 per cent in the NDP's first term in office and eliminated completely by 2010.

Table 7.3. Manitoba Income Tax Savings for Typical Taxpayers

Income ($)	Tax payable (refunds) 1999	Tax payable (refunds) 2011	Tax savings 2011	2011 savings over 1999 (%)	Cumulative savings over 12 years ($)
SINGLE PERSON					
10,000	88	(95)	183	207.0	1,397
20,000	1,369	1,099	270	19.7	2,290
40,000	4,012	3,318	694	17.3	5,780
70,000	9,153	7,230	1,923	21.0	15,360
100,000	14,572	12,450	2,122	14.6	17,684
FAMILY OF 4 – TWO EARNERS					
30,000	533	24	509	95.6	3,972
40,000	1,360	793	567	41.7	4,754
60,000	4,107	3,150	957	23.3	8,388
80,000	7,169	5,566	1,603	22.4	13,648
100,000	10,188	8,084	2,104	20.7	17,459

Source: Manitoba Government, Taxation Adjustments Budget 2011, http://www.gov.mb
.ca/finance/budget11/papers/taxation.pdf, C14

Overall marginal rates of taxation were relatively constant throughout the NDP's term in office. One exception was middle-income earners, for whom rates of taxation decreased from 16.2 per cent in 2001 to 12.75 per cent in 2011. For the NDP, paying attention to the interests of this group deflected criticisms that this group paid too much tax, while at the same time consolidating support from this growing segment of the urban population. Overall, however, changes to the structure of income taxes amounted to $540 million in lost revenue between 2000 and 2009. When cuts to property taxes are included, the total figure balloons to $830 million.[25] As indicated in table 7.3, the real dollar savings from income tax cuts were disproportionately enjoyed by middle- and upper-income Manitobans.

Decreases in taxation meant that spending priorities had to be carefully allocated, particularly given that balanced budget legislation meant that borrowing could not be used to offset revenue decreases. The government's spending priorities throughout much of the past decade have been fourfold: debt reduction, strategic investments in

Table 7.4. Manitoba Government Spending by Area ($000)

	1996	2004	% Change
Health	1,811,827	3,161,289	74.4
Education, Citizenship and Youth	1,155,477	1,648,071	42.6
Family Services and Housing	703,021	912,782	29.8
Community, Economic and Resource Development	699,590	967,781	38.3
Justice and Other	416,396	603,635	44.9
Debt Costs	575,000	238,681	−59.0

Source: Paul Egan, "Budget Central; NDP, Tory Governments Don't have much Political Room to Manoeuvre Left or Right at Budget Time," *Winnipeg Free Press*, 6 March 2005

health and education, tax cuts, and increasing the Fiscal Stabilization Fund (rainy day fund), combined with an ongoing commitment to balanced budgets.

At the end of the day, a typical budget under the NDP bore many similarities to budgets under the Filmon Conservatives. A comparison of operating budgets between 1996 under the Progressive Conservatives and 2004 under the NDP, conducted by the Winnipeg Free Press, illustrates this.

The priorities in the two budgets remain largely the same. The most notable changes are to found in spending allocated to health care and debt relief. Spending on health had increased nearly 75 per cent over eight years under the NDP, while spending on debt relief had decreased. Heath spending represented approximately 41.9 cents out of every budget dollar under the NDP, compared to only 34 cents under the Filmon Conservatives. Debt relief, by contrast, consumed nearly 11 cents of every budget dollar under the Conservatives, while this decreased to just 3 cents by 2004 under the NDP. Decreased debt relief spending, in part, allowed for modest increases in social spending in education and family services, although the bulk of this was consumed by health care. The NDP's neoliberalism earned it a second-place ranking among provinces for "fiscal responsibility" from the right-wing Fraser Institute.[26]

Cy Gonick has argued that the NDP's acceptance of neoliberalism has left very little scope for the party to pursue radical changes to social programs or aggressively pursue poverty reduction.[27] This is also true in most provinces where the NDP has formed govern-ment. Given the policy shifts of social democratic parties in British Columbia, Saskatchewan, Manitoba, Ontario, Nova Scotia, and the Parti Québécois in Quebec, transformative redistributive policies are no longer central to Canadian social democrats in government. Of course, for the NDP to completely avoid these issues (and other ques-tions of social inequality) would lead to a crisis for the social dem-ocratic party and its core supporters in the province. In Manitoba, the party has to be able to rely on the core support of the organized labour. At the same time, the province has a rich history of political radicalism and activism, which manifests in a vibrant anti-poverty and social justice community, particularly in Winnipeg. Community economic development organizations, anti-poverty activists, wom-en's organizations, and Aboriginal organizations all are important aspects of the party's core support.

Had the NDP failed to recognize this reality, it might have provided a political opening for third parties, including the Liberal Party to recover lost ground in the province. However, the politics of inoculation, and a Blairite Third Way orientation, allowed the party to address some of these issues and retain the support of its core constituencies. We now turn to examine the parameters of that strategy as it applied to core areas of NDP support.

Inoculation in Practice

Labour Law

It is generally taken for granted that the NDP can count on the sup-port of organized labour. Indeed, when Gary Doer and the NDP were elected in 1999 there were widespread expectations by organized labour that labour law reforms would be at the top of the new govern-ment's agenda. The fact that Gary Doer had previously served as pres-ident of the Manitoba Government and General Employees' Union certainly suggested that the government would be far more receptive to the interests of labour than the Progressive Conservatives. Under Gary Filmon, the government enacted reforms that had dramatically tipped the balance in labour relations in favour of employers. Most notably, the Filmon Tories had restructured public school teachers' bargaining rights, removing their right to strike. Workplace standards and occupational health and safety regulations were eroded, and most significantly, the rules for the certification of trade unions were changed to make it more difficult to organize a workplace. In particular, the automatic certification rule, which allowed for the awarding of bargaining rights to a union if it demonstrated that a majority of employees had signed union cards, was eliminated. All certification applications required a secret ballot of employees. Generally, the period of time between an application for certification and the holding of the vote often occurs when employers engage in tactics to discredit the union and to deter employees from supporting it.[28] A return to an automatic certification regime was a major expectation of organized labour with an NDP victory.

The NDP delivered on some aspects of the highly anticipated labour law reforms. In particular, automatic certification was re-established, although at a much higher threshold than in the past. Under the NDP's legislation, automatic certification would be granted only if 65 per cent of workers signed union cards, the highest threshold for automatic certification in Canada. These new rules were a far cry from the 55 per cent threshold that existed prior to its elimination in 1996. The move to extend workers' rights was counterbalanced by a high threshold that meant the reforms would potentially have a limited impact on rates of unionization in the province. While the proposals did result in an outcry from some business groups and the *Winnipeg Free Press*, overall this reform was not particularly contentious. Business itself was divided on the issue, and organized labour, while perhaps unhappy about the limited scale of the reforms, nevertheless was supportive, considering it a solid first step while hoping for further reforms in the future.[29]

On other labour issues, however, the government was quite clear that it would not be seen as a proxy for organized labour. In Donne Flanagan's terms, the government was clearly insulating itself from the traditional attack that the NDP was too sympathetic to organized labour. Members of the provincial NDP, at their annual convention, have consistently passed resolutions calling for the expansion of labour rights. Most notably these have included ongoing demands to reduce the rate for automatic certification to 50 per cent plus one, along with a call for the implementation of legislation prohibiting the use of replacement workers during a strike. The government steadfastly refused to implement these changes, with Gary Doer publicly stating that he opposed anti-replacement worker legislation and believed there to be no need for further changes to the certification rules.[30]

Inoculation in labour issues is also demonstrated in the controversy that surrounded the Red River Floodway expansion project, which was a major construction and infrastructure development project that would see the expansion of the Red River floodway. After the "flood of the century" in 1997, improvements to the floodway were widely viewed as a critical priority. The project itself involved widening of entire floodway channel, increasing the elevation of dikes, and making improvements to bridges and transmission lines in the area. The entire project costs were nearly $665 million and represented a significant boon to the Manitoba construction industry. Labour relations on the project were to be governed by a master agreement negotiated by the parties involved. Of course, this raised significant labour relations issues, particularly around the question of whether or not there would be a requirement for workers on the project to be unionized, and whether only unionized employers would be permitted to bid on the work. It was proposed that the labour agreement on the floodway expansion should require workers to become union members while employed on the project. This suggestion met with fierce opposition from business interests, particularly from construction associations throughout the province, Chambers of Commerce, and the Progressive Conservative Party.[31]

The NDP responded to the controversy by appointing Wally Fox-Decent, head of the Workers' Compensation Board, to develop a proposal for the management of labour relations on the project.[32] Fox-Decent's proposal, which was accepted by the government, is a classic example of an inoculation strategy. On the one hand, Fox-Decent recommended that the project be an "organization"-free zone. Union and non-union employers would be allowed to bid on the contract, and union and non-union workers would be allowed to work side-by-side. Recognizing that the construction trade unions would be deeply involved in negotiating and setting the terms and conditions of work on the project, Fox-Decent proposed that non-union workers be required to pay a fee, the equivalent of union dues, which would go into a trust fund. While Fox-Decent's proposal was meant to balance relations between union and non-union labour, it was clearly a neoliberal version of the Rand formula. This fund would be used to reimburse the relevant labour organizations for their services in negotiating terms and conditions of work that would benefit non-members. In this way, the problem of free riders, a major concern of the unions, would be eliminated. More significantly, though, no organizing of workers into trade unions would be permitted on the project. Effectively, Fox-Decent's proposals met the demands of employers, ensuring that non-union employers would have full access to the floodway project, and that there would be no pressure on their workers to become unionized. Some concerns of the unions would be attended to, although not in a fashion that would permit the expansion of union penetration into the construction industry. More fundamentally, however, it also ran counter to the underlying raison d'être of trade unionism, reducing the unions to a pay-for-service consultancy, rather than a democratic organization representing (and furthering) workers interests. For many, it was surprising that the NDP would take such a position, but it clearly reflected their willingness to put limits on their support of union activities.

Social Policy: Addressing Poverty in the Inner City

The government's approach to poverty and social issues in general also indicates a policy of inoculation. Poverty is a pressing issue in Manitoba, particularly in the inner city of Winnipeg. Table 7.5 provides data on selected indicators of poverty, drawn together by Jim Silver in his studies of the inner city.[33] These data clearly demonstrate the profound poverty of the inner city, but also that poverty in Winnipeg is spatially concentrated and profoundly racialized, with high concentrations of Aboriginal persons and visible minorities in the poorest areas of the city. The table compares Lord Selkirk Park, one of Winnipeg's poorest neighbourhoods in the North End of the city, with the inner city more broadly, and Winnipeg as a whole. Not only is poverty endemic, but rates of labour market participation are very low in the inner city, reflecting the absence of employment opportunities in these neighbourhoods. Education attainment rates are significantly lower than elsewhere in the city, and rates of youth unemployment are high. Overall poverty rates for households in Lord Selkirk Park border on 90 per cent, while the rate is nearly 45 per cent in the inner city generally. In the five poorest neighbourhoods of Winnipeg's inner city, Aboriginal people constitute 27.5 to 54.9 per cent of the population. Moreover, Aboriginal people plus other visible minorities constitute between 42.5 and 66.0 per cent of the population.[34] The average income in these neighbourhoods is $10,000 below the low-income cut-off (LICO), providing clear evidence of the depth of poverty in Winnipeg.[35]

Table 7.5. Poverty and Related Indicators 2001: Lord Selkirk Park, Winnipeg Inner City, Winnipeg

	Lord Selkirk Park	Winnipeg Inner City	Winnipeg
Median household income	$14,696	$26,362	$43,383
Household poverty rate	87.8%	44.1%	24.7%
Less than high school education (adults 20 years of age or older)	67.9%	36.0%	28.2%
Percentage one-parent households	47.7%	29.6%	18.5%
Adult unemployment rate	23.4%	9.0%	5.7%
Youth unemployment rate (15–24)	44.0%	13.0%	10.9%
Adult labour force participation rate	35.8%	63.0%	68.1%
Youth (15–24) labour force participation rate	44.0%	66.4%	71.3%
Aboriginal population as % of the whole	54.3%	18.3%	19.1%

Source: Jim Silver, "Segregated City: A Century of Poverty in Winnipeg," in *Manitoba Politics and Government: Issues, Institutions Traditions*, ed. P. Thomas and C. Brown (Winnipeg: University of Manitoba Press), 346

During its tenure in office the NDP government has certainly taken proactive steps to address poverty. One strategy has been to increase the minimum wage, which is certainly important and welcome. However, this fails to recognize the crisis of employment for many people in the inner city. There is simply an absence of jobs, and many individuals rely on welfare and other income-support programs for survival.[36] Given this reality, increases to the minimum wage accomplish little in addressing the deep levels of structural poverty that persist in the inner city. Moreover, during the same period the government was cutting personal and corporate taxes, welfare rates also decreased significantly. In 2005 in Manitoba a single employable recipient of social assistance received only 25 per cent of the LICO, while a couple with two children received 53 per cent of the LICO. Moreover, welfare income for single employable individuals fell by 33.2 per cent, in constant dollars, between 1989 and 2005. For a couple with two children, welfare income decreased by 16.7 per cent over the same period. While much of that decline came at the hands of the Progressive Conservatives, the NDP has not significantly reversed the trend.

From 2005 until 2010 some of the decline was reversed for single individuals, with welfare income increasing by 9 per cent for this group. Welfare income for a couple with children, however, continued its downward trend, decreasing a further 2.5 per cent.[37] This change was particularly troubling, given that child poverty rates in Manitoba are some of the highest in the country, and Manitoba has been repeatedly named the child poverty capital of Canada by the Social Planning Council.[38]

One particularly important program spearheaded by the NDP government was Neighbourhoods Alive, which was launched in 1999 with an initial budget of only $419,000.[39] The objective was to provide project-based funding to community development initiatives in some of the province's poorest communities. Funds were made available through a Neighbourhood Renewal Fund for projects geared to capacity building, neighbourhood stability, neighbourhood economic development, and general neighbourhood well-being. In addition, a separate pool of money for Neighbourhood Development Assistance was specifically targeted to community economic development and provided core funding on a five-year basis to locally administered Neighbourhood Renewal Corporations (NRCs). The NRCs are important community-based organizations that provide community leadership in development within their neighbourhoods. The final tier of the Neighbourhoods Alive program was the Neighbourhood Housing Assistance program, which provided financial assistance to support community-based home ownership and renovation. This fund also provided money to NRCs and other non-profit community housing corporations, as well as to private landlords/developers interested in renovating existing housing stock or constructing new housing units.

What was particularly important about Neighbourhoods Alive was that it explicitly adopted a community-led focus, incorporating many of the principles that underpin community economic development.[40] This differed from previous state-led and bureaucratically driven development programs. To this end, Neighbourhoods Alive has been a tremendous success.[41] Certainly the core funding provided to neighbourhood renewal corporations has been extremely important for the ongoing operation of these organizations, and many individual projects have been funded, including training and development, community gardens, and storefront rehabilitations. Having said that, the amount of funding for both NRCs and individual projects remains extremely small as compared to the size of the task.

In the first phase of the program, for example, Neighbourhood Renewal Corporations were entitled to $25,000 in start-up money and thereafter $75,000 annually in core funding. After 2006, in the second phase of the program, core funding was increased to $150,000 annually. Neighbourhood Renewal Corporations in the North End and Central neighbourhoods of Winnipeg each received higher amounts because those communities were larger ($350,000 and $225,000 respectively in 2009/10). Over the lifetime of the program, therefore, nearly $6.7 million has been spent on core funding for the NRCs.[42]

Nevertheless, evaluation of the program conducted in 2010 indicated that workers at the Renewal Corporations overwhelmingly felt that their levels of funding were inadequate to achieve their objectives. The core funding over a five-year period was certainly seen as beneficial, but the funding was also static throughout this period. Successful community development work often generates greater demands on organizations over time. Success in the early stages of development work leads to expectations and need to begin moving forward on more complex issues, which often are costlier. Moreover, the limited funding meant that staff salaries were often severely constrained in order to have sufficient program and operational funds available for community work.[43]

Another criticism of the Neighbourhoods Alive program was its overwhelming project-based focus. Over its ten years of operation, over $18 million was allocated for specific projects in the seven neighbourhoods targeted by the program. Although this certainly is not an insignificant amount, overall that money was spread across 570 projects. On average, then, projects funded by the program received approximately $32,500.[44] Again, given the depth of poverty that these communities face, these amounts are relatively small. Moreover, the one area where evaluations of the Neighbourhoods Alive program indicated a relative lack of success has been in developing long-term economic opportunities. In other words, Neighbourhoods Alive has not adequately addressed the crisis of employment in poor communities.

Neighbourhoods Alive, and indeed the government's entire anti-poverty strategy, while important, is a further example of inoculation. On the one hand, the program has become a vital funding source and the lifeblood for many community-based organizations. Without it, much important work in the inner city could not be undertaken. At the same time, the actual amounts of funding are, given the government's overall budget, and the size and depth of tax cuts and incentives to business, very small. Certainly it is inadequate if the government is to seriously undertake a comprehensive poverty reduction strategy. Significantly greater investment is required if these efforts are to be scaled up and generate real economic opportunities in the inner city.

In a similar vein, the government recently passed anti-poverty legislation committing itself to taking significant steps to reduce poverty. However, despite having done so, the government has refused to set concrete targets and goals under the legislation.[45] Community economic development (CED) has been acknowledged as important by the government, and even included in the priorities of a new Cabinet committee on economic development established by the NDP upon coming to power. However, the CED file was always clearly subordinate and somewhat of an afterthought, as compared to other economic development projects.[46] The government has been far more focused on bricks and mortar infrastructure, and megaprojects such as the downtown arena, the new football stadium, and the floodway, than local community economic development that addresses the needs of the inner city. Most community activists, then, argue that these initiatives, on balance, are reasons to continue supporting the NDP, for these opportunities were not present during the Conservatives' tenure. Certainly, their limits and inadequacies would not be the basis for withdrawing their support for the party, no matter how much the party is ultimately oriented towards supporting the business community first. The prospect of these programs disappearing should the NDP lose government are considered very real.

The same argument can be made on other social initiatives of the government. On Aboriginal issues, for example, the government moved fairly quickly after its election in 1999 to implement several recommendations of the Aboriginal Justice Inquiry,[47] which had largely been ignored by the Filmon government. They included establishing the Aboriginal Justice Inquiry – Child Welfare initiative, which oversaw the transfer of jurisdiction for child welfare to Aboriginal organizations. In Winnipeg alone, there are over seventy Aboriginal community-based organizations, created and run by and for Aboriginal people.[48] These include the Ma Mawi Wi Chi Itata Centre, a family and youth services agency, the Native Women's Transition Centre, the Urban Circle Training Centre, and a host of others. These organizations have done much to nurture and develop an urban Aboriginal leadership and enhance the capacities of and opportunities for Aboriginal persons in the inner city. Moreover, they have done so in a fashion that is consistent with and rooted in Aboriginal culture and traditions.[49] It is also important to recognize that, while these organizations may receive some state funding, they have developed largely on their own, and if anything, in response to the failure of state policies to grapple seriously and effectively with the legacies of colonialism and the poverty and inequality faced by Aboriginal people in the province.

Conclusion

The strategy of inoculation that has been described in this chapter is a particularly effective mode of conducting brokerage politics. In many respects, it owes much to the practice of Third Way politics developed by Tony Blair in his modernization of the British Labour Party. In the Manitoba context, the successful employment of this strategy has propelled the NDP to a position of electoral dominance. The success of the strategy requires knitting together fairly narrow electoral coalitions, and a reliance on the traditional and very well-established voting patterns that characterize Manitoba politics. Inoculation ensures the support of core constituencies, particularly among Aboriginal, activist, and working-class communities in Winnipeg. This permits the party to adopt a pro-business neoliberal economic policy that appeals to the growing middle-income and professional groups that make up the city. As a result, electoral outcomes turn on the results in a relatively few seats and have as much to do with the qualities of the party's leaders and the missteps and gaffes of their opponents.[50] The Manitoba NDP has benefited from the weakness of both the Liberal Party, which in many respects it has displaced, and disarray in the ranks of the Progressive Conservatives since the departure of Gary Filmon from the political scene.

The resignation of Gary Doer in the fall of 2009 marked a potential turning point for the NDP. Much of their success had depended on Doer's astute management of the party's political strategy and his own personal popularity. On 17 October 2009, the party selected Greg Selinger to replace Doer. Selinger had a background in social work and municipal politics. He had considerable credibility with community-based organizations and activists inside and outside the party. At the same time, as finance minister throughout the Doer era, he was also a key architect of the party's successful tenure in office. After having been sworn in as premier, it became evident that Selinger would operate in much the same fashion as Doer. NDP policy continued to be moderate, pragmatic, and cautious.

It is fair to say, however, that some cracks in the NDP's strategy are beginning to show. Under new leader Hugh McFadyen, the Progressive Conservative Party certainly seemed revitalized in the lead up to the 2011 provincial election. In March 2011 a public opinion poll showed the Progressive Conservatives with 47 per cent of the popular vote, compared to the NDP at 35 per cent. Even in September, just prior to the election, the Conservatives were still leading the NDP by 3 per cent in the popular vote.[51] As is the case with any government that has been in power for three consecutive terms, there was a general feeling of a need for a change. McFadyen played to that sentiment and tried to develop wedge issues, such as high rates of crime in the inner city. In what proved to be a very negative political campaign, the NDP was able to exploit fears that the Progressive Conservatives could not be trusted on privatization. The NDP resurrected the spectre of Conservative betrayals on privatization. The fact that McFadyen had been one of the architects of the privatization of MTS during the Filmon era meant that McFadyen's promises in 2011 that a Tory government would not contemplate privatizing Manitoba Hydro were less than convincing. As a result, the Conservatives lost much of their momentum and spent much of the campaign on the defensive. In the end, despite increasing in the popular vote, the Conservatives were not able to increase their seat total.

Notwithstanding its victory, there are signs that the Doer/Selinger approach is weakening. Although Manitoba weathered the current economic crisis fairly well, the surpluses of the Doer year have been replaced by a series of successive deficit budgets.[52] Of course, this has been the case for many provincial governments, as there has not been a shift from a fiscally conservative and neoliberal agenda. If anything, the depth of the economic crisis has meant that the Selinger government has found itself with less room to manoeuvre than in the 2000s. Third Way politics, as discovered by Tony Blair and Gordon Brown in Britain, is always more feasible in good economic times.

The fact that in 2011 the Progressive Conservatives increased their vote share so significantly illustrates the vulnerability of the NDPs electoral position. It was expected that a number of ridings in Winnipeg would be far closer than they were. Although they were not able to translate their increase in popular vote into an increase in seats, the Conservatives have continued to build momentum towards the next election in the fall of 2015 or spring of 2016. McFayden's resignation and subsequent election of Brian Pallister as the Progressive Conservative leader has continued the resurrection of the party. Pallister has deep Manitoba political credentials, having served both provincially under Gary Filmon and federally under Stephen Harper. Pallister's real strength is his appeal with the Conservatives' core constituency in rural Manitoba and with the business community.

The NDP's inoculation strategy has left it susceptible to single issues, scandal, and the politics of personality. The decision of the party to increase the provincial sales tax in the spring of 2014, for example, generated considerable public anger and gave the Conservatives an issue around which to mobilize anti-government sentiment. For the past decade, the NDP benefited from relatively weak leadership in both the Progressive Conservative and Liberal parties. For the Conservatives, Pallister has changed that equation. At the same time, the election of Rana Bokhari, a young and dynamic new leader of the Liberals, signalled an end to Jon Gerrard's fifteen-year tenure as leader of that party. The possibility of a reinvigorated Liberal Party in the next election changes the dynamics for the NDP considerably.

Finally, a very high-profile controversy between Selinger and Christine Melnick, former minister of immigration and multiculturalism, may prove costly for the party. The controversy, which centred on whether the premier's staff had ordered Melnick to use her ministerial authority to have client organizations attend a legislative debate, led to Melnick being demoted from Cabinet and ousted from the NDP caucus.[53]

The impact of these developments on the next election is uncertain. A Probe research poll conducted in April 2013 indicated the NDP had dropped 4 per cent to 35 per cent of the popular vote, while the Liberals had increased their popularity by the same margin to 15 per cent. The Progressive Conservatives continue to outpace the other parties at 42 per cent. However, the same poll predicts that the two main parties would likely win the same number of seats if an election were to be held in 2014. In this limited sense, the strategy of inoculation continues to offer the NDP protection. Whether the party continues to be electorally healthy, however, is an open question.

NOTES

1 I would like to thank my former colleagues at the University of Winnipeg, Peter Ives and Jim Silver, for their willingness to keep me updated and informed on developments in Manitoba. I am particularly indebted to

Jim Silver for introducing me to the concept of inoculation, and his astute observations on its implementation in practice. Thanks also to my research assistant, Mark Brister, for his tremendous contribution to this paper. Finally I would like to thank the anonymous reviewers of this chapter for their helpful comments, and Bryan Evans and Charles Smith for their patience.

2 Paul Thomas and Curtis Brown, eds., *Manitoba Politics and Government: Issues, Institutions, Traditions* (Winnipeg: University of Manitoba Press, 2010).

3 On the political culture of Manitoba generally, see Jared Wesley, "Political Culture in Manitoba," in Thomas and Brown, *Manitoba Politics and Government*, 43–72. See also the profiles of Manitoba premiers found in Barry Ferguson and Robert Wardhaugh, eds., *Manitoba Premiers of the 19th and 20th Century* (Winnipeg: Canadian Plains Research Center, 2010).

4 See Jim Silver, Cyril Keeper, and Michael McKenzie, *Electoral Participation in Winnipeg's Inner City* (Winnipeg: CCPA-Manitoba, 2005). For a discussion of the richness of Aboriginal politics in the inner city, see Jim Silver, *In Their Own Voices: Building Urban Aboriginal Communities* (Halifax: Fernwood, 2006).

5 Nelson Wiseman, "The Success of the New Democratic Party," in Thomas and Brown, *Manitoba Politics and Government*, 73–95. Also see Chris Adams, "Realigning Elections in Canada," in Thomas and Brown, *Manitoba Politics and Government*, 159–80.

6 Donne Flanagan, "Inoculating Traditional NDP Weaknesses Key to Doer's Success," 9 June 2003, *Straight Goods News*, http://www.straightgoods .ca/ViewFeature3.cfm?REF=255&Cookies=yes. See also Jim Silver, *The Inner Cities of Saskatoon and Winnipeg: A New and Distinctive Form of Development* (Winnipeg: CCPA-Manitoba/Saskatchewan, 2008); and Cy Gonick, "Gary Doer's Manitoba," *Canadian Dimension*, June 2007, http:// www.canadiandimension.com/articles/1785.

7 Silver, *Inner Cities of Saskatoon and Winnipeg*, 5–6.

8 Derek Hum and Wayne Simpson, "Manitoba in the Middle: A Mutual Fund Balanced for Steady Income," in Thomas and Brown, *Manitoba Politics and Government*, 294.

9 Ibid., 295.

10 Ibid., 296.

11 Adams, "Realigning Elections," 160.

12 Wiseman, "Success of the NDP," 88.

13 The inquiry concluded that PC party officials had funded independent Aboriginal candidates in Northern Manitoba to run against NDP

incumbents in the hope that vote splitting would allow Conservative candidates to win. See "Manitoba Tories Guilty of Vote Rigging," CBC News, 10 November 2000, http://www.cbc.ca/news/canada/story/1999/03/30/manitoba990330.html.

14 The difficulties in health care were, to a certain extent, the result of cuts to federal transfer payments. At the same time, the failure of the Conservatives to invest new funds into the sector was also blamed.

15 Paul Samyn, "MTS Sale Rings Alarm," *Winnipeg Free Press*, 1 November 1996; Errol Black and Paula Mallea, "The Privatization of the Manitoba Telephone System," *Canadian Dimension* 31 (March 1997): 11.

16 Janice Tibbetts, "Gary Doer, Manitoba's Premier in Waiting," *Postmedia News*, 22 September 1999.

17 Jared Wesley, "Stalking the Progressive Centre: An Ideational Analysis of Manitoba Party Politics," *Journal of Canadian Studies* 45 (Winter 2011): 155. See also Wesley, *Code Politics: Campaigns and Cultures on the Canadian Prairies* (Vancouver: UBC Press, 2011).

18 On the travails of the Liberal Party, see Paul Barber, "Manitoba's Liberals: Sliding into Third," in Thomas and Brown, *Manitoba Politics and Government*, 128–58.

19 Adams, "Realigning Elections in Manitoba," 171.

20 Anthony Giddens, *The Third Way: The Renewal of Social Democracy* (Cambridge, UK: Polity, 1998); Giddens, *The Third Way and Its Critics* (Cambridge, UK: Polity, 2000).

21 Byron Sheldrick, "New Labour and the Third Way: Democracy, Accountability and Social Democratic Politics," *Studies in Political Economy* 67 (2002): 133–44; Neil Bradford, "Renewing Social Democracy: Beyond the Third Way," *Studies in Political Economy* 67 (2002): 145–61.

22 Bryan Evans and Ingo Schmidt, eds., *Social Democracy after the Cold War* (Edmonton: Athabasca University Press, 2012).

23 Byron Sheldrick, "The British Labour Party: In Search of Identity between Labour and Parliament," in *Social Democracy after the Cold War*, ed. Bryan Evans and Ingo Schmidt, 149–82 (Edmonton: Athabasca University Press, 2012).

24 Byron Sheldrick, "The Contradictions of Welfare to Work: Social Security Reform in Britain," *Studies in Political Economy*, 62 (2000): 99–122; Alexandra Dobrowolsky, "Rhetoric versus Reality: The Figure of the Child and New Labour's Strategic Social Investment State," *Studies in Political Economy* 69 (2002): 43–73.

25 Manitoba Government, "Budget Paper C: Tax Adjustments 2011," http://www.gov.mb.ca/finance/budget11/papers/taxation.pdf.

26 Amela Karabegovic, Charles Lammam, and Milagros Palacious, "Fiscal
    Performance of Canada's Premiers," *Fraser Forum* 4 (January/February
    2011): 10–13.
27 Gonick, "Gary Doer's Manitoba." See also British Columbia,
    Saskatchewan, Nova Scotia, and Quebec chapters in this volume.
28 Sara Slinn, "The Effect of Compulsory Certification Votes on Certification
    Applications in Ontario: An Empirical Analysis," *Canadian Labour and
    Employment Law Journal* 10 (2003): 386–8. Slinn found that changes to
    mandatory voting in Ontario resulted in a 21.28 per cent drop in successful
    union certification applications. For similar conclusions, see also Chris
    Riddell, "Union Certification Success under Voting versus Card-Check
    Procedures: Evidence from British Columbia, 1978–1998," *Industrial and
    Labour Relations Review* 57 (2003–4): 493; F. Martinello, "Correlates of
    Certification Application Success in British Columbia, Saskatchewan,
    and Manitoba," *Relations Industrielles / Industrial Relations* 51 (1996): 544;
    Charlotte A.B. Yates, "Staying the Decline in Union Membership: Union
    Organizing in Ontario, 1985–1999," *Relations Industrielles / Industrial
    Relations* 55 (2000): 640; Andrew Jackson, "Rowing against the Tide: The
    Struggle to Raise Union Density in a Hostile Environment," in *Paths to
    Union Renewal: Canadian Experiences,* ed. P. Kumar and C. Schenk (Toronto:
    Broadview, 2006), 61.
29 David Kuxhaus, "Premier Tries to Placate Business Riled by Contentious
    Labour Law Changes," *Winnipeg Free Press,* 2 August 2000; Todd Scarth,
    "Business Lobby Cries Wolf over Manitoba's Labour Law Changes,"
    CCPA-Manitoba, 1 August 2000, http://www.policyalternatives.ca/
    publications/reports/business-lobby-cries-wolf-over-manitobas-labour
    -law-changes. See also Jason Foster, "Manitoba NDP Strengthens Provincial
    Labour Law," *Alberta Federation of Labour News,* http://www
    .telusplanet.net/public/afl/LabourNews/sept00-10.html.
30 Errol Black and Jim Silver, "Is Labour's Future in the Streets?," CCPA, *Fast
    Facts,* 10 October 2004.
31 Ibid.
32 Wally Fox-Decent, *Report on Certain Aspects of the Winnipeg Floodway
    Project* (Winnipeg: Manitoba Floodway Authority), 2004, http://www
    .floodwayauthority.mb.ca/pdf/wallyfox_decent_report.pdf.
33 Jim Silver, "Segregated City: A Century of Poverty in Winnipeg," in Thomas
    and Brown, *Manitoba Politics and Government,* 346.
34 Jino Distasio, Michael Dudly, Molly Johnson, and Kurt Sargent, *Neighbourhoods
    Alive!: Community Outcomes Final Report* (Winnipeg: Institute of Urban Studies,
    2005).

35 Jim Silver, "Inner Cities of Saskatoon and Winnipeg," 10.
36 Byron Sheldrick, Harold Dyck, Troy Myers, and Claudette Michell, "Welfare in Winnipeg's Inner City: Exploring the Myths," *Canadian Journal of Urban Research* 15, no. 1 (2006): 54–85.
37 National Council on Welfare, "Total Welfare Incomes, Manitoba," accessed 23 October 2011, http://www.ncw.gc.ca.
38 "Man. Named Child Poverty Capital," CBC News, 24 November 2009, http://www.cbc.ca/news/canada/manitoba/story/2009/11/24/mb -child-poverty-winnipeg.html. In 2009 roughly 18.8 per cent of children in Manitoba were considered to be living in poverty. See Campaign 2000, "2009 Report Card on Child and Family Poverty in Canada: 1989–2009," http://www.campaign2000.ca/reportCards/national/2009EnglishC2000 NationalReportCard.pdf.
39 Manitoba Government, "Manitoba Government Launches Neighbourhoods Alive! Program," news release, 21 December 1999, http://www.gov.mb.ca/ chc/press/top/1999/12/1999-12-21-03.html.
40 For a discussion the theoretical principles underpinning CED, see the collection of essays in John Loxley, ed., *Transforming or Reforming Capitalism: Towards a Theory of Community Economic Development* (Halifax: Fernwood, 2007). On the range of CED initiatives in Manitoba, see John Loxley, Jim Silver, and Kathleen Sexsmith, eds., *Doing Community Economic Development* (Halifax: Fernwood, 2007). See also Jim Silver, ed., *Solutions That Work: Fighting Poverty in Winnipeg* (Halifax: Fernwood, 2000).
41 Overall, the program has received very positive evaluation. See Ekos Research Associates Inc., *Neighbourhoods Alive! Community Outcomes Evaluation 2010, Final Report,* 24 September 2010, http://www.gov.mb.ca/housing/neighbourhoods/na_bg/pdf/ NACommunityOutcomesEvaluation2010.pdf.
42 Ibid., 31.
43 Ibid.
44 Ibid., 35.
45 Shauna MacKinnon, "How Will the Selinger Government Move Manitoba Forward?," *Fast Facts*, 14 October 2011, CCPA, http://www .policyalternatives.ca/publications/commentary/fast-facts-post -election-2011.
46 See Byron Sheldrick and Kevin Warkentin, "The Manitoba Community Economic Development Lens: Local Participation and Democratic State Restructuring," in Loxley, Silver, and Sexsmith, *Doing Community Economic Development*, 209–19.

47 The Aboriginal Justice Inquiry was established in 1988. In 1999 the Doer government established the Aboriginal Justice Implementation Commission. See the Aboriginal Justice Implementation Commission, http://www.ajic.mb.ca/index.html.

48 Silver, *In Their Own Voices*; Silver, *Inner Cities of Saskatoon and Winnipeg*.

49 Silver, *Inner Cities of Saskatoon and Winnipeg*.

50 Wiseman, "Success of the NDP," 73–4.

51 Polling data prior to the election have been compiled by the Election Almanac, http://www.electionalmanac.com/ea/manitoba-election -polls/.

52 On the current state of the Manitoba economy, see Fletcher Barager, *Report on the Manitoba Economy 2011* (Winnipeg: Canadian Centre for Policy Alternatives – Manitoba, 2011).

53 Larry Kusch, "Senior Staffers Were Involved in Inviting Agencies to Immigration Debate: Melnick," *Winnipeg Free Press*, 3 February 2014; Kusch, "Selinger Removes Melnick from Caucus," *Winnipeg Free Press*, 4 February 2014.

8 Saskatchewan: From Cradle of Social Democracy to Neoliberalism's Sandbox

AIDAN D. CONWAY AND J.F. CONWAY

Introduction

The uneven and contested rise of neoliberalism has been a global and pan-Canadian phenomenon. Yet as the editors demonstrate in their introduction to this volume, neoliberalism has everywhere been a product of particular "local" social relations, structural changes, and processes of political conflict, mobilization, and (re)alignment. In the case of Saskatchewan, coming to terms with the triumph of neoliberalism requires an attempt to understand the factors that (1) created and then eroded the social basis for a particular form of post-war social democracy; (2) provided conditions for the (mixed) successes of a series of conservative rollback policies that began in earnest in the 1980s (and consolidated new axes of political alignment in the 1990s with social democracy's market-conforming conversion); and (3) contributed to the continuing failure (or refusal) to reconstruct and reconstitute durable alternatives to neoliberalism thereafter.

This chapter outlines the triumph of neoliberalism in Saskatchewan, rooting it in the changing bases of political alignment and realignment in a particular and volatile form of Prairie capitalism. The chapter proceeds chronologically from the historical background and political economy of Saskatchewan's moderate post-war social democratic tradition; to the Conservative victories in the 1980s based on the fracturing of the social democratic coalition, the transformation of the rural economy, and a strategy of urban-rural electoral polarization; through the Roy Romanow NDP's embrace of neoliberalism in the 1990s, reflecting and reinforcing new patterns of political and ideological alignment and militating against the reconstruction of a social democratic coalition; and finally the stunning rise of a new potential "natural governing party" in the neoliberal mould following the Saskatchewan Party's march to power in the first decade of the twenty-first century. The chapter reflects on some of the underlying structural changes and pressures at work beneath the surface of Saskatchewan's political economy and political sociology that have shaped the rise of neoliberalism and will continue to condition its future prospects in the province.

Background: Region, Class, and Canadian Capitalism on the Prairies

Confederation and the National Policy that gave it substance provided a political and economic blueprint for the construction of a robust east-west national economy and a viable federated nation state committed to a strategy of internal imperial consolidation and industrial modernization. A strong federal state acquired the Prairie West as a colonial possession and borrowed capital, guaranteed investments, and provided grants of cash and western land to build a coast-to-coast railway. The Aboriginal populations were pushed aside in an ethnic cleansing whose chief instruments were consignment to reservations and threats of force. A modern industrial economy was nurtured in Central Canada behind a wall of protective tariffs that secured a national market for its products. Free homestead land lured a vast movement of migrants to settle the Prairie West as the basis for a capital-intensive, export-oriented agricultural economy and a lucrative captive market for Central Canada's industrial plants. The acquisition and settlement of the Prairies were therefore essential to the national economic design that came to full fruition with the "Wheat Boom" of 1896–1913.

By the end of the boom the structure of Canada's political economy was entrenched. As Central Canada's industrial foundation was laid, the place of the Prairie West was fixed: a producer of natural resource commodities for export to international markets through a marketing system dominated by large corporations; a tariff-secured market for the manufacturing and financial interests in Central Canada; a lucrative pool of captive clients for Canada's railway monopoly; and a vast market of assured customers for wholesale and retail chains. Success was guaranteed by federal and provincial governments dedicated to "creating conditions in which private enterprise might thrive," according to the report of the 1940 Royal Commission on Dominion-Provincial Relations.[1]

The Prairie West became an enclave of class and regional political ferment as western farmers, workers, and local business interests resisted elements of the development plan drafted by Canada's dominant economic and political class. The region witnessed aggressive class struggles by workers and farmers, alongside broader class coalitions protesting the region's maltreatment in Confederation. Class and regional grievances intersected, frequently reinforcing and heightening one another. The agrarian petite bourgeoisie that became the region's economic and political bedrock was ensnared in nation-building policies and accumulation strategies conceived and implemented by the dominant capitalist class. This atmosphere tempered their entrepreneurial outlook and made them open to a variety of radical, populist, and even "socialist" appeals and measures aimed at counterbalancing the power of capitalist business, and providing social protection against its depredations and the insecurity inherent in their market dependence.[2] The mechanisms for extracting wealth from farmers were varied and complex, from key government policies on trade and finance to one-sided marketing and transportation arrangements. The extraction of wealth from wage labourers was more direct. All capital wanted was their labour, as much as could be had at the lowest possible wage, with little concern for the lives or health of the workers. Given the rapidity of western settlement and its vital place in the national strategy, the process of accumulation and the resistance that it provoked was especially intense on the Prairie West, providing opportunities at times for building populist farmer-labour alliances.[3]

Class and regional agitations claimed modest victories as they peaked with the Winnipeg General Strike in 1919 and the agrarian political upsurge of the early 1920s, including minor modifications to the nation-building plan, concessions to farmers and workers, and gestures of conciliation to quiet regional outrage. These concessions became precedents in the contestation over Canada's political economy: the promotion of "free enterprise" on behalf of capital was now compelled to yield some small space to modest regulation in the interests of subordinate classes and the hinterland regions.

The agitations in the West abated after 1923 with a return of boom times. Many believed the good times would never end. They were wrong. On Black Tuesday, 29 October 1929, Wall Street crashed, ushering in the Great Depression of the 1930s. The Depression fell heaviest on farmers and other primary producers, especially in the Prairie West, and most particularly in Saskatchewan, heavily dependent as it was on the monoculture of wheat. Constitutionally responsible for relief but without the revenues to meet the crisis, provincial governments begged for federal support. In exchange, provincial governments were forced to retrench ever more deeply each year – cutting services and staff, rolling back wages and salaries, and raising the taxes that few could pay. By 1937 two-thirds of the rural population and one-fifth of urban dwellers were on relief.[4] Between 1930 and 1937 two dollars of every three in total provincial and municipal government revenues were spent on relief.[5] Governments, businessmen, and economic experts repeatedly claimed prosperity was just around the corner, mocking a desperate population as the Depression ground on remorselessly.

In 1932 the organized farmers of Saskatchewan went into politics, adopting a program of fundamental social and economic change, including socialist elements. In cooperation with the small Independent Labour Party (ILP), the United Farmers of Canada (Saskatchewan Section) first founded the Farmer Labour Party in 1932 and then the Cooperative Commonwealth Federation (Saskatchewan Section) (CCF) in 1935. From 1932 to 1944 a progressive farmer-labour coalition was formed and drove to power, winning decisively in 1944. Upon victory the CCF embarked on a radical program of policy innovation and economic experimentation in Saskatchewan, including controversial socialist measures.

The CCF gained a significant presence in the House of Commons and threatened to win power in British Columbia in 1941 and 1953, and in Ontario in 1943. The CCF was perceived as a much more serious threat to the status quo than Alberta's troublesome Social Credit movement, which failed to win support across the country. To that end, the establishment parties and the press subjected the CCF to an unrelenting red-baiting attack. In response the Saskatchewan CCF moderated its platform. After tense internal debates, by the 1952 election, the CCF had become a moderate social democratic party and the "natural" governing party of the province. Between 1944 and 2011 the party won twelve of eighteen elections, governing for forty-seven of sixty-eight years.

The importance of the CCF victory in Saskatchewan should not be underestimated. Aggressively using provincial powers, the CCF transformed the lives of citizens in ways never before believed possible, inspiring subordinate classes across Canada. Threatened by this popularity, the established pro-capitalist parties adopted features of the CCF's welfare state program. Without the CCF victory in Saskatchewan, it is unlikely that the federal welfare state would have been as progressive or as well-entrenched as it became. In 1957 John Diefenbaker's Tory government introduced a national version of the CCF's 1947 publicly funded comprehensive hospitalization plan. In 1966 Lester Pearson's Liberal government introduced a national medicare plan similar to the one pioneered by the CCF/NDP in Saskatchewan in 1962. These became anchors of the Canadian welfare state. In both cases, Ottawa used fiscal discipline to impose the plans on resistant right-wing provincial governments such as Ontario (chapter 6) and British Columbia (chapter 10). The same fiscal discipline forced provinces to adhere to national standards for social assistance, and, in the 1960s, to expand capacity and accessibility in post-secondary education.

Welfare capitalism made heady promises in the post-war decades and initially delivered on many. A greater share of the wealth produced was diverted from capital to labour through gradual increases in real wages and salaries and a broader "social wage" for all citizens. The dominant capitalist class resisted every step of the way, attempting to minimize the breadth of the programming and aggressively attacking anything considered inimical to "free enterprise," including public ownership and effective government regulation. Lamentations about anti-business intrusions and the unsustainable costs of the welfare state were ceaseless, even at the height of post-war welfare capitalism's "golden age." Popular demands redefined the policies of all political parties, but the days of capital's unfettered power were not forgotten. The welfare state was not yielded up voluntarily and all concessions were won under political threat. Crucially, the social democrats had to be prevented from winning federal power with its enlarged range of action. In capital's longer view, what Parliament can give, Parliament can take away. Hence, control of Parliament by either the Tory or Liberal Party was vital. Granting concessions and constructing a modest version of the welfare state was effective in denying the CCF/NDP power in Ottawa, though as chapters in this volume demonstrate, it was able to win power from time to time in British Columbia (chapter 10), Manitoba (chapter 7), Ontario (chapter 6), and Nova Scotia (chapter 3), while enjoying near political hegemony in Saskatchewan.

A Turning Point

The battle over the imposition of neoliberalism led to three of the most tumultuous decades of political contestation in Canadian history. Western provinces, notably Saskatchewan and British Columbia, with their history of polarized class-based political conflict and vulnerability to global economic forces, were at the centre of the drama. Conservative parties throughout Western Canada provided a dress rehearsal for imposing the neoliberal agenda from 1982 to 1986, testing the political will of neoliberal governments and the depth of popular opposition.[6] The battle in Saskatchewan was pivotal, given its strong social democratic tradition, incontestable importance in laying the political foundations for Canada's welfare state, and the general commitment to expanding the welfare state. Just as importantly, the Saskatchewan NDP in the 1970s demonstrated the possibility of using the state to intervene in the economy to channel the benefits of the province's resource wealth into collective forms of consumption and an expanded health and social security system. Buoyed by high resource prices, the Blakeney NDP government had pushed the envelope during the 1970s: a universal, publicly funded dental program for school-age children, with a promise to gradually expand it to cover all children to adulthood; discussion of a universal prescription drug program; the possibility of a universal dental program to cover the whole population; and comprehensive home and institutional care for the elderly. There was discussion of adding public universal day care onto the public school system, and of enhancing maternity leave benefits for working women. The Blakeney government also took half of the potash industry into public ownership, established an oil Crown corporation as a major player in the province's oil patch, and imposed public ownership shares on future developments in natural resources.[7]

Grant Devine's Tory sweep of Saskatchewan in 1982 – fifty-five seats and 54 per cent of the popular vote – reduced the New Democratic Party (NDP) under Alan Blakeney to nine seats and 38 per cent, the worst showing since 1938. The humiliation of the NDP in the cradle of Canadian social democracy was a watershed in Canadian politics. The province was "open for business," and the government catered to the business lobby with deregulation, a legislative attack on trade union rights, and a host of tax breaks for corporations, resource companies, and the affluent. Government support for free enterprise resulted in a stream of public money and loan guarantees to help big and small entrepreneurs develop projects, from manufacturing barbecue briquettes and shopping carts to pork plants and oil up-graders.[8]

The neoliberal revolution coalescing around the federal government of Brian Mulroney took a particular form in Devine's Saskatchewan. The long years of social democratic rule left the province with a comparatively well-developed social and health security system and a large public economic sector. The neoliberal assault was paced in two overlapping rollback phases: first, deep cuts in the social and health security system, and, second, a program of privatization of public assets. The Devine government attacked Saskatchewan's large Crown sector – the Crowns were curtailed, bled of revenues, hamstrung with hostile boards and CEOs, and deprived of their public policy role. Yet there were only a few minor privatization moves. The government denied it intended to privatize the Crowns, while preparing the way: "participation" bonds were sold in SaskOil, and eventually one-third of the oil Crown shares were sold at low prices; bonds were sold in the utility Crown, and small pieces of SaskPower's assets were sold. The Crown-owned Prince Alberta Pulp Co. (Papco) was sold back to the American multinational Weyerhaeuser. Meanwhile the government's accumulated deficit grew – the result of a combination of grinding recession, continued spending, and irresponsible cuts on the revenue side – from zero to over $1.7 billion in a short four years.[9] The civil service was purged of socialists and NDPers, but there were no cuts in its size. Despite efforts to steer a "moderate" right-wing course, while carefully preparing the ground for the future, public support for the Devine government began to weaken.

In response Devine devised his rural strategy, which was simple: ignore the urban centres as NDP strongholds and concentrate on rural and small-town Saskatchewan. In pursuit of this strategy the Devine government encouraged an unprecedented political polarization between rural and urban Saskatchewan. While slashing programs favouring urban residents, the Devine government tended to Saskatchewan's crisis-ridden farmers. Devine assumed the agriculture portfolio, promising to put the provincial treasury at risk to save rural Saskatchewan through a series of new programs: from cheap money to production cost relief; from hog incentives to farm purchase support; from loan guarantees to tax relief. The Premier's Office estimated that these expenditures amounted to $36,000 per farmer, totalling $2.4 billion.[10]

Devine's strategy paid handsome dividends on 20 October 1986 when thirty-three of thirty-six predominantly rural seats went Tory. A last-minute effort to win urban votes with mortgage relief and home improvement grants netted five of twenty-six urban seats, four of which were middle-class seats in Regina and Saskatoon. The NDP swept the major urban centres, while being decimated in the countryside, winning only two rural seats. The province was cleaved along urban and rural lines, reflecting the resurgence of the class, regional, and cultural divisions successfully overcome by the tenuous farmer-labour alliance constructed within and around the CCF.

In preparation for their second-term policy agenda, the Devine government quickly passed the Government Organization Act, granting Cabinet the power to make sweeping changes without debate in the legislature. Then in the spring of 1987 – "the year of the cutting knives" – the roll-out phase of neoliberalism began in earnest. The assault began on Saskatchewan's comparatively elaborate social and health security system, a system described by social services minister Grant Schmidt as "a hammock" in which "a lot of people [are] ... having a good time at the expense of a majority of taxpayers."[11] There was a blizzard of budget cuts issued by Order in Council. Then came the tax hikes on incomes and gasoline, and an end to controls on utility rates. In 1987, the Coalition for Social Justice, a united front of labour and social movement activists, organized the largest protest demonstration in the province's history.

A new Department of Public Participation implemented the Devine government's ambitious privatization plans. Throughout 1988 and 1989, there were a host of asset sales at fire sale prices. Public support for privatization plummeted, especially after the potash privatization, but public opposition hardened with the move to privatize the Crown natural gas utility and the general insurance arm of the Crown insurance company. The NDP Opposition, now under a new leader, Roy Romanow, provided only desultory resistance until public pressure grew. Finally Romanow acted when the privatization of the gas utility was proposed, boldly bringing the legislature to a procedural standstill. Devine backed off to re-examine his privatization strategy, and the big utility Crowns were saved.[12]

Despite neoliberalism's extravagant promises, the magic of the market did not produce the desired results. By any standards, many of the privatizations were either foolish business decisions or deliberate acts of raiding the public treasury to benefit private investors and corporations. In many cases, like Papco, the Potash Corporation, and SaskOil, the public assets were sold at a fraction of their real value, frequently because the sale took place during a low point in the market. Many entrepreneurs were given grants, low-interest loans, and loan guarantees, some of which were used to purchase public assets or were poor risks, and some were frauds. The list of abuses was extensive. Many of the megaprojects, back in fashion under the neoliberals, entailed huge public financial risks to backstop potential private gains while posing serious environmental threats.[13]

Just as the neoliberal revolution reached its apotheosis from 1986 to 1990, public support for Devine's government began to collapse. The economic facts were clear. Unemployment rates in Saskatchewan in the 1980s and early 1990s were the highest in twenty years.[14] Personal per capita income in Saskatchewan lagged far behind the Ontario average – in 1990, by about 33 per cent – and the brief closing of that gap during the 1970s disappeared. Net farm income continued to collapse while farm debt skyrocketed.[15] The growth in public opposition was complex, a contradictory cauldron of anxiety and fear. Partly it had to do with the economic failures of neoliberalism, though it was true that many of the causes of Saskatchewan's economic problems were beyond provincial government control – drought, the world wheat wars, and low and unstable global prices for virtually all export commodities. Much of what was needed was also beyond provincial control. But the neoliberals raised expectations that their strategy would work, bringing prosperity, diversification, jobs, and growth. Neoliberal extravagance with public funds for privatizations, economic development schemes, and tax concessions to the rich and to business, and the resulting deficits and debts, only increased the blame assigned to the government. A neoliberal government already long in power could not blame the ghosts of Trudeau in Ottawa or former NDP governments forever.

Having run up the debt, the Devine government now claimed it could not afford the expensive social and health safety net. In the context of growing economic anxiety, these claims provoked deepening public anger. It was evident that the origins of annual deficits and burgeoning provincial debt lay not in spending on social, health, and education programs, underfunded in real terms since the late 1970s. Rather, the origins lay in public spending to prop up the private sector, efforts to buy elections with subsidy programs, the high interest rates of the period (ranging from 9 to 19 per cent), and deep cuts on the revenue side, particularly tax breaks to corporations, the resource sector, and the affluent.[16]

Repeated scandals during its second term ultimately undermined the Devine government. Although Devine emerged personally unscathed by the revelations of patronage and corruption, he was roundly criticized for abusing power, showing contempt for democracy, and violating parliamentary norms and conventions.[17] Devine's most serious attack on democratic norms involved an effort to reproduce his rural strategy to retain power. A legislated gerrymandering had the effect of giving a greater weight to the rural vote than the urban vote – it took 121 urban votes to equal 100 rural votes.[18] The Saskatchewan Court of Appeal rebuked the Devine government for "spawning the divisive notion of rural and urban interests" and found the gerrymandering unconstitutional under the voting protections in the Charter of Rights and Freedoms.[19] Upon appeal the Supreme Court, encumbered with more conservative jurists appointed by Mulroney and increasingly resistant to constructive applications of the Charter, reversed the decision. Devine also "harmonized" the provincial sales tax with the hated federal GST to raise an additional $150 million annually. To advance his rural strategy, Devine took the unusual step of directing all of that additional revenue to the protection of farmers, the first time in Saskatchewan history a specific tax levied on everyone was openly targeted to benefit only one class of citizen. The most controversial measure to assure Devine's rural appeal was the last-minute Fair Share program proposing dramatic decentralization of government services and departments, and 2,000 jobs, from the capital of Regina to rural areas.

In Devine's final days, the abuses worsened. Facing mutiny in his caucus, Devine prorogued the legislature, leaving the budget and many bills unpassed. Rather than call an immediate election, he continued in power. Devine's government began routinely to spend money not approved by the legislature and continued to act as if unpassed bills were law. During the last days of the Devine government, the people suffered under a dictatorship with a time limit. An election was constitutionally required before 12 November 1991.

Attention was again focused on Saskatchewan as a key electoral test of public support for neoliberalism. The collapse of support for Devine was decisive. On 21 October 1991 Romanow won a convincing popular mandate, 51 per cent and fifty-five of sixty-six seats. The Tory party itself was totally discredited by 1993 as trials began in the Tory Caucus Fraud Scandal involving the fraudulent misappropriation of nearly $1 million from MLA communication allowances between 1986 and 1991. By the end of the trials sixteen were convicted or pleaded guilty, including fourteen former Tory MLAs, eleven of Cabinet rank, most prominently former deputy premier Eric Berntson.[20] Given the collapse of the Tories, Romanow could virtually count on two secure terms to carry out an aggressive social democratic strategy to turn back the neoliberal tide, undo the cuts, improve labour laws, and re-acquire sold-off public assets.

Saskatchewan's New Democrats in a Neoliberal Era

Expectations among NDP supporters were high after a decade of living under the New Right. Certainly the $850 million annual deficit and the $15 billion in public debt run up by Devine loomed large. The obvious social democratic remedies were clear: taxes on the wealthy and the corporations that benefited from the giveaways and privatizations; increased royalties on oil, potash, and uranium; the reacquisition of public assets, especially in potash and oil, proven cash cows for the province's revenues. Some suggested a retroactive windfall capital gains tax on all those who bought public assets at below market value prices.[21] As the Devine caucus fraud scandal unravelled, many expected the NDP government to convene a judicial inquiry into the scandalous privatizations where hundreds of millions in public assets, especially the Potash Corporation of Saskatchewan and SaskOil, were sold far below value. Romanow did none of these things.

Consumed by a narrow neoliberal view of the deficit and debt problem and without any commitment to reconstructing a progressive coalition, the NDP leadership could not but come to see their own party supporters and the labour movement as adversaries, and the business lobby and the media as allies. Upon election Romanow embarked on a neoliberal ideological offensive with dramatic speeches up and down the province to whip up public hysteria about the deficit and debt. That was followed by a three-year cycle of outright cuts in social, education, and health spending, involving hundreds of millions of dollars. Relief at Devine's defeat was replaced by anger, and by June 1994 the Romanow government's public support was crashing. In response Romanow made a sudden U-turn, declaring the battle against the annual deficit won and placing the larger problem of the public debt on the back burner. Declaring the worst over, Romanow promised no further cuts. Romanow made some minimal concessions to labour, most importantly an amendment to labour standards to allow senior part-time workers the right of first refusal on any additional hours of work (which passed but was never proclaimed).[22] Combined with reasonably good economic news, these moderately progressive laws helped turn things around, and Romanow called an election for June 1995. Most importantly, the anti-NDP vote remained divided between the declining Tories and the ascendant Liberals.

Romanow waged a tightly controlled and highly scripted campaign, exposing himself only to friendly groups, avoiding public rallies, and saying everything necessary to put the electorate to sleep. Throughout the campaign, Romanow moved to the centre-right to join the Liberals. In fact, all three parties presented nearly identical platforms, thoughtfully provided by the business lobby: cutbacks, lower taxes, non-interventionist government, and no new programs. The right-wing Fraser Institute endorsed the programs of all three parties. During the election Romanow solemnly promised not to raise either the minimum wage or taxes and resource royalties over the next four years, reassuring the business lobby. He also repeated his message of hope that the worst was over. There would be no further major program cuts.

The 1995 election was virtually a non-event. Voter apathy was epidemic. Only 64 per cent of voters bothered to cast a ballot, the lowest turnout in seventy years. Turnout was particularly low in the NDP's traditional strongholds in urban areas and the north. Although Romanow fell below the vote share won in 1991 and far below the NDP vote during the election losses of the 1980s, it was a clear victory. The truth was that it was the election of a government with no program beyond continuing the neoliberal agenda with a somewhat more human face. Romanow's New Democrats were content with being the least of three evils.

Romanow's last full term as premier (1995–9) witnessed the end of his political magic and the restructuring and unification of the right. In the summer of 1997 the Reform Party targeted Saskatchewan for a move into provincial politics. The Saskatchewan right panicked and quickly gathered a loose coalition of disgruntled Liberals and Tories into the Saskatchewan Party. On 9 August 1997 the Saskatchewan Party, with eight MLAs, replaced the Liberals as Official Opposition. Reform Party members rushed to join the new party, electing former Reform MP Elwin Hermanson as leader. There was a shift in mood on the right – from a defeatist conviction that Romanow was unbeatable to a sense that victory was within reach – that was manifest as the Saskatchewan Party mobilized popular support, especially in rural areas.[23]

Romanow strategists were convinced that the NDP could win in June 1999. The Saskatchewan Party was new and relatively untested. The Liberals would pull enough right-of-centre votes to help the NDP. Further, the NDP was convinced the public was deeply mistrustful of the extreme right-wing agenda of many in the Saskatchewan Party and uneasy about Elwin Hermanson as premier. The plan was derailed by the nurses' strike in April 1999. The Saskatchewan Union of Nurses (SUN) had built towards a potential strike since the first cuts in 1992. By 1999 bargaining reached an impasse and in April 8,400 nurses went on strike. Within hours Romanow pushed through a back-to-work law in the legislature. The nurses defied the government and embarked on a ten-day illegal strike. Relations between the NDP government and the labour movement deteriorated to the lowest point since 1982, as the government embarked on a negative propaganda campaign against the nurses while labour likened Romanow's unseemly rush to a back-to-work law as in the worst tradition of right-wing, anti-labour governments.[24] As the strike went on, public opinion shifted dramatically in the nurses' favour, the government caved, and a settlement was quickly achieved. But the political damage was done. The June election was postponed to September 1999.

Romanow was confident as the campaign started. In a *Globe and Mail* interview in late August, the premier was asked about his secret of success. "Call it Third Way or Tony Blair–style socialism," a confident Romanow replied.[25] Faced by growing anger in rural areas afflicted by the chronic farm crisis, Romanow played Pontius Pilate as he washed his hands, pointed the finger at Ottawa, and declared he would not put the province's treasury at risk as Devine had done in the 1980s. As in 1995, Romanow avoided large meetings in rural areas, opting for small gatherings of carefully selected rural supporters. Romanow counted on his captive vote in urban Saskatchewan, hoping to win just enough rural votes for a majority. The strategy failed. In an uncanny echo of the 1986 election, Romanow retained a tenuous hold on power, despite winning fewer votes than the Saskatchewan Party, which had united the anti-NDP vote and swept rural Saskatchewan. The NDP took twenty-nine of fifty-eight seats, the Saskatchewan Party twenty-six, and the Liberals three. The NDP won twenty-five seats in the four large cities, retained the two northern seats, one rural seat, and one seat that combined a small city and the surrounding rural area. Meanwhile the Saskatchewan Party won twenty-three rural seats and three seats that combined small cities and surrounding rural areas. Turnout was lowest in urban and highest in rural ridings. To keep power, Romanow cobbled together a coalition with two Liberals and announced his retirement. He led the party from a major victory in 1991, when over 83 per cent of the electorate voted, to a near defeat in 1999, when just 65 per cent turned out.

Assessing the Romanow Premiership:
plus ça change, plus c'est la même chose

A common view among Romanow's critics on the left is that he lost his nerve and refused to reverse the neoliberal agenda, repair the damage done by Devine, and steer the government in a moderate social democratic direction.[26] The evidence suggests a harsher conclusion. Romanow deepened the neoliberal agenda and completed elements of it that Devine had left unfinished. From 1991 to 1994 he finished the privatization of the Potash Corporation of Saskatchewan (PCS) by selling off 22 million shares at the same price as 1989. In 1989, when the PCS was privatized, the province received 35 million shares, immediately selling 13 million of them. Romanow had the tools necessary to reverse the privatization, given the 22 million shares still held by the government. More than that, Romanow removed the concessions Devine had been politically compelled to make during the 1989 privatization battle – all persons or groups, except the government of Saskatchewan, were restricted to holding no more than 5 per cent of shares, and non-residents of Canada could not own more than 45 per cent of the shares, thus ensuring effective domestic control. The loss between 1989 and 1996, both in the underselling of assets and lost dividends, amounted conservatively to half a billion dollars. Over the lifetime of the potash industry, the losses have constituted and will continue to constitute a flood of forgone public revenues.[27]

Between 1991 and 1996 Romanow reduced the province's stake in Cameco, a partnership with the private uranium industry, from 30 to 10 per cent. In 1997 Romanow sold the province's 50 per cent interest in Saskfor, a forestry partnership with Macmillan, thus depriving the province of average annual dividends of $6 million. In 1998 he sold the province's shares in the Crown Life Insurance Company ($150 million) and those in the Lloydminster Upgrader ($308 million) just as the latter was finally becoming profitable after years of government assistance; it has since proven to be a highly lucrative operation.[28] Clearly, Devine began the privatization of public assets, but Romanow completed it.

Defenders of privatization argue that the most important source of resource revenues is from royalties and taxes, while the dividends paid from ownership hardly compensate for the public capital frozen in the asset and the market risks associated with public ownership. The evidence, however, contradicts this defence. For example, between 1976 and 1988 PCS paid provincial taxes and royalties of over $372 million and dividends of over $228 million, and the province still owned its investment.[29] That total came close to the one-time payment received for privatization. The Crown oil company, SaskOil, was financially profitable. Despite arguments that royalties delivered the real benefits without the risk, Devine had cut royalties for all resources dramatically. For example, under the Blakeney government the provincial treasury took 50 per cent of the total sales of oil as royalties and taxes. Devine cut this to 27 per cent. But Romanow went further, cutting it to 17 per cent. Back in 1979–80 the Blakeney government obtained about 21 per cent of its total revenues from resource rents (royalties and taxes on oil, potash, uranium, and others). Certainly Devine changed that dramatically, but by 1994–5, given Romanow's refusal to reverse Devine's reductions, Saskatchewan obtained just over 8 per cent of its total revenues from resource rents. A return to a resource rent policy approximating Blakeney's, and a re-acquisition of cash-producing public assets, would have more than offset Devine's deficits and debt from the 1980s (which were largely created by tax and royalty cuts), and meaningfully sheltered the province from the federal cuts of the 1990s. But Romanow not only retained Devine's cuts in resource rents, he actually deepened them in 1998.

On labour law there was more continuity than discontinuity between the Devine and Romanow regimes. Romanow legislated striking power workers back to work in 1998 and striking nurses in 1999. He refused to amend labour laws to tilt the relations of power one bit from capital to labour. He rejected anti-scab laws. Romanow refused to include workers in large agro-industrial enterprises in rural areas, like hog barns and feedlots, under the province's labour code. He routinely rejected individuals recommended by labour as representatives on boards and commissions. Symbolic of the relationship was the fact that the amendments to labour standards to help part-time workers get more hours and benefits were passed but never proclaimed, sitting forlornly on permanent public display as a solemn promise unfulfilled.

Upon election in 1991, Romanow pushed the party hard to the right and decisively abandoned its founding principles. As a convert to neo-liberalism, Romanow cut health, education, and social programs mercilessly, while embracing the business lobby (including the historic turn to accepting corporate donations). In fact, his program of cuts went farther, faster than Devine ever dared. Overall, as political economist John W. Warnock concluded in a 2003 study, in each and every policy area – privatization, deregulation, agriculture and rural development, taxation, labour, social programs, the environment – "the Romanow government decided to continue the restructuring of capitalism as demanded by the business community," while jettisoning the "promised … return to the social democratic orientation of the Blakeney government."[30]

The Calvert Recalibration?

Romanow's departure in 2001 led to renewal and a slight shift to the left in the NDP.[31] Many disgruntled members and supporters returned to the fold to support Lorne Calvert, widely viewed as a moderate social democrat in the Blakeney tradition. After an unexpected four-ballot leadership victory, Calvert became premier in 2001. From then until he sought his own mandate in November 2003, Calvert distanced himself from the Romanow legacy – a little more went into health and education, the Crowns were somewhat re-centred in government policy, and there was more social democratic talk. But he was still an unelected premier finishing Romanow's mandate, relying on the coalition with the Liberals.

When Calvert called the election in 2003, pundits predicted defeat. Calvert turned slightly left, very publicly called home the disillusioned among the party's faithful, defended public ownership with zeal, and promised to make health and education top priorities. Surprising many, Calvert won 45 per cent of the vote, the Saskatchewan Party 39 per cent. This translated into a narrow victory in seats of thirty to twenty-eight. His appeal and his promise of a new left-leaning direction worked beyond the expectations of most – voter turnout jumped to 71 per cent, and the NDP vote increased dramatically.

Yet, by 2005, Calvert had not broken with the Romanow legacy of neoliberalism and submission to the business lobby. In fact, Calvert caved on the most important issues that ultimately defined his government. When he moved to proclaim the "most available hours" law[32] that Romanow had left sitting on the books, the business lobby and the Saskatchewan Party launched a massive attack. Calvert surrendered and promised not only not to proclaim the law, but also to wipe it off the statute books. The message to Calvert was clear – implacable opposition would meet even modest pro-worker measures. Calvert continued to lower royalty rates on resources, especially oil and potash. Indeed, while the share of oil sales the province took as revenues fell to 17 per cent under Romanow, Calvert's additional concessions brought it down to 14 per cent.

Under Romanow the NDP government was neoliberal in both words and deeds. Under Calvert the NDP government staggered one day in a moderate social democratic direction and the next day, pressured by the business lobby, lurched in a neoliberal direction.

The Saskatchewan Party Triumphs

Brad Wall, a protégé of Grant Devine, replaced Elwin Hermanson as leader of the Saskatchewan Party and won two back-to-back landslide victories, with thirty-eight of fifty-eight seats and 51 per cent of the vote in 2007, and forty-nine of fifty-eight seats and 64 per cent in 2011.[33] The once-proud NDP, viewed since 1944 as the province's "natural governing party" (holding power from 1944 to 1964, 1971 to 1982, and 1991 to 2007), was reduced in 2011 to nine seats and 32 per cent of the vote. Wall appears determined to make history by winning a third term in 2016 and replacing the NDP as the natural governing party.

The Saskatchewan Party's victories confirm that Saskatchewan has become a stronghold for neoliberalism in Canada. Wall's party has successfully combined economic neoliberalism, social conservatism, and considered ideological pragmatism in the electoral march from its rural stronghold into the province's booming cities. Wall had solemnly promised not to privatize the province's big Crowns, so he largely contented himself with fiscal conservatism, a series of small downsizing measures against the Crowns, and a slightly bigger push than under Romanow and Calvert towards privatization of selected aspects of health-care delivery. A singularly benign fiscal and economic environment has so far allowed the Wall government to avoid the turn to austerity that has engulfed much of the world in the wake of the global financial crisis, and thereby to keep its friends and avoid making too many new enemies.

In the area of social policy Wall actually improved the situation of some of the most needy by increasing welfare benefits to the disabled and poor seniors, and taking thousands of low-income earners off the provincial income-tax rolls. The biggest moment of his first term was his violation of free market ideology by opposing the hostile takeover of the Potash Corporation of Saskatchewan by Australian-based multinational BHP Billiton, and successfully lobbying the Harper government to deny the takeover. Such actions did not sit well with some members of his party and elements of the business lobby. He is increasingly (if quietly) criticized for his NDP-like spending habits and his lack of sufficient enthusiasm for strict neoliberal economic orthodoxy. These sections of the Saskatchewan party base, which include the old far right from the Reform Party, deeply committed right-wing Tories, and right-of-centre Liberals will join the business lobby to pressure Wall to implement more tax cuts, especially for business, and to lead a bigger push for privatizations in health care and the Crowns.

On one key feature of neoliberalism, however, Wall has been zealous, and this has earned him strong support from the business lobby and anti-labour voters. Upon election in 2007 Wall declared war on the labour union movement and has passed the most anti-union labour laws in Canada (it was the CCF that pioneered progressive, pro-union labour laws in 1944).[34] Angered by the ad campaign against his government by the province's trade unions, upon victory in 2011 Wall announced his intention to seek legislative means to prevent unions from using members' dues for political purposes. The war between organized labour and the Wall government is likely to continue, even if the pace of such an escalation remains far from clear.

Structural Change, Political Realignment, and the Triumph of Neoliberalism

The uneven and contested rise of neoliberalism has been a global and pan-Canadian phenomenon but has everywhere been a product of particular "local" social relations, structural changes, and processes of political conflict, innovation, and realignment. Despite the complexity of the history of "actually existing neoliberalism," it is both possible and worthwhile to highlight some of the deeper causal relations – both structural and contingent – underlying what is in retrospect an epochal shift in the political economy of our times. In the case of Saskatchewan, understanding the triumph of neoliberalism requires recognizing the factors that eroded the social basis for a particular form of post-war social democracy; those that provided conditions and institutional pathways for the (mixed) successes of the conservative counter-offensive that began in earnest in the 1980s; and those that have contributed to the continuing failure (or refusal) to reconstruct and reconstitute durable alternatives since the 1990s.

The triumph of moderate social democracy in Saskatchewan emerged initially as the product of a uniquely successful progressive farmer-labour coalition constructed in the late 1930s and early 1940s and sustained, if in increasingly tenuous form, until the 1970s. The wrenching long-term transformations underway in the agricultural sector – farm consolidation, social differentiation among farmers, rapid technological change, and growing "agri-business" integration – were in evidence as early as the 1950s. By the 1970s they had become particularly salient politically in debates over transport and marketing policies, and by the end of that decade there could be little doubt that on key questions "a free enterprise and more openly capitalist ideology, often championed by large farmers, [increasingly] carried the debate signalling the demise of the hegemony of agrarian populism."[35]

The consolidation of the farm sector into far fewer and much larger operations accelerated markedly beginning in the late 1970s and, along with rural depopulation, it contributed to the political de-radicalization of rural Saskatchewan. By the 1980s, "the Conservatives were able to play to an increasingly receptive rural audience in Saskatchewan, not because neoliberalism *per se* was attractive, but because of the decline of social democratic populism."[36] Devine's victory in 1982 depended on an urban breakthrough accomplished by appealing to right-wing populist pocketbook issues (such as mortgage rates and gasoline prices). His winning of a crucial second term depended on the Conservatives' rural strategy in the context of the electoral implications of increasing urbanization for the respective weight of urban and rural seats. The Conservatives were able to position themselves as the party of a rural Saskatchewan in crisis, channelling anxiety among an aging population about the closure of rail lines, grain elevators, rural hospitals, and the more general viability of rural communities, into a right-wing populism that combined regional grievances and resentment with hot-button social and cultural wedge issues.[37]

Between 1981 and 2006, the proportion of farms with gross receipts under $50,000 was cut nearly in half. Since 1991, the only category of farm to experience any relative growth was that with more than $100,000 in gross receipts. Since 2001, that honour has belonged exclusively to farms with upwards of $250,000 in receipts (see figure 8.1), and since 2006, to those with more than $500,000 in receipts. According to preliminary results from the 2011 Census of Agriculture, the number of farms with less than $500,000 in receipts has decreased by 21.6 per cent since 2006 while the number with more than $500,000 in receipts rose 44.9 per cent between 2006 and 2011. These very large farms account for just 12.9 per cent of all farms, but they were responsible for 60 per cent of all farm receipts in Saskatchewan in 2010.[38]

Figure 8.1. Distribution of Saskatchewan Farms by Size, Gross Recipients, Constant 2005 Dollars, 1981–2006

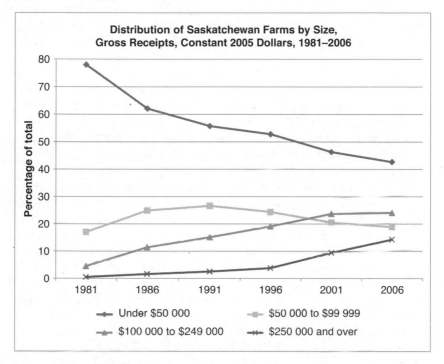

Source: Statistics Canada, Census of Agriculture

Under Blakeney the NDP had itself opened the door to its defeat at the hands of Devine in important ways. In the 1970s it had completed the transition to a predominantly urban party and had alienated rural Saskatchewan by failing to move aggressively on promised rural rebuilding. At the same time, the party leadership, more and more composed of civil servants, teachers, lawyers and other professionals, as well as credit union and co-op managers, increasingly insulated itself from labour influence. Enthusiastic support for wage controls and growing conflict with public-sector unions (including back-to-work legislation targeting hospital workers just prior to the 1982 election) spoke to a definite estrangement between the party and organized labour, and perhaps to early efforts to recast a more middle-class urban electoral bloc in place of the crumbling farmer-labour alliance. Environmentalists and peace activists were outraged by the government's support for uranium mining, and feminists were angry at the government's weakness on reproductive choice in the face of a social conservative lobby and the lack of progress on day care. The Blakeney NDP had, by deed or inaction, offended or alienated nearly every component of the traditional NDP coalition, while its traditional opponents – the business lobby, large farmers, the wealthy, and especially the private resource companies – regrouped behind the Tories and poured money into the effort to unseat the NDP.[39]

On its return to power in 1991 the NDP declined to even attempt to reconstruct a broad progressive coalition. This development was virtually assured by the leadership's commitment to tackling the deficit on the basis of neoliberal orthodoxy and to aggressively courting the business community, since it turned important parts of the traditional NDP base into the government's natural adversaries. Organized labour and the activist left were increasingly marginalized by the NDP in power as the party leadership cleaved towards Third Way–style social liberalism, adopted key aspects of the right-wing's economic policy agenda, and subordinated policy innovation and coalition building to narrow electoral pragmatism. In keeping with this cynical project, the party organization itself completed the turn in the 1990s to a professional electoral machine tightly controlled by party cadre and with a smaller and more passive membership role.[40] The NDP under Romanow repeatedly ignored pleas from the NDP's traditional constituencies – labour, the progressive farmers' movement, the activist left, environmentalists – refusing them any major concessions while paying devoted attention to the demands of business. The left, labour, farm activists, and environmentalists left the party in large numbers or drifted into inaction.

Instead, the party opted to batten down the hatches on its increasingly urban base (both electorally and in terms of party cadre) in the "new" urban middle class of white- and pink-collar workers and professionals. This constituency tends to support the public services they depend on in health and education, but is lukewarm on redistributive measures that might impinge on their powers of private consumption, and favour single-issue activism and individual identity/lifestyle politics over the "old" left/right or class-based politics.[41]

The relative growth of the private sector, encouraged throughout the Devine and Romanow-Calvert years through privatization, subsidies, and tax/regulatory relief (and boosted by the resource and real estate

Figure 8.2. Sectoral Composition of the Employed Labour Force

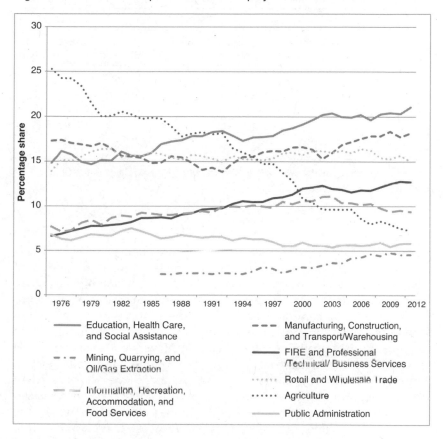

Source: Calculated from Statistics Canada, CANSIM, table 28220008

booms of the 2000s) has, alongside the more general trend towards a service-based occupational structure, added complexity to the urban social forces available for electoral appeals and coalition building (see figure 8.2). The share of the labour force employed in education, health care, and social assistance experienced strong growth in the late 1980s and again in the late 1990s – providing a pillar of urban support for the NDP's recapture and retention of power. Between 1976 and 2012 this sector's share of the labour force grew by 43 per cent.

But even more dramatic has been the growth, from a lower initial level, of the share of employment found in finance, insurance, and real

Table 8.1. Urban Seats Won in Saskatchewan Elections, 2003–11

	2003		2007		2011	
	Saskatchewan Party	NDP	Saskatchewan Party	NDP	Saskatchewan Party	NDP
Prince Albert	0	2	1	1	2	0
Moose Jaw	0	2	1	1	2	0
Regina	0	11	3	8	8	3
Saskatoon	3	9	5	7	8	4
Total	3	24	10	17	20	7

Source: Elections Saskatchewan, *Statement of Votes* (Regina: Office of the Chief Electoral Officer, 2004, 2008, 2012)

estate (FIRE) and in professional, technical, and business services. These categories of primarily urban and private-sector workers and petit bourgeois professionals grew twice as fast, nearly doubling as a share of the labour force between 1976 and 2012. Together with overwhelming support from confident business lobbies,[42] it seems reasonable to hypothesize that the growth in size and influence of this more solidly neoliberal urban grouping, along with employers and workers in the favoured resource-extraction and construction industries, has been an important contributing factor in the Saskatchewan Party's steady urban breakthrough in recent elections. The party's success has been based more generally on its ability to associate in the public consciousness the province's boom in resource industries and real estate with its brand of pro-business boosterism in economic policy (even if global economic forces, including a commodity super-cycle, and domestic flows of credit into residential real estate have been the primary drivers).

Epilogue: A Fundamental Realignment?

The Saskatchewan Party's urban breakthrough has been truly dramatic and raises the question of whether Saskatchewan has witnessed a fundamental political realignment on a par with what swept the CCF to power in 1944. Saskatchewan may well be on the cusp of embracing the Saskatchewan Party as the new "natural governing party." The unprecedented victory of Brad Wall in the 2011 election – at 64 per cent, the highest popular vote victory in the province's history – suggests this is the case. Wall swept city, town, and country, decimating the NDP. The previous victories of anti-CCF/NDP, pro-business election coalitions – Ross Thatcher's Liberals in 1964 and 1967, Grant Devine's Tories in 1982 and 1986 – proved ephemeral, ending in large victories for the NDP after two terms (Blakeney in 1971 and Romanow in 1991). The Saskatchewan Party's assault on the NDPs twenty-seven-seat base in urban areas garnered no seats in 1999, three in 2003, ten in 2007, and twenty in 2011. While the political realignment in rural Saskatchewan is clear and apparently permanent, the twenty-seven urban seats remain contested terrain.

At the party and electoral level, the next election will test the extent to which the realignment has staying power in urban Saskatchewan. Should Wall win a third majority government in 2015 or 2016 with a continuing solid foundation in urban Saskatchewan, it can be reasonably concluded that the 2011 election involved a critical and structural realignment of politics in the province. Wall's soft neoliberalism, combined with the care he has taken not to provoke an urban/rural polarization like that engineered by his mentor Grant Devine, might well sustain a substantial urban base.

At the ideological level the political realignment in Saskatchewan arguably occurred following Romanow's 1991 victory. After winning a large majority based on promises to reverse the neoliberal agenda, Romanow embraced neoliberalism and continued its aggressive implementation. Calvert's brief flirtation with a left turn to polarize the 2003 election aside, from then on both major parties supported neoliberalism, and the social democratic option largely disappeared from electoral politics. After their defeat in 2007, the NDP narrowly rejected the centre-left social democratic vision of Ryan Meili in leadership contests in 2009 and 2011, selecting Romanow's former deputy premier Dwain Lingenfelter in 2009 and Cam Broten in 2011, both of whom adhered to the mainstream NDP commitment to neoliberalism. Under its current leader, the NDP will take a cautious, traditional electoral approach, criticizing the Wall government on the margins while waiting for the government to stumble or the economy to weaken. Neoliberalism will therefore remain hegemonic in Saskatchewan electoral politics. Should Wall win a third term, the NDP may go through a major internal battle between the more opportunist neoliberal wing and those with a residue of the social democratic principles who continue to enjoy significant sway among many in the rank and file and in the broader populace.

Of course, developments outside the party system and the electoral arena will be critical in shaping future developments, including whether or not the labour movement can revive itself from its defensive sclerosis and experiment with new approaches to organizing and political coalition building, becoming in the process more relevant to younger workers outside its areas of traditional strength. Future developments will also depend on whether extra-parliamentary social movements can gain traction as the contradictions of Saskatchewan's booming capitalism become more apparent. Of particular importance in this regard will be the extent to which the province's large and growing young Aboriginal population throws up new forms of political representation and mobilization, a possibility hinted at by the "Idle No More" protest movement that flowered briefly in 2012–13.

Events in Saskatchewan cannot be understood in isolation. As numerous chapters in this volume demonstrate, the last three decades have been a tumultuous period of conflict and accommodation that has reshaped Canada's political culture. These political, economic, and social transformations have led to neoliberal ideological hegemony among all political parties and a decline of alternative political subjectivities among growing numbers of Canadians who have been presented less and less with meaningful political and economic alternatives. With the narrowing of acceptable political discourse, growing numbers of (especially younger) people have lost faith in the democratic system – a final triumph for those seeking to convince the public to surrender the notion that they could use the system to collectively reshape their communities and deliver social and economic (and crucially, today, ecological) justice. But the very scale and scope of the transformations that have accompanied the triumph of neoliberalism and its ushering in of a new "bourgeois epoch" in Saskatchewan and elsewhere in recent decades at the same time belies overly fatalistic assumptions about the solidity, let alone the permanence, of our neoliberal present. As inveterate students of capitalism's contradictory dynamism noted long ago, it is the "constant revolutionizing of production, uninterrupted disturbance of all social conditions, everlasting uncertainty and agitation [that] distinguish the bourgeois epoch from all earlier ones. All fixed, fast-frozen relations, with their train of ancient and venerable prejudices and opinions, are swept away, all new-formed ones become antiquated before they can ossify."[43] Residents of Saskatchewan, like others around the globe, will no doubt have occasion to face with sober and critical senses their real conditions of life and their relations with one another in ways that may once again lead them beyond the cramped horizons represented by neoliberalism.

NOTES

1 *Report of the Royal Commission on Dominion-Provincial Relations (Rowell-Sirois Report), Book I* (Ottawa: King's Printer, 1940), 61.
2 For a more complete discussion of the ideological instability in the politics of rural and farm populations see J.F Conway, "Populism in the United States, Russia and Canada: Explaining the Roots of Canada's Third Parties," *Canadian Journal of Political Science* 11, no. 1 (March 1978): 99–124; Conway, "The Prairie Populist Resistance to the National Policy: Some Reconsiderations," *Journal of Canadian Studies* 14, no. 3 (Fall 1979): 77–91; Conway, "Agrarian Petit-Bourgeois Responses to Capitalist Industrialization: The Case of Canada," in *The Petite Bourgeoisie: Comparative Studies of the Uneasy Stratum,* ed. Frank Bechhofer and Brian Elliott, 1–37 (London: Macmillan, 1981).
3 For classic investigations of western labour radicalism during this period, see H. Clare Pentland, "The Western Canadian Labour Movement, 1897–1919," *Canadian Journal of Political and Social Theory* 3 (1979): 53–78; David J. Bercuson, "Labour Radicalism and the Western Industrial Frontier, 1897–1919," *Canadian Historical Review* 58, no. 2 (1977): 154–77; and A. Ross McCormack, *Reformers, Rebels, and Revolutionaries: The Western Canadian Radical Movement, 1899–1919* (Toronto: University of Toronto Press, 1977). For analyses of the prairie agrarian movement, see, among many others, Seymour Martin Lipset, *Agrarian Socialism: The Cooperative Commonwealth Federation in Saskatchewan* (Berkeley: University of California Press, 1950); David Laycock, *Populism and Democratic Thought in the Canadian Prairies* (Toronto: University of Toronto Press, 1990); and the chapters assembled in Murray Knuttila and Bob Stirling, eds., *The Prairie Agrarian Movement Revisited* (Regina: Canadian Plains Research Center Press, 2007).
4 *Submission of the Government of Saskatchewan to the Royal Commission on Dominion-Provincial Relations (Rowell-Sirois) (Canada, 1937)* (Regina: King's Printer, 1937), 187; Alma Lawton, "Urban Relief in Saskatchewan during the Years of the Depression, 1930–37" (MA thesis, University of Saskatchewan, 1969), 46.
5 *Rowell-Sirois Report,* 164.
6 J.F. Conway, *The West: The History of a Region in Confederation* (Toronto: Lorimer, 2006), 45–178. On the important British Columbia case, see Bryan

D. Palmer, *Solidarity: The Rise and Fall of an Opposition in British Columbia* (Vancouver: New Star, 1987).

7 John Richards and Larry Pratt, *Prairie Capitalism: Power and Influence in the New West* (Toronto: McClelland and Stewart, 1979), chap. 10; Jocelyne Praud and Sarah McQuarrie, "The Saskatchewan CCF-NDP from the *Regina Manifesto* to the Romanow Years," in *Saskatchewan Politics: Into the Twenty-First Century*, ed. Howard Leeson (Regina: Canadian Plains Research Center Press, 2001), 150–3.

8 Lesley Biggs and Mark Stobbe, eds. *Devine Rule in Saskatchewan* (Saskatoon: Fifth House, 1991); James M. Pitsula and Ken Rasmussen, *Privatizing a Province: The New Right in Saskatchewan* (Vancouver: New Star, 1990).

9 Conway, *The West*, 246–67.

10 J.F. Conway, "The Distribution of Benefits of the 1986 Saskatchewan Farm Production Loan Program" (paper presented to the Canadian Association of Rural Studies, Learned Societies, Laval University, June 1989).

11 Bart Johnson, "Schmidt Stresses Attitude Change," *Leader-Post*, 9 October 1990.

12 "Devine Shuffles Cabinet, Rethinks Privatization," *Globe and Mail*, 4 October 1989.

13 Pitsula and Rasmussen, *Privatizing a Province*, chaps. 3–5 and 8–10.

14 Canada, *Economic Reference Tables*, August (Ottawa: Department of Finance, 1992), 31 and 58.

15 Saskatchewan, *Ministry of Agriculture, Agricultural Statistics 1991* (Regina: Ministry of Agriculture, November 1992), 3 and 13.

16 Mark Stobbe, "Political Conservatism and Fiscal Irresponsibility," in Biggs and Stobbe, *Devine Rule in Saskatchewan*, 15–32.

17 Merrilee Rasmussen and Howard Leeson. "Parliamentary Democracy in Saskatchewan, 1982–1989," in Biggs and Stobbe, *Devine Rule in Saskatchewan*, 49–65.

18 J.F. Conway, "The Saskatchewan Electoral Boundaries Case, 1990–91," paper presented to the Canadian Political Science Association Annual Meeting, 1993.

19 *Reference Re Provincial Electoral Boundaries,* Saskatchewan Court of Appeal (1991), 90 Sask. R. 174, 78 DLR (4th) 449; *Reference re Prov. Electoral Boundaries (Sask.),* [1991] 2 SCR 158.

20 J.F. Conway. "The Devine Regime in Saskatchewan, 1982–1991: The Tory Caucus Fraud Scandal and Other Abuses of Power," in *(Ab)Using Power: The Canadian Experience,* ed. Dorothy E. Chunn, Susan C. Boyd, and Robert Menzies, 95–109 (Halifax: Fernwood, 2001).

21 Details on the sales of assets for less than market value are provided in Pitsula and Rasmussen, *Privatizing a Province,* chap. 9, "Privatization: Saskatchewan for Sale," 157–79, and chap. 10, "Privatization: The Momentum Shifts," 180–200.

22 For an account of the uneasy relationship between the labour movement and the CCF/NDP over the years, see J.F. Conway, "Labour and the CCF/NDP in Saskatchewan," *Prairie Forum* 31, no. 2 (Fall 2006): 389–426. ·

23 Raymond B. Blake, "The Saskatchewan Party and the Politics of Branding," in *Saskatchewan Politics: Crowding the Centre,* ed. Howard Leeson, 165–88 (Regina: Canadian Plains Research Center Press, 2008).

24 For details of the nurses' strike, see Conway, *The West,* 330–2. For the shift to a paradigm of coercion in dealing with trade unions under neoliberalism, see Leo Panitch and Donald Swartz, *From Consent to Coercion: The Assault on Trade Union Freedoms,* 3rd ed. (Aurora, ON: Garamond, 2003). For details on how this shift was also supported by the Saskatchewan NDP governments of Romanow and Calvert, see Charles W. Smith, "The 'New Normal' in Saskatchewan: Neoliberalism and the Challenge to Workers' Rights," in *New Directions in Saskatchewan Public Policy,* ed. David McGrane, 121–52 (Regina: Canadian Plains Research Center Press, 2011).

25 David Roberts, "NDP Bets on 'Third Way' to Third Term," *Globe and Mail,* 31 August 1999.

26 David McGrane, "Which Third Way? A Comparison of the Romanow and Calvert NDP Governments from 1991 to 2007," in Leeson, *Saskatchewan Politics,* 143–64.

27 Saskatchewan Institute for Social and Economic Alternatives, *The Privatization of the Potash Corporation of Saskatchewan: A Case Study* (Regina: Saskatchewan Institute, June 1996).

28 See David Hanly, "Husky Energy," *Encyclopedia of Saskatchewan,* http://esask .uregina.ca/entry/husky_energy.html; and Husky Energy Inc. president and CEO presentation to the Annual Meeting of Shareholders, 2007, accessed 14 June 2012, http://www.huskyenergy.com/investorrelations/presentations .asp.

29 Saskatchewan Institute for Social and Economic Alternatives, *The Privatization of the Potash Corporation of Saskatchewan.*

30 John W. Warnock, *The Structural Adjustment of Capitalism in Saskatchewan* (Ottawa: Canadian Centre for Policy Aleternatives, 2003), 9–10.

31 McGrane, "Which Third Way?," 143–64.

32 For details of this law designed to extend benefits and some degree of job and income security to part-time workers, see Jim Warren and Kathleen

Carlisle, *On the Side of the People: A History of Labour in Saskatchewan* (Regina: Coteau, 2005), 263–5.

33 For details on the 2007 election, see David McGrane, "The 2007 Provincial Election in Saskatchewan," *Canadian Political Science Review* 2, no. 1 (March/April 2008): 64–71; Howard Leeson, "The 2007 Election: Watershed or Way Station?," in Leeson, *Saskatchewan Politics*, 119–40.

34 J.F. Conway, "Wall Declares War on Organized Labour in Saskatchewan," *Bullet*, 13 July 2009, http://www.socialistproject.ca/bullet/239.php; Charles Smith, "'New Normal' in Saskatchewan."

35 Bob Stirling and J.F. Conway, "Fractions among Prairie Farmers," in *The Political Economy of Agriculture in Western Canada*, ed. G.S. Basran and D.A. Hay, 73–86 (Saskatoon: University of Saskatchewan Social Research Unit, 1988).

36 Howard Leeson, "The Rich Soil of Saskatchewan Politics," in Leeson, *Saskatchewan Politics*, 7.

37 John W. Warnock, *Saskatchewan: The Roots of Discontent and Protest* (Montreal: Black Rose, 2004), 366–7; Kevin Wishlow, "Rethinking the Polarization Thesis: The Formation and Growth of the Saskatchewan Party, 1997–2001," in Leeson, *Saskatchewan Politics*, 186.

38 Statistics Canada, Census of Agriculture, 2011, "Highlights and Analyses: Farm Data and Farm Operator Data," http://www.statcan.gc.ca/pub/95-640-x/2012002-eng.htm.

39 Lorne Brown, Joseph Roberts, and John Warnock, *Saskatchewan Politics from Left to Right, 1944–1999* (Regina: Hinterland Publications, 1999), 25–7; J.F. Conway, "From 'Agrarian Socialism' to 'Natural' Governing Party," in *The Prairie Agrarian Movement Revisited*, ed. K. Murray Knuttila and Robert Sterling (Regina: University of Regina Press, 2007), 228–9.

40 Praud and McQuarrie, "Saskatchewan CCF-NDP," 162–4.

41 Ken Rasmussen, "Saskatchewan: From Entrepreneurial State to Embedded State," in *The Provincial State in Canada: Politics in the Provinces and Territories*, ed. Keith Brownsey and Michael Howlett (Peterborough: Broadview, 2001), 255–7.

42 Simon Enoch, *Mapping Corporate Power* (Regina: Canadian Centre for Policy Alternatives – Saskatchewan, 2012).

43 Karl Marx and Friedrich Engels. *The Communist Manifesto*, chapter 1, "Bourgeois and Proletarians," http://www.marxists.org/archive/marx/works/1848/communist-manifesto/ch01.htm#007.

9 The Politics of Alberta's One-Party State

STEVE PATTEN

Introduction[1]

Stereotypes abound in popular imaginings of politics in Alberta. Having elected Progressive Conservative (PC) governments in every election since 1971, and gained a reputation for leading the charge in Canada's neoliberal revolution during the 1990s, the province is now identified as Canada's most conservative. Commentators regularly portray Alberta as having a homogeneously conservative political culture that smothers progressive political dissent. According to the *Globe and Mail*'s national affairs columnist, Jeffrey Simpson, "Alberta has a weird political culture ... All the currents of dissent happen within the conservative world."[2]

One popular depiction of the character of Alberta politics labels the province a resource-rich "one-party state." Although the province has all the trappings of democracy that are found in other Westminster-style parliamentary systems, a single political party with a conservative political agenda has triumphed year after year. Alberta's governing Conservatives seem to have the political and institutional capacity to marginalize opposition parties and left-of-centre political movements that champion progressive social reform. The *Edmonton Journal*'s Shelia Pratt describes Alberta as "a long-time one-party state – where Tory MLAs are mostly silent and dissent is discouraged."[3] Mark Lisac depicts the province as a "one-party state with a virtually obsolete legislature and an increasingly apathetic electorate."[4]

Yet how useful are these portrayals of Alberta to the serious student of comparative provincial politics? What insights are revealed through an analysis of Alberta as a one-party state? Is it accurate to describe Alberta as deeply conservative and devoid of left-leaning voices of political dissent? What are the social forces, institutions, and political economic conditions that sustain and perpetuate the unique character of Alberta politics? Are the patterns of one-party state politics unalterable, or might Alberta be entering a period of political change – one in which progressive voices will become more significant to partisan politics or, perhaps more likely, a new party of conservatism (the Wildrose Party) will challenge Progressive Conservative dominance?

This chapter aims to answer these questions while deepening our understanding of the character of politics in Alberta in an era of neoliberalism. It offers an interpretation of the usefulness of the one-party state label and then explores the long-term political economic relations, social processes, and institutional mechanisms that preserve the power relations associated with a democratic one-party state. While rejecting the notion that Alberta is homogeneously conservative and devoid of progressive political voices, the chapter concedes that the province's community of progressive activists is small and limited in influence. Finally, the chapter concludes with speculation about the possibility that Alberta recently entered a period of change that could undermine the solidity of its one-party state politics or, possibly, see the Wildrose Party as Alberta's new "governing party" without significant alterations to the patterns of neoliberal one-party state politics.

A Democratic One-Party State?

In democratic contexts, the term *one-party state* identifies an electoral situation in which only one party has a realistic chance to win elections and form governments. Students of electoral politics and party systems often use the label "dominant party system" to avoid any suggestion that the system is undemocratic and authoritarian or has only one political party. In such contexts opposition parties continue to contest elections, but they are weak, ineffective, and command insufficient electoral support to threaten the governing party. As Evans and Smith show in their chapter, for forty-two years from 1943 to 1985 Ontario was also a dominant one-party system, with only the Progressive Conservative Party forming government. In Canada today, however, "Alberta stands out as in a class by itself as a genuinely one-party dominant system."[5]

The electoral dominance of a single party has long been a fact of political life in Alberta. The Social Credit Party governed without significant opposition from 1935 to 1971, and the PCs have formed majority governments since then. But the one-party state label should be taken to imply *more* than consistent electoral domination. In this chapter the term is used, first and foremost, to evoke notions of a melding of party and state, a situation in which the quality of democratic life is compromised by the fact that the elected legislature is marginalized and the governing party has the capacity to shape political discourse and popular understandings of the public interest. Yet the political economy of oil and gas extraction has also meant that relations between the government and the energy sector are characterized by a high degree of mutual dependence. Moreover, popular interpretations of politics and political news coverage tend to privilege a discursive framing of policy and governance that serves the political interests of the governing party *and* the material interest of those powerful social economic forces that are tightly connected to that party. As such, the social, political, and economic implications of one-party state politics extend well beyond the capacity of the governing party to win elections.

Perpetual electoral dominance leads to a sense of entitlement to govern and expressions of disdain for opposition parties and activists with alternative political agendas. Dominant parties tend to view the levers of power and institutions of the state as belonging to the governing party, and this makes it difficult to maintain the separation of public administration and partisan politics. In Alberta, wide swathes of politics (and sometimes even aspects of the public service) are imprinted with the partisan signifiers of the governing party. Over the past four decades the PC Party has left its mark on the public service and shaped Alberta's political culture in a manner that ensures the party's dominance is viewed as inevitable, even natural and legitimate.

In one-party states the governing party's policy agenda is socially and politically entrenched as a hegemonic governing paradigm. When a governing paradigm is hegemonic it need not be actively imposed on the public. Even though critics will claim that governing policies are designed to serve the interests of the dominant party or powerful economic interests, these policies are widely perceived as being in the public's interest – it is as if the political and policy interests of the government and prominent economic actors are so widely embraced that they become internalized in the political consciousness of significant segments of the general population. As a result, policy challenges emanating from alternative political visions appear, by their very nature, to be narrow and lacking legitimacy. In Alberta, the political elite has propagated a powerful narrative about how, as a result of the significance of oil and gas extraction to the provincial economy, the core political interests of all citizens are defined by a shared interest in the profitable extraction of a single dominant commodity.[6] The power of this industry shapes the political narrative of the province, which enthusiastically acknowledges the fact that the Alberta political economy is what some call a "petro state." Challenging the policy agenda of Alberta's petro state or the dominance of oil and gas production is condemned as contrary to the political and economic interests of the *people* of Alberta.

In reality, hegemonic paradigms may not be as widely internalized as this characterization proposes. Often the views of the population are more diverse than suggested by popular images of a political community. There is evidence, for example, that Albertans' "identification with the energy industry may well be exaggerated."[7] But popular narratives often persevere in media and academic commentary, even in the face on contrary evidence. This has allowed Alberta's governing Conservatives to conceptualize the province as a politically homogeneous population – a perspective that appears to legitimize privileging the interests of the energy sector and governing in a manner that is often single-mindedly ideological. For two decades now, the governing ideology in Alberta has been neoliberalism, which, despite its nominal association with the progressive ideas of the social or welfare *liberalism* of the twentieth-century welfare state, is an ideological orientation that draws on classical pre-welfare-state liberal notions of individualism and free enterprise (see introductory chapter). In Canada, neoliberalism has been more fully embraced by nominally "conservative" parties (as in British Columbia, Saskatchewan, Ontario, Quebec, and most of Atlantic Canada). In Alberta, for example, neoliberalism has been manifested in recent Progressive Conservative governments' dogged commitment to highly profitable natural resource extraction, balanced budgets, flat and reduced taxes, unfettered markets, and shrinking of the role of government through privatization and deregulation. While this chapter will stress the importance of cautious, nuanced analysis that avoids over-simplification, it is argued that since the early 1990s, Alberta has been a neoliberal democratic one-party state governed by a Conservative political party.

Conservative Dominance and Alberta's
Neoliberal Revolution, 1971–2013

The election of Peter Lougheed's Progressive Conservatives in 1971 marked the end of a thirty-six-year Social Credit Party dynasty. While power was being transferred from one conservative party to another, the Lougheed PCs were a more modern and urban party. Moreover, as was typical of "progressive" conservatives in that era, Lougheed was more willing to use the powers of the state to achieve core policy objectives. Flush with rising provincial revenues from an unprecedented boom in the oil and gas sectors, the Lougheed governments of the 1970s modernized the machinery of government, expanded the public service, established new Cabinet decision-making processes, and invested in hospitals, education, social assistance, and social services. Furthermore, between 1973 and 1976, the Alberta government began to engage in what has been called interventionist "province building" – investing in economic initiatives and public works that benefited the province's business community and growing urban classes.[8] This included setting up the Alberta Energy Company, purchasing Pacific Western Airlines, providing equity investment in the giant Syncrude oil sands project, and establishing the Heritage Savings Trust Fund to invest surplus government revenues. When contrasted with that of other provinces, Alberta government spending was high, but plentiful resource revenues allowed Lougheed to ensure corporate taxes remained among the lowest in the country.

The political economic context of the 1970s allowed the Conservatives to engage in a form of market-friendly interventionism. Premier Lougheed deepened ties between his government and the energy sector, while also winning over more of the urban middle class and gaining new support in areas of Social Credit strength in rural and southern Alberta. As the energy sector boomed, the PCs averaged 60 per cent of the vote and over 90 per cent of legislative seats in the 1975, 1979, and 1982 elections. Assured of electoral victory, Lougheed came to define and dominate Alberta politics. Despite protests from opposition politicians who felt their capacity to access information and influence governing priorities was being undermined, Lougheed moved policymaking power from the legislature to Cabinet and the Premier's Office.[9] Also, while engaged in a series of political battles against federal energy and constitutional policies in the late 1970s and early 1980s, Lougheed portrayed himself as the sole representative of Albertan's collective political interests.

The positive economic conditions that made political life easy for the Lougheed Conservatives began to unravel in the 1980s. An economic recession and skyrocketing interest rates combined with declining oil prices and the federal government's National Energy Program weakened Alberta's economic and fiscal climate. In response, the Conservative government began to curtail its interventionism – public enterprises such as Pacific Western Airlines were privatized, and political attention turned to downsizing the public sector. By the time Don Getty replaced Lougheed as PC leader and premier in 1985, world oil and gas prices were plummeting. As boom turned to bust, natural resource revenues fell off, and by 1987 the provincial government recorded its first deficit since the early 1970s. The downside of a single-resource political economy was hitting home.

The Getty government struggled unsuccessfully to reduce expenditures while maintaining support for besieged economic sectors. But it was clear that a new "politics of scarcity and conflict" was replacing the "politics of plenty and consensus" that had benefited the governing PCs during the Lougheed era.[10] The Conservatives lost fourteen seats in the 1986 election, and two more in 1989. Between 1982 and 1989 the party fell from 62 per cent to 44 per cent of the popular vote. Within the governing party, unrest was brewing, and prominent Conservatives were openly challenging Getty's leadership as the Alberta Liberals were gaining in popularity under the leadership of former Edmonton mayor Laurence Decore. When Getty finally resigned as premier and party leader in 1992, the Conservatives still led in opinion polls, but there was considerable uncertainty about the solidity of Alberta's dominant party system. The Alberta Liberals were within striking distance of winning the next provincial election, and many political observers predicted the end of the Conservative dynasty. In fact, even after Ralph Klein replaced Getty as leader of the Alberta PC Party, the Liberal threat concerned Progressive Conservative strategists – no one anticipated Klein's capacity to change the political landscape in a way that further benefited the ruling Conservatives.

A one-time television journalist and former mayor of Calgary, Klein was relatively new to provincial politics when he became premier in 1992. Having proven himself a competent but not particularly distinguished environment minister, Klein's selection as party leader was rooted in strong backing from caucus colleagues, a campaign team that was very effective at selling new memberships and mobilizing support, and a promise of back-to-basics problem solving combined with a grass roots–oriented style of governance.[11] Yet nothing about Klein's ascendance to the leadership of the PC Party suggested that a new golden era of Conservative dominance was just over the horizon. Indeed, even though the Conservatives won the 1993 election, it was with a further reduced majority – and the Liberals were only five percentage points behind the PCs in popular vote. Over the next decade, however, Klein reasserted Conservative electoral dominance by first developing a unique personal rapport with a significant portion of Albertans, and then exploiting an economic boom cycle in the oil and gas sector to advance the notion that his Conservative government best understood the collective economic benefits associated with increasing the pace of natural resource extraction. As Klein's hold on power tightened, Conservative political messaging tied the political economy of resource extraction to economic growth, prosperity, and, importantly, the province's capacity to lead a neoliberal ideological revolution that would transform politics and governance in Alberta.

Neoliberalism is, as has been stated throughout the book, an ideological commitment to free enterprise and small government. As increasing numbers of nominally conservative politicians gravitated towards neoliberal policy prescriptions in the 1980s and 1990s, governments focused on rolling back government spending, cutting programs, deregulation, and privatization. For the neoliberals of the 1990s, a single fiscal policy goal – balanced budgets – dominated the policy agenda. But, as champions of individualism and self-reliance, neoliberals also promote an understanding of politics that privileges market identities and dismisses organized social interests and defenders of activist government as self-interested "special interests." To the extent that citizens came to understand themselves as consumers and taxpayers while viewing defenders of activist government as narrowly self-interested, neoliberal policies could be sold to Albertans as governance in the public interest. Critics of neoliberalism – including left-leaning policy think tanks, organized labour, and environmental groups concerned about the pace of carbon resources extraction – could thus be dismissed as "un-Albertan"; they simply failed to understand the neoliberal political economy of what the Klein government called the "Alberta Advantage."

Prior to assuming leadership of the Alberta PCs in 1992, Ralph Klein had shown little enthusiasm for a decisive neoliberal policy agenda. However, during his first months in power and in the lead up to the 1993 provincial election Klein sensed a desire for political change. He tapped into the neoliberal enthusiasm generated by the federal Reform

Party and reinvented himself and his party as Alberta's deficit slayers. In fact, Klein openly criticized the gratuitous spending of Don Getty's government and vowed to tackle the deficit "crisis" by abandoning the excesses of his predecessor.[12]

Following the 1993 provincial election, Ralph Klein set out to transform the substance and style of Alberta politics. The first pillar of Klein's revolution was shrinking the provincial state through strict budget controls and privatization. The second pillar was lower and flatter taxes. The third pillar was centralized political control and premier-centred politics.[13] Critics argued that Klein's fixation on unchecked expenditures was a misdiagnosis of government deficits that had actually been caused by low energy prices, economic recessions, and political decisions to flow subsidies to the corporate sector.[14] But Klein persevered. During his first mandate Klein oversaw dramatic cuts in health, social services, and environmental protection programs. His government privatized retail liquor sales and motor vehicle licensing, deregulated electricity markets, maintained low corporate tax and energy royalty rates, and in 2001 replaced Alberta's progressive income tax system with a 10 per cent across-the-board flat tax.

Just as important to the character of Alberta politics, Klein introduced Cabinet decision processes that further marginalized the legislature and concentrated power in the Premier's Office. Given Klein's capacity to dominate media coverage of provincial politics and develop a rapport with Albertans, concentrating power and personalizing provincial politics improved the Conservatives' electoral position. The Klein PCs won 52 per cent of the vote in 1997 and 62 per cent in 2001. Reflecting the extent to which Conservative victories were the result of Klein's personal popularity – and perhaps hinting at the extent to which political power had become concentrated in the Premier's Office – Klein began his 2001 victory speech with a very telling quip: "Welcome to Ralph's world."

Not long after the 2001 election, Klein's focus and enthusiasm began to wane. With the province experiencing another oil and gas boom, provincial revenues were increasing to unprecedented levels, deficits were a thing of the past, and annual surpluses had the province on track to retire its provincial debt by 2004. After a decade of single-minded deficit cutting and support for expanded oil and gas extraction, there was a sense that Klein's government lacked direction and purpose. In the 2004 provincial election Klein won another majority, but many of his traditional supporters simply stayed home, and support for his government declined to 47 per cent of the electorate. It was clear to most observers that it was time for another leadership change. After receiving support from a mere 55 per cent of delegates during a routine leadership review vote at a party convention, Ralph Klein sensed it was time to step down and that he must do so before it became even more apparent he was being pushed out of office. The Klein era came to its formal end in 2006 when Ed Stelmach was selected PC leader and premier. In power from 2006 to 2011, Stelmach showed himself to be more conciliatory and less interested in political control and premier-centred politics than Klein. But Stelmach failed to initiate significant changes to the focus or character of Alberta politics. While willing to explore the possibility of modest adjustments to resource royalty and tax regimes to ensure that Albertans received their "fair share" from energy development – a move that angered corporate players in the oil patch and many right-wing conservatives – Stelmach's view of the Alberta political economy precluded any moves to limit or manage the pace of resource extraction or pursue policy innovations that would differentiate his government from Klein's. Thus, continuity won out over change; Alberta retained premier-centred politics and an essentially unreformed approach to the political economy of energy, but with a weaker premier.

Stelmach's failure to provide decisive leadership or reinvent his party allowed discontent to grow within conservative political circles. The most striking result of this discontent was the 2008 founding of the Wildrose Alliance Party, a party that was more ideologically conservative than the PCs, more willing to champion neoliberal free market ideas, create space for socially traditional conservatism, and commit even more strongly to governing in support of the oil and gas sector. But even within Stelmach's own party, right-wing PC activists began to organize in favour of a reinvigorated commitment to something akin to the free market and small-government-oriented conservatism of Klein's 1990s neoliberal revolution. Indeed, it was a dispute over growing budget deficits between Stelmach and his ideologically driven minister of finance, Ted Morton, that precipitated Stelmach's 2011 decision to step down as premier and party leader.

The 2011 Progressive Conservative leadership race was an interesting and important one. The front-runner was a former Klein-era Cabinet minister, Gary Mar. Ted Morton ran as the candidate of the ideological right, essentially calling on the PCs to undermine the upstart Wildrose Party by outflanking them on their own ideological turf. Candidate Doug Horner encouraged party members to embrace the party's more "progressive" tradition, which is often characterized as a return to the politics of Peter

Lougheed. In the end, however, Alison Redford won the leadership by mobilizing more new members and earning the second-preference support of those members who supported candidates who were removed from the race during preferential balloting. Although initially labelled a "red Tory" and clearly unwilling to pursue an aggressive neoliberal agenda on issues such as privatization in funding and delivery of health-care services, Redford's leadership was never out of step with the Alberta Conservatives who governed before her. The political economy of oil and gas continued to be a prime determinant of government policy and priorities, and Redford steadfastly refused to consider reducing the provincial state's reliance on the resource sector by introducing a provincial sales tax or abandoning the flat tax introduced under Ralph Klein.

When Premier Redford called a general election for April 2012 it was clear she and her PC campaign team had their work cut out for them. The Wildrose Party and its leader, Danielle Smith, were rising in the polls, particularly in rural Alberta. There was a sense that after four decades of Conservative governments it was a time for change. Through much of the campaign Wildrose led the Conservatives in opinion polls. But as some of the more stridently social conservative Wildrose candidates captured media attention, moderate Albertans backed away from Smith and her party. With Redford articulating a more modern and cosmopolitan social perspective, the PCs stopped bleeding support to Wildrose. Although Conservative support fell to 44 per cent of the electorate – the lowest level since 1989 – the peculiarities of the vote split and the single-member plurality electoral system allowed Redford to win a substantial majority of legislative seats.

There was, for a time, a sense that Redford was reinventing the Conservatives as more urban and socially progressive. She came to power with surprisingly strong support from nurses, teachers and professors, and public servants. But much of that support slipped away as the Redford government attacked public-sector unions, took a hard line on teachers' salaries, and dramatically reduced post-secondary funding. Ironically, however, unchecked spending in other areas and a temporary decline in resource revenues ensured that fiscal conservatives were also frustrated with Redford, particularly since Wildrose – which was busy distancing itself from socially conservative policies and candidates – seemed significantly more committed to fiscal prudence and balanced budgets. To make matters worse, Redford's imperious leadership style and sense of entitlement – evidenced by personal spending on travel and accommodation – angered her caucus and, eventually, the public at large. As popular support plummeted and party fundraising faltered, a simmering caucus revolt forced Redford to resign as premier in March 2014. The contest to select a new PC leader (and premier) is only beginning as this chapter goes to press, but it is clear the next Conservative leader must cleanse the party of its accumulated sense of entitlement and respond intelligently to a partisan landscape in which the PCs' main rival (Wildrose) comes from the ideological right. Conservatives must refocus on preserving the one-party state politics that have kept them in power for over forty years.

Preserving the Power Relations of a One-Party State

Alberta has had two governing parties and eight premiers since 1935. Four of those premiers were transitional and less consequential to the character of provincial governance: Harry Strom (1968–71), Don Getty (1985–92), Ed Stelmach (2006–11), and Alison Redford (2011–14). The real political heavy weights were premiers William Aberhart (1935–43) and Earnest Manning (1943–68), who governed during the era of the Social Credit Party dynasty, and Peter Lougheed (1971–85) and Ralph Klein (1992–2006) of the Progressive Conservatives. It was these four premiers who did the most to shape Alberta's dominant party system and cement the one-party state. But strong and popular political leadership is not enough to sustain the politics of a one-party state. To understand the unique character of Alberta politics we must explore the ways in which the province's one-party state is sustained and perpetuated by a series of power relations embedded in established political economic linkages, social processes, and institutions. Alberta is a socially complex and democratic province, so caution must be exercised to avoid oversimplified analysis or overstating the extent to which the province's politics is an example of the pure form of a democratic one-party state. The label is apt, but the analysis to follow seeks to avoid exaggerated stereotypes. The goal is to deepen our understanding of the factors that have helped to preserve the power relations of one-party state politics, particularly since Peter Lougheed won power and established Alberta's Progressive Conservative dynasty.

Party, State, and Powerful Economic Interests

Political economists have long agreed that business interests are in a privileged position when it comes to influencing governments. State policymakers know that political stability and government finances depend on business confidence and a strong economy. This reality is never truer than in the context of a single-commodity, resource-dependent economy like Alberta's. For decades oil and gas extraction has been the motor that drives the Alberta economy. The energy sector directly accounts for approximately 27 per cent of the provincial GDP and contributes significantly to the vitality of other sectors of the economy. A recent study estimates that without the cumulative impact of the oil and gas sector over the past fifty years, the Alberta economy would be less than half its current size.[15] Governments and citizens alike are aware that low taxes and government spending are made possible by booms in Alberta's resource economy. The 2012 provincial budget indicates that fully 28 per cent of government revenue came directly from non-renewable resources. It is also widely known that despite substantial variation – often due to fluctuating commodity prices – Alberta has regularly led the nation in GDP, population, and employment growth. What is less well understood is that although Alberta's unemployment rate is approximately 2 per cent below the national average and incomes are, on average, nearly 15 per cent above the national average, Alberta has higher levels of income inequality than other provinces.[16]

Yet polling suggests that Albertans caught in low-waged work or otherwise feeling squeezed by economic circumstances tend to believe they are an exception to a broader pattern in which resource-led economic growth is improving standards of living.[17] Thus, when the economy cycles from boom to bust, the collective mind focuses on responding to what the energy sector says is required to kick-start another boom. The politics of economic policy becomes less about alternative ideas and policy choices than it is about the economic elite of the energy sector, governments, and much of the public getting behind a policy agenda in support of accelerated oil and gas extraction. This political economic equation empowers the corporate elite of the oil patch, while creating the perception that the political interests of the governing party and the public mirror the economic interests of the oil and gas sector. Moreover, by reinforcing the perceived legitimacy of the dominant party's agenda of supporting the oil and gas sector, this political economic equation also sustains the politics of Alberta's one-party state.

Even though Alberta's Conservative governments have talked a lot about diversifying the provincial economy, there has been little agreement on what that means, and even less on how this goal could be achieved.[18] For decades the oil and gas sectors have attracted more capital investment than other sectors (ranging from 24 to 43 per cent).

This pattern of investment stimulates supporting and supplying industries but does little to alter the extent to which the fate of the provincial political economy is tied to the boom-bust cycle of energy resources. The Alberta political economy is as energy-centred today as it was in Lougheed's era – Alberta remains a petro state in which government priority setting is dominated by concern for the future of the oil and gas sectors. As such, when questions are raised about the social or environmental consequences of resource extraction, Alberta's political elite feel personally challenged, as if the very legitimacy of the provincial state – even the provincial identity – had been disputed. Having become a champion of the notion that Albertans share a material interest in supporting oil and gas extraction, Alberta's Conservative governments rarely rise above the politics and economics of resource extraction to consider broader social and environmental interests. Instead, the government aligns itself with the energy sector and assumes that those who raise concerns about the social or environmental impacts of oil and gas extraction are somehow engaged in anti-Albertan challenges to the provincial state.

In addition to the systemic or structural ways in which the political economy of oil and gas extraction reinforces Alberta's one-party state, there are also explicit and instrumental ties between the oil patch and the governing Conservatives. Powerful economic interests support the dominant party system through personal ties and financial support provided to the governing party. Peter Lougheed, Ralph Klein, and certain Alberta energy ministers were known to have informal "kitchen cabinets" of advisors from the energy sector. Furthermore, data from 1993 to 2003 reveal that political donations from large oil and gas companies favour the governing Conservatives over other parties by a ratio of more than 2:1.[19] Critics of the government have long argued that these material and instrumental ties between oil and gas interests and the governing party buttress the energy sector's privileged position in Alberta politics and governance.

A Compromised Parliamentary System

Parliamentary systems of government afford premiers and members of their Cabinets control over significant aspects of the legislative agenda, while also exercising executive power associated with the dispersal of government revenue and the implementation of government programs and legislative initiatives. Given this concentration of power, respect for the principle that the government of the day is permitted to govern only so long as it can maintain the confidence of the legislature is the cornerstone of parliamentary democracy. The legislature must have ample opportunity to review government-sponsored legislation, scrutinize the spending and activities of government departments, and hold the government to account for its policies and actions. For democracy to prevail, the premier, Cabinet, and central executive agencies must treat the processes, offices, and members of the legislative assembly with respect. In the context of Alberta's one-party state, however, the governing Conservatives do not take the functions of the legislature seriously. There is a long tradition of the government limiting the legislature's role, dominating legislative processes, and restricting the capacity of opposition members to play an effective role in Alberta's parliamentary system.

Two decades ago Leslie Pal commented on the extent to which Alberta's legislature was weak and marginalized: "The real debate and discussion over policy took place in caucus; the real decisions were made in cabinet."[20] Indeed, in 1975 Peter Lougheed struck a series of "legislative committees" within the governing party's caucus and began to empower backbench Conservative MLAs at the expense of opposition members of the legislature. The role of the legislature as a forum for public debate continued to decline through the 1980s and 1990s. The number of sitting days in legislative sessions was reduced, government ministers displayed strikingly dismissive attitudes towards opposition members during the daily question period, and the time allocated to the annual review of departmental spending estimates by the Public Accounts Committee was curtailed. Perhaps most frustrating to opposition members was the disbanding of all-party standing committees for reviewing legislation and studying public policy options. Critics claim these efforts to curtail opposition influence amount to a conscious strategy to compromise the quality of parliamentary democracy.[21]

In 1993 Ralph Klein established a series of standing policy committees (SPCs) to replace the legislative committees of caucus that had been created under Peter Lougheed. The SPCs were hybrid Cabinet committees that included Cabinet ministers and backbench Conservatives who were not formally members of Executive Council. Meeting in secret, these SPCs received executive briefings from public servants and heard representations from advocacy organizations, professional groups, and industry associations. As the most significant forum for debating new policy initiatives and scrutinizing proposed legislation, the SPCs created an institutionalized opportunity for backbench Conservatives to supplant the opposition parties and serve as a sort of informal (un)official opposition to the government of the day. These committees effectively replaced public debate in the legislature by involving Conservative MLAs in Cabinet decisions in a manner that blurred the distinction between legislative and executive functions. Given the power of SPCs and the marginalization of the legislature, John Williams, a former Conservative MP with an interest in democratic accountability, described the Alberta government under Ralph Klein as "executive government, not democratic government."[22]

Under pressure to address the democratic deficit, Ed Stelmach renamed the SPCs Cabinet policy committees (CPCs) – a more honest label. In a 2007 agreement worked out with the opposition Liberals and New Democrats, his government also agreed to re-establish an active role for all-party policy committees within the legislative assembly. At the same time, there was an agreement to enhance the power and capacity of the opposition-chaired Public Accounts Committee. These were potentially important democratic advances, but they have not had the impact that was hoped for. The tradition of government dominance of the legislature continues, as it is the government that determines whether legislation will be referred to an all-party policy committee or, alternatively, to the committee of the whole. Similarly, improvements in the functioning of the Public Accounts Committee have been limited. Indeed, at one point Conservative members of the committee threatened to undermine the significance of the tradition of having this committee chaired by an opposition member by requiring that all correspondence from the chair be co-signed by the Conservative vice-chair. After replacing Stelmach in 2011, premier Alison Redford disbanded the Cabinet policy committees and spoke of her desire to ensure the legislature and its committees have a fuller role in public policy debates. But during her time in power there was little evidence of the sort of culture shift among her caucus and Cabinet that were required to realize this goal. Thus, despite the Stelmach reforms and Redford's more democratic rhetoric, the manner in which the legislature functions continues to assist the preservation of Alberta's Conservative one-party state.

Centralization, Politicization, and the Executive Structure of Government

During the Social Credit era prior to 1971 the style of politics and the executive structure of government were thoroughly premier-centred. These were, in a very real sense, the governments of Aberhart and Manning. The melding of party and state was both real and personal. During the 1970s, Lougheed created Cabinet policy committees, modernized Cabinet decision-making, and restructured Alberta's executive central agencies. Following the federal government's example, Lougheed expanded the Premier's Office and built greater capacity in an Executive Council Office that could manage the affairs of Cabinet and offer government-wide leadership on implementation of the government's agenda. Political life and the government of Alberta remained very premier-centred, and the Lougheed Conservatives were not above political appointments to bureaucratic posts or acting as if the institutions of the state belonged to the governing party. But notwithstanding these centralizing features, Keith Brownsey contends that the distinction between partisan and bureaucratic executive functions was clearer in the context of Lougheed's "institutional" decision-making processes than it was under Social Credit governments.[23]

Under Ralph Klein the Alberta governance structure reverted to a simpler, non-institutional executive style. Authority was centralized in the Premier's Office, and partisan control reasserted so that the "distinction between the Executive Council Office and the Office of the Premier continued only on paper."[24] This led to questions about the politicization of Alberta's executive structure. Of course, politicization within the most senior reaches of government is not uncommon in Canada. Even after a century of efforts to safeguard the integrity of the public service through merit-based hiring and a commitment to non-partisanship, first ministers and their governments rightly retain the capacity to design the machinery of government, play a role in approving the appointment of deputy ministers, and ensure that the political executive is supported by an executive support structure appropriate to their approach to governance. Given this, vigilance is required to ensure the executive structures of government are not inappropriately politicized.

Alberta is probably no worse (or better) than many other jurisdictions in avoiding partisanship in the executive structure of government. In fact, under the leadership of Ron Hicks, Klein's final deputy minister of executive council, an institutionalized executive style – including efforts to maintain the distinction between Executive Council and the Premier's Office – was re-established. An effort was also made to ensure the appointment of deputy ministers would be open, transparent, and free of partisanship. But the blurring of partisan politics and public administration is a recurring reality of governance in one-party states. The legitimate imperative for public servants to serve the government of the day is easily distorted, and the line between the partisanship of the governing party and the apolitical bureaucracy can be blurred by simple things, such as assumptions about the inevitability of the governing party remaining in power. But in Alberta there are also blatant cases of politics seeping into the bureaucracy. For example, shortly after the 2012 provincial election, the recently defeated MLA and agriculture minister, Evan Berger, was hired into a civil service post as senior policy adviser to the deputy minister of his former department. The deputy minister saw this as a perfectly acceptable hiring, despite Berger's refusal to rule out running for re-election and conflict of interest guidelines that forbid former ministers from accepting such contracts or benefits for a year after leaving their post.[25]

Not long after assuming the premiership, Stelmach reverted to something more akin to the post-institutional executive style of the Klein era. This did not immediately result in a significant intensification of the politicization of the bureaucracy, but, as is always the risk in a one-party state, it heightened the possibility that the executive structure of government would be used in the service of the partisan interests of the Conservative government. It is with this in mind that observers watched executive-level developments under Alison Redford very closely. The number of political staff in the Premier's Office increased dramatically, as did the size of the policy coordination unit of Executive Council (Cabinet Office). There were, moreover, indications that the Redford team was doing what it could to learn from the example of Stephen Harper in centralizing and politicizing issue and communications management.[26]

Media Relations and Public Affairs Management

In the late 1970s, when the Lougheed Conservatives were winning massive majorities and the legislative opposition was particularly weak, the publisher of the *Edmonton Journal* declared that major daily newspapers must support careful investigative journalism and be willing to serve as a sort of unofficial opposition to the government.[27] Twenty years later hardly a trace remained of this sort of approach to political journalism. During the recession of the early 1990s, investments in political news coverage were reduced, and the press gallery lost much of its gravitas as the more senior reporters covering Alberta politics moved on to new responsibilities. Moreover, the editorial policies at the *Edmonton Journal* and *Calgary Herald* took a decidedly conservative turn, and the right-leaning *Sun* newspapers and Corus Radio talk shows contributed to the emergence of a more government-friendly media environment.

As a former television news reporter, Ralph Klein understood the media. He and his powerful chief of staff, Rod Love, expanded the government's capacity to manage public affairs and worked to ensure the premier set the news agenda. While the legislature was in session, Klein participated in a daily media availability session that allowed him to deflect attention from the legislature's daily question period and set the political news agenda. As reporters came to rely on this regular access to the premier, political news coverage came to be as premier-centred as Klein's executive style. At the same time, Love transformed the province's Public Affairs Bureau (PAB) into a powerful media relations machine capable of protecting and furthering the political interests of the Conservative government.

The PAB was created in 1973 to provide information on government to Albertans. Its original mandate did not include media relations or political support to the government of the day, but the PAB gradually expanded into these roles. In 1992 Klein brought the PAB into Executive Council to ensure its reporting lines into the Premier's Office.[28] Through the 1990s the PAB's budget and staff expanded dramatically. In addition to the central PAB staff, each government department has a PAB-appointed communications director and small staff. Until 2012 these public servants were responsible for all aspects of public affairs, from media enquiries and news management, to speech writing and government advertising.

Nowhere in the Alberta government has the potential politicization of the public service been clearer than in the Public Affairs Bureau. PAB staff members are public servants, but until 2012 when Alberta Cabinet ministers first began to hire press secretaries onto their own personal political staff, they provided speech writing, media relations, and political messaging advice to ministers whose personal offices had very limited capacity in this area. Departmental communications directors work with their ministry's executive team and report to their deputy minister, but they are appointed by and also report to the PAB's managing director, who works within Executive Council and closely with the Premier's Office. This structure allows for improved coordination of political messaging and media relations. But the centralization of news and information management, and the close relationship between the PAB and the Premier's Office convinced observers such as Jonathon Rose that the Public Affairs Bureau was little more than the "propaganda arm of the government designed to support the political actions of the Alberta premier and his cabinet."[29]

Under Alison Redford there was at least as much emphasis put on centralizing communications and political message control as in the past. But the 2012 decision to have press secretaries on the personal political staff of Cabinet ministers has clarified the separation of the political communications function of ministers' offices from the role of communications staff in the Alberta public service. Optimists hoped this move was made in recognition of the inappropriateness of allowing the government to rely on a large bureaucratic infrastructure with an annual budget of over $14 million rather than locating speech writing and political messaging functions in the offices of the premier and her ministers. But critics suggest that the creation of the press secretary role was motivated by a desire for *more* political control of messaging. Thus, it may be too early to know whether Alberta's Public Affairs Bureau – particularly its central offices in Executive Council – will step back from its role in shaping political debate and buttressing Alberta's one-party state model of governance.

Apathy, Fear, and the Political Culture of Consent

Building on the notion that Alberta is uniquely homogeneous and conservative, it is often argued that the province's one-party state politics are facilitated by a political culture that supports the Conservative government's neoliberal agenda and rejects the value and legitimacy of political opposition and dissent. There is evidence, however, that such assumptions are misplaced. In her analysis of Alberta political culture, Doreen Barrie contends that the political values of Albertans are similar to those of Canadians in other provinces.[30] Stewart and Sayer agree. Their examination of public opinion on matters such as activist government, environmental protection, and public funding for health care reveal that Albertans are not uniquely or especially conservative.[31] Opinions vary, and many Albertans hold views that run contrary to Conservative government policy.

Why then the lack of political dissent? The answer lies in an examination of apathy and fear. Dennis Soron is adamant that one-party dominance should not be understood as resulting from political enthusiasm or ideological unanimity. He contends that Albertans acquiesce because they are disengaged and de-politicized.[32] Years of neoliberal one-party state politics has marginalized the legislative opposition, limited the scope of democratic participation, and privatized social relations to an extent that citizens are naturally apathetic and politically inefficacious.

Neoliberalism emphasizes personal initiative and private sector solutions, while downplaying the importance of politics and essentially depoliticizing the issues associated with the democratic deficit in a one-party state. Thus, it is unsurprising that voter turnout in Alberta is extremely low (turnout dipped as low as 41 per cent in 2008, then rebounded to the still low rate of 57 per cent in 2012). There is little sense that the character of provincial politics will change through political engagement. Albertans, Soron suggests, offer little more than disinterested acquiescence to the governing agenda of the Conservatives.

But many political observers tell a darker story; they argue the lack of political dissent in Alberta is the result of fear and intimidation. While the stories are often difficult to validate, it has been claimed that government MLAs and ministers regularly make it clear to school boards, municipal administrators, social services providers, and others that their funding could be threatened and their access to government denied if they publicly challenge government policy.[33] One small-town mayor and former Progressive Conservative MLA claims there is "a culture whereby most municipalities will not be critical for fear it will come back to haunt them."[34] Stories abound of organized interests being warned to refrain from criticism and not affiliate with vocal opponents of the government. The head of the Alberta Federation of Labour, for example, claims that in his first meeting with Alberta's employment minister he was told "good things would happen" if he stopped criticizing the government in the media. He continued to criticize, and the minister refused to meet with him thereafter.[35] The executive director of the Alberta Council of Women's Shelters reports that she received a dressing down from a senior official when word leaked of her plan to speak at an event organized by a vocally critical public interest advocacy group.[36] Even the conservative-minded Canadian Association of Oilwell Drilling Contractors found itself in receipt of a sharply worded letter from the Alberta energy minister when it invited the leader of the Wildrose Party to address its annual Anniversary Luncheon in 2010.[37]

Although it is difficult to measure the impact of fear and intimidation on the preservation of Alberta's one-party state, an active observer of provincial politics cannot help but be struck by the regularity of news stories on this theme. When the chief medical officer at the Palliser Region Health Authority spoke out in favour of the Kyoto Protocol in 2002, he was fired. In 2007 Alberta's Energy and Utilities Board hired private investigators to pose as disgruntled landowners and infiltrate a citizens' group that had lawfully organized to oppose a new 500,000-volt power line at public hearings. In 2011 an Edmonton-area lawyer engaged in challenges to provincial land use legislation claiming that the Conservative government is more interested in loyalty than active public discussion of policy issues. He contends there is a "culture of fear" in rural Alberta that makes it difficult to challenge the priorities of the province's one-party state.[38] In 2012, Alison Redford's minister of municipal affairs wrote the president of the Alberta Urban Municipalities Association (AUMA) chastising her for criticizing the government's provincial budget and informing her that as a result of this open criticism he and his Cabinet and caucus colleagues would be boycotting the AUMA's annual political breakfast meeting. These examples, and others, contribute to the notion that a culture of intimidation contributes to silencing opposition to the Conservative government.

It is clear that a full and careful analysis of Alberta's neoliberal one-party state cannot rest on simplistic depictions of the province as an inherently homogeneous and conservative political culture that actively supports the governing Progressive Conservatives. Political economic realities, social forces, and institutional mechanisms combine to preserve the power relations of one-party state politics. The unique situation of a political economy dominated by a single commodity deepens the ties between government and a single economic elite, while also creating the impression that the economic interests of the oil and gas sector are shared by all Albertans. The province's compromised legislative system, its highly centralized and sometimes politicized executive structure of government, and very effective media relations and public affairs management all favour the continued dominance of the governing party. Finally, the active silencing of opposition through intimidation combines with the reality of an apathetic and inefficacious electorate to create an overstated impression of public support for the governing party's policy agenda. There has often been considerable support for the governing PCs, but it is a mistake to ignore the reality of ideological diversity and currents of political dissent.

Political Dissent and the Future of Alberta's One-Party State

The form and character of political dissent in Alberta began to change about a decade ago, first on the ideological right, and then on the left. In the 2004 general election the PCs' share of the total vote dropped by 15 per cent. While many disaffected Tories simply opted not to vote, a significant number threw their support behind the upstart Alberta

Alliance Party, giving this new right-wing challenger 8.7 per cent of the vote and its first seat in the legislature. In 2008 the Alberta Alliance merged with another right-wing party (the Wildrose Party) to form the Wildrose Alliance Party. The Wildrose Alliance Party (now known simply as the Wildrose Party) soon developed into a well-organized and effectively led partisan advocate of a revitalized neoliberal agenda. On the left there have been initiatives ranging from calls for greater cooperation between the Liberals and NDP, to the creation of the Alberta Party as a centrist advocate of a more progressive form of public interest politics. This chapter concludes with a brief examination of these developments and the possibility Alberta has entered a period of change that could eventually undermine the solidity of one-party state politics.

The Wildrose Party's Challenge to the Conservative One-Party State

When the Alberta Alliance challenged the PCs in 2004, there was a growing sense that premier Ralph Klein was out-of-touch, autocratic, and no longer committed to the neoliberal principles that had guided him over the previous decade. Many Alliance supporters felt some allegiance to the PC brand but could no longer support the party under Klein's leadership. In fact, when Klein succumbed to pressure to resign in 2006, the leader of the Alberta Alliance encouraged party members to (re)join the PCs and support Ted Morton, the right-wing leadership candidate viewed as most likely to recommit to a decisively neoliberal agenda.

The fact that Ed Stelmach won the leadership disappointed both Alliance supporters and the more deeply conservative Tories. Of particular concern was the fact that Stelmach seemed to have bought into the argument that the existing structure of energy royalties and taxation of the oil and gas sector was too generous to energy companies and failed to collect Albertan's fair share of the wealth generated by the province's abundant natural resources. It was no surprise then that the ideological right attacked Stelmach for appointing an expert panel to make recommendations on changes to the royalty and tax regime. What did surprise observers was the aggressiveness of the energy sectors' attacks on Stelmach's 2007 proposal for modest changes to energy royalties and taxes. Frustrated as much by their apparent loss of influence as by the content of the policy, key players in the energy sector turned on the PCs and supported political change by financially supporting the founding of the Wildrose Party.

Although Wildrose was ill prepared for the 2008 provincial election, the party soon matured into a real electoral threat. In 2009 the party won a Calgary by-election, selected the articulate and media-savvy Danielle Smith as party leader, and celebrated public opinion polls that, for the first time, put Wildrose ahead of the governing Conservatives. Then, in 2010, three PC MLAs – including two former Cabinet ministers – crossed the floor to sit as Wildrose members. Sensing mounting political pressure, Stelmach reversed several aspects of his 2007 royalty and tax regime and worked to repair his government's frayed relationship with the oil and gas sector. But Stelmach never fully recovered. The ideological right remained sceptical, and Stelmach seemed unable to alter negative views of him and his government. Thus, when Stelmach resigned in 2011, the dominant issue in the leadership race was how to undermine Wildrose's momentum. Ted Morton championed recommitting to a more right-wing conservatism, but he failed to win even the level of support he had in 2006. Instead, PC Party members elected Alison Redford, who advocated a more "progressive" conservatism and the building of a more centrist electoral coalition.

In the 2012 election, Redford held the Wildrose to 34 per cent of the vote and seventeen seats by positioning herself as a modern centrist committed to a more urban and cosmopolitan conservatism. She also successfully portrayed Danielle Smith as a right-wing extremist who embraced socially conservative views that most Albertans were unwilling to embrace. But Redford soon lost control of the discursive framing of Alberta politics. Wildrose has shed much of its socially conservative baggage while successfully characterizing the Conservatives as being irresponsible and politically entitled after too long in power. By the time of Redford's resignation in 2014, Wildrose was again well ahead in opinion polls, and the future of the governing Conservatives and the solidity of the province's one-party state was on shaky ground. It remains to be seen whether the next PC leader can rescue Alberta's long-term governing party from defeat.

The Potential Dynamism of Progressive Political Dissent

One point of this chapter has been to argue that Alberta is not as homogeneously conservative as stereotypes suggests. Indeed, Alberta has a progressive left-leaning political community that is, in many ways, similar to what is found in other provinces. The Alberta Federation of Labour and several prominent unions and professional associations – particularly the United Nurses of Alberta, the Health Sciences Association, and the Alberta Teachers Association – are actively engaged in provincial political advocacy. They are supported by progressive think tanks such as the Parkland and Pembina Institutes. The Council of Canadians is active in the province, as are the Sierra Club and Green-peace. Women's groups, LGBTQ activists, and non-profit social service agencies are politically engaged in many Alberta communities, and at the provincial level Friends of Medicare and Public Interest Alberta have become prominent voices for progressive policies and strengthened public services.

What is unique about Alberta is the extent to which progressive organizations and social interests have been marginalized and excluded from mainstream politics by the processes that reinforce Alberta's one-party state. Progressive voices are regularly denied access to government and sometimes openly attacked by the governing party. The Klein years were particularly tough for left-leaning activists. Indeed, for a time there was a sense that activism was futile and, as a result, mobilizing new, particularly younger recruits to progressive causes was difficult. Centrist and left political parties experienced similar frustrations, as supporters believed an electoral breakthrough was nearly impossible.

The 2004 election was a low point for Alberta progressives. Even though Klein's personal popularity had dropped and there was considerable evidence that Albertans were less than enthusiastic about their government, the PCs won another majority. Over the next few years progressive Albertans engaged in a lot of soul searching. Then, as the rise of the Wildrose was destabilizing the ideological right, there were a number of interesting developments on the centre-left of partisan politics in Alberta. Among them were the Democratic Renewal Project (DRP) and Reboot Alberta. The DRP's initial goal was to orchestrate a formal electoral coalition that would have Liberals and New Democrats sign a non-competition agreement to ensure that just one progressive candidate would run in each electoral district. Despite some high-profile support within the Liberal Party, this initiative failed and the DRP has since turned its attention to the more limited goal of encouraging strategic voting in provincial elections. During 2009 and 2010, Reboot Alberta brought together a number of disaffected red Tories and centre-left supporters of the Liberals and New Democrats to engage citizens in defining a new progressive agenda for the province. Concrete results were few, but there was a sense that centrist and progressive Albertans were coming together in unprecedented ways and laying the foundations for future collaboration. The partisan landscape was unaltered, but it was clear for the first time in decades that efforts were afoot to lay the foundations for new approaches to advancing progressive agendas in partisan politics.

Perhaps the most ambitious initiative was the 2010 launch of the Alberta Party, a centrist alternative that organizers hoped would succeed where the Liberals and New Democrats had failed. Although the Alberta Party gained a member in the legislature when a sitting Liberal MLA crossed the floor, and it managed to attract the popular mayor of Hinton, Glenn Taylor, as its first leader, the new party failed to win a seat in the 2012 election and now faces an uncertain future. With few New Democrats wanting to cooperate with a more centrist partisan grouping, and Alberta Liberals struggling to survive under the shaky leadership of a former PC MLA, the Alberta Party may represent nothing more than a further splintering of progressive partisan voices. All the same, the fluidity on the partisan centre-left suggests there is potential for new partisan formations or alliances, should the governing Tories falter under their next leader. If the Wildrose seems destined to govern and the PCs cannot shake the perception they are tired and entitled, it is difficult to predict which party would be best positioned to win the support of Albertans who are unwilling to support Wildrose.

While progressive partisans have yet to have anything like the impact the Wildrose has had on partisan politics, other efforts to advance left-leaning public interest politics are having some success. Environmental and social justice activist organizations are more vibrant than they have been for some time. The Pembina Institute's research on sustainable energy and environmental protection plays an increasingly significant role in public policy debates. The once vilified Parkland Institute's research into progressive policy alternatives is gaining increased attention and legitimacy in the media. And Public Interest Alberta has brought new focus and dynamism to advocacy in favour of strengthened public services. Moreover, the victories of the centre-left mayoralty candidates in Calgary (Naheed Nenshi in 2010) and Edmonton (Don Iveson in 2013) are evidence of an inchoate longing for political change that, perhaps, progressive forces can take advantage of at the provincial level. None of this is equivalent to the rise of Wildrose; however, it does suggest progressive politics is considerably more vital in Alberta than suggested by popular portrayals of the province as homogeneously conservative.

Conclusion

After four decades of single-party dominance, Alberta stands alone as Canada's only democratic one-party state. It is a mistake, however, to explain Alberta's uniqueness with reference to myths about the province's homogeneously conservative – òr Progressive Conservative – population. There is more ideological diversity in Alberta than is often assumed, and even the province's left-leaning progressive community is not dissimilar to those in other provinces. Thus, understanding Alberta's one-party state requires analysis that de-emphasizes ideology and political culture, and focus instead on the character of the provincial political economy and the unique configuration of social forces and institutional mechanisms that preserve the power relations of one-party state politics. This chapter has explored how a political economy dominated by a single commodity, a compromised legislative system, highly centralized and sometimes politicized executive structure of government, very effective media relations and public affairs management, and sometimes voter apathy and political intimidation can buttress the power of the governing party and create overstated impressions of public support for the governing party's policy agenda.

With well-entrenched political economic, social, and institutional forces favouring continued one-party dominance, political change is difficult to achieve. Yet there is considerable evidence of transformation on the ideological right and left of Alberta politics. As of spring 2014, Wildrose leads in public opinion polls. Moreover, the sense of tiredness and entitlement that hangs over the Progressive Conservatives seems both new and significant. There are parallels to 1993 when Don Getty resigned and Ralph Klein stepped in to rejuvenate Alberta's Conservative one-party state. This could happen again. If, however, the Wildrose Party wins the next provincial election, the Tory dynasty could come to an end. The result might be something akin to a two-party or multi-party system. However, if Progressive Conservatives fail to rebuild and implode in the context of Wildrose electoral success, we may witness little more than a change at the helm of Alberta's neoliberal one-party state. The melding of party and state, the compromising of democratic life, and the high degree of mutual dependence between government and the energy sector may continue. The one-party state is sustained and perpetuated by a series of power relations embedded in established political economic relations, social processes, and institutions. Given how many of the key backers of Wildrose were once Alberta Tories, Danielle Smith and her party may be well placed to establish a new conservative dynasty, just as the PCs did when Albertans threw the Social Credit out of power in 1971.

NOTES

1 This chapter benefited from the willingness of several individuals to participate in research interviews: Ricardo Acuna and Diana Gibson of the Parkland Institute, Larry Booi and Bill Morre-Killgannon of Public Interest Alberta, David Eggen of Friends of Medicare, and Sheila Pratt of the *Edmonton Journal*.
2 Jeffrey Simpson, "End of a Dynasty: Conservative Ferment Is Fertile Soil for Wildrose," *Globe and Mail*, 22 January 2010.
3 Sheila Pratt, "Social Media Gang Hopes to Reboot Democracy in Alberta: Growing Groups of Disenchanted Red Tories, Frustrated Liberals Try to Fill the Centre-Left Vacuum," *Edmonton Journal*, 7 March 2010.
4 Mark Lisac, *Alberta Politics Uncovered: Taking Back Our Province* (Edmonton: NeWest, 2004), 4.
5 David K. Stewart and R. Kenneth Carty, "Many Political Worlds? Provincial Parties and Party Systems," in *Provinces: Canadian Provincial Politics,* ed. Christopher Dunn (Peterborough: Broadview, 2006), 105.
6 Gurston Dacks, "From Consensus to Competition: Social Democracy and Political Culture in Alberta," in *Socialism and Democracy in Alberta,* ed. Larry Pratt (Edmonton: NeWest, 1986), 187–90.
7 David K. Stewart and Anthony M. Sayers, "Alienated and Conservative? Continuity and Change in Alberta Political Culture" (paper presented at the Annual Meeting of the Canadian Political Science Association, Concordia University, Montreal, 2 June 2010).
8 Larry Pratt, "The State and Province-Building: Alberta's Development Strategy," in *The Canadian State: Political Economy and Political Power,* ed. Leo Panitch, 133–64 (Toronto: University of Toronto Press, 1977).
9 Ron Chalmers, "Insults to Democracy during the Lougheed Era," in Pratt, *Socialism and Democracy in Alberta*, 172–85.
10 Peter J. Smith, "Alberta: Experiments in Governance – From Social Credit to the Klein Revolution," in *The Provincial State in Canada: Politics in the Provinces and Territories,* ed. Keith Brownsey and Michael Howlett (Peterborough, ON: Broadview, 2001), 291.
11 David Stewart, "Klein's Makeover of the Alberta Conservatives," in *The Trojan Horse: Alberta and the Future of Canada,* ed. Trevor Harrison and Gordon Laxer, 24–47 (Montreal: Black Rose Books, 1995).

12 Stewart, "Klein's Makeover of the Alberta Conservatives."

13 Lisac, *Alberta Politics Uncovered*, 22–3.

14 Kevin Taft, *Shredding the Public Interest: Ralph Klein and 25 Years of One-Party Government* (Edmonton: University of Alberta Press, 1997).

15 Robert L. Mansell and Ron Schlenker, "Energy and the Alberta Economy: Past and Future Impacts and Implications," paper 1 (Calgary: Alberta Energy Future Project of the Institute for Sustainable Energy, Environment and Economy at the University of Calgary, 15 December 2006).

16 Dan Schrier, "Mind the Gap: Income Inequality Growing," *Business Indicators* 12, no. 1 (January 2012): 1–4.

17 Diana Gibson, research director, Parkland Institute, University of Alberta, interview with author, 15 March 2010.

18 Allan Tupper, Larry Pratt, and Ian Urquhart, "The Role of Government," in Pratt, *Socialism and Democracy in Alberta*, 31–66.

19 Trevor W. Harrison, "The Best Government Money Can Buy? Political Contributions in Alberta," in *The Return of the Trojan Horse: Alberta and the New World (Dis)Order*, ed. Trevor W. Harrison (Montreal: Black Rose Books, 2005), 101.

20 Leslie Pal, "The Political Executive and Political Leadership in Alberta," in Pratt, *Socialism and Democracy in Alberta*, 21.

21 Kevin Taft, *Democracy Derailed* (Calgary: Red Deer, 2007).

22 Sheila Pratt, "Meaningful Debate Hard to Find in Alberta's Alleged Democracy," *Edmonton Journal*, 9 October 2005.

23 Keith Brownsey, "The Post-Institutionalized Cabinet: The Administrative Style of Alberta," in *Executive Styles in Canada: Cabinet Structures and Leadership Practices in Canadian Government*, ed. Luc Bernier, Keith Brownsey, and Michael Howlett, 208–24 (Toronto: University of Toronto Press, 2005).

24 Ibid., 213.

25 James Wood, "Hiring Defeated PC Minister an Act of Cronyism: Wildrose," *Calgary Herald*, 17 August 2012.

26 Mark Lisac, "One Year Later: A New Style of Governing," *Insight into Government: Alberta's Independent Newsletter on Government & Politics* 27, no. 9 (19 October 2012): 2. One of the closest observers of Alberta politics observed on the anniversary of Alison Redford's swearing in as premier that "centralized power has been a dominant theme in Redford's first year" in office.

27 Shannon Sampert, "King Ralph, the Ministry of Truth, and the Media in Alberta," in Harrison, *Return of the Trojan Horse*, 40.

28 Taft, *Democracy Derailed*, 105–6.

29 Charles Rusnell, "Premier Controls Information with Iron Fist," *Edmonton Journal*, 15 May 2004.

30 Doreen Barrie, *The Other Alberta: Decoding a Political Enigma* (Regina: University of Regina, Canadian Plans Research Center, 2006).
31 Stewart and Sayers, "Alienated and Conservative?"
32 Dennis Soron, "The Politics of De-Politicization: Neoliberalism and Popular Consent in Alberta," in Harrison, *Return of the Trojan Horse,* 65–81.
33 Rich Vivone, *Ralph Could Have Been a Superstar* (Kingston: Patricia Publishing), 105–20.
34 Ernie Isley, cited in Sheila Pratt, "The Fear Factor in Alberta Politics," *Edmonton Journal,* 24 April 2011.
35 Sheila Pratt, "How the Code of Silence Works," Edmonton Journal blogs, 5 May 2011, http://blogs.edmontonjournal.com/2011/05/05/how-the-code-of-silence-works/.
36 Larry Booi, president, Public Interest Alberta, interview with author, 3 March 2010.
37 Pratt, "Fear Factor in Alberta Politics."
38 Sheila Pratt, "You Are with Us or against Us," *Edmonton Journal,* 24 April 2011.

10 British Columbia: Right-Wing Coalition Politics and Neoliberalism

DENNIS PILON

Introduction

British Columbia was arguably the first province in Canada to experiment with neoliberal reforms. It was the province's pioneering "restraint" program of 1983, introduced by the just re-elected Social Credit government, where all the familiar themes of neoliberal rhetoric were first paraded before Canadians: austerity, public-sector wage restraint, program cuts, balanced budgets, privatization, deregulation, and attacks on unionized workers. At the time, Stan Persky argued it was "the most sweeping and ideologically extreme program to be visited upon a North American jurisdiction."[1] Philip Resnick claimed that under "restraint" the "provincial government committed itself to a program of rollback in government activity the likes of which postwar Canada has never known."[2] And Rand Dyck suggested that in its execution of the restraint program, the BC government was "generally more extreme than that practiced by U.S. president Ronald Reagan or British Prime Minister Margaret Thatcher."[3]

With hindsight, we now know that this early period of reforms in BC represented only the rollback phase of neoliberal restructuring, focusing primarily on cuts to public-sector wages, employment, government programs, and regulations related to those policy areas. The rollout phase of neoliberalism, the one that would author a fundamental restructuring of the province's political economy, would have to wait nearly two decades to be fully implemented. The reasons for the delay were political, reflecting a fractured and competitive political dynamic in the province that was deep and abiding, despite appearances to the contrary.

Politics in British Columbia has long been defined by successive struggles to craft and maintain a winning coalition on the right to marginalize the province's class-based political left. Early on, the weakness of the left allowed provincial Conservative and Liberal parties to either ignore them or take their support for granted. With the emergence of a stable and electorally popular political party of the left in the 1930s, however, the dynamics of political competition in the province changed considerably. Since then, the centre-right in BC has dominated elections and the government benches, winning eighteen of the twenty-one elections between 1941 and 2013. But such dominance has not been produced automatically. It has required the concerted effort of political and economic elites to actively fashion a winning coalition, either between different parties or within a single party. Despite their winning record, the centre-right have often struggled to contain the contradictory elements of their necessary coalition. Whenever they have failed, the results have been unpredictable, allowing either a new political party to emerge (Social Credit in 1952, BC Liberals in 1991) and/or the left to gain power (NDP in 1972, 1991, and 1996). Thus, despite their apparent dominance, the right in BC remain beholden to multiple and sometimes antagonistic constituencies, somewhat limiting their ability to act decisively on matters that might affect any component of the coalition. Such political machinations affected the timing of neoliberal transformations in the province.

This chapter will demonstrate how furthering neoliberalism in BC has required a fundamental realignment of political forces within the broad coalition of the political right. This will be accomplished by reviewing the province's historic party and state systems and paying particular attention to the most recent Social Credit, NDP, and Liberal eras of government.

BC's Historic Party and State System

Accounts of BC politics often highlight its freewheeling frontier populism, ideological polarization, and, more recently, rising importance of so-called post-material issues (e.g., social rights claims and the environment).[4] Yet when we turn to BC elections, the key opening to state power for rival parties has consistently pivoted on just one dimension: the electoral threat from the left, specifically how a left government might reconstruct the economy of the province.[5] Why has the left appeared so threatening to its opponents? Because BC's party system has been less than stable since its origins in the nineteenth and early twentieth centuries. Indeed, since 1903 BC politics has been defined largely by the challenges inherent in establishing and maintaining different political coalitions for office. Prior to 1933, both Liberal and Conservative coalitions struggled to maintain their shape, with the former challenged by labour and the latter by rural and farmer interests in different periods.[6]

With the arrival of the Cooperative Commonwealth Federation (CCF), the coalition making challenges shifted, and Liberals and Conservatives struggled to dominate but retain a non-left electoral and governing coalition. This movement received particular impetus with the results of the 1941 election, when the CCF came first in the popular vote, followed by the other two main parties. From 1941 to 1951 a Liberal-dominated coalition of the two right parties ruled, replaced in 1952 by an arguably rural conservative–dominated coalition in the form of Social Credit. But Social Credit could never secure the urban portion of the non-socialist vote, which remained with the remaining Liberal MLAs. Only the election of the NDP in 1972 finally forced a real coalition of the two major federal forces, which emerged with a renewed Social Credit in 1975 that had absorbed the urban Liberals. But this new coalition was destabilized under the leadership of Bill Vander Zalm and ultimately fell apart in 1991. A new centre-right coalition tried to form behind a rejuvenated Liberal Party but struggled to absorb the residual non-lower-mainland centre-right vote. This challenge cost the Liberals the 1996 election. By 2001 the centre-right coalition was put back together, though with a much-weakened rural contingent.

Analysing these processes over time, it is clear that the business-friendly forces in the province have consistently constructed a centre-right coalition and prevented the centre from shifting into alliance with the left. They have done this through a number of means: development decisions, institutional safeguards, and strong support in civil society. Yet their dominance could never simply be assured. An effective centre-right majority required careful attention to the different elements of the coalition, both corporate and small business, urban and rural, as well as a selective poaching of popular policies from the left. Though the character of the right and left coalitions has changed over time, its broad contours and competitive position has remained remarkably constant.

What is striking about BC experience historically is the important role of regionalism as a challenge for the centre right. From 1941 to the mid-1980s this was managed through government-directed aid and investment in regional economic development. With the rise of neoliberalism, combined with changes to the rurally biased electoral map, this pact between Howe Street (BC's version of Bay Street) and Main Street came under strain. A neglected area of concern in this period has been the impact of federal competitive pressures on the BC scene.[7] However, with the shift of the federal Liberals towards neoliberal economic policies in the 1990s, and the split of the traditional federal right along populist and social conservative lines, the pressures eased somewhat.[8] Today's centre-right coalition in BC still faces some regional challenges, but their impact within the coalition has weakened considerably.

Another distinctive factor in BC has been the centre-left's apparent inability to shift centrist support over to their camp, as New Democrats appear to have done in Saskatchewan (chapter 8), Manitoba (chapter 7), and briefly in Nova Scotia (chapter 3). Stuck at around 42 per cent of the popular vote, the BC NDP seems to come to power only when the centre-right vote spreads across more than one party. The shift of former Liberal leader Gordon Wilson over the NDP in the late 1990s suggested that some Liberal support could go left, but so far it has never been enough to allow the party to win a two-horse race.

The state in BC followed fairly conventional Canadian development patterns, coloured by the populist and class hues of its political competition from the 1930s on. A focus on patronage and resource exploitation gave way to more active, state-directed industrial strategies from the mid-1940s on, mirrored by a shift from a residual to more institutional welfare state. The Liberal-Conservative coalition government of the 1940s began investing in developing the province's interior and northern economy while introducing social programs like hospital insurance (only the second province to do so after Saskatchewan).[9] With the Social Credit government of the 1950s and 1960s, BC joined a host of federally sponsored shared-cost programs, including medicare, income supports for the poor and elderly, and the expansion of post-secondary education. But as Michael Prince notes, Social Credit (similar to Conservatives in Ontario) was not enthusiastic about expanding the government's capacity to either direct the province's economy or the social development of its citizens. As a right-wing populist party, Social Credit's biases tapped individual entrepreneurship and market-driven policies as the solution to most social problems.[10]

The dividing line in BC party competition and state development can be marked with the election of the NDP to government in 1972. Victory for the party made real what had been only a threat – at times real, at times empty – before. In the 1930s and 1940s perceived electoral support for the left moved governments of the right to promote jobs and social programs, even as they dragged their feet legislatively. The threat that the left would benefit from a vote split between competing former coalition partners even hastened the introduction of new voting system designed specifically to prevent that outcome.[11] But at other times, as throughout much of the 1960s, right-wing parties simply raised the "socialist bogey" as a convenient way to rally the troops and muddy discussions of substantive policy. The NDP election victory in 1972 dramatically altered the trajectory of provincial politics because as the province's right wing found itself outside the corridors of state power for the first time, the price of its own internal dissension became clear.

In power the NDP moved quickly to promote their agenda. They modernized the legislature and the public service while introducing a flurry of new policies. The party nationalized auto insurance, created an agricultural land reserve to protect the province's dwindling farmland, and raised income support for the poor and elderly. While the 1970s NDP policy mix was hardly radical when compared to other social democratic governments of the period, their drive and enthusiasm about what they were doing was shocking to the province's traditional media and political elites.[12] Very quickly after the party took power a relentless campaign of vilification began, sponsored by the province's business community and seemingly with the full support of the local media.[13] At the same time, midway through the government's mandate, the first great economic crisis of the post-war period began, slashing government revenues and creating competing pressures to both expand and cut government services. When the NDP stumbled from power in 1975, both the BC party system and the economic landscape were fundamentally changing. Managing the change would prove an unpredictable challenge for the province's right-wing political coalition.

The Modern Social Credit Era, 1975–91

Social Credit's return to power in 1975 witnessed a modernized but not radically reformed populist right-wing party. As one commentator noted, the old Social Credit regime was "a horse-and-buggy government largely run by one man, W.A.C. Bennett."[14] Bennett Jr modernized the party and the government, adopting up-to-date campaign methods, new Cabinet and policymaking structures, and paying lip service to "liberalizing" the party and moving it closer to the political centre.[15]

But the populist conservative philosophy of Social Credit remained the party's ballast, despite its temporary outreach to centrist Liberals. In fact, Bennett's centrism was tactical, designed to cement his winning coalition. But with each electoral victory, the need to placate the political centre seemed to diminish. By 1986, an academic study of the party demonstrated that members were still largely rural, anti-Vancouver, self-employed, and socially conservative.[16]

The "modern" Social Credit party won elections in 1975, 1979, 1983, and 1986, with each succeeding administration more conservative than the last. Bill Bennett's first government had proceeded cautiously after defeating the New Democrats for fear of alienating centrist voters. Their first order of business was discrediting the NDP government's financial record. In a novel move, the government hired an independent auditor to review the financial records and prepare a report. Though the report hardly damned the NDP, Bennett and a friendly media were largely successful in using it to shape public perceptions that the NDP had been poor fiscal managers. Beyond that, the government did not aggressively attempt to roll back what the NDP had accomplished in power. Social Credit did raise fees on auto insurance, BC ferries, and BC Hydro while also reducing a host of government services and attempting to revise parts of the NDP's union-friendly labour code. More surprisingly, the government established a provincial ombudsperson and auditor general.[17] Thus when the parties returned to electoral battle in 1979, the modern Social Credit's first term appeared somewhat temperate, even to unsympathetic observers.

The Social Credit victory in 1979 confirmed a two-party polarization of the electorate, with the NDP trailing by a mere 2 per cent of the popular vote.[18] In their second term Social Credit quickly became mired in scandals. First, reporters uncovered an ongoing "dirty tricks" campaign in which Social Credit party members were encouraged to write letters to the media under false names, either to praise the party or damn their critics. Then information came to light suggesting that high-ranking Cabinet minister Grace McCarthy may have attempted to improperly influence an electoral boundary commission to add more Socred supporters to her riding in 1978. These were followed by numerous allegations of improper influence, usually involving business interests getting special access to government contracts and decision-making.[19] Economically, the world economy continued to stagnate, tipping into a deep recession in the early 1980s. Social Credit's policy response tended towards mega-projects, with plans to revitalize Vancouver's harbours and build a stadium. But in 1982 the government introduced a "restraint" budget that cut government programs and placed limits on public-sector wage increases. The government strongly defended the budget, though it would back down on other initiatives, like Bill Vander Zalm's proposed reorganization of municipal government, or the strongly pro–Social Credit redistribution of provincial riding boundaries prepared in 1982.[20]

In May 1983 Social Credit was elected to a third term, again on a largely polarized vote between themselves and the NDP. The failure of the New Democrats to displace the Socreds despite poor economic times, government cutbacks, and numerous scandals emboldened Bennett to push further to the right, especially as the province's political centre seemed unable or unwilling to organize itself separately. In the July 1983 Social Credit budget, finance minister Hugh Curtis introduced a sweeping set of cuts, along with a host of bills that would fundamentally rewrite the province's post-war social contract. In this new version of "restraint," the government clearly sought to weaken the unionized public service and introduce what were then radical neoliberal policies like deregulation, privatization, contracting out, and user payment for government services. Organized opposition quickly arose in the form of the Solidarity Coalition, comprising community groups and public- and private-sector unions. Solidarity launched initiatives to mobilize public opinion against the cuts throughout the summer and in the fall scheduled escalating walkouts by sectors of the provincial workforce. The province seemed headed for a general strike when the premier was able to negotiate a cooling-off period and then a negotiated deal (the Kelowna Accord) with BC Federation of Labour president Art Kube and other labour leaders. In the end, however, Bennett managed to separate the private-sector workers from the public sector ones in the coalition, fatally weakening the opposition.[21]

From 1984 to 1986 the government operated on twin tracks economically: further cutbacks in the public service, while investing in megaprojects like stadiums, fairs, and highways. The 1984 provincial budget witnessed a 25 per cent reduction in the public-sector workforce, and in 1985 the government dismissed the Vancouver School Board for refusing to implement budget cuts. Meanwhile funds were readily found to build BC Place stadium, sponsor an international fair – Expo 86 – and build a new highway linking the premier's riding with the Lower Mainland. Yet the premier's hubris in imposing self-serving mega-projects and austerity budgets seemed to take a toll on the government, with polling numbers slipping in the spring of 1986.[22] When Bennett hastily announced his retirement in 1986, the party chose controversial ex-Cabinet minister Bill Vander Zalm as its leader. In the subsequent election Vander Zalm was able to lead his party to their fourth victory at the polls and push the party even further to the political right.

The inability of the New Democrats to defeat Social Credit in 1986 has been blamed on many things. Unlike Social Credit, the NDP's new leader, Bob Skelly, did not perform well in the media – many commentators credit him with the loss. But the media circus surrounding Bill Vander Zalm, both in the run-up to the leadership race and the election itself, was undoubtedly a factor in his party's resurrection in the polls. Vander Zalm smoothly characterized himself as the man that would lead the province away from its penchant for polarized confrontation. Why this seemed plausible, given his record in government, was hard to fathom. As the minister of human resources, Vander Zalm had called for a radical neoliberal reform of welfare, suggesting that all able bodied-men on welfare be given shovels. As minister of municipal affairs he had floated a reform package that would have stripped local government of much of its power. As minister of education, he had tried to gut the BC Teacher's Federation of any substantive role in the education system.[23] In fact, just about everywhere he went, Vander Zalm had a knack for polarizing opinion and alienating even his own allies. But his views did play well with a Social Credit membership base that often rankled at the compromises that seemed required of government.[24]

Ironically, Vander Zalm had campaigned on ending the confrontation that was seemingly endemic to BC politics. Similar to neoliberal reformers who would come after him (such as Ralph Klein in Alberta, Gary Filmon in Manitoba, Grant Devine in Saskatchewan, and Mike Harris in Ontario) Vander Zalm quickly managed to polarize the province on social issues and deepened the rift between organized labour and the government. Unlike that of many others, however, Vander Zalm's polarizing influence also sparked a series of resignations from his Cabinet by high-profile ministers. On social issues, Social Credit had always been socially conservative but the party leadership had worked hard to keep such issues out of the limelight. But six months into his term Vander Zalm made abortion a key issue of his government, eventually delisting the procedure from those covered by medicare. More than a year later, Vander Zalm was forced to backtrack by the courts but not before the issue stirred the first voluble dissent against his leadership from backbench MLAs and a few Socred riding presidents.[25]

Perhaps the hallmark of neoliberal reforms has been alterations to the labour relations regime (see chapters on Saskatchewan, Manitoba, Ontario, Nova Scotia, and Newfoundland and Labrador). Not surprisingly, Vander Zalm decided to weigh into arguably the main division in the province, the one between organized labour and big business, by sponsoring a radically revised labour code. While many Socreds did not shy away from limiting labour's power, Vander Zalm managed to split his own caucus in the process by tasking his labour minister with exploring reform while secretly delegating the task to a senior civil servant and a group of anti-labour lawyers from the private sector. The result was a new labour code that even big business was not sure it could support.[26] The labour code debacle was just one of series of events in which it became apparent that Vander Zalm was effectively running a one-man government. His ministers began to complain that they found out about policy changes with everyone else – by reading the headlines.

After a series of scandals, Vander Zalm was forced to resign in 1991.[27] Although Vander Zalm left, there was no revival of Social Credit as the coalition vehicle for centre-right voters. Liberals might have been prepared to accept neoliberal economic policies, but they balked at socially conservative ones. By the 1991 election, a centrist Liberal Party had been revived and attracted more votes than the defeated government, now headed by Vander Zalm loyalist Rita Johnston. This time, even choosing a new leader did not save the party, particularly from their poor record on the economy. The Socreds had campaigned on the necessity of restraint and cutbacks in government social services to get the provincial economy moving throughout the 1980s, but the economy seemed as mired in its cyclical and structural boom and bust as ever.[28] Meanwhile, despite restraint, money flowed freely for mega-projects – BC Place Stadium, Expo 86, and the construction of the Coquihalla Highway – that would shift considerable amounts of public money into private hands. The fact that all such projects lost money or represented poor investments did not capture the media headlines.[29] More importantly, they did nothing to alter the basic dependent and vulnerable political economy of the province.

In October 1991 the second and final Socred era came to an end, with the party slipping to third place in both seats and the popular vote behind the victorious New Democrats and a revived provincial Liberal Party. Longtime Socred Grace McCarthy tried to rebuild the party, but when she failed to win a 1994 by-election in what had long been a Socred safe seat, her remaining MLAs left to form a provincial version of the popular federal Reform Party.[30] More importantly, Social Credit's business supporters and backroom operatives had already fled, opting instead to take over the opposition Liberal party as the most viable anti-NDP vehicle for the centre-right.[31] Vander Zalm's efforts to accelerate the pace of neoliberal reform (such as rewriting the provincial labour code) while simultaneously attempting to push the province in a more socially conservative direction contributed to the unravelling of his right-wing coalition.

The NDP Era, 1991–2001

Unlike NDP governments in Saskatchewan and Ontario, the BC NDP came back to power in fortuitous circumstances in the fall of 1991. The economic downturn affecting central Canada did not have the same impact in BC, the opposition was divided, inexperienced, and largely ineffective, and the media, particularly those that had surprisingly endorsed Harcourt in the election (e.g., the *Vancouver Sun* and *Province*), seemed willing to grant the new government some breathing room.[32] On the other hand, the internal pressure on the party was enormous after sixteen years in opposition.

The NDP had groomed itself for office in the previous half decade by downplaying its historic links to labour, excising "socialism" from any public links to the party, and branding itself as a modern, centrist party with a social conscience. Mike Harcourt was central to this makeover. The story of the party's previous failures among some activists, popular writers, and academics was one of a party failing to modernize. The party needed to reach out to the centre, the critics claimed, and Harcourt, Vancouver's unthreatening consensus-oriented mayor, was just the person to do it.[33] As Harcourt himself claimed, "I became leader because people saw that we had to become more mainstream and broaden our base and get rid of a lot of the old dusty policies that were out of date."[34]

The only problem with the story was that it was wrong in a number of important respects. First, centrism was hardly a new strategy for the CCF/NDP. Arguably ever since the CCF lost the pivotal election to Social Credit in 1952, the party had been actively reaching out to the centre. Reporting on the 1960s, Martin Robin claimed that the "NDP strained terribly in the 1963 contest to present itself as a nice middle

class party and leader Strachan appeared everywhere mouthing pleas-
antries and attired in the garb of a Royal Trust bond salesman," while
in the 1969 election new leader Tom Berger was quoted as saying that
"responsible free enterprise" would be safe if he formed government.[35]
Then, in government, Barrett's disastrous decision to order a number of
unions back to work just before the 1975 election was designed to establish his centrist credentials, while in 1979 and 1983 the party operatives
behind the campaigns had him run on vague and bland programs precisely to avoid accusations that the party harboured any grand plans if
they took office.[36] Second, the NDP did not win in 1991 as the result of
any perceived centrism, they won on a vote split between the remaining right-wing parties, just as they had done in 1972.[37] The NDP under
Harcourt was actually *less* popular than the previous versions, wining
just 41 per cent of the vote in 1991, compared to 43 per cent under Skelly
in 1986 and 45 per cent under Barrett in 1983. The misplaced faith that
centrism had won them the election left the government ill-prepared to
defend itself or its policies over the next decade.

Shortly after taking office, the NDP signalled a shift from the previous government in a host of policy areas. It increased funding for
child-support programs, promised pay equity for the civil service,
added sexual orientation to the list of prohibited grounds of discrimina-
tion in the Human Rights Code, and made access to abortion easier by
funding procedures performed at free-standing abortion clinics.[38] But
across-the-board social spending increases were cut short by the government's discovery that the Social Credit's books were in much worse
shape than they had claimed. Borrowing a trick from his opponents,
Harcourt called in an independent auditor to assess the state of the
province's finances. The report castigated the previous government for
lousy and misleading accounting practices and revealed a significant
debt and deficit. At the same time, federal cuts to provincial transfer
payments destined for social programs limited the NDP's fiscal room.
The government's first budget in March 1992 increased taxes to maintain existing levels of public services, though business and the wealthy
would pay more.[39] For the most part then, the NDP in government
accommodated itself to the general climate of neoliberal restraint, even
if it chose not to advance it further.

Similar to NDP premiers Roy Romanow (Saskatchewan) and Bob Rae
(Ontario), Mike Harcourt also moved quickly on his promise to develop
major policy changes collaboratively, setting up consultative bodies to
help craft new legislation on labour relations, health-care delivery, and

resource/environmental planning and management. The results were a new labour code, a decentralization of health-care administration to a regional level, and the creation of a Commission on Resources and Environment (CORE) to help balance the development and preservation of the province's staple economy. But here the NDP over-estimated how much consensus was possible in the province's polarized political climate. For instance, just like Bob Rae in Ontario (see chapter 6), the NDP yielded to small-business concerns and rejected sectoral bargaining for the service sector in its new labour code. Notwithstanding this concession, the business press lambasted the new labour laws.[40] In giving up on sectoral bargaining, the NDP relinquished a key legislative strategy for reversing the decline of union membership in the private sector, but got nothing in return.[41]

By 1993, despite a divided and weak opposition, the NDP government found itself under constant fire, particularly from the media. A series of unbalanced media reports about rampant welfare fraud put the government on the defensive. In a televised address in 1993 Harcourt joined the welfare bashing, denouncing "welfare cheats, deadbeats and varmints."[42] To signal a tougher line on finances and social issues, Harcourt shuffled his Cabinet, shifting perceived left-wingers like Joan Smallwood and Glen Clark out of Social Services and Finance, replaced by others seen as more conservative (such as Elizabeth Cull).[43] Giving up the illusion of pursuing a rather lean social democracy, Harcourt's government now surrendered to both the rhetoric and substance to the dominant neoliberal economic agenda, shifting to more post-material concerns in the latter part of its term, particularly environmental and indigenous issues. But these proved to be hardly less contentious. Throughout 1993 and 1994 the government was embroiled in a "war of the woods" as it tried to manage disagreements between environmentalists and loggers. Later it would face armed First Nations blockades and incendiary anti-land-claims rallies – both, in their own way, responses to the halting movement on negotiating Aboriginal treaty rights.[44]

The issue that broke the Harcourt government was a scandal, eventually dubbed "Bingo-gate." Harcourt had already faced down a few scandals in his government, mostly the product of poor judgment rather than naked self-interest of different ministers, and they were easily dealt with. But Bingo-gate could not be brushed aside so easily. The scandal involved a non-profit charity bingo society, run by NDPers, that used funds to help out good causes and "promote socialism." The practice had its roots in the 1950s but intensified in the 1960s when the Social Credit government outlawed union contributions to political parties (though business contributions were still allowed). Barrett's NDP repealed the restrictions on union funding in 1973, but the party's links to the charity bingos remained. When a story broke in the early 1990s that some money from the bingos had been diverted to the party illegally, Harcourt moved quickly to pay back any funds that should have gone to charity and sever the party's links to such practices. Yet the scandal dragged out for a long period and eventually uncovered that a long-time NDP politician had personally benefited from the bingo funds, building himself a luxury island cottage with the proceeds. Though the politician was a federal MP and not a member of his government, Harcourt decided that he could not distance himself from the scandal and announced he would resign for the good of the party and government on 15 November 1995.[45]

Glen Clark won the NDP leadership contest that followed by clearly signalling a departure from Harcourt's consensus style of governing. Clark effectively rallied the base of the party into activity with his pointed attacks on big business and their strong links to Gordon Campbell's Liberal Party.[46] In 1996 he led the NDP to a surprising victory in the provincial election, the first back-to-back win for the party in BC. The media and the opposition Liberal Party were stunned, especially as the Liberals had actually won more votes than the NDP (42 per cent to 39 per cent). Here the NDP continued to benefit from the new electoral map, first introduced for the 1991 election, and the splits that remained on the centre-right of the political spectrum. BC's old electoral map had over-represented areas where the centre-right had the advantage, while the new one was more even-handed, allowing the NDP to more efficiently turn votes into seats.[47]

Glen Clark's government quickly dispensed with Harcourt-style consensus in favour of Barrett and W.A.C. Bennett–style "decisive leadership." And like Bill Bennett in his later years, Clark was convinced that getting results quickly was key. The second NDP term focused on economic development in both old and new ways. A new highway stretching down Vancouver Island was finished on time, clearly demonstrating the continued resiliency of old-style highway politics. But Clark also broke with tradition in attempting to expand the province's shipbuilding capacity by having local firms and workers build new fast ferries for provincial use. If successful, the investment would have represented a departure from the centre-right's reliance on mega-projects, low-wage service jobs, and resource exploitation as the base of BC's economy. Indeed, it would have represented an important break with the increasingly consolidated neoliberal orthodoxy across the country. But Clark's economic counteroffensive proved superficial, poorly planned, and subject to his whims, which often seemed influenced by contingency and polling results. For instance, desperate for cash in the face of federal government cutbacks, his government (similar to those of Ontario and PEI) also opportunistically sanctioned the expansion of gaming in the province to raise funds.

The Clark NDP government was scarcely re-elected before it came under attack, this time for the claims made about its economic record during the election. Clark had campaigned strongly on his party's balanced budgets while in office, but shortly after the election it was revealed that an accounting error meant that the budget was actually in deficit. The press and the opposition claimed that Clark had lied during the campaign, while the premier protested that it was an honest mistake. A subsequent auditor general's report lamented the government's sloppy accounting but stopped short of claiming that a cover-up had occurred.[48] Pushed by right-wing interest groups, the media, and business, the "fudgit budget" issue haunted the NDP during its second term in office.[49]

By 1999 Clark was coming under fire for his leadership style, which focused on getting results at any costs. The strategy backfired when the fast ferry plans proved costly and not structurally sound. The "fast ferries fiasco" appeared to confirm media and opposition claims that the government was economically incompetent. Gaming also came back to haunt Clark when he became embroiled in a scandal in which it was alleged he used his office to get a friend a government-issued casino licence in return for free work on his house and cottage. Though he was subsequently cleared of any wrongdoing, the media circus generated by the scandal forced Clark to resign.[50]

Subsequent NDP leaders tried to turn things around for the government, but it soon became clear that no revival of party fortunes was likely. In the 2001 provincial election NDP support slumped to 22 per cent, securing it just two seats in the legislature. Though the party had governed for nine years, it seldom looked like it was in charge, often appearing weak and vulnerable.[51] For some, having the NDP in power did make a difference. Organized labour had done fairly well under the NDP, at least in legislative changes, but social movements were less successful, particularly if their demands involved money.[52] More importantly, NDP governing in BC did not break decisively with the neoliberal consensus being entrenched across the country. Nor did its "moderation" deliver votes or elite support: its political strategy of centrism failed to woo centre voters or gain concessions from the business community or their press.[53]

The Liberal Era, 2001–12

In May 2001, the Liberal Party under Gordon Campbell won seventy-seven of seventy-nine legislative seats in the BC election, the most lopsided victory in the province's history. The result was not entirely surprising. For almost two years the Liberals had been taunting the New Democrats to hold an election, vowing to reverse whatever legislation might be passed in the interim. Their confidence was based on a number of factors. First, the NDP victory in 1996 was weak, based on just 39 per cent of the vote. Second, the Liberals were clearly the sole choice on the centre-right in 2001, unlike in 1996. Finally, polling had put the party ahead of the NDP as early as 1997, a lead they never surrendered.[54] Such a decisive victory allowed the incoming Liberals to act boldly, quickly, and with seeming legitimacy. The popular vote was less one-sided than the seat totals but still clearly majoritarian: 58 per cent of those voting chose the Liberals, with just 22 per cent backing the NDP. The dramatic spike in Green support to 12 per cent, up from just 2 per cent in the previous election, was muted by their failure to win any seats. BC's centre-right was firmly back in power and determined to use it.

The restoration of BC's traditional ruling coalition took a bit longer to put together in the 1990s than it had in the 1970s. After the NDP came to power in 1991, many thought it would just be a matter of identifying which party on the right was best placed to win and then get the word out. The remnants of Social Credit quickly stumbled, morphed into a provincial version of the federal Reform Party, and ceased to be a credible contender for provincial power. That left the revived provincial Liberal Party, which had surprisingly risen from nowhere to become the official opposition. Former Socreds and the province's business elite quickly took over the party, installed Vancouver's pro-development mayor, Gordon Campbell, as leader, and then poured money into the party.[55] By 1996, they were confident that as Bennett had regrouped the centre-right around Social Credit in 1975, Campbell and the BC Liberals would do the same in 1996. But they did not. Part of the problem was Campbell's misunderstanding of the coalition he represented. Promises to cut government services, sell off publicly owned utilities like BC Hydro and BC Rail, and restructure the interior and northern economies did not go down well with right-wing voters outside the Lower Mainland. Many opted to stick with the remnants of the old Social Credit party, now running as BC Reform. Campbell's clear (and open) endorsement of what amounted to roll-out neoliberalism cost him the election.[56]

Between 1996 and 2001, the BC Liberals worked hard to woo the remaining hold-outs on the right by adjusting their policy mix: stiffer opposition to native land claims, an end to discussions about privatizing BC Rail and other government utilities, and a strong critique of NDP governing practices with a promise of democratic reform. By 1999 the BC Reform MLAs had resigned or jumped ship to the Liberals, while the centrist PDA's one elected member, Gordon Wilson, dissolved his party to join the NDP. Meanwhile, another four years of NDP government convinced whatever hold-outs remained on the right that the Liberals were the only viable force to defeat the left.

Upon taking office, the Liberals moved quickly on their agenda. The day after they were sworn in, they introduced across-the-board 25 per cent cuts in personal income taxes. Eight weeks later they added significant cuts to business taxes as well. As with previous governments, the Liberals also prepared to discredit their opponent's economic record, though they found themselves stymied by a booming economy and reports claiming healthy budget surpluses from the outgoing NDP. However, a handpicked group of business advisors were eventually assembled (in contrast to an accounting firm, as was the practice previously), who dutifully declared that the NDP had wrecked the economy, a message that was repeated ad nauseam throughout the Liberal time in government. Ironically, when it came time to prepare their first full budget, it was the Liberals' commitment to cut taxes at any cost that pushed the government into deficit.

Between 2001 and 2004 the Liberals embarked on a massive series of market-oriented reforms, both political and economic. Politically, the Liberals moved on their right-wing populist democratic reform package, which included fixed election dates, open Cabinet meetings, and a greater use of referenda to gain public input into policy. The first of these was a mail ballot referendum on First Nations treaty rights that opponents claimed was one-sided and racist.[57] Economically, the government took aim at organized labour and the civil service, tearing up contracts, imposing wage cuts, and reducing the workforce through service cuts, privatization, and contracting out. Unions and the diminished

NDP opposition tried to resist these changes but ultimately did little to slow the pace of market-oriented reform.[58]

As the cuts came down, many of these initiatives were popular with Liberal supporters – until they started to affect them personally. Indeed, it came as a surprise to many Liberal voters when government cuts led to school and hospital closures in their ridings. Here the Liberals were using their huge majority to impose a major shift in the balance of power within the province.[59] The changes in the electoral map had already weakened the rural dominance in the centre-right coalition. Now Campbell sought to break with the traditional social contract that had been established between the government and the non–Lower Mainland parts of the province.[60] For instance, changes to the Forestry Act allowed companies to avoid using local mills, leading to a centralization of lumber processing along the major truck routes to the Lower Mainland, and a dramatic decline in employment.[61] Cuts to government services and closures of local offices, schools, and hospitals left many interior and northern communities reeling.[62] The combination of the weakening power of his rural constituency within the BC Liberals, combined with his super-majority in the legislature, allowed Campbell to move aggressively with a set of roll-out neoliberal reforms that went far beyond the proposals that cost him the election in 1996.

The new Liberal government also enjoyed a long honeymoon with the provincial media, who gave little coverage to government critics and often seemed to simply paraphrase government press releases in their coverage.[63] But a series of scandals, beginning in 2003, tarnished their polished image. It all began with the drunk driving arrest of Premier Campbell while on vacation in Hawaii in January 2003, though when Campbell apologized the media seemed to lose interest. Then an unprecedented RCMP raid of the BC Legislature occurred later that year, connected to allegations that Liberal Party insiders had leaked details of the secret bidding for the government-owned BC Rail to friends of the party who represented rival bidders. This time Campbell and others deflected questions by claiming the issue was before the courts. But the damage was there. By the time the next provincial election was in sight, polls were showing that the NDP support had recovered and was rivalling the Liberals'.

The 2005 election was a test for both parties. The Liberals were supremely confident that the public approved of their actions and dismissed anti-government demonstrations as unrepresentative of the electorate. The NDP was also confident that the Liberal cuts would mobilize its base and bring swing voters over to the party. The new NDP leader was Carole James, a long-serving school trustee, Metis activist, and self-described moderate. She claimed that she was business-friendly and favoured distancing her party from its historic links to organized labour.[64] She was everything the media had counselled the party to adopt. And 2005 would also serve up a populist reform opportunity because voters would cast a ballot on whether to change the province's mode of election. After losing the 1996 election, Campbell opened the doors of the Liberal Party to all manner of populist reform causes, including voting system reform. While most of Campbell's democratic reforms – open Cabinet meetings, for instance – would prove empty and soon abandoned, the voting system was treated more seriously.[65] In late 2004 a citizens assembly recommended switching from BC's traditional first-past-the-post voting system to a proportional system called the single transferable vote (STV), which was to be part of a province-wide referendum.[66]

In the end, the Liberals won the 2005 election but received a serious rebuke from the electorate, losing thirty-one seats and shaving 12 per cent from their popular vote. Meanwhile, the NDP rebounded from its disappointing 2001 showing, winning thirty-three seats and returning to its historic levels of support with 42 per cent of the popular vote. The NDP revival was not that surprising. Academic survey work had shown that the NDP and Liberals did not trade much voting support. In other words, NDP voters in 2001 did not turn to the Liberals – most simply stayed home. In 2005, they came back.[67] The last surprise was the majority vote in favour of the new voting system, STV. Nearly 58 per cent of voters endorsed the new system, though it was not enough to pass as the government had insisted on a super-majority for any change. However, with such strong support, the government eventually agreed to hold another vote on the issue.

The election results, for the politicians and the voting system, suggest how upset BC voters were with the breakneck speed of neoliberal reform as practised by the Liberals. Visibly shaken by their results, the government rebranded themselves in their second term, de-emphasizing neoliberalism and embracing the post-material issues they had once decried. Or at least they appeared to. Over their second mandate, the Liberals focused each budget on a significant social theme: housing, the environment, and new social investments. The government had already reversed themselves on First Nations issues, breaking with their original anti-treaty position prior to the election. The term witnessed politicians formerly hostile to indigenous rights actively seek to advance the treaty process, and a formerly anti-union government successfully negotiating new contracts with the public-service unions. Finally, the government that had voted down support of the Kyoto accords in 2003 introduced a widely respected carbon tax in 2007.[68] A kinder, gentler Gordon Campbell seemed to have replaced the more ruthless previous version.

Yet not everyone was convinced. Upon inspection, the socially themed budgets were really just more thinly veiled tax cuts. Thus the "housing budget" offered tax cuts that people *could* apply to housing, if they wished. Such a market-oriented policy approach did little to help those genuinely in need of housing. The deals with the public service were motivated largely by the government's need for labour peace during upcoming mega-events, like the 2010 Winter Olympics.[69] The First Nations land claims process had little to show for itself after many years. And even a marquee policy like the carbon tax, which had been lauded by a broad array of groups (most not typically Liberal supporters), was calibrated at such a low level that it would not produce the results it was designed to achieve.[70] Most importantly, the neoliberal reforms to BC's economy implemented in their first term – changes to the Forestry Act, deregulation economic development, and weakening of the provincial labour code – remained.

Meanwhile, in other more subtle ways, the Liberals' neoliberal agenda was still alive and well. In their 2007 "conversation on health" with the public, the government did most of the talking, peddling a deliberately alarmist portrait of the provincial health-care system and pitching market reforms as the answer. The public was not buying.[71] More quietly, they signed the TILMA agreement with Alberta (later joined by the Saskatchewan government of Brad Wall under the banner of a "New West Partnership"), essentially creating a neoliberal free trade zone between the Western provinces. And of course there were more scandals (like the ongoing BC Rail corruption case) and economic blunders (like the cost overruns on the Vancouver Trade and Convention Centre) that were given rather light treatment in the press.

The policy shifts in this second Liberal term convinced many in the media that Gordon Campbell's government had moved to the centre. Whether such policies were substantial or not, they created friction within the governing coalition as northern and interior supporters vocally opposed the reversal on native land claims and the environment. For a time, it appeared that the Liberals might be facing a rural revolt over their carbon tax.[72] As a result, the NDP decided to come out against the carbon tax in the hopes of gaining more traction with non–Lower Mainland voters. Strategically, the Liberals hoped to hold the right and appeal to the centre with their new post-material commitments to social peace and the environment. Meanwhile, the NDP tried to steer BC's populist regionalism into its camp by vigorously opposing the carbon tax while keeping its traditional bases of urban support.[73] Both parties were taking risks to expand the breadth of their political coalitions.

Election day 2009 returned the Liberals to power again, with both parties simply reproducing their 2005 vote shares. All the political calculations and risk-taking had not altered the political status quo. Of course, for the Liberals, this worked well, as they remained in power with a comfortable majority. For the NDP, it was a major blunder. Instead of building on the palpable anti-neoliberal public response to the Liberals' first term that had been registered in the 2005 election, the NDP spent the Liberals' second term offering vague criticism and promises, while trying to appear "business-friendly."[74] The party's cynical embrace of a populist, neoliberal, anti-tax campaign in 2009 failed to return it to power.[75] Seemingly bereft of original ideas or compelling leadership, the party could only hope that the existing government would implode, leaving it as the only governing alternative. The status quo remained for the voting system as well when the second referendum went down to defeat with only 39 per cent of voters now supporting STV.[76] In the end, the Liberals did not appear to pay any price in the 2009 election for their aggressive pursuit of roll-out neoliberalism over the previous two terms.

Government implosions are not typical immediately after an election victory, but the Liberals nearly snatched defeat from the jaws of victory with their ill-fated decision on a new tax. Just days after winning re-election, they signed an agreement with the federal government to adopt a new harmonized sales tax, or HST. They had said during the election that they were not considering such a measure and would not pursue it if proposed by the federal government. But the speed with which a complicated tax agreement between two levels of government was signed shortly after election day made a host of observers suspicious.[77] Criticism of the HST quickly began to mount. Anti-HST rallies led by former Socred premier Bill Vander Zalm drew thousands of people throughout the fall of 2009.[78] By 2010, an organized anti-HST campaign had emerged and decided to use the province's cumbersome initiative referendum legislation to seek its repeal. Pundits quickly declared it would fail. But the spring campaign gathered 700,000 signatures and forced a referendum to be scheduled.[79]

The Liberals and their big business supporters thought the opposition would fizzle, just as it had for the carbon tax. But even the unrelenting media blitz surrounding the 2010 Olympics could not divert the public's hostility. In the end, amid resignations and plummeting polling numbers, the successful centre-right coalition represented by the Liberal Party appeared to be unravelling.[80] To forestall the momentum, Gordon Campbell resigned in November 2010.[81] The decision may have saved his party, but it did not save the HST, which was defeated in a mail-in ballot referendum in August 2011.[82]

As with Bill Bennett's Social Credit before them, the BC Liberal Party had created a stable coalition of the political centre and right within one party, able to govern with confidence and strong media support. It helped that media proved more forgiving of Liberal economic blunders and less interested in their scandals than those of the previous NDP administration.[83] Still, cracks in this most recent coalition emerged from time to time, along various cleavage lines: rural vs urban, small vs big business, and social vs fiscal conservative. The HST battle highlighted them clearly, pitting the party's big business contributors, mostly urban, against their small business and non–Lower Mainland supporters. The choice of Christie Clark as the new Liberal leader – an urban-based, socially liberal former MLA and talk show host – appeared only to exacerbate these divisions.

In contrast to the Liberal show of strength, the NDP continued to struggle to build a winning coalition in the 2000s, rather than simply wait to inherit power through a right-wing implosion. Victory by the latter route would leave the party vulnerable to media-based attacks and unable to govern effectively. But here the party continued to fail in analysing their strategic political situation. Party leaders and the party's few positive media commentators continued to offer centrism as the key to victory, seemingly unaware of its signal failure to deliver the goods on repeated attempts. Centrism failed because as the party tried to move to the centre, the centre line would simply be moved further right by the media and the NDP's political opponents. Throughout the 2000s, moreover, it was also clear that the electoral "centre" was now firmly embedded within a neoliberal consensus between the two main parties. The BC NDP failed because electoral history suggests that not enough centre voters were willing to embrace the party, no matter how "reasonable" (or neoliberal) it attempted to be.

Carole James was a case in point. She was everything the media said the NDP should look for in a leader but they still failed to endorse her. Her centrism did not bring out the swing voters either – she lost twice, contributing to grumblings about her leadership. Just a month after her nemesis Gordon Campbell had resigned, James was forced to resign as well.[84] On the other hand, the party did make gains electorally when it recruited new voters into the political system. For instance, in both 1972 and 1979 – elections that witnessed a surge in NDP support – new voters were as important as or more important than the swing votes from other parties. In his bid to become NDP leader, Adrian Dix had made recruiting support from the 50 per cent of BC non-voters a key priority, suggesting a break with the party's traditional losing strategy.[85]

From her victory in early 2011 to the election of 2013, Christie Clark's tenure as premier and leader of the BC Liberals appeared to be unsteady as she lurched in different directions attempting to appease all the constituencies in her party's coalition. After a brief bump in polling numbers accompanying her win, Liberal support slumped and remained between 10 to 20 points behind that of the opposition NDP. The 2013 election campaign featured an NDP confident of victory, so confident in fact that they offered few concrete policy promises. Meanwhile Clark's relentlessly upbeat campaign, one that refused to countenance the possibility of losing, appeared to media observers as desperate and doomed. Most polls just two days before the election had the NDP ahead of the Liberals by 7–10 per cent, a seemingly insurmountable lead. When the Liberals easily won re-election, commentators, politicians, and the public were shocked.[86]

The year 2013 turned out not to be a repeat of 1972, 1991, and 1996 for one main reason – no credible alternative to the Liberals emerged for right-wing voters. In polls during the previous two years, many had parked their support with the BC Conservatives, but in the run-up to the campaign and in the televised leaders' debate the party appeared amateurish and too far to the right on social issues for BC voters.[87] Though they were clearly unhappy with the government, such voters held their nose and supported them in the absence of a credible alternative to the neoliberalism of the Liberal party. The NDP, by contrast, suffered both from over-confidence and a lack of ambition. Its inability to mobilize the large non-voting elements of the public, NDP leader Adrian Dix's hesitant opposition to the Kinder Morgan pipeline, and its general unwillingness to make the economy a key issue left it struggling once more to gain traction with centrist voters, a strategy that has been a reliable failure.

Conclusion

British Columbia arguably inaugurated the era of neoliberal transformation in Canada with its infamous "restraint" program of the early to mid-1980s. But this early innovation in the rollback phase of neoliberalism later stalled as repeated attempts to push through to the roll-out stage failed for political reasons, resting primarily on the coalition dynamics of the provincial right. Though dominant politically, governing for all but thirteen years of the province's history, BC's political centre and right have sometimes struggled to maintain unity, either in coalition or behind a single party. Since the NDP's breakthrough to government in the 1970s, its opponents have typically rallied – successfully – behind a single party. But to do so placed constraints on the successful government, as it had to balance very different urban and rural interests, ones that often divided on political economy and social conservatism. For instance, attempts by Bill Vander Zalm to push the province in a more socially conservative direction in the late 1980s led to the demise of the Social Credit as a vehicle that could unite the centre and right, while calls by Gordon Campbell's Liberals to diminish state support for BC's interior and northern economies arguably cost him rural support and the 1996 election.

The introduction of neoliberalism in BC was affected fundamentally by the political dynamics of coalition building on the centre and right of the political spectrum. Once Social Credit was confident that an independent political centre was dead in the form of a competing party, they had more latitude to move on early rollback forms of neoliberalism. Later, Gordon Campbell's Liberal Party faced a similar problem, unable to move on the roll-out aspects of neoliberalism until competing forces on their right representing holdout rural economic interests had been marginalized. The weakening of rural interests within the Liberal Party coalition (due in part to changes in the province's electoral map) and the lopsided legislative victory for the Liberals in 2001 (seventy-seven of seventy-nine seats) allowed Campbell to aggressively roll out neoliberal reforms with impunity. The failure of the BC NDP to fundamentally contest either phase of neoliberal restructuring meant that the Social Credit in 1986 and the Liberals in 2009 and 2013 paid only a modest electoral price for their unpopular market-oriented policies.

NOTES

1 Stan Persky, *Fantasy Government: Bill Vander Zalm and the Future of Social Credit* (Vancouver: New Star, 1989), 10.
2 Phillip Resnick, "Neo-Conservatism on the Periphery: The Lessons from B.C.," *BC Studies* 75 (Autumn 1987): 12.
3 Rand Dyck, *Provincial Politics in Canada* (Scarborough, ON: Prentice Hall Canada, 1996), 619.
4 See David J. Mitchell, *W.A.C. Bennett and the Rise of British Columbia* (Vancouver: Douglas and McIntyre, 1983); Bob Plecas, *Bill Bennett: A Mandarin's View* (Douglas and McIntyre, 2005); Donald E. Blake, "Value Conflicts in Lotusland: British Columbia Political Culture," in *Politics, Policy and Government in British Columbia*, ed. R.K. Carty, 3–17 (Vancouver: UBC Press, 1996).
5 Martin Robin, "British Columbia: The Politics of Class Conflict," in *Canadian Provincial Politics*, ed. Martin Robin, 27–68 (Scarborough, ON: Prentice-Hall Canada, 1972); Philip Resnick, "Social Democracy in Power: The Case of British Columbia," *BC Studies* 34 (Summer 1977): 3–20.
6 John Douglas Belshaw, "Provincial Politics, 1871–1916," in *The Pacific Province. A History of British Columbia*, ed. Hugh M. Johnston (Vancouver: Douglas and McIntyre, 1996), 137–46.
7 For an exception to this focusing on the 1940s, see Donald Alper, "The Effects of Coalition Government on Party Structure: The Case of the Conservative Party in BC," *BC Studies* 33 (1977): 40–9.
8 For appraisals of the federal Liberal Party and its changes in policy, see Stephen Clarkson, *The Big Red Machine* (Vancouver: UBC Press, 2005); and Brooke Jeffrey, *Divided Loyalties* (Toronto: University of Toronto Press, 2010).
9 John R. Wedley, "Laying the Golden Egg: The Coalition Government's Role in Post-war Northern Development," *BC Studies* 88 (Winter 1990): 58–92.
10 Michael Prince, "At the Edge of Canada's Welfare State: Social Policy-making in British Columbia," in Carty, *Politics, Policy and Government in British Columbia*, 253.
11 Dennis Pilon, "Democracy, BC Style," in *British Columbia Politics and Government*, ed. Michael Howlett, Dennis Pilon, and Tracy Summerville (Toronto: Emond Montgomery, 2010), 93–4.

12 The most comprehensive and balanced account of the NDP's time in power in the 1970s can be found in Geoff Meggs and Rod Mickleburgh, *The Art of the Impossible: Dave Barrett and the NDP in Power, 1972–1975* (Vancouver: Harbour Publishing, 2012).

13 See G.L. Kristianson, "The Non-partisan Approach to B.C. Politics: The Search for a Unity Party – 1972–1975," *BC Studies* 33 (Spring 1977): 13–29; Meggs and Mickleburgh, *Art of the Impossible*.

14 Plecas, *Bill Bennett*, 30.

15 Donald E. Blake, "The Politics of Polarization: Parties and Elections in British Columbia," in Carty, *Politics, Policy and Government in British Columbia*, 74.

16 Donald E. Blake, R.K. Carty, and Lynda Erickson, *Grassroots Politicians* (Vancouver: UBC Press, 1991), 26, 48–9.

17 Stan Persky, *Bennett II: The Decline and Stumbling of Social Credit Government in British Columbia* (Vancouver: New Star, 1983), 35, 37.

18 Blake, "Politics of Polarization," 73–4. The provincial Liberal and Conservative parties remained dormant as their voters largely endorsed Social Credit. Meanwhile, the NDP improved their result by picking up a few stray social Liberals, but most of their gains came from new voters, particularly youth.

19 Persky, *Bennett II*, 58, 102–3.

20 Ibid., 205, 224, 237.

21 William K. Carroll and R.S. Ratner, "Ambivalent Allies: Social Democratic Regimes and Social Movements," *BC Studies* 154 (Summer 2007): 47–8. For more detailed examinations of these events, see Bryan Palmer, *Solidarity: The Rise and Fall of an Opposition* (Vancouver, New Star, 1987); and Ted Richmond and John Shields, "Reflections on Resistance to Neoliberalism: Looking Back on Solidarity in 1983 British Columbia," *Socialist Studies* 7, nos. 1–2 (Spring/Fall 2011): 216–37.

22 Persky, *Fantasy Government*, 4.

23 Vander Zalm's many controversial political initiatives are detailed in Persky's three books on Social Credit.

24 For a breakdown of Socred delegate views at the 1986 convention, see Blake, Carty, and Erickson, *Grassroots Politicians*, 99–112.

25 Persky, *Fantasy Government*, 154–5, 164–5, 168.

26 Ibid., 105–6, 118–21.

27 Ibid., 214–56. See also Daniel Gawthrop, *Highwire Act: Power, Pragmatism and the Harcourt Legacy* (Vancouver: New Star, 1996), 8–15.

28 Persky, *Fantasy Government*, 16–17.

29 William K. Carroll and R.S. Ratner, "Social Democracy, Neo-Conservativism and Hegemonic Crisis in British Columbia," *Critical Sociology* 16, no. 1

(1989): 41. As Carroll notes, "In strict economic terms, Expo '86 amounted to a highly inefficient Keynesian public works project, generating a local mini recovery through the large number of predominantly low-wage jobs and inflow of tourism income."

30 Gawthrop, *Highwire Act*, 121–3.

31 Stephen Phillips, "Party Politics in British Columbia: The Persistence of Polarization," in Howlett, Pilon, and Summerville, *British Columbia Politics and Government*, 117.

32 Richard Sigurdson, "The British Columbia New Democratic Party: Does It Make a Difference?," in Carty, *Politics, Policy and Government in British Columbia*, 328.

33 Phillips, "Party Politics in British Columbia," 116.

34 Gawthrop, *Highwire Act*, 6.

35 Robin, "British Columbia: The Politics of Class Conflict," 68.

36 Persky, *Bennett II*, 48.

37 As Erickson notes, the 1991 election witnessed Social Credit support collapse, with much of it moving to Liberals, not the NDP. Nonetheless, the vote split allowed the NDP to come to power. See Lynda Erickson, "Electoral Behaviour in British Columbia," in Howlett, Pilon, and Summerville, *British Columbia Politics and Government*, 132.

38 Gawthrop, *Highwire Act*, 59–60.

39 Ibid., 61.

40 William K. Carroll and R.S. Ratner, "The NDP Regime in British Columbia, 1991–2001: A Post-Mortem," *Canadian Review of Sociology and Anthropology* 42, no. 2 (2005): 167–96; Rodney Haddow, "How Malleable Are Political-Economic Institutions? The Case of Labour-Market Decision-making in British Columbia," *Canadian Public Administration* 43, no. 4 (December 2000): 387–411.

41 Gawthrop, *Highwire Act*, 63–8.

42 Ibid., 239–40.

43 Ibid., 148–9.

44 See Steven Bernstein and Benjamin Cashore, "Globalization, Four Paths of Internationalization and Domestic Policy Change: The Case of Eco-Forestry in British Columbia," *Canadian Journal of Political Science* 32 (March 2000): 67–99; Roger Hayter, "The War in the Woods: Post-Fordist Restructuring, Globalization, and the Contested Remapping of British Columbia's Forest Economy," *Annals of the Association of American Geographers* 93, no. 3 (2003): 706–29.

45 For a detailed treatment of the scandal, see Gawthrop, *Highwire Act*, 279–97.

46 Phillips, "Party Politics in British Columbia," 117–18.
47 For a review of the events preceding the development of the new electoral map, see Norman J. Ruff, "The Cat and Mouse Politics of Redistribution: Fair and Effective Representation in British Columbia," *BC Studies* 87 (Autumn 1990): 48–84. Meanwhile, the opposition Liberals lost a number of seats to vote-splits, either on the right to the populist BC Reform or the centre to Gordon Wilson's Progressive Democratic Alliance.
48 Will McMartin, "Fiscal Fictions," in *Liberalized*, ed. David Beers (Vancouver: New Star Books, 2005), 123.
49 Phillips, "Party Politics in British Columbia," 119.
50 Michael Howlett and Keith Brownsey, "British Columbia: Politics in a Post-Staples Political Economy," in *The Provincial State in Canada: Politics in the Provinces and Territories*, ed. K. Brownsey and M. Howlett (Peterborough: Broadview, 2001), 323–4.
51 For a detailed review of how government insiders understood this lack of control, see Carroll and Ratner, "NDP Regime in British Columbia," 167–96.
52 Sigurdson, "The British Columbia New Democratic Party," 337.
53 Joanna Burgar and Martin Monkman, *Who Heads to the Polls? Exploring the Demographics of Voters in British Columbia* (Victoria: BC Stats, March 2010), 41. Throughout the 1990s, electoral participation continued to decline, particularly amongst working-class and the poor voters, just those the NDP would need if they were ever to return to office.
54 Erickson, "Electoral Behaviour in British Columbia," 136.
55 Phillips, "Party Politics in British Columbia," 117.
56 For more details on this, see Dennis Pilon, "Assessing Gordon Campbell's Uneven Democratic Legacy in British Columbia," in *The Campbell Revolution: Power and Politics in British Columbia from 2001 to 2011*, ed. Tracy Summerville and Jason Lacharite (Vancouver: UBC Press, forthcoming).
57 David Rossiter and Patricia K. Wood, "Fantastic Topographies: Neoliberal Responses to Aboriginal Land Claims in British Columbia," *Canadian Geographer* 49, no. 4 (2005): 352–66.
58 For some of these responses, see Marcy Cohen, "The Privatization of Health Care Cleaning Services in BC," *Antipode* 38, no. 2 (June 2006): 626–44; Carroll and Ratner, "Ambivalent Allies," 56; Marge Reitsma-Street and Bruce Wallace, "Resisting Two-Year Limits on Welfare in British Columbia," *Canadian Review of Social Policy* 53 (Spring/Summer 2004): 170–7.
59 Chris Tenove, "In the Hurtland," in Beers, *Liberalized*, 38–70.
60 Tracy Summerville, "The Political Geography of BC," in *British Columbia Politics and Government*, ed. Michael Howlett, Dennis Pilon, and Tracy Summerville (Toronto: Emond Montgomery, 2010), 76–7.

61 Nathan Young, "Radical Neoliberalism in British Columbia: Remaking Rural Geographies," *Canadian Journal of Sociology* 33, no. 1 (2008): 1–36.

62 Phillips, "Party Politics in British Columbia," 121.

63 David Beers, "The Big Swerve," in Beers, *Liberalized*, 8.

64 Phillips, "Party Politics in British Columbia," 124. For more on the shifting relationship of organized labour and the NDP, see Dennis Pilon, Stephanie Ross, and Larry Savage, "Solidarity Revisited: Organized Labour and the New Democratic Party," *Canadian Political Science Review* 5, no. 1 (January 2011): 20–37.

65 Norman Ruff, "Executive Dominance: Cabinet and the Office of the Premier in BC," in Howlett, Pilon, and Summerville, *British Columbia Politics and Government*, 207–8.

66 Pilon, "Democracy BC-Style," 99–102.

67 Erickson, "Electoral Behaviour in British Columbia," 137, 140.

68 Ibid., 146.

69 Carroll and Ratner, "Ambivalent Allies," 58–9.

70 Marc Lee, *Fair and Effective Carbon Pricing* (Vancouver: CCPA – BC Office, February 2011), 32.

71 Alan Davidson, "Sweet Nothings: The BC Conversation on Health," *Health Policy* 3, no. 4 (May 2008): 33–40.

72 Tom Barrett, "Carbon Tax Screws BC's North?," Tyee, 4 April 2008, http://thetyee.ca/News/2008/04/04/CarbonTaxNorth/.

73 Tom Barrett, "A Carbon Tax Backlash?," Tyee, 23 June 2008, http://thetyee.ca/News/2008/06/23/CarbonTax/.

74 The choices of the BC NDP are not out of step with those of social democrats elsewhere in Canada or across the Western world. See William K. Carroll and R.S. Ratner, eds., *Challenges and Perils: Social Democracy in Neoliberal Times* (Halifax: Fernwood, 2005); for a Canadian and comparative discussion of these trends, see Dennis Pilon, "The Long Lingering Death of Social Democracy," *Labour / Le Travail* 70 (Fall 2012): 245–60.

75 Andrew MacLeod, "Carbon Tax Opposition Lacked Vision: Former NDP MLA," Tyee, 12 May 2009, http://thetyee.ca/Blogs/TheHook/BC-Politics/2009/05/12/CarbonCubberley/.

76 Pilon, "Democracy BC-Style," 103–4.

77 "Documents Show B.C. Negotiated HST Pre-election," CTV News, 2 September 2010, http://www.ctvnews.ca/documents-show-b-c-negotiated-hst-pre-election-1.548727.

78 "Thousands Rally against HST," CBC News, 9 September 2009, http://www.cbc.ca/news/canada/british-columbia/thousands-rally-against-hst-1.790004.

79 "B.C. Anti-HST Petition Arrives in Victoria," CBC News, 30 June 2010, http://www.cbc.ca/news/canada/british-columbia/b-c-anti-hst-petition-arrives-in-victoria-1.898439.

80 Monte Paulsen, "Lekstrom Quits BC Liberals over HST," Tyee, 11 June 2010, http://thetyee.ca/Blogs/TheHook/BC-Politics/2010/06/11/Minister-Lekstrom-quits-BC-Liberals-over-HST/.

81 Andrew MacLeod, "'Politics Can Be a Nasty Business': Campbell Steps Down," Tyee, 3 November 2010, accessed February 27, 2011, http://thetyee.ca/News/2010/11/03/CampbellResigns/.

82 "BC Votes 55 Percent to Scrap HST," CBC News, 26 August 2011, http://www.cbc.ca/news/canada/british-columbia/b-c-votes-55-to-scrap-hst-1.1011876.

83 An excellent example would be the media's double standard in judging the Liberal and NDP economic records, particularly on budget projections. For a laudible exception, see Will McMartin, "Worst Fudge-It Budget Proven, But Free Ride from Media," Tyee, 12 July 2010, http://thetyee.ca/Opinion/2010/07/12/FudgeBudget/.

84 Andrew MacLeod, "Carole James Quits 'in Best Interests of the Party,'" Tyee, 6 December 2010, http://thetyee.ca/News/2010/12/06/CaroleJamesResigns/.

85 Andrew MacLeod, "What Separates Top Three NDP Leadership Candidates?," Tyee, 7 April 2011, http://thetyee.ca/News/2011/04/07/NDPLeadershipCandidates/.

86 "Christy Clark Leads B.C. Liberals to Surprise Majority," CBC News, 15 May 2013, http://www.cbc.ca/news/canada/british-columbia/christy-clark-leads-b-c-liberals-to-surprise-majority-1.1315526.

87 Angus Reid, "What Went Wrong with the Polls in British Columbia?," Maclean's, 8 July 2013.

PART FOUR

New Opportunities and Old Problems: The North

11 Managing the Moraine: Political Economy and Political Culture Approaches to Assessing the Success of Nunavut

AILSA HENDERSON AND GRAHAM WHITE

Introduction

The creation of Nunavut has been described as a bold, innovative step towards improving Aboriginal peoples' lives, empowering them by establishing a governance system that they control and that serves their interests. How might one evaluate whether things are going well or poorly in a new political jurisdiction such as Nunavut? For political scientists, this might mean examining levels of political engagement, the government's ability to balance its books, its effectiveness in delivering programs and services, the openness and fairness of the policy process (or the people's belief that it is open and fair), and economic indicators such as unemployment levels or economic growth rates. Certainly, other measures could also be used. Reaching a conclusion about the success of Nunavut depends in part on the criteria used.

We could identify the goals of those who wanted to create a new polity and determine whether they have been met. The creators of Nunavut expected, for example, that the new territory and land claim would produce economic advances and a cultural renaissance for the Inuit population. Alternatively, we could focus on criteria derived from different theoretical approaches. For political culture researchers, levels of political engagement or the integration of Inuit values into the operation of the civil service would be of obvious interest. From a political economy perspective, we might consult indicators that help us to evaluate who holds political and economic power and the standards of living in the territory. The original land claim advocates emphasized goals that fall under the rubric of political culture as well as political economy. With Nunavut into its second decade, we attempt in this chapter to reach some conclusions of its success by evaluating four aspects of political life in Nunavut: political participation, the functioning of its civil service – including the extent to which Nunavut is an Inuit government – economic development, and standards of living. This enables us to determine whether things have changed, and if so, if they have changed for the better. Looking at these matters sheds light on the transformation of politics in Nunavut as well as the utility of our two conceptual frameworks.

The concept of political culture encompasses the basic attitudes toward politics – and behavioural norms within them – that underpin a society. While political culture is not static, it is stable, powerfully influencing not only day-to-day politics but also the institutional foundations of government and the political order. Political economy stresses the importance of societal divisions, especially those rooted in economic conditions; it sees the distribution of political power as reflecting the distribution of economic resources and the configuration of economic interests in society. In the abstract these approaches to understanding politics may seem very different but, as we conclude in the case of Nunavut, they are linked in important ways.

Juxtaposing political culture and political economy perspectives is especially apt for Nunavut in light of the far-reaching social change that has affected Inuit society in recent decades. Both perspectives help explain how new resource development projects currently underway (or expected) portend profound economic transformation across the territory. As recently as the 1940s and 1950s, most Inuit lived a nomadic existence, depending heavily on hunting and fishing, with little exposure to permanent settlements or the wage economy. Many of the social ills that plague Nunavut today, such as alcoholism and suicide, were all but unknown. The shift to life in settled communities and close integration into modern, high-tech society has brought significant material benefits and government services, but it has been accompanied by severe social dislocation, often reflecting cultural loss. At the same time, important elements of traditional Inuit society, not least widespread use of Inuktitut, the Inuit language, continue to underpin society and politics in Nunavut.

Economic development, badly needed in Nunavut, is a multifaceted process, but by far the most promising – and at once the most troubling – prospects arise from large resource extraction projects, for Nunavut has enormous deposits of gold, diamonds, iron ore, oil and gas, and other non-renewable resources. Many in Nunavut, including the Government of Nunavut, are banking heavily on the economic potential of mining for jobs, infrastructure, and government revenue. At the same time, concern is widespread over the environmental costs of large resource extraction projects and the potential political influence of large multinational mining firms. Moreover, the mining industry is notorious for cycles of "boom and bust," giving rise to far-reaching economic and political problems.

Nunavut: An Overview

Nunavut came into being on 1 April 1999 when the Inuit-dominated Eastern Arctic was split off from the Northwest Territories (NWT). The principal reason for the creation of Nunavut was to provide for the people of the Eastern Arctic what other Canadians had long enjoyed: a government that they controlled, which would be located in and be knowledgeable about their communities. Prior to division in 1999, as part of the NWT, Inuit and other residents of the Eastern Arctic did send elected representatives to the NWT Legislative Assembly, but disliked being governed from a capital thousands of kilometres (and two time zones) away, where precious few public servants could communicate with them in their own language. In addition to a desire for a local rather than distant government, however, the Inuit wanted a government they could control in order to ensure the survival of their culture and to protect their rich but fragile land. From the first concrete proposal for an Inuit homeland – Nunavut ("our land" in Inuktitut) – in 1976, it took a quarter century of difficult negotiations with the federal government to reach a resolution of the Inuit demands in the form of the Nunavut Land Claims Agreement (NLCA).

Nunavut thus represents an unusual combination of a fresh and hopeful start-up with an extensive legacy of unique social and demographic characteristics, as well as political and economic structures inherited from the NWT. Hence the appeal of the moraine metaphor – moraines being distinctive landforms composed of earth, rocks, and other debris left when the glaciers retreated.

To be sure, every province and territory – indeed, every political jurisdiction – is unique, but within the Canadian context, Nunavut is decidedly distinctive. We suggest, accordingly, that understanding Nunavut requires analysis of both its political culture and its political economy.

Covering some two million square kilometres – roughly the size of Western Europe, one-fifth of Canada's landmass – Nunavut is home to about 36,000 residents. Though the Arctic has experienced far more environmental change because of global warming than the rest of the planet, Nunavut's climate remains harsh. Winters are much longer, and typically colder than elsewhere in Canada. When trees are coming into bud throughout southern Canada, Nunavut remains snow- and ice-covered, and of course there are no trees to bud in the Arctic tundra.

Approximately 85 per cent of Nunavummiut (the people of Nunavut) are Inuit, of whom 60–80 per cent speak Inuktitut, depending on the definition used. The population is dispersed across twenty-five communities, no two joined by roads. The largest is Iqaluit, the capital, with a population approaching 7,000 according to the 2011 census. Only two others have as many as 2,000 residents and nearly half have fewer than 1,000.[1] Nunavut's demographic profile differs tremendously from that of southern Canada in age: whereas about 17 per cent of the Canadian population is younger than fifteen years old, in Nunavut this cohort represents over 40 per cent of the population.[2] With the highest fertility rate in the country, Nunavut's population continues to expand significantly. The territorial population – and thus the government – faces pressing social and economic needs. Rates of suicide are by far the most disturbing, the highest of any jurisdiction in Canada and among the highest in the world. As the data in table 11.1 highlight, levels of infant mortality, drinking, smoking, and food insecurity are the highest in the country, while access to doctors and high school graduation rates are the lowest. Incarceration rates and the severity of crime are far above overall Canadian levels. High levels of unemployment and low average household income mean that the territorial government faces severe economic challenges. In terms of economic activity, the public sector is by far the largest employer in the territory. The territorial government has a surprisingly large bureaucracy. and there is a much smaller, yet still sizeable and certainly influential federal presence as well. The private sector is weak and underdeveloped by comparison.

Table 11.1. Health and Socio-economic Indicators in Nunavut

	Canada	Nunavut	Worst
Health indicators			
Infant mortality (deaths/1000 live births)	5.0	12.1	Nunavut
Heavy drinking (%)	19.0	26.1	NWT (31.2)
Daily smokers (%)	15.6	53.0	Nunavut
Population with regular doctor (%)	84.7	12.7	Nunavut
Socio-economic indicators			
Incarceration rate/100,000	89.9	586.4	NWT (935.6)
Crime severity index	85.3	469.3	Nunavut
High school graduation rate (%)	71.0	32.0	Nunavut
Food insecurity (%)	7.7	31.6	Nunavut
Human Development Index	0.91	0.82	Nunavut

All data from Statistics Canada, except Human Development Index (Elspeth Hazell, Kar-Fai Gee, and Andrew Sharpe, *The Human Development Index in Canada: Estimates for the Canadian Provinces and Territories, 2000–2011* [Ottawa: Centre for the Study of Living Standards, Ottawa, May 2012], 33). Most indicators are for 2011; some are for 2007/8.

Politically, Nunavut is at once very similar to and very different from the other territories and provinces. The Government of Nunavut (GN) is a Westminster-style "responsible government" elected by all territorial residents (Inuit or not), supported by a hierarchical, merit-based public service organized into conventional departments (Finance, Education, Health, Justice, etc.). At the same time, Nunavut's very existence is rooted in a comprehensive land claim, the significance of which can hardly be overstated. Briefly, comprehensive land claims are modern treaties by which Aboriginal peoples formally convey ownership of their traditional lands to the Canadian state in return for certain benefits (cash, ownership of selected lands, extensive governance arrangements, and a wide range of other provisions such as mineral royalties and employment guarantees). Once ratified by a vote of Aboriginal people and authorized by acts of Parliament and the provincial/ territorial legislature, finalized land claims agreements become constitutionally protected by virtue of section 35 of the Constitution Act, 1982. Many provisions of the land claim relate to institutional governance arrangements, from a set of powerful wildlife and environmental regulatory co-management boards to formal status in various government processes for Inuit land claim organizations.

Another distinctive feature is the explicit commitment the GN has made to operate according to traditional Inuit values – *Inuit Qaujimajatuqangit* (*IQ*, "that which has been long known by Inuit"). Yet another distinctive feature of governance in Nunavut is the remarkably influential role played by Nunavut Tunngavik Incorporated (NTI), the territory-wide Inuit land claim organization and the three regional Inuit associations, which represent all Nunavut Inuit. These organizations might appear to be interest groups – unusually influential interest groups to be sure, but interest groups nevertheless. Such a categorization, however, grossly underestimates their importance in the governance of Nunavut. NTI is not – nor does it think of itself as – an alternate government, yet it does perform a number of governance functions, such as nominating and appointing members to the powerful "institutions of public government," such as the Nunavut Impact Review Board, and delivering social services to its members, such as through a hunter support program and what amounts to a pension program for Inuit elders. In short, NTI plays a significant role in territorial politics.

It is important to understand the political implications of Nunavut's status as a territory, as opposed to a province. Canada's three territories are best understood as "proto-provinces," lacking the formal constitutional status of provinces, but exercising most – though not all – of the jurisdictional and taxation powers that provinces enjoy. For example, unlike the provinces, territories have no role in constitutional amendment processes; moreover, they could, technically, be abolished or amalgamated simply by an act of Parliament, though politically this is all but inconceivable. The territories have most of the taxing powers as the provinces: personal, sales, and corporate taxes, "sin taxes" on cigarettes and alcohol, and so on. Like their provincial counterparts, the territorial governments are responsible for such major policy fields as health, education, social welfare, housing, municipal government, and renewable resources.

In one fundamentally important respect, territorial governments are disadvantaged when compared to the provinces. Whereas Crown – that is, public – land in southern Canada is owned and controlled by the provincial governments, in the territories, the federal government retains ownership and effective control of Crown land. Even taking into account the massive land holdings of the Aboriginal organizations such as NTI, this means that Ottawa owns and controls the vast bulk of land in the territorial North (relatively little land is privately owned). Among the implications of this ownership regime is that the substantial – and potentially massive – royalties from oil and gas production and mining flow to Ottawa rather than into territorial coffers (in southern Canada, royalty rates are set by and collected by provincial governments). Both Yukon and the Northwest Territories have reached "devolution" agreements with the federal government giving them administrative responsibility for lands and non-renewable resources, although in neither case have the territorial governments gained ownership of the land. Since Nunavut is entirely shut out of the lucrative royalties arising from development of its non-renewable natural resources, and since the small private sector provides only a limited tax base, Nunavut, like the other territorial governments, receives a large unconditional grant from Ottawa to fund its operations. This "territorial formula funding" provides as much as 90 per cent of the GN's revenue.

The GN and NTI have been pressing Ottawa to negotiate a devolution deal to enhance Nunavut's political and financial autonomy and to put Nunavummiut closer to an even footing with other Canadians. Yet progress has been glacial. The federal and territorial governments and NTI signed a negotiation protocol on devolution in 2008, but negotiations have yet to begin. Ottawa argues that Nunavut is not yet "ready" and lacks the capacity to take on such an important set of responsibilities, a stance that infuriates Nunavut leaders.[3] The failure of Ottawa to come to the table to work out a devolution agreement not only has huge financial implications for the GN, it also means that the federal government plays a far more influential role in natural resource development in Nunavut than it does in the provinces. However, some of the governance institutions established by the claim provide the opportunity for substantial Inuit involvement in decision-making on resource development, and of course Inuit collectively own and control extensive tracts of land.

Before embarking on our analysis we might ask how those most affected – Nunavummiut themselves – evaluate Nunavut. Thanks to a major study commissioned by the GN we have a detailed answer, and it is a sobering one. Shortly after taking office in late 2008, the government led by newly elected premier Eva Aariak engaged an independent consulting firm to produce a "report card" on the GN's performance at its ten-year anniversary. In conducting their review, the consultants held meetings in twenty-five communities and through these meetings, online surveys, and other methods heard from more than 2,100 people, a substantial proportion of Nunavut's adult population. The ensuing report, *Qanukkanniq? The GN Report Card: Analysis & Recommendations*[4] pulled no punches in recounting how Nunavummiut perceived their government:

> While many were happy with the progress being made in certain areas, most were disenchanted with, and some were profoundly discouraged by, directions taken by the government in others. Often people described governance in Nunavut as a vision not yet realized and, at times, a vision derailed. Without doubt, the expectations most people had of Nunavut at its inception have not yet been met ... we heard people speak critically of the government's performance in the areas that matter most to them. Many of these views were shared by public servants who expressed frustration that more was not being done. In fact, GN staff knew better than anyone the government's shortcomings, expressing deep concern about key but dysfunctional elements of the government's internal operating environment ... when Nunavut was created, people expected better interaction with government and that they would be involved in decisions that affect them. Today, they say that government has never seemed so distant ... they believe strongly that general service levels have dropped over the last ten years.[5]

Significantly, for all the criticism and disappointment voiced by Nunavummiut, goodwill remains: "While much of the commentary was critical of the government's performance, people everywhere said they supported Nunavut, and remained inspired by the dream that had created it. Many acknowledged that it was still early days for Nunavut and that ultimately government performance would align with public expectations."[6]

We now turn to our two conceptual approaches, political economy and political culture, to determine how they enable us to evaluate the political success of Nunavut.

Political Economy in Nunavut

Political economy and political culture approaches to understanding politics are by no means mutually exclusive, but they emphasize different elements of the political system. As the editors note in the introduction, political economy focuses on the linkages between politics – the distribution and use of political power – and social forces, most notably the economic divisions and groupings in society. The interests and activities of different economic strata, typically defined in terms of income, occupation, and class, are seen as especially important drivers of politics. Political economists include among the factors determining politics economic processes and structures outside the jurisdiction, such as international economic conditions and trends, and the extent to which control of economic resources and economic institutions (corporations, financial institutions) lies beyond the jurisdiction's borders. In a federal country like Canada, the economic – and thus the political – influence of corporations and governments located outside the jurisdiction may be greater than that of international factors. Central to the political economy approach is attention to the nature and effectiveness of mechanisms such as trade unions and political parties for mobilizing political action. In analysing politics, political economists pay special attention to state policies affecting the control and distribution of economic wealth and the provision of services contributing to the material welfare of the population, especially those who are most economically disadvantaged.

Sadly, Nunavut is well supplied with economically disadvantaged residents. An interconnected syndrome of social ills affects a substantial proportion of Nunavummiut – primarily Inuit. High rates of poverty, evident in high levels of food insecurity, are linked to over-crowded housing and poor health, and levels of family violence and suicide are worryingly high. Just as these social problems are inextricably intertwined, their causes are reflected in historical inequity and present-day neoliberal economic realities. As with Canada's other Aboriginal peoples, colonization profoundly affected the Inuit. Residential schools and resettlement, sometimes forcible, into permanent communities contributed to far-reaching cultural dislocation – the skills required of a good hunter are not readily transferable to office settings. In terms of economics, physical isolation, distance from markets, high transportation, and other costs all limit development prospects, as do low levels of education. While education outcomes are slowly improving (especially for women), lack of adequate education remains a major barrier to those attempting to climb out of poverty (in this regard, it is worth noting that Canada is the only Arctic country that does not have a Northern university). And while exploitation of Nunavut's enormous deposits of valuable natural resources represents strong economic development potential, even here, the social downsides are substantial. As a recent analysis of the Nunavut economy argued,

> The effect of a mining boom on social inclusion and the potential deterioration of Nunavut community well-being [is a notable risk]. At issue is the rise in income disparity that is a guaranteed outcome of economic growth and the possibility that community cohesion could suffer in the face of rapid economic and social change. The modernization that will take place in communities through rapid economic change tends to erode social ties. At the same time, both the perception and the reality of new inequalities are most likely increasing while the social institutions that might otherwise help people understand and cope with these changes are deteriorating.[7]

From the overview offered in the previous section, we might assume that *standard* political economy approaches are less helpful in understanding Nunavut than they are elsewhere in Canada. The imposition of the wage economy on Nunavummiut is a relatively recent development and indeed, a substantial proportion of the population remains only weakly tied to the wage economy. Key features of the traditional subsistence economy, which until only a few decades ago dominated what is now Nunavut, run fundamentally counter to essential elements of the capitalist economy, which has long held sway in Canada, namely the lack of interest in capital accumulation and the emphasis on community-wide sharing of resources. The latter is linked to the often ambivalent attitude of Inuit to unions; most government employees are unionized, and labour-management strife, including strikes, is not unknown, but discomfort is sometimes expressed that confrontational union behaviour "is not the Inuit way." Nunavut has only a small private sector. Notably, the most powerful private economic interests – resource development companies – are almost entirely owned and controlled by interests located outside Nunavut, often large multinational corporations. The Inuit land claims organizations and the extensive web of commercial corporations that they own, which differ substantially in their objectives and activities from privately owned firms, are important players in the economy.

Nunavut's economy is dominated by public-sector employment and activity. The private sector is limited largely to small retail, construction, and service (primarily hospitality/tourism and business services) sectors. Nunavut has virtually no manufacturing enterprises, though arts and crafts – mostly Inuit carvings and prints – provide supplementary income to many households. The traditional economy – hunting, fishing, and gathering – brings in little or no income but contributes substantially to many families' sustenance needs (and provides far more nutritious food than the expensive perishable food that has to be flown in from Ottawa, Montreal, or Winnipeg). In addition, traditional harvesting activities remain of huge cultural significance. Agriculture is entirely absent, but commercial fishing holds significant economic potential, though federal government policies impede the realization of that potential in two respects. First, the Department of Fisheries and Oceans assigns much of the quota for valuable species in waters adjacent to Nunavut to companies from Newfoundland and Labrador and Nova Scotia (and with the minister of fisheries and oceans typically representing a riding in one of these provinces, changing this policy is an uphill fight). Second, the lack of infrastructure – in this case, suitable harbour facilities – means that even Nunavut-based fishing vessels must often offload their catches and have them processed in southern Canada or even in Greenland.

This latter point is worth pursuing briefly. All but one of Nunavut's twenty-five communities are on the ocean, so that the absence of roads and the expense of air freight, almost all non-perishable supplies – vehicles, construction supplies, fuel, furniture, even bulk groceries – arrive by sea-going ships. Astonishingly, however, not a single community has docking facilities to handle even moderate-size ships, let alone large ocean-going transport ships.[8] Accordingly, cargo must be transferred onto barges that unload on local beaches when the tides are right; this is costly, inefficient, and dangerous. Nunavummiut rightly point out that their government cannot afford expensive infrastructure projects and that earlier in Canadian history it was the Government of Canada that built the wharves, docks, railways, canals, and other infrastructure needed to promote local economic development in the provinces.

Conventional political economy approaches are clearly relevant to understanding important elements of Nunavut politics. In particular, the difficult social and economic conditions of many Nunavummiut raise critical questions about the state's role in providing for the people's material well-being. In addition, a political economy approach highlights an important question about where Nunavut is heading in equality of economic condition: is the land claim and the creation of

Nunavut producing a class division within Nunavut society between a small Inuit elite doing well for itself and a large Inuit underclass struggling with poverty and social dysfunction?

Political Culture in Nunavut

Political culture researchers are fundamentally interested in the attitudinal and behavioural norms of political life. Typically, researchers are interested in attitudes towards government: whether citizens hold it in high regard, trust it to do what is right, feel that as citizens they can make a difference, or that the political system as a whole is responsive to their influence. Other indicators include measures of political engagement such as voting, standing for office, contacting politicians, or more "protest" behaviours such as attending rallies or signing petitions. Sometimes researchers examine the institutions about which individuals hold views, or the institutions that structure the way citizens participate. We can distinguish, therefore, between approaches that look at objective aspects of political culture, such as patterns of political recruitment, and subjective aspects such as citizen attitudes.

Political culture is a property of the political system as a whole. It is often measured by looking at indicators that are available at the individual level, but these are only partial ways of forming an impression of the overarching system. Political cultures can be fairly homogeneous, where the norms reinforced by institutions and held by elites and the rest of the electorate are fairly similar. These norms can also be heterogeneous, where clear differences distinguish, for example, the views of elites and "masses," or the subjective expectations of citizens and the behavioural norms of political institutions.

The political culture approach has much to offer those interested in Nunavut politics.[9] If you were to ask people about the unique features of political life in Nunavut, it is likely that they would refer to values or symbols relevant to political culture such as the layout and design of the debating chamber, consensus government, and the absence of parties, or maybe even the fact that government departments refer to policy fields such as "elders." The care and attention devoted to a sustainable environment might also receive a mention. In fact, political culture in Nunavut reflects a number of influences, some at cross-purposes, others mutually reinforcing, some clearly imposed and foreign, but some quite similar to values or behaviours in pre-contact society. Some wield greater influence over the political norms of citizens, while others have more do to with the working culture of institutions. Disentangling them is not easy.

Over several decades, the process of institutional creation has been a battleground for competing visions of political culture, and the current territory bears the hallmarks of four distinct cultural visions: first, the approaches to communal "political" life that dominated pre-contact and early contact life among Inuit in the eastern Arctic; second, the cultural influences of the federal government and government agents who sought to integrate Inuit in Canadian political life in the 1950s and 1960s; and third, the culture of a territorial administration, evident from the 1970s onwards as it established itself in Yellowknife after its 1967 relocation and, after 1999, in Iqaluit. We see now a fourth vision in the effort to ensure that Inuit values are at the centre of political decision-making.

In the first half of the twentieth century, Inuit did not have political institutions as we would recognize them, and the distribution of a small and nomadic population across the eastern Arctic produced distinct variation in practice by region. We can see in communal life a clear reliance on rules and codes of behaviour, with punishment for those found to be in breach, great emphasis on environmental stewardship, and an inherent conservatism that prioritised survival of the group. We can see also a distinction between spiritual leaders and secular camp leaders, between those who think and those who are obeyed,[10] or between those who hunted and those who took a more active role in the life of the settlement.[11] These secular camp leaders may be seen as precursors to contemporary politicians; in traditional society their role was less the policing of social behaviour than the steady supply of food and shelter.

In the 1960s the federal government promoted a political culture that sought to integrate Inuit as political citizens on a southern-Canadian model. Subsequently, in the pre-division Northwest Territories a distinctive Northern political culture developed, structuring the institutional working culture of the legislature and its civil service. The impact of these two components can be contradictory. The working culture of territorial institutions, for example, is a hybrid of institutional working practice common in Western liberal-democratic systems and adaptations specific to the North that reflect both accident and design. The most obvious manifestation is what has come to be termed "consensus government." In the NWT, and now Nunavut, candidates for office run as individuals rather than as representatives of political parties. Cabinet ministers are elected from among the successful candidates by all members of the legislative assembly (MLAs) rather than by the premier. This poses obvious challenges for Cabinet cohesiveness or solidarity. As in all Westminster systems, power resides principally with the premier and the Cabinet, but MLAs (both individually and through an all-MLA "caucus") have unusual scope for policy influence. This political system was, until 1999, unique to the NWT; since division, it prevails in Nunavut as well.

A fourth political cultural vision seeks to imbue the bureaucratic, liberal-democratic, Westminster form of government with more traditional approaches to Inuit governance. *Inuit Qaujimajatuqangit*, which can be seen as an attempt to transform the way decisions are reached or which priorities should be valued, can also be seen as a way to restructure a civil service and a polity, to alter the institutions that influence the lives of citizens to reflect better the way individuals relate to one another and the land that sustains them. It is, in part, a process of untangling cultural influences. Identifying those elements that are foreign or traditional, are helpful or unhelpful, is, however, not always clear. But *IQ* captures a desire to put Inuit values and priorities at the centre of policy and institutions and in this it highlights neatly both the dominant trends and challenges in Nunavut political culture. Such efforts face several challenges, not least the very powerful and established norms of the existing institutional arrangements. In addition, there is, perhaps not surprisingly, no uniform view of the "traditional approaches to Inuit governance" that might supplant existing practices.

Evaluating the Success of Nunavut

Having outlined some of Nunavut's salient features and set out how political economy and political cultures might be brought to bear, let us turn to an evaluation of Nunavut's success, recognizing that in many ways it is still very early in its economic and political development.

Political Engagement

One basic tenet of political culture research is that democratic polities require minimum levels of political engagement. Typically such research focuses on participation during elections, for it provides an opportunity to examine the most common form of political activity in which citizens engage – voting – as well as more "gladiatorial" activities such as standing as candidates for office. Elections in Nunavut operate slightly differently from the way they do in most other jurisdictions in Canada, though they are organized on the same "first-past-the-post" electoral system as elsewhere in the country. Since candidates run not as representatives of political parties but as independents, this raises the "costs" of participation for both candidates and voters. Candidates lack the institutional, organizational, and financial support that parties can provide. This can include anything from institutional knowledge acquired over several campaigns, or something as basic as lists of likely or sympathetic voters. Voters lack the cues that parties provide them in casting their ballots and must wade through the competing claims of different candidates to identify issues that are of interest to them, evaluating the proposals of each potential legislative member, as well as the candidates' personal qualifications and characteristics. One important upside is that, unlike elsewhere in Canada, where candidates other than those officially representing a major political party are rarely elected, anyone with a modicum of local support and modest financing can run for office with some prospect of winning.

In such a system it is difficult to identify issues that attract the attention of the entire electorate. This has both positive and negative aspects. Since candidates lack incentives to serve as aggregators of interest across the polity, territory-wide discussion of policy issues is often lacking. This not only means that it is difficult for the electorate to feel part of a cohesive whole, but also that important "big picture" issues may not be adequately addressed. Instead, candidates are more likely to identify local issues to attract the interest of local voters and in so doing raise the profile of what in other elections might be considered insignificant issues. At the same time, this can be of considerable benefit to local communities, whose concerns might not be highlighted in other types of campaigns. Data from a survey of all eighty-two candidates in the 2004 Nunavut election confirm the local orientation of territorial elections: when asked why they were running, 44 per cent mentioned local concerns, 20 per cent cited personal reasons, 15 per cent said they wanted to work on specific (non-local) issues, 15 per cent wanted to contribute to politics on a territory-wide basis, and 7 per cent mentioned ethnic concerns.[12]

Given all this, we might expect that levels of turnout would be lower than in other jurisdictions in Canada, or that the number of people putting themselves forward to contest seats would be lower. This expectation is premised on Nunavut's lack of one key agent of political recruitment and mobilization – political parties – that seek to identify or attract prospective candidates and to get voters out to the polls. As the results below demonstrate, however, this is not necessarily the case.

First, with respect to turnout and similar to smaller political communities in southern Canada such as PEI, levels of political engagement in Nunavut have typically been described as among the highest in the country, with recorded rates of turnout exceeding 100 per cent in some communities in the first two elections in 1999 and 2004. It should immediately be said that a careful review of the data reveals that turnout is far lower than the official figures suggest and that no community approaches, let alone exceeds, 100 per cent. The official figures are misleadingly high for two reasons. First, voters are allowed to register on the day of the election and cast their ballots. This in itself is not remarkable, but when the official turnout figures are calculated, the number of ballots cast is divided by the number of electors on the voting list compiled prior to the election. Thus a surge in last-minute voters can cause the turnout numbers to increase beyond 100 per cent. Second, variations in enumeration practices across communities produce voting lists that vary to differing degrees from the permanent voters list used for federal elections. In some communities, the federal and territorial lists have relatively similar numbers of potential voters. In others, whether because enumeration was done when more citizens were out on the land and away from the community or because individuals did not respond to requests for information, the territorial list has far fewer names.

Table 11.2 records turnout levels across the constituencies in Nunavut over the first four territorial elections. For the first three elections there were nineteen constituencies, which expanded to twenty-two for the 2013 elections. The changes brought a fourth constituency in Iqaluit, eliminated the unpopular Akulliq constituency (where candidates had to spend two days travelling between its two communities – Kugaaruk in the Kitikmeot region and Repulse Bay in the Kivalliq region), divided some of the larger communities such as Igloolik and Arviat, and moved smaller communities with different larger neighbours to accommodate population shifts. Across the four elections we can see higher levels of engagement, in both turnout and candidates, for 1999 and 2004 and far lower levels in 2008.[13] The number of candidates increased for 2013 but the level of turnout dipped below that in 2008. From a political culture perspective, do these figures give us reason to worry about political engagement in Nunavut?

Table 11.2. Levels of Political Engagement, 1999–2013

	1999		2004		2008		New constituency (blank if unchanged)	2013	
	Turnout (%)	Candidates	Turnout (%)	Candidates	Turnout (%)	Candidates		Turnout (%)	Candidates
Akulliq, Repulse Bay, Kugaaruk	78.01	2	93.33	5	78.1	5	See Netsilik		
Amittuq, Igloolik, Hall Beach	85.11	5	120.10	5	59.2	2	Amittuq, Igloolik South, Hall Beach	60.5	2
							Aggu, Igloolik North	49.4	3
Arviat	92.68	2	81.10	6	66.1	3	Arviat North, Whale Cove	75.9	5
							Arviat South	76.6	3
Baker Lake	103.01	3	89.50	4	67.1	3		70.7	2
Cambridge Bay	115.07	4	102.13	4	Acclamation	1		101.7	3
Hudson Bay, Sanikiluaq	79.01	2	96.09	5	81.6	3		76.1	4
Iqaluit East	97.67	2	112.4	3	73.2	3	Iqaluit Niaqunnguu	65.0	6
Iqaluit Centre	114.94	4	101.73	6	69.7	4	Iqaluit Tasiluk	72.1	5
							Iqaluit Sinaa	50.3	4
Iqaluit West	82.38	3	101.13	2	90.2	2	Iqaluit Manirajak	67.4	4
Kugluktuk	87.67	4	134.33	3	68.2	2	–	Acclamation	1
Nanulik, Coral Harbour, Chesterfield Inlet	90.61	5	77.78	4	86.3	3	Aivilik, Coral Habour, Repulse Bay	64.0	2

(*Continued*)

Table 11.2. (Continued)

	1999		2004		2008		New constituency (blank if unchanged)	2013	
	Turnout (%)	Candidates	Turnout (%)	Candidates	Turnout (%)	Candidates		Turnout (%)	Candidates
Nattilik, Taloyoak, Gjoa Haven	85.56	6	107.04	7	83.6	4	Netsilik, Taloyoak, Kugaaruk	Acclamation	1
							Gjoa Haven	70.2	4
Pangnirtung	80.99	6	83.95	2	54.7	2		80.0	4
Quttiktuq, Grise Fiord, Resolute Bay, Arctic Bay	67.99	6	81.34	6	63.8	2		72.7	2
Rankin Inlet North	78.94	3	Acclamation	1	Acclamation	1	Rankin Inlet North, Chesterfield Inlet	64.0	4
Rankin Inlet South (RI + Whale Cove)	85.67	3	78.48	5	63.9	2	Rankin Inlet South	56.9	2
South Baffin, Cape Dorset, Kimmirut	91.23	3	109.17	3	58.7	0 (4)		82.4	5
Tununiq, Pond Inlet	88.24	5	90.22	3	70.8	3		68.8	2
Uqqummiut, Clyde River, Qikiqtarjuaq	83.28	3	143.34	7	84.9	3		77.9	5

As table 11.2 also demonstrates, some constituencies have experienced a clear decline in the number of candidates standing for office. In 1999 and 2004 there were five and six candidates contesting the seats in Amittuq and Quttiktuq constituencies respectively, and only two each in 2008 and 2013. This could indicate a genuine decline in political interest levels among potential candidates or it could mean that, as patterns of Nunavut politics develop, potential candidates are taking a more measured assessment of their prospects of winning. Evidence for the latter interpretation would include the fact that in 2008 and 2013 sitting MLAs in four ridings were returned by acclamation (as opposed to one in 2004 and none in 1999), suggesting an unwillingness to take on strong, popular legislative members. Similarly, elections for top posts in NTI and the regional Inuit associations continue to attract substantial numbers of candidates. In Iqaluit, there were nineteen candidates seeking election in the four new constituencies in 2013, including former premier Eva Aariak, who lost her seat, and former premier Paul Okalik, who returned to the legislature. The experience in the nearby constituency of South Baffin in 2008, however, points in the other direction: when nominations closed, no one had come forward as a candidate, and the election had to be postponed pending a second nomination period, which produced four candidates.[14]

In terms of popular participation, the 2008 elections were held at both the territorial and federal levels, and the two lists of electors appear far more similar than in the past, a trend that continued in 2014. This suggests that the apparent declining rate of participation is in fact a product of the improved accuracy of the enumeration process, rather than declining levels of engagement.

An Effective – and Inuit – Government?

One of the most basic questions to be asked of any government relates to its effectiveness in delivering high-quality programs and services for its residents. Like any modern government, the GN can and should be measured by how well it performs its basic functions such as managing its finances, ensuring quality health care and education, protecting the environment, processing government cheques in a timely and accurate fashion, providing shelter and safety to those vulnerable or in need, and promoting economic growth. In addition, Nunavummiut judge their government by one of the primary goals of the Inuit leaders who for so many years pushed for the creation of an Inuit territory: a government operating according to Inuit values and practices and thus promoting and enhancing Inuit culture.

Realizing either set of goals has been difficult for the GN, not least because to some extent, at least in the short term, they conflict. While all governments encounter problems recruiting and retaining good staff, these essential elements of good governance have proven especially troublesome in Nunavut. Many of the more important – and better-paying – jobs in government require specific educational qualifications and/or extensive managerial experience that are in short supply among Inuit. Moreover, the GN faces stiff competition for talented Inuit from the land claims organizations, the private sector, and the federal government, all of which may offer more attractive salaries and benefits. It is expensive and difficult to attract qualified staff from southern Canada, so that since its first day the GN has been bedevilled by high vacancy rates. When bringing forward his 2010–11 budget Nunavut finance minister Keith Peterson acknowledged that some 900 GN jobs – nearly a third of the total – were vacant.[15] A blistering report from the auditor general of Canada (whose office audits all three territories) took the GN severely to task for systematic inadequacies in dealing with vacancies, revealing, for example, that on average it took 318 days to fill a vacancy and that half of GN job competitions failed to result in hiring.[16] With so many positions unfilled, and with the high rate of staff turnover that gives rise to many vacancies, it is difficult for the GN to discharge its responsibilities effectively, though paradoxically the money saved as a result of understaffing helps to keep the budget balanced.

The issue of Inuit staff levels within the GN is an especially important and sensitive one. Article 23 of the land claim contains an explicit provision requiring that Inuit hold "representative" levels of government positions in all employment categories. ("Government" in this instance encompasses the federal as well as the territorial government.) Since Inuit constitute well over 80 per cent of the population, this same proportion of Inuit should fill government jobs. Article 23, however, imposes no deadline, and a decade and a half on, the GN is little closer to achieving "representative levels" than it was when it opened for business. The goal, agreed by the three parties to the claim (Canada, the Government of the Northwest Territories, and the Tungavik Federation of Nunavut [NTI's predecessor]) was to have 50 per cent of GN employees be Inuit at start-up, and this goal was met. Subsequently, however, the level fell below 50 per cent, and although it recovered slightly, it remains mired at or just above that level.[17] Overall rates of Inuit hiring are only part of the story; the distribution of Inuit across employment categories is no less important. And here the record is even more disappointing. A recent count found 39 per cent Inuit in the very small executive cadre but only 20 to 26 per cent in the senior management, middle management, and professional categories; by contrast, the two lowest categories in the bureaucratic hierarchy, paraprofessionals and those in administrative support, were 72 and 91 per cent Inuit respectively.[18]

Article 23 was designed to ensure that Inuit would benefit economically from the creation of Nunavut through well-paid, stable employment in the public sector. A related objective was to create a government that operated according to traditional Inuit values and practices. A truly Inuit government in this sense would entail more than simply a government staffed by Inuit. Given the centrality of language to culture, the GN has committed to making Inuktitut the working language of government by 2020 and has brought in sweeping language legislation (the Official Languages Act and the Inuit Language Protection Act) to elevate the status of Inuktitut across the territory but especially in government. Inuktitut dominates in the legislative assembly; many front-line government services and forms are available in Inuktitut; some offices operate primarily in Inuktitut, and important documents are translated into Inuktitut. By and large, however, the GN operates in English, especially at its higher reaches. Achieving a government operating primarily in Inuktitut will not be easy with non-Inuit, very few of whom are fluent in Inuktitut, comprising nearly half the GN's workforce (and substantially more than half at higher levels). Moreover, given the GN's extensive interactions with other jurisdictions, notably but not exclusively the federal government, English will continue to be prominent within the Nunavut bureaucracy.[19]

So too, imbuing a large organization, whose structures and processes are very much determined by Western bureaucratic precepts, with Inuit values and approaches has proven challenging. The predominance of English is an obvious and important barrier, but even more fundamental is the lack of clarity as to what a government operating on *IQ* principles would look like. Government departments have *IQ* coordinators and committees, and the Department of Heritage and Culture (formerly the Department of Culture, Language, Elders, and Youth [CLEY]) has been assigned lead responsibility on the *IQ* initiative. However, progress on anything like a transformation of government services and bureaucracy has been limited.

In many ways the structure of the GN public service is conventional, in keeping with the premise recalled by John Amagoalik, the influential Inuit leader who chaired the commission that designed the GN: "We did not want to introduce anything that people did not really understand. We did not want to try to re-invent the wheel. We knew that up here people understood the territorial form of government and that was what they expected."[20] Establishing a department like CLEY was certainly innovative, and the retention of the NWT's non-partisan "consensus government" approach distinguishes Nunavut from party-based southern Canadian models.

Economic Development

Hope for a brighter economic future for Nunavut largely rests with the territory's non-renewable resources. Although massive oil and gas deposits have been discovered in Nunavut's Arctic Islands, daunting logistical and financial barriers have thus far stymied development. Mining holds more immediate promise, though hardly any instant solutions. Nunavut has extensive deposits of diamonds, gold, coal, iron ore, silver, uranium, and other valuable minerals, but the history of its mining industry is replete with problems and false starts. Some mines simply come to the end of their productive life – the Rankin Inlet nickel mine, iron ore at Nanisivik, the zinc mine on Little Cornwallis Island – while others fall victim to high operating costs and unstable markets: Nunavut's first diamond mine lasted less than two years before closing in response to unsustainable losses (it subsequently reopened under new ownership but the new owners soon closed it again and literally disappeared, leaving unpaid bills and clean-up costs). As of early 2014, only one mine was operating in Nunavut, though many other projects were at various stages of exploration and planning.

Potential ventures require huge capital investments and often demand extensive publicly funded infrastructure and are thus vulnerable to shifting international economic conditions that slow or altogether halt their development. The Baffinland Iron Mines Corporation's project at Mary River in North Baffin Island involves what is said to be the largest untapped top-quality iron ore body on the planet but requires billions of dollars of capital. Baffinland's original plan included construction of a 150-kilometre railway across very difficult terrain and of a deep-water port. Early in 2013, Baffinland drastically scaled back its plans; at the time of writing, the revised proposal is before regulatory authorities.

The Baffinland project highlights basic questions about who gains and who loses from non-renewable resource extraction in Nunavut. Three sets of issues are in play. First, who will get the jobs – often high-paying jobs – at the mines? For many years the history of mining (and of oil and gas projects) in the far North was marked either by outright exclusion of local Aboriginal people from employment or by relegating them to the lowest-paid jobs. More recently, Aboriginal organizations and territorial governments have insisted that industry train and hire substantial numbers of Aboriginal workers and direct as much subcontracting to Aboriginal firms as possible. Still, despite notable improvement along these lines, Inuit generally lack the formal education for the management and high-end technical mining jobs. Second, which level of government collects the huge royalties from profitable mining operations? As noted above, with Crown land owned by the federal government, royalties on mining accrue to the national treasury, not to the GN, though the GN taxes the economic activity that mining generates.

The third question is the most important and the most difficult: what will be the environmental consequences of widespread resource extraction? Not only is the Arctic ecosystem singularly fragile, but mining activities directly threaten the fundamental foundation of Inuit culture: a deeply spiritual connection to the land and the animals. Potentially irreversible damage to sensitive caribou calving grounds, marine mammal habitat, and spiritually significant places are of deep concern to many Nunavummiut. As one Inuit leader told a recent mining symposium, "We're still here after the mines close [but] it's next to impossible for the land to be the way it was before."[21] While the Mary River project could bring hundreds of much-needed jobs to the region, residents of communities such as Igloolik strongly oppose the prospect of dozens of massive ore-carriers, with their potential for catastrophic oil spills, plying nearby waters.

Inuit and other Nunavummiut do have mechanisms for influencing major resource development projects. The land claim created a series of co-management boards ("institutions of public government," or IPGs) with guaranteed Inuit participation and rigorous processes for reviewing and modifying – and occasionally blocking – such projects. While many board recommendations require agreement of federal or territorial ministers, few have been rejected or modified, so that in most instances they effectively determine whether roads, mines, or even mineral exploration projects go ahead. In 2010 the Nunavut Impact Review Board (NIRB), one of the IPGs, recommended to the federal government that a major coal-mining project proposed for Ellesmere Island be rejected entirely (or very substantially modified), on the grounds that it "may have significant adverse effects on the ecosystem, wildlife habitat or Inuit harvesting activities ... [and that it] may have significant adverse socio-economic effects on northerners."[22] Ottawa accepted the recommendation and the project was cancelled.

Important as the IPGs can be, they by no means guarantee that Inuit concerns over the environmental and social costs of development will be heeded, not least because there are significant divisions within Nunavut and within Inuit organizations and communities over the relative costs and benefits of non-renewable resource development. By way of illustration, at the time of writing, NIRB was engaged in a protracted review, which included public hearings, on a proposed uranium mine near Baker Lake, a project that brought out deep divisions within Nunavut over resource extraction. Many local residents, supported by broad-based wildlife associations and citizens groups, entirely reject the idea of introducing such a toxic element to their environment and warn that if one mine is approved, others are likely to follow. Others argue that the economic benefits are worth the risks. A local environmental interest group, Nunavummiut Makitagunarningit, claimed that the NIRB process favoured the company over the Inuit of Baker Lake.[23]

Among those promoting not just large resource development projects but those involving uranium have been Inuit land claim organizations. After much debate, in 2007 NTI reversed its long-standing opposition to uranium mining. It subsequently granted approval for uranium prospecting on certain Inuit-owned lands and in 2010, along with two of the three regional Inuit associations, established the Nunavut Resources Corporation. This company, whose aim is to give Inuit greater involvement in and economic benefit from their non-renewable resources, participates in joint ventures in two uranium exploration projects. Subsequently, spurred on by concerns raised in debates about the Baker Lake project, NTI announced a review of its uranium policy, though in late 2011 it decided not to alter it. The GN, after a perfunctory review conducted by the consulting firm that had earlier worked on the proposal for the Baker Lake mine, declared itself in support of uranium mining. One analyst has written, "The story of how Nunavut was opened up to the nuclear industry stands as a warning to indigenous peoples elsewhere: the settlement of indigenous rights claims can result in the emergence of a managerial and petty bourgeois elite whose class instincts are to cozy up to capital."[24]

If the Inuit land claims organizations' involvement in uranium mining may be surprising – and indeed to some in Nunavut, disturbing – their status as major economic players is not. Under the land claim the Inuit received $1.14 billion over a fifteen-year period in partial compensation for giving up title to their traditional lands. Following the practice in other comprehensive land claim agreements, this money was not divided up among Inuit beneficiaries but transferred to NTI (which also holds title to the 350,000 square kilometres of Inuit-owned lands specified under the claim) and invested in a trust fund. Land claim monies have been used to create a vast network of companies operating across the North that not only provide jobs and training to Inuit but also keep profits in Nunavut. In addition to Atuqtuarvik Corporation, which provides expertise and loans to Inuit-owned businesses, NTI, through its holding company, Nunasi Corporation, owns outright or has partnership arrangements in a wide variety of business ventures including retail, transportation, manufacturing, insurance, travel, education, multimedia, fuel distribution, digital communications, medical boarding facilities, contracting, and real estate.[25] For example, Nunasi and the Inuvialuit Development Corporation, Nunasi's equivalent for the Inuvialuit of the NWT, jointly own NorTerra, which in turns owns two of Northern Canada's most important transportation enterprises, Canadian North airline and Northern Transportation Company Limited. The three regional Inuit associations have similar economic development "birthright" corporations.

Important as these Inuit-owned firms unquestionably are for the Nunavut economy, their size and economic clout pales beside the huge multinational corporations (MNCs) that dominate the mining sector. From this perspective, conventional political economy approaches, which stress the scope and power of neoliberal globalism in the form of massive, highly mobile capital investments by MNCs, have clear relevance to Nunavut. With exploration and start-up costs for a major mine often running into hundreds of millions of dollars, only large, powerful multinationals can afford to be in the game. Nor is it surprising that foreign-owned companies are at the forefront of mining development in Nunavut, companies such as ArcelorMittal, said to be the world's largest steelmaker, which owns 70 per cent of Baffinland Iron Mines; AREVA, the French nuclear giant behind the proposed Kiggavik uranium mine near Baker Lake; and MMG Limited, a subsidiary of China Minmetals Corporation, an arm of the Chinese government, which owns two large tracts of mineral-rich land in Western Nunavut.

The potential jobs arising from these projects are very attractive, but the social and environmental risks are substantial. What is more, not everyone welcomes the prospect of much of the value of Nunavut's natural resources leaving the territory in the form of corporate profits or Ottawa-bound royalties. The questions of how much benefit the people of Nunavut receive from mining developments and what sort of controls are needed to regulate these mining giants have led to internally conflicted responses from the GN, Inuit organizations, and local communities. It might be expected that conflict over resource development pits the federal government and the MNCs against the GN, the Inuit organizations, and local communities. Not so: both the GN and NTI favour increased mining activity and, as discussed, local people in the communities are often deeply divided over the prospect of resource development.

Quality of Life Indicators

Advocates of the land claim and territorial division argued that the creation of Nunavut would bring two types of benefits. One involved cultural emancipation for the Inuit population, including improved opportunities to pursue education in Inuktitut, greater chances to work in Inuktitut, greater representation of Inuit in the public service, greater representation of Inuit values in the legislature and the public service, greater opportunities to pursue life on the land for those who so wished, and, in general, greater voice for Inuit. A second set of expected benefits were material, on the premise that the land claim would provide a much-needed infusion of capital and the political control required to improve standards of living in the Eastern Arctic. These were ambitious goals, and it is worth considering the time frame for assessing success. What level of improvement over what length of time would be necessary for the territory to be considered a success? Would five years be sufficient? Would Nunavut be considered a success if standards of living remained comparable to before 1999, in other words if they did not decline? Or would we expect an appreciable increase in levels of economic activity or the quality of life indicators such as adequate housing?

Table 11.3. Economic Indicators and Language Use in Canadian Inuit Communities, 1996–2006

	1996				2006			
	Western NWT (NWT)	Eastern NWT (Nunavut)	Nunavik	Nunatsiavut	NWT	Nunavut	Nunavik	Nunatsiavut
Housing (%)								
Old	43.6	45.9	18.3	51.7	50.6	47.0	41.0	39.3
In need of major repair	16.4	21.5	11.2	31.1	25.3	24.9	40.9	29.7
Crowded	15.4	25.8	25.4	17.4	8.9	21.5	28.5	3.2
Education (%)								
No degree, diploma, or certificate	53.4	57.6	65.1	51.2	58.9	61.3	62.1	47.3
High school	4.5	2.8	4.1	7.2	12.0	8.8	10.3	17.2
Trade or college	23.8	21.3	12.5	23.3	20.2	20.0	19.8	26.5
University	6.4	5.6	8.3	7.0	5.1	6.0	5.8	5.6
Economic vitality								
Pre-tax income	$22,542	$19,611	$19,396	$15,320	$20,613	$18,258	$20,601	$18,136
Economic participation rate	69.2	62.4	65.3	56.1	65.9	63.0	69.6	56.3
Language (%)								
Aboriginal mother tongue	20.1	79.5	91.0	11.9	17.9	79.2	91.9	12.8
Use Aboriginal language at home	4.5	71.1	90.0	4.4	4.2	61.5	88.3	3.6

Sources: Statistics Canada census 1996, 2006, community profiles

The data in table 11.3 provide four indicators relevant to both sets of goals: the quality of housing, educational attainment, economic activity, and language use. The table presents figures from 1996 and 2006 for the Inuit populations in the four regions numerically dominated by Inuit: Nunatsiavut (Labrador), Nunavik (northern Quebec), the Inuvialuit region of the NWT, and Nunavut. If we look only at the figures for Nunavut, we see no appreciable change in economic activity and language use and some change in housing and education. The proportion of overcrowded houses decreased slightly, but the proportion of housing stock in need of major repair increased. With respect to education, the proportion of residents completing high school has risen dramatically. The figures remain low, but between 1996 and 2006 there was a threefold increase in the proportion of individuals who have obtained high school diplomas.[26]

These figures could, of course, be looked at in another way. We can examine the figures for Nunavut in light of the data for the NWT, Nunatsiavut, and Nunavik. This will help us to understand the changes in context. Land claim advocates argued that a land claim and division were necessary so that Inuit could have greater control over policy and create policy better tailored to the needs of the local population. If the results in Nunavut are improved *relative* to the results in other communities, if they improved while others remained stable, or if they remained stable while all others fell, then even the more muted results discussed above might be considered a success. Each of the other regions saw an increase in rates of those obtaining high school diplomas, so we should be cautious attributing the increase in Nunavut to the creation of the territory itself. The absence of an improvement in language use mirrors results across the other Inuit regions, while the absence of economic improvement in Nunavut can be evaluated in light of a decreasing rate of participation in the NWT and an increase in Nunavik. Whether such changes are within the control of the government or are subject to other economic "legacies" is, of course, a matter for debate. Lastly, the decrease in overcrowded housing, which seems impressive when we look only at Nunavut, seems more muted when compared to Nunatsiavut, where the proportion of crowded houses fell from 17 to 3 per cent in ten years.

How do Inuit of Nunavut compare with those in other jurisdictions? Are Nunavut Inuit significantly better off? Are they significantly worse off? In both 1996 and 2006 there were statistically significant differences across the communities on all indicators except for the proportion with university degrees, the economic participation rate, and pre-tax income. In several instances this is not because the Nunavut communities distinguished themselves at either the high or low end of the scale, but because of remarkable results in other regions. The data in table 11.3 indicate no dramatic variation in four sets of cultural and economic indicators before and after the creation of Nunavut, which is to say that the people of Nunavut, while not noticeably better off after 1999, are not noticeably worse off than they were before.

In-depth studies of such social policy fields as housing, suicide and suicide prevention, and education policy consistently reveal that the GN continues to struggle to provide basic social services and to deal with far-reaching social problems.[27] The continuing demographic pressures, together with the GN's limited room for financial manoeuvre, mean that progress on these and other fronts will be slow. And of course the GN's ongoing capacity deficit further complicates the process of improving the cultural and material well-being of Nunavummiut.

Conclusion

While up-to-date hard data are difficult to come by, a growing sense of disappointment and frustration with Nunavut's success is evident among Nunavummiut, as evidenced by the North Sky "report card." Systematic analysis of survey data from Nunavut's first few years uncovered an emerging trend of dissatisfaction with the GN, no doubt partially reflecting the widely held yet clearly unrealistic expectations (especially among Inuit) as to how implementation of the land claim and creation of Nunavut would improve their lives.[28] Initially, Nunavummiut were clearly judging Nunavut and the land claim on their cultural rather than economic merits.[29] By the 2004 election, though, popular concern with economic issues far outpaced interest in cultural concerns: when asked "What is the biggest challenge facing Nunavut?," 47 per cent of respondents to the Nunavut Household Survey mentioned aspects of territorial economic vitality, whereas only 11 per cent cited cultural vitality of primary importance.[30]

Judging by the indicators analysed in this chapter – political participation, the functioning of its civil service, the extent to which Nunavut is an Inuit government, and standards of living – Nunavut's record of success is indeed mixed. So too, whether Nunavut's success is analysed from a political economy or political culture perspective, the results are mixed.

A final point about political culture and political economy is important. Although we have examined Nunavut through the separate lenses they offer, we recognize that the two are linked. Their interconnection was brought home in a commentary on an early draft of this chapter by Jim Bell, long-time editor of Nunavut's principal newspaper, *Nunatsiaq News*, and an astute observer of territorial politics. Bell argued that despite the heavy dependence of Nunavummiut on government and the pressing need for better government services, many Inuit harbour intense resentment and suspicion of government, reflecting a populist, deeply conservative political culture. Success in establishing the goal of an Inuit-dominated territory, Bell wrote, "created more of the thing that so many Inuit hated, and still hate: government."[31] If, as many would agree, strong state action is required to confront Nunavut's problems, and Bell's interpretation of present-day Inuit political culture as significantly anti-government is correct, it is little wonder that many Nunavummiut are conflicted about the way forward.

While it is fair to observe that the territory and its government are only sixteen years old and have faced difficult circumstances from the outset, it is too easy to dismiss lack of progress by reference to growing pains and inexperience and to hope that things will improve. And yet, harkening back to a key conclusion of the North Sky "report card," a substantial residue of goodwill and optimism remains among Nunavummiut. Four decades ago, few in the Eastern Arctic or elsewhere would have believed that a far-reaching land claim could be settled or an Inuit-dominated territory established. Whether the promise of Nunavut set out by the visionary Inuit leaders who made the land claim and the territory a reality – a promise of fundamental importance to all Nunavummiut – will be fulfilled remains an open question.

NOTES

1 See Statistics Canada, "Population and Dwelling Counts, for Canada, Provinces and Territories, and Census Subdivisions (Municipalities), 2011 and 2006," http://www12.statcan.gc.ca/census-recensement/2011/dp -pd/hlt-fst/pd-pl/Table-Tableau.cfm?LANG=Eng&T=302&SR=1&S=51&O =A&RPP=9999&CMA=0&PR=62.
2 Conference Board of Canada, *Northern Outlook: Economic Forecast* (Ottawa: Conference Board, January 2010), 4.
3 On devolution, see Tony Penikett, "Destiny or Dream Sharing Resources, Revenues and Political Power in Nunavut Devolution," in *Polar Law Textbook II*, ed. Natalia Loukacheva, 199–213 (Copenhagen: Nordic Council of Ministers, 2013); Anthony Speca, "Nunavut, Greenland and the Politics of Resource Revenue," *Policy Options*, May 2012, 62–7.

4 North Sky Consulting Group, *Qanukkanniq? The GN Report Card: Analysis & Recommendations* (Iqaluit: North Sky, October 2009).

5 Ibid., 2–5.

6 Ibid., 1.

7 Nunavut Economic Forum, *2010 Nunavut Economic Outlook: Nunavut's Second Chance* (Iqaluit: Nunavut Economic Forum, October 2010), 59.

8 One modest dock project was recently completed at Pangnirtung, and the federal government plans to turn the former Nanisivik mine site, which has good harbour facilities, into a docking and refuelling centre for the military. Other deep-water ports have been discussed in connection with possible mining activity. For a sympathetic analysis of the lack of wharves and docks in Nunavut, see Senate of Canada, Standing Committee on Fisheries and Oceans, *Nunavut Marine Fisheries: Quotas and Harbours* (Ottawa, June 2009), 18–26.

9 For an analysis of Nunavut political culture, including the three separate strands influencing contemporary political culture, see Ailsa Henderson, *Nunavut: Rethinking Political Culture* (Vancouver: UBC Press, 2007).

10 Marc Stevenson, *Traditional Inuit Decision-Making Structures and the Administration of Nunavut* (Ottawa: Royal Commission on Aboriginal Peoples, 1993).

11 Henderson, *Nunavut*, 48.

12 Ibid., 121–2.

13 The figure for the 2008 election includes two persons who were ruled ineligible to be candidates because they failed to meet residency requirements, but not the four candidates in South Baffin by-election required because no candidates were nominated at the general election. See Annis May Timpson, "The 2008 Nunavut Territorial Election" (paper presented at the Annual Meeting of the Canadian Political Science Association, Carleton University, Ottawa, June 2009).

14 See ibid.

15 Jim Bell, "Nunavut Holds the Line in 'Stable' 2010–11 Budget," *Nunatsiaq News*, 8 March 2010.

16 See Office of the Auditor General of Canada, *Report of the Auditor General of Canada to the Legislative Assembly of Nunavut 2010: Human Resource Capacity – Government of Nunavut*, March 2010.

17 As of June 2014, 50 per cent of permanent GN employees (departments, agencies, boards, and corporations) were Inuit. See Government of Nunavut, Department of Finance, "Towards a Representative Public Service: Statistics as of June 30, 2014," 4.

18 Ibid.

19 On language policy in Nunavut, see Annis May Timpson, "Reconciling Settler and Indigenous Language Interests: Language Policy Initiatives in Nunavut," *Journal of Canadian Studies* 43 (Spring 2009): 159–80.

20 John Amagoalik, *Changing the Face of Canada: The Life Story of John Amagoalik,* ed. Louis McComber (Iqaluit: Nunavut Arctic College, 2009), 128.

21 Gabriel Zarate, "Nunavut Mayors Warned to Look beyond Immediate Benefits of Mining" *Nunatsiaq News*, 21 April 2010.

22 Lucassie Arragutainaq, NIRB chairperson, to Chuck Strahl, minister of Indian and northern affairs, 22 February 2010.

23 Nunavummiut Makitagunarningit, "NIRB Has Failed Us," 24 March 2011, news release, http://makitanunavut.wordpress.com/press-releases/.

24 Jack Hicks, "The Dissociative State of Nunavut," *Canadian Dimension*, May–June 2013.

25 For a listing of Nunasi's holdings, see Nunasi Corporation, http://www .nunasi.com/wp-content/uploads/2013/06/2014-04-21-nunasi-info -package-sm.pdf.

26 Entries in the table are progressive, that is, they indicate the highest level of education received by an individual.

27 See Frank Tester, "Iglutaasaavut (Our New Homes): Neither 'New' nor 'Ours': Housing Challenges of the Nunavut Territorial Government," *Journal of Canadian Studies* 43 (Spring 2009): 137–58; Jack Hicks, "Toward More Effective Evidence-Based Suicide Prevention in Nunavut," in *Northern Exposure: Peoples, Powers and Prospects in Canada's North*, ed. Frances Abele, Thomas J. Courchene, and F. Leslie Seidle, 467–95 (Montreal: Institute for Research on Public Policy, 2009); Derek Rasmussen, "Forty Years of Struggle and Still No Inuit Right to Education in Nunavut," *Our Schools / Ourselves* 19 (Fall 2009): 67–86; Nunavut Tunngavik Incorporated, *Annual Report on the State of Inuit Culture and Society 05/06, 06/07: Kindergarten to Grade 12 Education in Nunavut* (Iqaluit: Nunavut Tunngavik, 2007).

28 Henderson, *Nunavut*, 201–12.

29 Ibid., 212.

30 Ibid., 124.

31 Advocatus Diaboli [Jim Bell], "The Nunavut Territory: Populist, Conservative, Conflicted," 16 September 2010, www.titiraqti.wordpress .com/2010/09/16/the-nunavut-territory-populist-conservative-conflicted/.

12 The Northwest Territories: A New Day?

GABRIELLE A. SLOWEY[1]

Where else in the world would you find such excellent aboriginal economic models and rich resources?

Bruce Valpy[2]

The question of devolution (the transfer of power and control over land, resources, and water from Ottawa to the territorial government) in the Northwest Territories (NWT) has a long history. After a century of petitions and eleven years of negotiations, in January 2011, the federal government and the Government of the Northwest Territories (GNWT) announced that a deal (agreement in-principle or AIP) had been achieved. Members of the territorial legislature ratified the agreement on 5 June 2013 (only Michael Nadli, the MLA for the Dehcho region, voted against the agreement). Premier Bob McLeod, minister of Aboriginal affairs and northern development Bernard Valcourt, and leadership from the Inuvialuit Regional Corporation, the NWT Metis Nation, the Sahtu Secretariat Inc., the Gwich'in Tribal Council and the Tlicho Government added their signatures to the final agreement. The NWT Lands and Resources Devolution Agreement was signed in Inuvik on 25 June 2013 with the final transfer of powers taking place 1 April 2014.

While the majority of residents of the NWT agree with devolution in principle and the achievement of a devolution agreement is certainly laudable, the question this chapter asks is: does it represent a new day for the NWT? This chapter argues that the devolution deal is not a panacea for the NWT because, as it stands, its terms are far from ideal. Although devolution may represent an important step in the

348 Gabrielle A. Slowey

political and economic evolution of the territory, it does not promise to significantly alter the path of development for the territory. In fact, as I shall further show, the results may prove just the opposite. In the end, devolution means that the Government of Canada's (GOC) embedded neoliberalism is simply being reproduced at the local level. As a result, devolution only transforms the GWNT into another colonizing government.

Looking at changes that have occurred over the past forty years, this chapter argues that delays in devolution have significantly impeded economic development. Instead, the federal government has remained heavily invested and involved in regulating the lives and the economy of the NWT. All of that may change as devolution takes hold. Yet even though there is market demand for increased oil and gas activity, obstacles to further economic growth (like environmental reviews and government regulatory processes) continue to frustrate industrial proponents and locals alike. Consequently, what is revealed is the paradox of neoliberalism for the north. While neoliberalism promises less government intervention, the NWT's path to economic development remains tied to activist government intervention.

Tracing political and economic developments, this chapter considers the role that devolution plays in the history of the Canadian north in general and in the NWT in particular. It charts the rocky road to devolution and cautions that the agreement, once portrayed as a cure-all for territorial problems, may in fact lead to new and different problems for the population while also exacerbating underlying tensions. In addition, the focus on economic development eclipses many of the social needs that continue to plague the territory. The pursuit of devolution has not been just about improving the economic condition of the region but also represents an important step towards developing solutions to local problems. In many ways the realization of devolution and changes to the federal regulatory process reflects the broader extent to which the federal government continues to guide the development of the NWT in particular, with an eye to Canadian economic development more generally. This reality further exposes the historic colonial status of the territory within Canada. As Frances Abele has put it, "To this day, northern development policy follows very old patterns set by the National Policy of 1879."[3] I conclude that although the territory has experienced some important changes, its development and prosperity continue to be controlled by the GOC.

Political Development and Devolution

It was only in 1870 that the land "northwest" of Rupert's Land was transferred to the control of the Dominion of Canada (a full three years after Confederation). Over the course of the next fifty years the land previously known as the northwestern territory was eventually chiselled away to allow for the development of the Prairie Provinces. From the beginning, the territory appealed for devolution (transfer) of power from Ottawa because under the terms of the Constitution (1867), territories are creatures of the federal government. That is, they do not represent their own order of government as a province does. Instead, the territories remain under the tutelage and control of the federal government. In 1967, this dream of devolution for the Northwest Territories came one step closer to reality with the creation of Yellowknife as the territorial capital and home to the GNWT.[4] Until that point, the territory had been governed directly by civil servants in Ottawa. While there was a territorial council, its main function was to act as advisor to the territorial commissioner, the local representative of Ottawa. After the creation of responsible government in the territory, the seat of government moved to Yellowknife, with the first fully elected legislative assembly being realized in 1975.

Similar to the governance structures in Nunavut, the territorial legislature remains distinctive in that there are no elected parties represented. Individuals are elected to the government as independents, and a Cabinet and premier are chosen from among those elected. Government also runs by consensus instead of by majority rule, which is also tied to the lack of party system. Among the nineteen-seat legislature, many Aboriginal peoples have been elected as representatives, reflecting their strong demographic presence in the territory (representing 50 per cent of the total population). Yet despite the formation of a local government in 1975, the GNWT had very little autonomy. That came only later in the 1970s and 1980s when Ottawa began to devolve some political authority to the territory.

Over the years, subsequent premiers have pushed Ottawa to grant the territory more province-like powers. While devolving power to Yellowknife was certainly viewed as an important step for the territory, it has occurred only piecemeal. With the political and economic shift to neoliberalism in the 1980s and 1990s, the federal government began to transfer program control over matters like forestry management, education, social welfare, and housing to the territorial government, which then assumed decision-making and administrative responsibility. During this period it also introduced territorial formula financing (TFF), which is reviewed every five years. Until 1985 all fiscal decisions were decided directly by Ottawa; elected politicians in the NWT had no role in this process. In 1986, after territorial formula financing was introduced, the GNWT was free to spend this amount at their discretion.[5] Yet, despite the apparent increase in autonomy, the federal government maintained political control in the territory. To clarify, while administrative duties associated with health care and resources were also transferred to the territory, the federal government retained all decision-making power in these areas. At the same time that the federal government offloaded administrative responsibility, it retained strict fiscal control over the territory's finances, with the consequence that the growth rate of expenditures has been higher than revenues. As Peter Eglington and Lew Voytilla explain in a 2011 report, "The federal government plays a huge role in financing GNWT. The principal source of GNWT own-financing is a combination of personal income taxes, corporate income taxes and payroll taxes, which however only account for 13.7% of total revenues. The (territorial) Grant and other transfer payments account for close to 80% of revenues. The federal government keeps the territory on a tight leash and in addition it limits the net debt of GNWT to $500 million."[6]

The experience with devolution so far has been an increase in responsibility without increased fiscal capacity. There has also been an accompanying increase in the number of government offices across the territory, yet most of these new government officials are limited in their ability to address socio-economic conditions.

When coupled with the emergence of regional land claim boards and governance agents like the Inuvialuit Regional Council and its community representative bodies, the general increase in government agencies has resulted in the territory now boasting "more public officials than any other jurisdiction in Canada."[7] For instance, one need only roam around the hamlet of Tuktoyaktuk (population 935 according to the 2011 data of the NWT statistics bureau) to find as many as five levels of government (federal, territorial, hamlet, Tuktoyaktuk community corporation, and Inuvialuit regional corporation) operating in the community. In addition to the increased physical presence of different levels of government across the territory is the consolidation of federal power across the territory vis-à-vis the conditional access to jurisdictional authority and program delivery within self-government agreements. Although in many respects the GNWT sets its own priorities, greater autonomy and control remains elusive, as the federal government continues to retain a strong presence in the overall administration and governance of the territory.

More recently, in 2009 the GOC under the leadership of Stephen Harper announced a formal, four-pronged northern strategy that prioritizes sovereignty, sustainable development, environmental protection, and devolution. Setting the stage for the strategy, the 2007 Speech from the Throne announced,

> [The Conservative] government will bring forward an integrated northern strategy focused on strengthening Canada's sovereignty, protecting our environmental heritage, promoting economic and social development, and improving and *devolving governance*, so that northerners have greater control over their destinies.
>
> To take advantage of the North's vast opportunities, northerners must be able to meet their basic needs. [The] government will work to continue to improve living conditions in the North for First Nations and Inuit through better housing. [emphasis added][8]

On the surface, it would seem that the Conservative government is interested in transferring power and control to the territories. Yet, upon closer inspection, what is revealed is the extent to which the federal government continues to drive devolution, in essence laying out the terms of any deal to the territory and ultimately retaining significant financial control. Pursuant to the new strategy, in January 2011 the Harper government signed a devolution deal agreement-in-principle (AIP) with Floyd Roland, the premier of the Government of the Northwest Territories. While this latest development initially appeared as a step forward, it came almost a decade after devolution was achieved in the Yukon, at a time when no formal strategy was yet in place.

As chapter 13 in this volume demonstrates, the Yukon stands alone as the most "devolved" territory in the north. As far back as 2001, the federal government and the Yukon signed the Yukon Northern Affairs Program Devolution Agreement that transferred formal power on 1 April 2003. In 1998, province-like authority for oil and gas was devolved under the Canada-Yukon Oil and Gas Accord (YOGA). Feehan clarifies that this agreement does not, however, extend to offshore reserves that may exist in the Beaufort Sea, where the federal government retains control.[9] In that area, the Yukon is seeking a shared management regime, including a revenue-sharing agreement. An important catalyst to devolution in the Yukon was the 1992 Umbrella Final Agreement (UFA) between the GOC, Yukon territorial government, and the Council of Yukon Indians (now Council for Yukon First Nations, or CYFN), which created a new regime for land rights, mineral rights, and self-government in the territory. Important to this development is that about 9 per cent of the area of the Yukon now belongs to Aboriginal peoples. Feehan explains that attached to this area are subsurface as well as surface rights, which means "that petroleum and other subsurface minerals belong to the relevant Aboriginal community and not the Crown."[10] Of course, as Feehan also points out, despite these resource agreements, there has been relatively little to share.[11] While there is some oil and gas production, royalties from these accrue to the territory's First Nations. The extraction of natural resources in the territory, however, is fairly insignificant, representing only 3 per cent of the territory's GDP. The key therefore lies in the potential of these agreements in areas of future development. Yet as Kirk Cameron points out,[12] what is really up for discussion is the transfer of control rather than the transfer of ownership of natural resources. As ownership remains with the federal government, the territory ultimately remains subject to federal domination. In this way, the important differences between the Yukon and the NWT boil down to the resource wealth of the NWT (and the revenues that accrue to Ottawa) and the willingness of the Yukon territorial government to work with indigenous governments to achieve devolution.[13]

In contrast, the Nunavut Land Claim (as Henderson and White examine in chapter 11 of this volume) established public government and awarded some title to land that includes mineral rights. However, in terms of devolution of jurisdiction over Crown lands and natural resources, Feehan suggests that little progress has been made and it may be some time in coming. Part of the explanation for the delay is that the Nunavut government wants devolution to include offshore areas and 100 per cent of natural resource revenues.[14]

Another factor to consider in Nunavut is certainly the fact that the federal government has been extremely reluctant to begin serious negotiations. Certainly the prospect of hydrocarbon resources offshore makes it unlikely that the Nunavut government will succeed in its claim. So, in essence, only the Yukon has been delegated jurisdiction in this area, but it is limited to onshore resources and revenue-sharing agreements that Feehan argues are quite "ungenerous."[15] Critics of the NWT devolution agreement concur, questioning the "generosity" of a deal that offers the GNWT only 50 per cent of all resource revenue collected up to a maximum of $65 million (with the remainder returned to the GOC through adjustments to transfer payments, of which 25 per cent must be set aside for indigenous governments).[16] As Irlbacher-Fox put it,

> While everyone agrees that devolution – the transfer of authority over Crown lands and resources to Northern governments (read: Indigenous governments and the GNWT) – is desirable, the deal ... has garnered considerable criticism by Indigenous governments and independent observers. The resource revenue sharing deal associated with that devolution agreement allows Canada to keep most resource revenues under a resource royalty regime that sells oils and minerals far too cheaply. And when you sell it that cheap – you cannot share, it would seem. So while Northern governments will see small benefits from that deal, they are a pittance compared to what Canada gets to keep. Those who observe that the NWT receives a huge transfer payment from Canada every year are correct – but that criticism incorrectly forgets to take into account how much less the NWT would cost Canada if only the resource royalty regime would be changed.[17]

The historic lack of ownership and control has been frustrated, in part, by the fact that the provinces have constitutional authority over resources (section 92A of the Constitution Act, 1982) while the territories do not. While this constitutional reality has not proven to be much of an impediment for the Yukon, many indigenous peoples in the NWT have viewed the GNWT as an agent of the federal government and not as a government in its own right. Challenging this view, in 1999 Justice Vertes of the NWT Supreme Court ruled that the territorial assemblies do not act as agents or delegates of the GOC and possess a "sovereign-like legislative character," thereby providing for the most substantive constitutional recognition of the territories in Canadian history.[18]

Despite this proclamation to the contrary, however, the fact remains that the GNWT has not owned the land or resources within its geographic boundaries. Of course, who owns the land is critical to indigenous people as they engage in land claims negotiations and self-government agreements. As Dacks observed over twenty years ago, where the Yukon waited patiently to achieve devolution until after agreements were finalized with the territorial Aboriginal groups, the NWT has been more aggressive in pursuing devolution and the transfer of powers to the GNWT, which may challenge local relationships as issues of land management come to the fore.[19] Indeed, in contrast to the Yukon experience, the GNWT entered devolution negotiations without the support of, or consent of, the Aboriginal community (and claimants to outstanding land claims remain concerned about how that process will unfold in a post-devolution era). What this means is that the devolution deal was achieved despite the lack of public consultation or indigenous input. What the current devolution deal reflects therefore is also the ongoing paternalistic way the GNWT has acted, similar to other colonizing governments. As CBC reporter Elizabeth McMillan recounted, quoting MLA Bromley, "We [GNWT] can make decisions without asking."[20]

Indeed, the negotiation of the deal between the GNWT and the federal government led Aboriginal peoples to fear a significant reduction in their voice and power in the territory. The general concern regarding the Harper government's embrace of this neoliberal form of devolution was made apparent when Aboriginal groups responded to the news in January 2011 that the territory was a step closer to devolution. Upon learning that premier Floyd Roland had signed an AIP with the Harper government, Aboriginal leaders immediately criticized the GNWT for its lack of consultation. In a territory with a total population of only 40,000 people, over half of whom are indigenous, it was surprising to many when Roland "snubbed a request from the communities to sit down and discuss the issues."[21] Upon learning that the AIP had been signed, Dene regional chief Bill Erasmus stated that the "agreement represented a step backwards for Aboriginal communities and was a bad business deal to boot."[22] These concerns initially prompted a meeting of regional chiefs in Yellowknife in late January 2011 to pressure the territorial government to forgo the deal. Despite the protest, the territorial government proceeded to sign the AIP, consulting with territorial residents and Aboriginal groups only after the fact. For their part, two of the territorial groups, the Inuvialuit and Metis, signed on to the deal in January and February 2011 respectively. The Sahtu signed in May 2012, while other Aboriginal groups like the Gwich'in Tribal Council filed a lawsuit against the territorial government and the GOC for failing to consult prior to signing the AIP.[23] Even though the majority of indigenous groups eventually signed the final agreement, this failure to consult with Aboriginal groups reflects an ongoing internal tension within the GNWT that has festered over the years.

This tension rose to the surface in 2010 when the GNWT tried to impose a hunting ban on Bathurst caribou. In response to the GNWT action, a court case was launched that called into question the very legitimacy of the territorial government. As Fred Sangris, head of the Yellowknives caribou committee explains, "They [the GNWT] are not a province, they forget that some times. They forget that the natives here have more rights than the GNWT does."[24] While the debate about the power or legitimacy of the GNWT is not new, what is new is the notion that Aboriginal self-government could further devolve power away from a territorial government struggling to preserve its power. What this means is that the territorial government is increasingly caught between the GOC and local demands for Aboriginal self-government. However, as the Yukon experience demonstrates, working together on a government-to-government basis to achieve territorial goals could ameliorate the GNWT situation.

Self-Government vs Territorial Government?

Self-government agreements are practical arrangements with the GOC that recognize the jurisdiction of indigenous governments over human services such as education, health, justice, and social services.[25] Although four land claims have been settled in the territory (Inuvialuit, Sahtu, Gwich'in, and Nunavut), only one First Nation, the T'licho in 2003, has finalized a self-government agreement (though a few more are forthcoming). The Inuvialuit were the first group to settle a land claim in 1984, followed by the Gwich'in in 1992 and the Sahtu in 1993. All communities within the Sahtu region are now engaged in ongoing self-government negotiations, as are the Inuvialuit and Gwitch'in. The sole outstanding agreement remains in the DehCho territory, whose status remains uncertain in the new devolution era. For instance, it was announced in October 2011 that while settling land claims is a priority for the DehCho, the GOC has clawed back one million dollars from the land claim budget, thus adding another barrier to the completion of a deal that has been in negotiation since 1995. The lack of progress on the land claim, coupled with cutbacks suggests that, despite the rhetoric, the GOC is not interested in achieving a deal with a group that privileges territorial integrity over development. Rather, the Conservatives maintain (and reinforce) the colonial model of paternalism and governance "by remote control."[26]

The current federal government's disinterest in real reform is demonstrated in multiple areas. For one, while the devolution deal does include a framework agreement for resource development and revenue sharing, it does so at the cost of undermining new Aboriginal governments. According to one self-government negotiator, when it comes to resource sharing, an arbitrary 25 per cent will be shared with Aboriginal governments, which does not necessarily correspond to the degree of government responsibilities that may be taken on by Aboriginal governments.[27] In effect, the federal government has left Aboriginal groups to work out any administrative flaws in the deal with the territorial government. More specifically, as a result of devolution, the GNWT will assume those legislative powers, programs, and responsibilities for land and resources associated with the department's Northern Affairs Program (NAP) that now include:

- Powers to develop, conserve, manage, and regulate surface and subsurface natural resources in the NWT for mining and minerals (including oil and gas) administration, water management, land management, and environmental management;
- Powers to control and administer public land with the right to use, sell, or otherwise dispose of such land; and
- Powers to levy and collect resource royalties and other revenues from natural resources.[28]

Given the unequal distribution of resources between Aboriginal groups, the territorial government, and the federal government, it is highly problematic that many settled claims award similar levels of administrative duties and powers to individual Aboriginal groups. Initially Dene communities denounced any transfer of powers to the GNWT, because "at the same time that they negotiate agreements to get out from under colonial practices, agreement implementation is still a federal responsibility."[29] And as both the federal government and indigenous groups with settled claims and new government arrangements across this country already know, the real challenge is not in formalizing a deal but in implementing and administering the terms of the deal.

With respect to the relationship between indigenous groups and devolution, former territorial environment minister J. Michael Miltenberger argues that the recent trend towards self-government has destabilized the territory's already ambiguous governmental grip. As he explains it, because the GNWT's authority is delegated from Ottawa and because the GOC retains control over Crown lands and non-renewable resources, the "territorial government's authority is constantly being questioned and its financial independence is constantly foiled."[30] The suggestion by Miltenberger that increased Aboriginal governments will compromise territorial government authority ignores concerns of Aboriginal peoples that devolution undermines land claims and self-government agreements in the territory.

Aside from the argument that the deal does not provide a large enough share of resource royalties, many Aboriginal groups fear their own land claims and self-government negotiations are in jeopardy. A self-government negotiator in the territory explained that, under the devolution deal, Canada will transfer land claim implementation responsibilities to the territory and away from the federal government.[31] This is significant because promises that have been made by the Crown will become the responsibility of the territorial government. In addition, intergovernmental cooperation on land management will pivot around the territorial government assuming regulatory control. Finally, this neoliberal form of devolution threatens to preclude or narrow potential arrangements for unsettled land and introduces another level of government, the GNWT, into negotiations.[32]

Economic Development and the Politics of Resource Control

If the politics of GNWT are tied to a federal offloading of responsibility to the territorial and Aboriginal governments, then economic change is tied to federal support for resource development, a new commitment to royalty sharing, and an increasing disparity between "have" and "have-not" indigenous groups. Resource development in the territory, remains the primary economic driver for the region, as it has been for most of its history. Indeed, the NWT has long been regarded as a land of opportunity. In the 1970s the quest for oil and gas promised to open up the region to great opportunity and even greater investment. The report of the Berger inquiry in the 1970s, however, called for a ten-year moratorium on all exploration and development until land claims and treaties could be settled with local Aboriginal peoples.[33] Almost forty years later, with many land claims agreements settled, and the potential for many new self-government arrangements on the horizon, the quest for oil and gas development persists but remains unrealized. In the interim, diamond mines have been operating with great success for the past seventeen years (the Ekati Diamond Mine was first opened in 1998) but have already entered the sunset years. In theory, the Mackenzie Valley gas project (MVGP), which centres on the construction of a pipeline across the territory to ship natural gas to national and international markets, remains the best opportunity to throw off the shackles of federal dependence and develop an autonomous economic future. Moreover, it offers some Aboriginal groups an opportunity to participate for the first time in resource exploration, either as an investment partner in the Aboriginal Pipeline Group (APG), as a shareholder in a land claim settlement, or as an employer in construction or pipeline development. This is important because economic independence of the territory and for Aboriginal peoples is required to fund numerous social programs.

To be sure, the MVGP could transform the NWT. Yet when the federal Cabinet in Ottawa approved the agreement in early 2011, it did so without offering financial support for the project. The lack of federal subsidies surprised proponents of the project, who felt the government should treat the MVGP as a nation-building exercise that will open up the Arctic for greater exploration in the same way the railway linked the east to west in the late 1800s. However, as a possible consequence of devolution, the burden may now fall on the GNWT and Aboriginal groups to negotiate with some of the largest natural gas and oil companies in the private sector in order to ensure the building of the pipeline. This means that any benefit from resource exploration will now be muted by the need to subsidize development in order to attract multinational companies to the region. This was the conclusion reached by the Joint Review Panel (JRP) when it determined that a new revenue sharing agreement was required between Canada and the GNWT because the GNWT will carry the chief burden of costs in dealing with the project. In its final report, the JRP determined that "the GNWT would receive little Project revenue directly and, to the extent that its revenues are increased, much of this increase would be offset by the Territorial Funding Formula (TFF)."[34] Eglington and Voytilla reach a similar conclusion, stating that the NWT governments will bear the costs and risks of development post-devolution.[35] The authors also argue that these added costs (and risks – both financial and environmental) will increase with the level of development activity that is realized and that, post-devolution, the federal government will share none of these risks. To that end, they recommend in their report that the TFF be renegotiated, advising, "The shortcomings of TFF and the pressure exerted by the federal government to keep a lid on GNWT Grant revenues, sometimes by unilateral actions, should be a concern to Aboriginal groups who are contemplating the devolution of government responsibilities, or sharing responsibilities with GNWT."[36] In other words, after only recently becoming partners in the natural gas development project, Aboriginal peoples may now have to offset those benefits with corporate subsidies and infrastructure development, which they are presently ill equipped to do.

One key tenet of neoliberalism is that governments should reduce expenditures and increase market solutions to public problems (see introductory chapter). Given the increase in territorial government responsibility, a corresponding increase in revenue is required to ensure that the continuity of programs can be provided. If the shortfalls are not addressed, austerity and further market incentives are likely to occur. As Dickerson writes, "Without a constant course of public revenue, the territorial government will not be able to respond to problems in the region, and without developing a resource base of its own, the 'autonomy' of the government will always be in question."[37] This is especially critical if Ottawa continues to reduce the level of financial support and transfer of dollars it provides to the provinces and territories. Similar events occurred, as Eglington and Voytilla point out, in 1995–6 when the TFF was frozen at 1994–5 levels and then reduced by 5 per cent. These were arbitrary federal actions related most likely to the creation of the Canada Health and Social Transfer (CHST), which amalgamated and then dramatically reduced funding for Canada's social welfare state.[38]

In light of a decision in late 2010 by the National Energy Board to approve the development of the Mackenzie Valley Pipeline (and subsequent approval by Cabinet), it now appears that the project will go ahead, assuming that the companies backing it proceed with development. Consequently, the economic prospects for the GNWT are strong. The NWT's geological resources are vast and include an array of minerals, including gold and diamonds, as well as hydrocarbon potential in oil and natural gas. Already the NWT has the highest per capita gross domestic product (GDP) of all provinces or territories in Canada. What this means is the NWT has the potential to become the first "have" territory in Canada.

While the new deal has the potential to transform the territory, it could similarly accelerate a growing tension between indigenous groups. Nowhere is this strain more noticeable then among those groups with settled claims and strong economic development plans ready to proceed. As one editorial put it, "The Inuvialuit, Gwich'in, Sahtu and Tlicho leaders and entrepreneurs – all with settled land claims – are aching to do business and have proven themselves solid business partners. The Inuvialuit Development Corporation has hundreds of millions of dollars worth of airline, construction and oil and gas development companies. There are 46 registered Gwich'in-owned businesses and 28 registered Sahtu-owned companies. The Tlicho Investment Corporation has 16 divisions involved in ventures ranging from hydro-power to trucking to explosives and much more."[39]

In a stagnant economy where people are desperate for work and living off the land is increasingly difficult, some Aboriginal groups and proponents for further devolution argue that increased territorial power and settled land claims create a business environment from which everyone profits. But, as Irlbacher-Fox cautions, what the prospect of devolution as well as development reveals is that there are "have" and "have-not" regions emerging throughout the territory. Simply put, the ongoing politics of natural resource extraction is creating class divisions among and between indigenous groups and the remaining residents of the territory. For instance, the people of the Sahtu region are unlikely to benefit at all from any pipeline development. Irlbacher-Fox points out that "the differences in economic power and consequent social impacts, and the reality of checkerboard wealth and capacity could ultimately have destabilizing consequences both politically and economically in the territory."[40] This increasing dichotomy is further reflected in the fact that some communities choose not to engage, even if the opportunity arises. In other cases, even when indigenous groups (like the Sahtu) try to balance extraction with environmental protection by referring drilling projects to territorial environmental agencies, when those companies (like Shell and MGM) threaten to pull out it has the intended disciplinary effect and development proceeds unimpeded, without any environmental assessment.

For other First Nations groups like Lutsel K'e, interest in development is eclipsed by concern that it will undermine their traditional economies and cultural values. Indeed a "major flaw in the devolution vision is an absence of relation to big picture – how devolution fits with development."[41] In essence, in the rush for devolution and development there is a significant risk that greater disparity and inequality in the NWT will be revealed between indigenous groups. This inequality will be perpetuated because those regions with greater access to resources, with greater governance capacity and economic readiness will take advantage of development while those less fortunate (that is, without a settled claim or institutional capacity), those desperate for jobs that accompany development or those that choose not to participate will continue to suffer.

In the interim, proponents of the Mackenzie Valley Pipeline who have already invested heavily in the region and who have already weathered an extensive government and regulatory process now appear unsure about if or when development will proceed. In the summer of 2011, the multinational oil and gas company Shell Canada announced that it was selling its estimated 11 per cent stake in the project to focus on the development of shale oil and gas reserves.[42] Indeed the location and development of the Canol, a new shale oil basin located in the Mackenzie region, has refocused the oil and gas industry in the territory and kept the prospects for a pipeline dormant. Hence, the future of the MGVP remains uncertain as companies explore and develop oil and gas potential in other areas of the territory, including the Beaufort Delta and around Norman Wells.

While the industry insists this development is improving the territorial economy, across the sector observers point to the fact that royalties continue to accrue only to the federal government and not the territory. They add that the benefits of development are localized and hence do not necessarily benefit the territorial population as a whole.[43] Others point out that government red tape needs to be cut to foster investment.[44] As John Hogg, vice-president of explorations and operations at Calgary's MGM Energy Corp., which has several holdings in the NWT, stated, "Already drilling in the NWT is more complicated than in any other jurisdiction in Canada." He explained that "the territory continues to be, and always has been, more of a challenge."[45] Indeed, companies like MGM have threatened to withdraw drilling applications from the Sahtu region, arguing that MGM Energy "simply cannot justify the allocation of resources to pursuing a regulatory process that is uncertain both in terms of requirements and time lines, and thus cost." As MGM Energy president Henry Sykes said in a press release, "We believe it is premature to invest substantial and indeterminate time, money and resources in this regulatory process at the exploratory phase of the Canol shale oil play. As the play advances, the time for such a process may come, but that time is not now."[46]

Even today the MGVP remains mired in the regulatory process because there are more than 6,000 permits required before construction can commence. Moreover, the potential delay in drilling due to lengthy regulatory hearings that have frustrated some anxious Aboriginal groups and oil companies alike may further prove to be a catalyst for conflict among Aboriginal groups in the region. The 2010 disaster in the Gulf of Mexico where a British Petroleum (BP) rig sank, leading to an offshore oil spill (which prompted the United States government to call for a moratorium on offshore drilling) shook the confidence of many northern residents regarding offshore drilling in the Beaufort Sea. However, some Aboriginal groups, such as the Inuvialuit, remain supportive of prospective offshore drilling. As Mervin Gruben, the mayor of Tuktoyaktuk, told the CBC, "A lot of our people are optimistic it's still going to happen."[47] He added that the BP spill "hasn't turned people against drilling. It's just taught people to be more aware."[48] Strong proponents of devolution and development, the residents of Tuktoyaktuk and Inuvik appear most eager to look beyond the pipeline for sources of investment and jobs. In some circles, the offshore option is being cast as "plan B" in the event that the MVGP falls through. Currently working as a consultant for the Inuvialuit, Doug Matthews is conducting a research project called Base for the Beaufort. The project is "looking at what assets need to be put in place to help Inuvik and Tuktoyaktuk become supply bases for ongoing Beaufort exploration."[49] At the same time, there are groups of Aboriginal people in the NWT, such as the community of Lutsel K'e, that remain reticent about any prospective drilling occurring on or around their traditional lands, not only for the potential environmental impacts, but also out of a desire to protect the integrity of sacred sites.

Conclusion

Referencing the work of Mark Dickerson, Doug MacArthur writes, "Decentralization has been a primary force underlying change in the NWT."[50] The question this chapter asks is: does devolution represent a new day for the NWT? Since the 1970s, the promise of development has fuelled hope that the economic fortunes of the territory could improve. However, significant development has yet to begin. Since the 1980s the powers of the GNWT have increased somewhat and with them the presence of government in the territory. While the increase in decision-making powers in some key areas has been important, the absence of power in the areas of land and resource ownership means critical decisions remain within the GOC's jurisdiction. Consequently, a neoliberal form of devolution is not likely to reduce the role of the federal government in the territory.

As has always been the case, the GOC is quite capable of and interested in making deals and agreements with indigenous groups and territories. Yet the devil is in the details, and ultimately it is not devolution per se that signals a new day for the NWT but rather how or whether that devolution is implemented in a way that leads to meaningful change in the way that indigenous governments, the territory, and the GOC interact. As Irlbacher-Fox suggests, meaningful change requires more than just a devolution deal; it requires a "reconfiguration of power sharing and increased cooperation among governments and agencies [which] will be the hallmark of institutional change in the NWT in the immediate future."[51] Indeed, in an area with successful Aboriginal economic models and rich resources, the NWT has all the potential to be a real engine of economic growth in the Canadian Arctic if its governments and its citizens can find new and innovative ways to work together.

NOTES

1 This chapter includes data collected from the project A Renewed North: Resources, Corporations and First Nations, which was supported by an SSHRC Northern Development Research Grant (2006–9). I would like to thank Graham White for his feedback on the original draft. I would like to thank Stephanie Irlbacher-Fox for her time, friendship, and many conversations regarding this chapter. Her experience and insight into the politics of the NWT is invaluable and her work represents a significant contribution to this chapter. Thanks also to the book's editors for their comments.

2 Bruce Valpy, "Northern Bashing," *Northern News Services Online*, 3 May 2010, http://www.nnsl.com/frames/newspapers/2010-05/may7_10edit.html. Thanks to Graham White for directing me to this editorial and quotation.

3 Frances Abele, "A Strong North Must Be Prosperous," *Ottawa Citizen*, 15 June 2009.

4 Mark Dickerson, *Whose North? Political Change, Political Development, and Self-Government in the Northwest Territories* (Vancouver: UBC Press, 1992), 90.

5 Peter Eglington and Lew Voytilla, *Report re Fiscal and Self-Government Issues in Connection with Devolution, Prepared for Richard Nerysoo, President Gwich'in Tribal Council of Inuvik*, 5 February 2011, Legislative Assembly of the Northwest Territories, http://www.assembly.gov.nt.ca/tabled -documents/report-re-fiscal-and-self-government-issues-connection -devolution-prepared-richard.

6 Ibid.

7 Dickerson, *Whose North?*, 122.
8 Government of Canada, Speech from the Throne, 16 October 2007.
9 James P. Feehan, "Natural Resource Devolution in the Territories: Current Status and Uresolved Issues," in *Northern Exposure: Peoples, Powers and Prospects in Canada's North*, ed. F. Abele, T. Courchene, L. Seidle, and F. St-Hilaire (Montreal: Institute for Research on Public Policy, 2009), 348.
10 Ibid., 349.
11 Ibid.
12 Kirk Cameron, "There *Is* a Northern Crown," *Policy* Options (March 2000): 57–8.
13 Gabrielle Slowey, "The Yukon: A New Era of First Nations Governance and Intergovernmental Relations," this volume.
14 Feehan, "Natural Resource Devolution in the Territories," 367.
15 Ibid.
16 Government of the Northwest Territories, "Results of the Public Engagement on the Proposed Northwest Territories Lands and Resources Devolution Agreement," May 2013, Legislative Assembly of the Northwest Territories, http://www.assembly.gov.nt.ca/tabled-documents/results-public-engagement-proposed-northwest-territories-lands-and-resources.
17 Stephanie Irlbacher-Fox, "Northern Governance and the Economy: Thinking about the Big Picture," *Northern Public Affairs*, 13 November 2012, http://www.northernpublicaffairs.ca/index/irlbacher-fox-northern-governance-and-the-economy-thinking-about-the-big-picture/#more-1920.
18 Cameron, "There *Is* a Northern Crown," 58.
19 Gurston Dacks, *Devolution and Constitutional Development in the Canadian North* (Ottawa: Carleton University Press, 1990), 4.
20 Elizabeth McMillan, "Bromley: GNWT chose paternalistic way typical of colonizing govt's, hey ppl we have authority, we can make decisions w/o asking #nwtpoli," Twitter, 5 June 2013, https://twitter.com/elizmcmillan/status/342399754996695040.
21 Jessica Murphy, "N.W.T. a Step Closer to Devolution," *Toronto Sun*, 26 January 2011, http://www.torontosun.com/news/canada/2011/01/26/17042761.html.
22 Ibid.
23 "Dene Nation Won't Go to Court over Devolution Deal," CBC News, 25 February 2011, http://www.cbc.ca/news/canada/north/story/2011/02/25/dene-nation-devolution-resolution.html.
24 Patrick White, "A Caribou Herd in Decline: A Way of Life in Jeopardy," *Globe and Mail*, 5 May 2010.
25 Stephanie Irlbacher-Fox, "Governance in Canada's Northwest Territories: Emerging Institutions and Governance Issues," main paper for Plenary

on Arctic Governance, 3rd Northern Research Forum, Yellowknife, September 2004.

26 Peter Clancy, "Politics by Remote Control: Historical Perspectives on Devolution in Canada's North," in Dacks, *Devolution and Constitutional Development*, 13–42.

27 Stephanie Irlbacher-Fox, email correspondence to author, 24 April 2011.

28 Irlbacher-Fox, email correspondence to author.

29 Clancy, "Politics by Remote Control."

30 White, "Caribou Herd in Decline."

31 Irlbacher-Fox, email correspondence to author.

32 Ibid.

33 Thomas Berger, *Northern Frontier, Northern Homeland: The Report of the Mackenzie Valley Pipeline Inquiry* (Ottawa: Minister of Supply Services, 1977). It is important to note that, with the Norman Wells pipeline in the 1980s, development has long since begun.

34 Joint Review Panel for the Mackenzie Gas Project, *Foundation for a Sustainable Northern Future: Report of the Joint Review Panel for the Mackenzie Gas Project* (December 2009), 11–15, http://www.reviewboard.ca/upload/project_document/EIR0405-001_JRP_Report_of_Environmental_Review _Executive_Volume_I_1263228660.PDF.

35 Eglington and Voytilla, *Report re Fiscal and Self-Government Issues*, 55.

36 Ibid., 42.

37 Dickerson, *Whose North?*, 124.

38 Eglington and Voytilla, *Report re Fiscal and Self-Government Issues*, 16.

39 Valpy, "Northern Bashing."

40 Irlbacher-Fox, email correspondence to author.

41 Stephanie Irlbacher-Fox, "A major flaw in the devolution vision is an absence of relation to big picture – how #devolution fits w/ development, NWT governance, etc.," Twitter, 25 April 2013, https://twitter.com/ IrlbacherS/status/327496200230158336.

42 Josh Wingrove, and Nathan Vanderklippe, "In the North, Energy is the Future," *Globe and Mail*, 19 July 2011.

43 Stephanie Irlbacher-Fox, "Gahcho Kué Economic Impacts and NWT Devolution," *Northern Public Affairs*, 4 May 2012, http://www .northernpublicaffairs.ca/index/irlbacher-fox-gahcho-kue-economic -impacts-and-nwt-devolution/.

44 Wingrove and Vanderklippe, "In the North."

45 Ibid.

46 "#NWT Chamber cries ... over yesterday's Sahtu #fracking pull-out by #MGM #Energy," *Northern Clipper*, 9 November 2012, http://

mediamentor-circumpolar.blogspot.ca/2012/11/nwt-chamber-cries-over-
yesterdays-sahtu.html.

47 Nathan Vanderklippe, "Far North Residents Weigh Offshore Drilling's Risk-
Reward Equation," *Globe and Mail*, 23 August 2012, http://m.the
globeandmail.com/report-on-business/far-north-residents-weigh-offshore
-drillings-risk-reward-equation/article1988764/comments/?service=mobile.

48 Ibid.

49 Ibid.

50 Doug MacArthur, "The Changing Architecture of Governance in the
Yukon and the Northwest Territories," in Abele, Courchene, Seidle,
and St-Hilaire, *Northern Exposure*, 189.

51 Irlbacher-Fox, email correspondence to author.

13 The Yukon: A New Era of First Nations Governance and Intergovernmental Relations[1]

GABRIELLE A. SLOWEY

Introduction

There are no "cook book" models for the path that we are on in self-government in Yukon. We are all learning as we are going, but I feel we have covered a lot of ground very productively, and am optimistic about the future.[2]

Joe Linklater, former chief of the Vuntut Gwitchin
First Nation (Old Crow, Yukon)

The politics of the northern territories is among the most politically dynamic and exciting anywhere in the country. Nowhere does this statement carry greater resonance than in the Yukon. When the territory settled the bulk of land claims in 1995, Kirk Cameron and Graham White reported, "Governance in the Yukon had entered a new era and the next challenge would be to work out the interplay of self-government and public government in the context of uncertain federal financial support."[3] Indeed, in contrast to previous speculation that the Yukon public government would experience significant erosion or that Aboriginal self-government would prove divisive and not economically feasible,[4] over the past seventeen years, the Yukon and the First Nations groups in the territory have shown the rest of the country just how indigenous and public governments can work together to produce new policy plans and meaningful results. The Yukon is best known as the land of the Gold Rush and the midnight sun, yet in an era of global neoliberalism, the exploration of natural resources (minerals, oil, and gas) by large multinational companies has become the key economic driver of the territory. Yet the Yukon has become increasingly recognized for its rich and impressive economic, political, and social transformation. Beginning in the 1970s, Yukon First Nations came together to articulate a new vision for the future that culminated in 1995 with the settlement of almost all the land claims put forward in the territory (eleven of fourteen First Nations have settled their claims). The Yukon was also the first territory to achieve devolution, which was finalized in the Yukon Act in 2003. And though the original days of the Klondike are memories of a distant past, today the Yukon appears to be on the brink of another significant mining development boom that will bring new opportunities and new challenges to the territory.

When one considers all these changes, an important question to address is: what does the Yukon look like today? And how have First Nations and the territorial governments risen to the challenge of governing together? This chapter argues that, despite its small size and remote location (or perhaps because of it), the Yukon is, in many ways, years ahead of the rest of northern Canada because of its devolution status, resolved land claims, self-government agreements, and the prospective inclusion of indigenous peoples in the pending economic boom. Put simply, the Yukon has risen to the challenge presented by state-imposed neoliberalism, which has focused on the settling of land claims to produce a stable investment environment and opening up the North to new markets. Embracing this new relationship between the territory and the First Nations has created a new era of inter-governmentalism. That is, as the federal government bows out of its management role in the territory as part of its broader policy approach that includes devolution and offloading, the territorial governments, both public and indigenous, are demonstrating new ways where local governments can fill an important void. With strong leadership and a vision for the future, the result has been a significant transformation in the territory's political and economic condition over the past decade.

Devolution: Building Intergovernmental Relations

Although the Yukon is the smallest territory (in size) and located the farthest distance from Ottawa, it has only recently achieved a significant level of independence. It also has a relatively small population of only 30,000 people, most of whom reside in Whitehorse or other "urban" locations across the territory (such as Dawson City, Watson Lake, Haines Junction, Mayo, Carmacks, or Carcross). In contrast to the Northwest Territories and Nunavut where indigenous people represent a majority of the population, in the Yukon Aboriginal peoples have long been a minority. In fact, the first Klondike gold rush proved catastrophic for First Nations. As one former territorial leader explains, "They were down to 25 percent of the Yukon population, probably half of the permanent population, certainly half of the rural population."[5] In other words, the First Nations lost their majority, if not after the Gold Rush, then certainly after the building of the Alaska Highway in 1942.

Today, there are fourteen First Nations scattered across the territory representing eight different language groups.[6] However, despite their relatively smaller population, the Yukon First Nations are among the first in Canada to have resolved outstanding land claims and moved forward to achieve self-government. Indeed, although Whittington suggests that the reason land claims were completed in 1995 is partly because the bulk of First Nations in the territory are located in relatively remote areas of the territory and therefore subject to low land use competition, one cannot discount the fact that the push towards self-government was actually launched by the First Nations themselves.[7] As early as 1973 the Yukon elders made their intentions clear when they presented their statement, *Together Today for Our Children Tomorrow*, to the federal government. What they presented to Prime Minister Trudeau in effect was a "statement of grievances and an approach to settlement."[8] Hence, in large part a result of the determination and drive of the Yukon First Nations and the willingness of government to listen, the finalization and subsequent implementation of these agreements formed an integral part of the transformation and political evolution of the territory.

For the bulk of its history, the Yukon has been a colonial outpost of Ottawa. As Douglas MacArthur describes it, "Until the 1970s, administration in northern Canada was modeled on the British colonial system. The Aboriginal population [was also] under the protection and tutelage of a distant government [and] the region was valued almost solely for its resources and contribution to the external economy."[9] As a result, between 1900 and 1978, the elected legislative council in the territory was "governed" by a ten-member body that did not govern per se but instead acted as an advisory body to the commissioner, who was appointed by Ottawa.[10] The Government of Canada (GOC) was thus directly responsible for all policy and administration throughout the territory. Following the passage of the 1977 Yukon Elections Act, however, the territorial council was replaced by the current legislative assembly, which was first elected in 1978.

Today the Yukon legislature seats eighteen members and is the only legislature among Canada's northern territories where politics are organized along party lines. As Ken Coates writes, "In the Yukon, party politics emerged relatively early in the game. The political affiliation of most territorial politicians was well known in the Yukon, but before the mid-1970s, no formal party mechanism had been established. The 1974 decision of the New Democratic Party to run a slate of candidates in the territorial election, however, convinced the Liberal and Conservative Parties (now the Yukon party) to organize at the territorial level."[11]

Consequently, the territorial election of 1978 was the first one run along party lines in which the Conservatives won. Throughout the 1980s, the Conservatives dominated Yukon party politics by advancing a pro-development platform, while the New Democratic Party (NDP) typically formed the official opposition. In effect, the Conservative party and the NDP have been the two main "combatants" in the territory, "each representing strongly contrasting views of the role of the government in the North."[12]

Since 1978 the Conservative Party (which in 1992 renamed itself the Yukon Party) has formed the government six times (1978, 1982, 1992, 2002, 2006, and 2011). The NDP has been in power three times (1985, 1989, and 1996), while the Liberal Party has formed the government once (2000). For the most part, the Conservative approach has centred on traditional notions of individualism and less government intervention, while the NDP has focused on a planned economy and restoring rights to First Nations. The shifting success of the two parties in many ways reflects the underlying demographic trends in the region that is composed of relocated southerners looking for a meaningful northern experience, Whitehorse government workers, European (primarily German) immigrants, and Aboriginal peoples. Continued political polarization also reflects a deeper tension over the preferences for economic development in the territory that oscillates between resource development and environmental protection.

In contrast to the anxieties voiced by opponents of self-government that it would erode public institutions and territorial authority, and in contrast to other jurisdictions in Canada (both provincial and territorial), the Yukon is a leader in resolving land claims and coordinating policy with indigenous governments in the territory. What is unique about this set of circumstances is that, as one former territorial official explains, unlike other regions in Canada, resource extraction was not a particularly strong driver in the Yukon in providing a stimulus for self-government and land claim negotiations. Instead, the key was the election in 1985 of an NDP government that was absolutely committed to picking up the stalled claims process and to delivering on the claim with a social justice agenda. As former premier Tony Penikett explained it to the author, "Because the settlements that the James Bay and the Inuvialuit both won were driven by the judicial mega-project drivers toward land claims settlement, the state wanted clear indigenous title. The Yukon started the same way, but the pipeline project pretty well evaporated by the time they got serious [so that by the] time Canada got involved in this land claim, land claims negotiations [were] projects in [their] own right, as social policy, economic policy, [and] political bonus[es]."[13]

Even in the absence of immediate resource-development pressures, there was a sense by many in the territory that the north was on the verge of a resource boom. This sense of optimism coupled with political momentum led to the first attempt at a final agreement in 1984. However, somewhat surprising to the government officials involved, the terms of the agreement were rejected by the indigenous community. In retrospect, one former territorial official acknowledges, "The correct analysis was done on the failure of the 1984 agreement that was the agreement required the consensus of all First Nations. The problem was with an omnibus agreement you needed to include provisions that were particular to each First Nation in a way that all could buy into, and that was just structurally hard to do."[14]

After the failure of the 1984 negotiations it was apparent that new tactics needed to be adopted. As a first priority, negotiators considered the notion of having a broad framework agreement that set out the universal principles of the claim but also gave enough flexibility for individual First Nations to reach agreements reflecting their own priorities. This new approach allowed for two things: important issues at the negotiation table could be separated into two piles, and negotiators could create a process (not without difficulty) that, if accepted, would allow individual First Nations to be dealt with on a First Nation by First Nation basis. For instance, it allowed those First Nations that were ready to come to the table early (like the Vuntut Gwitchin First Nation [VGFN] of Old Crow, northern Yukon) to do so without having to worry about other First Nations that had myriad concerns or who needed time to prepare their claim before formally entering negotiation. That is, while some groups needed time to work out substantive issues over land rights and jurisdiction (as some First Nations territory in the southern Yukon includes parts of northern British Columbia), others were able to reach agreement much more quickly.

This new approach created a dynamic that allowed for completion of the umbrella final agreement in 1995. At that time, there were not development pressures from government or the private sector. However, there were a number of developments occurring outside the Yukon (that is, the proposed Alaska Highway gas pipeline and the Mackenzie Valley Pipeline project next door in the NWT) that were destined to have an impact on the Yukon. Yet it was the spectre of devolution and the growing power of the territorial government that really spurred the negotiations. Simply put, the territorial government was engaged in devolution and assertive of its right to devolve power further. Moreover, it was sensitive to the fact that the drive for devolution meant the territory was required to attend to the First Nations' interests in the process.

Because the process of land claims was relaunched under the Penikett government, there was concern that when it lost power to the Yukon Party in 1992, the claims process would be derailed. At the time, concerns arose from the fact that Yukon Party leader John Ostashek's approach to First Nations' issues had run on the need to fix the claims process. Ostashek's decision to vest the Yukon Government negotiators with a continuing mandate to follow the Penikett negotiation structure proved to be critical. As one observer commented, "There was a process in place, it was a politically charged decision of the Yukon Party to carry on with the mandate, but they respected the process. It might not have, they may not have liked all the elements of it, but they respected the process."[15]

Throughout the 1980s and early 1990s, three critical elements came together to transform the status of the Yukon. First, Tony Penikett was elected territorial leader under the banner of the NDP. As a leader, he had a vision for the Yukon that was "pretty powerful ... about people working together and about pride and about place."[16] Second, Penikett selected a small group of powerful Cabinet ministers with whom he did not necessarily get along but who were able to capture his vision in specific community terms. For instance, David Porter, who was minister of renewable resources, is credited for having represented the First Nation agenda very strongly in council but was also instrumental in championing a broader regional development agenda. Third, Penikett made an inspired choice when he asked Barry Stewart to step down from the judiciary in order to be the Yukon Government's chief negotiator through the start-up phase of negotiations. The confluence of these factors led to a "perfect storm" and allowed the territory to successfully negotiate the Umbrella Final Agreement in 1995 and a subsequent devolution agreement with Ottawa in 2003. Consequently, in the territorial North, the Yukon stands alone as the most "devolved" territory with province-like authority for many natural resources, including oil and gas. This power includes the collection of royalties for all oil and gas dispositions, a portion of which is shared with First Nations' governments.

Although officials credit their desire to remedy injustice and restore political balance in the territory as the motivation for land claims, sceptics caution that "government motivations tend to be overwhelmingly economic in nature."[17] Indeed, in a report produced by the Fraser Institute (a conservative think tank that focuses on access to markets and the benefits of neoliberal economics as a means to improve quality of life) in 2011, the Yukon was ranked fifteenth in terms of representing one of the most attractive jurisdictions in the world for mining exploration and development, placing it well ahead of neighbouring territories (the NWT was ranked forty-fourth and Nunavut was ranked fifty-second).[18] The report credited Yukon's political climate with its streamlined mining and environmental process (not split between local and federal levels of government) and the settlement of land claims as factors that create stability and attract mining companies to the region. As one author of the report pointed out, "If you're in the exploration stage, you're more worried about what's going to happen five years from now when you start making money. What the Yukon has managed to do is create a stable regime where people have faith in the future."[19]

Although the ranking reflects the success of the Yukon thus far, the authors of the report concluded that the Yukon could continue to rise in the ranks if it was able to settle outstanding land claims in the territory. Indeed, the creation of a stable investment environment as an outcome of the settlement process that can attract more exploration and extraction capital is certainly a bonus for the territory, even if it was not initially a driving factor in the land claims process. While the resolution of the bulk of land claims has certainly improved the current economic prospects for the territory, it was the determination of the indigenous leaders, coupled with the political will and vision of subsequent territorial governments, that originally inspired settlement.

Notwithstanding the success of the land claims process, the Yukon continues to struggle with intergovernmental conflict. On these questions,

Cameron and White's assessment is largely correct in that intergovernmentalism after 1995 has been a challenge.[20] However, their concern recognizes that intergovernmental conflict was a challenge even before the finalization of agreements and has been a factor since initial negotiations began. As one former Territorial official remarked, "I think the essence of First Nations' self-government agreements being part and parcel of the claims process is that it established intergovernmental relationships. It wasn't a community working with government, it wasn't a collective of individuals, or it wasn't individuals working with government, it was governments working with governments."[21]

In effect, those First Nations engaged in self-government negotiations came to the table as governments, and this was recognized early in the process. They are no longer simply wards of the state or stakeholders in development projects but participants in the decision-making process that affects their people, their communities, their land, and issues across the Canadian Arctic. This has significantly changed the political landscape in the Yukon, because self-government has provided First Nations a different avenue for dealing with the territorial government. Whether these negotiations occur through the Yukon Forum (a political body created in 2005 and established through legislation in 2006) or another avenue to formalize cooperation in governance between the territorial government and the Council of Yukon First Nations (CYFN – which represents the majority of First Nations in the territory), or the signing of bilateral intergovernmental accords with individual First Nations, it is clear that these new agreements, institutions, and initiatives reflect a new policymaking environment in the territory.

To elaborate, a recent policy exercise to reform the Yukon education system was concluded with consultation of First Nations' governments. As is the case in many communities across Canada, Aboriginal students in the Yukon lag behind the national average in educational attainment. So it was in 2007 that the long-awaited Yukon Education Reform report was finally released. The *Education Reform Project: Final Report* represents the findings of the government, along with the Council of Yukon First Nations and educators, which spent over three years reviewing the Education Act and putting the 250-page report together. The goal of the report was to find better ways to include First Nations in the territory's public school system. This was considered imperative, because some First Nations like the Kwanlin Dun First Nation had threatened to pull out of the education system, given its historic failure to meet the needs of Aboriginal students. Working together, the report ultimately recommended more First Nations' involvement in developing curriculum and greater community participation. As the CYFN representative said, "What we're trying to do is improve education."[22] But beyond the obvious benefit that an improved education system could provide First Nations' students, another clear benefit of the process was the successful collaboration of public and Aboriginal governments. As then education minister Patrick Rouble, put it, "Having our officials working so closely together has been a real strong benefit to understanding a lot of the issues."[23] With the mutual aim to improve educational achievement for all Yukoners, the education reform project represents a new phase of intergovernmental cooperation and joint decision-making no longer reflective of the traditional paternalistic approach to policymaking.

While policy development is critical to addressing some of the socio-economic challenges that plague First Nations in the territory (beyond education, these include poverty, addictions, and abuse), land management represents another important challenge. As former chief Linklater explains it,

> In the past, affected First Nations had very little, if any, say in how land and environmental management worked in the traditional territories. These practices and the ties to the land had a very important role in First Nation life and still do today. The First Nations' traditional practices of land management were largely ignored by government and exploration companies, who instead chose to impose the Western European values of the time for land management through ownership and exploitation for profit. Exploration companies would come into First Nation areas with Federal Land Use Permits allowing them to explore for various resources, and the affected First Nation would have no voice when it came to expressing concern about the socioeconomic impacts these activities had on their lifestyle.[24]

Linklater points out that, since self-government, the VGFN is no longer at the mercy of the GOC in deciding what issues they will address or how they will be concluded. Further highlighting the benefits of self-government for the VGFN, Linklater explains how, although the VGFN government had been promoting economic development, its role as a government had been limited prior to the finalization of its self-government agreement. Historically, the VGFN government played a supporting role, creating an environment conducive to economic development, as opposed to initiating economic development per se. With self-government in place, the powers of the VGFN government have been significantly expanded, and it is currently engaged in economic development in addition to new projects involving housing, health care, and education, as well as dealing with infrastructure and intergovernmental relations. Recently, the VGFN was active in a territory-wide curriculum review (see the Yukon Education Reform Project, 2007, mentioned above) and also in devising a new land-use planning model. In short, it is busy tackling the day-to-day business of governance in the region and in its traditional territory as a government.

Another example of intergovernmental coordination that stands out is the introduction of land use planning commissions in the territory. Since October 2010, the Yukon Land Use Planning Council has assisted and guided newly formed regional planning commissions like the Dawson Regional Planning Commission, which was developed in consultation with the Yukon government, the Tr'ondek Hwech'in, Nacho Nyak Dun, and Vuntut Gwitchin First Nations. This new commission represents a coordinated approach to land use planning and is the direct result of chapter 11 of the Yukon First Nation Final agreement, which made a commitment to conduct land use planning in the Yukon in cooperation with local First Nations. According to the territorial government, "The underlying rationale for doing a land use plan is to facilitate land uses that will promote orderly development that considers the values of the land, provide for economic, social and environmental well-being of the residents of the region, and to reduce or avoid conflicts between different land uses."[25] The land use planning exercise also represents the first time a dialogue between First Nations and the Yukon Territorial Government has occurred on questions such as: What areas should be off limits to development? What areas should development be allowed in? How much development should be allowed? And how do First Nations show ideas on maps and make them clear to everyone from elders through to land management technicians in government? Currently there are eight commissions throughout the territory, with each commission comprising government and First Nations nominated representatives. The Department of Indian and Northern Affairs in Ottawa appoints each commissioner to these bodies. As MacArthur argues, the portioning of land into First Nations settlement lands and general Yukon lands is yet another remarkable feature of the Yukon agreements: "Under the UFA, First Nations in the Yukon play an integral role in land and resource management through a series of territory-wide management boards, councils and committees, which in most cases include 50 percent First Nations representation. These bodies are expected to bring about a dramatic change in the way that land-use planning, resource regulation and management and the assessment of developments are undertaken."[26] No longer will politicians or public servants be able to make decisions on land use independent of First Nations. This is especially important, given the mounting development pressures (from corporations and First Nations alike) occurring on settlement lands.

Development: The Yukon as Mining Camp

Although the Yukon has a rich history of resource extraction, government is the major single source of economic activity. Indeed, the latest statistics available for employment in the Yukon indicate that government services account for 31 per cent of total employment in the territory.[27] This means is that the territorial economy and the majority of territorial residents (both centred in Whitehorse) are sustained to a large extent by government. Government control over the economy means that employment in various government sectors provides well-paying, long-term jobs for many Yukon residents. To a much lesser extent, tourism also offers economic opportunities. Each year the territory hosts an array of cultural and sporting events that draws tourists from all over the world. Its pristine natural environment and northern location also attract tourists interested in exploring the mountain ranges, catching a glimpse of caribou, or just travelling along the famed Dempster highway.

However, mining still has the greatest potential to improve the overall economic health of the territory. Recent reports suggest that the Yukon gold deposit along the Rackla gold belt in central-eastern Yukon could house decades' worth of gold.[28] Forecasting another Klondike gold rush, activity at the 2011 Prospectors and Developers Convention in Toronto further suggests that another boom is likely for the territory. At a conference with over 26,000 delegates from 125 countries, the Yukon was a hotbed of interest and activity. As the acting mineral services manager explained, "More than 80,000 mining claims were staked in the territory last year [2010] so that should guarantee a busy exploration season."[29] In fact, more than $160 million was spent on exploration in the Yukon in 2010 with an anticipated equal amount to be spent in 2011. All of this investment means that the Yukon is now viewed as a "bright spot" in the North American economy. Even the Conference Board of Canada forecast suggested the territory's GDP would rise by 4.9 per cent in 2011.[30]

Clearly the growing demand for metals and the opening of two more mines is responsible for this "robust economic expansion." Yet reports of an anticipated housing shortage in Dawson and new government incentives for the construction of privately owned rental suites reflect the toll another boom is taking on infrastructure and social support in the territory. And what this implies is that there is increasing pressure on the territorial government to reopen devolution discussions with the federal government. The Yukon territorial leadership is now seeking new devolution agreements with the intention of securing a larger share of the resource royalties it claims it needs to pay for "the territory's growing pains."[31] With the prospect of increased exploration and mineral activity in the territory, former premier Dennis Fentie told the Canadian Broadcasting Company, "If there's more operating mines in the Yukon, there's better growth, there's better GDP, there's more peripheral economic development. It generates necessary cash flow to drive other economic engines."[32] So as the Yukon prepares for a boom it similarly seeks an increase in the revenue-sharing pie that can be used to alleviate the growing pains it anticipates will soon arise.

In terms of new employment opportunities, exploration and extraction has provided local employment across First Nations and non–First Nation communities. However, as one former territorial official concedes, "There was a history that wasn't always kind to First Nation people [but] First Nations people adapted to it in one way or another."[33] Certainly the negative effects have had a significant impact on the communities. As one First Nations leader explained, they are still suffering the effects of the last oil boom, which saw a dramatic rise in fetal alcohol syndrome and the abuse of drugs in the communities. "The exploration for mineral and hydrocarbon resources in Northern Canada from the 1940s through to the 1970s took place at the same time another system was taking its toll on First Nations people: the brutal system of residential schools, in which families were often torn apart so that the children could be taken away from their communities to be taught the 'white man's way,' thereby, more quickly assimilating them into the broader Canadian society. The First Nations people never really had a chance to give their input into the process of exploration within their traditional territories, until recently."[34]

Again, the settlement of land claims and the development of self-government mean that First Nations communities are better prepared to take advantage of an economic boom and to participate more effectively in the process. They are active investors in the region and working towards increasing their self-sufficiency. As one official with a First Nation corporation explained, "If you want a materialistic view, the greatest success is achieving self-sufficiency and moving forward and able to gain the confidence of the citizens."[35]

Clearly some First Nations seek to become the economic drivers in the territory. The focus is creating the conditions necessary for self-sufficiency in order to generate wealth, which can then be used to operate government: "Once we are able to fund our own investments, we are going to be able to grow at a very rapid pace."[36] To that end, some First Nations are focused on diversification and controlling multiple economic levers, which can yield rewards on investment, while also remaining under local control. Again, as one corporate executive puts it, "Let's say there was a pipeline: the people coming up to work on the pipeline would have to get up here. They would fly with our airline. When they got on the ground, they would communicate through our communication, and then we would have our equipment moving the dirt."[37] And, of course, there is the underlying reality that First Nations now have the opportunity to develop their own resources any time they need to. For some like the Vuntut Gwitchin First Nation, this means they can even consider drilling in their own backyard, which includes the prized Eagle Plains area.

Located in northern Yukon, the Eagle Plains region is estimated to have six trillion cubic feet of natural gas and more than 400 million barrels of oil. The Vuntut Gwitchin partnership is leading a feasibility study and the development of a business plan for the distribution of Eagle Plains gas on behalf of the Vuntut Gwitchin, Trondek Hwechi'in, and Nacho Nyak dun First Nations, as well as the Gwitchin Tribal Council. The Vuntut Gwitchin Limited Partnership has committed $33,375 to the project (with a general commitment to about $90,000), while the territorial government is reported to have committed $35,000 to the study.[38] Of course, this interest in oil and gas exploration surprises many who are familiar with the international campaign the VGFN has waged against any drilling in the nearby Arctic National Wildlife Refuge.[39]

The interest in furthering natural resource extraction highlights a tension between traditional environmental and land concerns of the territory's First Nations and global capitalism's (and its largest multinational companies') thirst for oil and gas. To a large degree it is the First Nations in the north that are caught between participating in the global economy and (or while) trying to maintain traditional ties to the land. Today, the VGFN remains a very traditional community, reliant on caribou and other natural resources for subsistence. Since finalizing their self-government agreement, however, the VGFN has gained full control over its settlement lands and has developed mechanisms to influence the management of Crown lands. Further, conservation regimes have been established and the land use management strategy approved. As Linklater explains, these agreements "provide us with considerable assurance that appropriate resource management practices are being put in place in our traditional territory." He adds, "Given these inter-governmental arrangements in North Yukon, we are prepared to look more carefully at economic development opportunities that will benefit our people as well as other Yukoners and Canadians more generally."[40]

Having said this, Linklater qualifies that the Vuntut Gwitchin government (VGG) is aware of the benefits that may come from economic development. He suggests that economic development be viewed as one positive step towards achieving self-determination and self-reliance for First Nations people, cautioning that "decisions made for any community should not hinge on economic factors alone. The long-terms effects on a society must be treated as a priority. Any mistakes we make today will be paid for by our children in the future."[41] Clearly economic incentives are important, but remaining at the root of any development decision are the cultural values that continue to inspire and inform governments throughout the territory.

Conclusion: People Can Make a Difference

Clearly there has been a seismic shift in the way the state and First Nations interact in the Yukon. It began with the settlement of land claims and self-government agreements. The achievement of devolution soon thereafter further set the stage for a real evolution in the system of governance in the Yukon. Finally, new prospects for mineral development loom on the horizon and offer new opportunities (and significant challenges) to territorial and Aboriginal governments alike. That is, while many communities work to protect their traditional culture and activities, the new environment also offers them the chance, if they so choose, to participate in development projects on their own terms (and even on their own land).

In a span of only fifty years, the territory and the First Nations have passed from a state of colonial wardship to free and self-governing territory. While fifteen years of self-government and inter-governmentalism is a relatively short period of time, preliminary evidence and stakeholder observations suggest that important progress is being made and results are being achieved.[42] As all orders of government work quickly to adjust to the new ways of doing business in the Yukon, they similarly work to develop effective public policy instruments in an environment of good will, innovation, and flexibility. The key, it would appear, is a respect for jurisdiction and a desire to work together to shape the Yukon of tomorrow.

NOTES

1 This chapter includes data collected from the project A Renewed North: Resources, Corporations and First Nations, which was supported by an SSHRC Northern Development Research Grant (2006–9). I would like to thank Graham White for his feedback on the original draft. I would like to thank those people who were interviewed for their contributions to the chapter. Their experience and insight into the politics of the Yukon is indeed invaluable. Thanks also to the book's editors for their comments.

2 Joe Linklater, "The Perspective of a Settled Aboriginal Land Claim 'Stakeholder': Realities to Date in Terms of Oil and Gas Operations and Exploration" (paper presented at the conference "Extending Oil & Gas into the Yukon and the NWT," Calgary, September 2000), 6–9.

3 Kirk Cameron and Graham White, cited in Doug MacArthur, "The Changing Architecture of Governance in the Yukon and the Northwest Territories," in Northern Exposure: Peoples, Powers and Prospects In Canada's North, ed. F. Abele, T. Courchene, L. Seidle, and F. St-Hilaire (Montreal: Institute for Research on Public Policy, 2009), 190.

4 Ibid., 188.

5 Tony Penikett, personal interview, Ottawa, 20 September 2009.

6 Gurston Dacks, "Implementing First Nations Self-Government in the Yukon: Lessons for Canada," Canadian Journal of Political Science 37, no. 3 (2004): 671–94.

7 Michael Whittington, paraphrased. Chris Alcantara, "Explaining Aboriginal Treaty Negotiation Outcomes in Canada: The Cases of the Inuit and the Innu in Labrador," Canadian Journal of Political Science 40, no. 1 (2007): 204.

8 See Chris Alcantara, "Explaining Aboriginal Treaty Negotiation Outcomes in Canada: The Cases of the Inuit and the Innu in Labrador," Canadian Journal of Political Science 40, no. 1 (2007): 185–207.

9 MacArthur, "Changing Architecture of Governance," 187.
10 Gabrielle Slowey, "The NWT: A New Day?," this volume.
11 Ken Coates, "Yukon and Northwest Territories: The Emerging North of Native and Non-Native Societies," in *The Challenge of Northern Regions*, ed. Peter Jull and Sally Roberts (Casuarina, Darwin: North Australian Research Unit, Australian National University, 1991), 175.
12 Ibid.
13 Penikett, personal interview.
14 Anonymous former Yukon government official, personal interview, Toronto, 20 August 2007.
15 Anonymous Vuntut Gwitchin economic development officer, personal interview, Whitehorse, 12 October 2007.
16 Penikett, personal interview.
17 McCormick, cited in Chris Alcantra, "To Treaty or Not to Treaty? Aboriginal Peoples and Comprehensive Claims in Canada," *Publius* 38, no. 2 (2007): 355.
18 Fred McMahon and Miguel Cervantes, *Fraser Institute: Survey of Mining Companies 2010/2011*, 2011, http://www.fraserinstitute.org/uploadedFiles/fraser-ca/Content/research-news/research/publications/mining-survey-2010-2011.pdf.
19 "Yukon Given Good Grade in Mining Survey," CBC News, 4 March 2011, http://www.cbc.ca/news/canada/north/story/2011/03/04/yukon-mining-fraser-institute.html.
20 As cited in MacArthur, "Changing Architecture of Governance," 190–1.
21 Anonymous former Yukon government official, personal interview.
22 "Long-Awaited Yukon Education Reform Report Released," CBC, 8 February 2008, http://www.cbc.ca/news/canada/north/story/2008/02/08/educ-reform.html.
23 Ibid.
24 Linklater, "The Perspective of a Settled Aboriginal Land Claim 'Stakeholder.'"
25 Yukon Territorial Government, "Energy, Mines, and Resources: Regional Land Use Planning," http://www.emr.gov.yk.ca/lands/frequently_asked_questions.html.
26 MacArthur, "Changing Architecture of Governance," 198–9.
27 Yukon Bureau of Statistics, "Survey of Employment, Payroll and Hours, 2013," http://www.eco.gov.yk.ca/stats/pdf/seph_2013.pdf.
28 "Yukon Seeks Devolution Deal Changes," CBC News, 17 February 2011, www.cbc.ca/news/canada/north/story/2011/02/17/yukon-devolution-talks-fentie.html.

29 Ibid.
30 "Mining to Boost Northern Economies: Report," CBC News, 11 August 2010, http://www.cbc.ca/news/canada/north/story/2010/08/11/north-mining-conference-board.html.
31 Ibid.
32 Ibid.
33 Anonymous former Yukon government official, personal interview.
34 Linklater, personal interview.
35 Anonymous former Yukon government official, personal interview.
36 Anonymous Vuntut Gwitchin economic development officer, personal interview.
37 Ibid.
38 "Eagle Plains Natural Gas Study Gets $300K," CBC News, 8 March 2008, http://www.cbc.ca/news/canada/north/story/2011/03/08/yukon-eagle-plains-gas-study.html.
39 Gabrielle Slowey, "America, Canada and ANWR: Bilateral Relations and Indigenous Struggles," *Native Americas* 18, no. 2 (2001): 26–32.
40 Linklater, personal interview.
41 Ibid.
42 MacArthur, "Changing Architecture of Governance," 199.

Epilogue: Mapping the Neoliberal Transformation in Canada's Provinces and Territories

BRYAN M. EVANS AND CHARLES W. SMITH

This survey of thirteen rather distinct sub-national states that compose the Canadian federation reveals how complex the emergence and implementation of "neoliberalism in one country" can be. The centrality of region in Canadian politics is well established and is further affirmed by the accounts of neoliberal restructuring presented here. While each of the provinces and territories shares certain institutional similarities derivative from the Westminster parliamentary tradition and are allocated the same administrative and policy responsibilities by the constitution, each is also distinctive. The history of formative political events, class structure and relations, demography, and the economic structure of each jurisdiction vary considerably. Canada's sub-national states provide thirteen laboratories where each contributes in its own way to shape the contours of neoliberal restructuring across the country. Broad similarities across several jurisdictions are discernible at certain historical points, while rather starkly divergent narratives are expressed in others. Of course, the territories are most distinctive as a consequence of their constitutional status as creatures of the Government of Canada. Lack of provincial status places significant constraints on the territories' capacity to act autonomously. Moreover, the political economy of the North is shaped in unique ways because comparatively large Aboriginal and First Nations populations have demanded greater autonomy over land and natural resources.

When examining the provinces and territories, what can be concluded is the importance of political economy, as an intellectual approach, to identifying and explaining neoliberal transformations across Canada. Taken as a whole, the chapters presented here appreciate that changes in government are only one factor among many in explaining broader transformation within institutions, policies, and societal relations. Building on these themes, each author argues that social transformation occurs through political, economic, and social struggles that have no predetermined outcome. Rather, social transformation is shaped by history and by a confluence of unpredictable events. In the current era, society has been shaped by the forces of neoliberalism and thus has fundamentally transformed the provincial and territorial state. The focus of this book has been to highlight those changes and offer new avenues of inquiry that can assist students of both political economy and provincial politics. These are highlighted below. The epilogue concludes with some preliminary observations regarding future research on the provincial and territorial state.

Transformation of the Provincial and Territorial State under Neoliberalism

As identified in the introduction, the book highlights four broad themes that emerge explicitly (or implicitly) from the canvassing of Canadian sub-national experiences. These include (1) the broad changes in the accumulation and distribution of wealth, which have occurred through changes in public policy, changes in labour law, and in many cases, direct assault on workers' rights; (2) the transformation of political parties, most noticeably in the changes to Canada's social democratic parties in government; (3) the restructuring of state institutions, especially by centre-right political coalitions that have concretized neoliberalism in numerous provinces and territories; (4) broad societal change, including popular resistance to restructuring from workers, social movements, Aboriginal peoples, and a host of others. All of these themes present some paradoxical aspects of neoliberal transformations across the country while also opening up political space to challenge both public and private power.

In the wake of the Great Recession of 2008, public sector austerity was rolled out as part of the strategy to deal with the deficits accumulated when governments of all political persuasions transferred billions to private corporations and banks. However, government-imposed wage rollbacks, wage freezes, and legislative interventions are not unique to this period. Indeed, the most prominent characteristic of neoliberalism in the provinces and territories has been a drastic restructuring of how wealth is accumulated and redistributed. Throughout the post-war period, the social welfare state and strong private- and public-sector unions allowed for a modest redistribution of wealth across the country. Today that reality has been transformed by neoliberal governments. This was a particularly prominent feature of the rollback phase of neoliberalism (fiscal retrenchment, privatization, marketization of public service, and deregulation) witnessed in the 1980s and 1990s.

The arsenal of weapons available to governments was significant as changes in policy led to downward pressure on social assistance recipients (as in Ontario, Alberta, Saskatchewan, and British Columbia), cutting personal and corporate income taxes (as occurred almost everywhere), and the termination or radical reframing of public policies originally intended to restrict market forces in such policy domains as housing and health care. In addition, a regulatory framework providing some degree of protection from market failure or other risks, as with environmental regulations, was redesigned to accommodate investment. In other areas, governments clawed back public-sector salaries and wages, as seen in PEI (7.5 per cent rollback in 1994), Ontario (5.0 per cent cut in wages and salaries in 1993), and Alberta (government workers received a 5.0 per cent wage cut between 1994 and 1997). Other provinces chose to freeze public-sector wages for an extended period of time, as in Newfoundland in what became a four-year wage freeze in 1991. In 2005, Quebec froze wages for two years, and Ontario froze wages for non-union public sector workers in 2010 (the freeze is still in place as of 2014).

Where workers resisted austerity, governments resorted to legislative interventions through back-to-work legislation (as in British Columbia, Alberta, Saskatchewan, Quebec, and Ontario).[1] And in many cases, it was not simply the parties that have historically been aligned to business interests that have implemented public-sector austerity policies and sought to balance budgets on the backs of their own public-sector workers. The New Democrats in Saskatchewan, BC, Ontario, and Nova Scotia, as well as PQ governments in Quebec, have all imposed back-to-work legislation and other legislative strategies to discipline their public-sector workforces. Of course, unlike with the centre-right parties, the political ramifications have been more serious, given that organized labour constitutes an important component in the electoral base of these parties.

For parties of the ostensible centre-left, alienating and attacking labour has often been a critical moment leading towards electoral defeat. This is most spectacularly the case with Ontario's NDP government led by Bob Rae. The imposition of the Social Contract Act fractured the most important component of the Ontario party's electoral base, the labour unions, into two opposing camps, one that remained loyal to the party and the other composed of the major public-sector unions and the Canadian Auto Workers union, who turned to strategic voting to defeat hard-right Conservatives. The bitterness of the divide was so deep and enduring that the Ontario NDP did not recover their pre-1990 levels of electoral support until 2011. Less dramatically, New Democrat governments in Saskatchewan, Manitoba, and Nova Scotia through the 1990s and 2000s expressed considerable alignment to fiscal austerity and a retreat from more redistributive policies.

Recognizing these changes within Canada's social democratic parties is a second recurring theme in this volume. The high point of social democracy in Canada was the decade of the 1970s. New Democrats governed three provinces (Saskatchewan, Manitoba, and British Columbia), while the PQ formed government in Quebec in 1976. These governments presented the most progressive face of Keynesian capitalism, but it was their misfortune to govern through a decade of paradigm change. All three NDP governments were relegated to the opposition benches by the early 1980s as a consequence of their initial embrace of austerity measures, including the adoption of wage controls. With the ascent of neoliberalism through the 1980s, social democracy in Canada and elsewhere accommodated itself to neoliberalism.[2] In every province where social democratic parties formed government they abandoned core Keynesian policies and replaced them with supply-side policies centred on skills acquisition at the individual level, retreated from progressive taxation, and cut public expenditures.[3] As Byron Sheldrick demonstrates in his chapter on Manitoba, this ideological victory was so complete that by the end of the 1990s, social democracy had accepted distinct versions of Third Way neoliberalism.[4] So complete has been the transformation of social democratic politics that, as this volume goes to print, in the heart of industrial Ontario the NDP has embraced a form of right-wing anti-populism where it has positioned its tax and policy proposals to the right of Kathleen Wynne's Liberals. The PQ underwent similar transformations throughout the 2000s and in 2014 embraced a conservative form of nationalism, abandoning many of its progressive roots.

A third theme is the role of the sub-national state in driving capitalist economic development and shaping neoliberalism. It comes as no revelation to anyone familiar with the history of Canadian political economy that the state, whether federal or sub-national, has always had a significant role in directly or indirectly intervening to encourage economic development and to institutionalize neoliberalism. From John A. Macdonald's National Policy in the nineteenth century to Dalton McGuinty's or Gary Doer's Third Way–inspired sectoral industrial policies, green energy strategy, and new planning and delivery institutions for Manitoba or Ontario in the twenty-first century, there is a continuous role for the state in attracting investment, aiding capital accumulation, and creating new markets. In the current period, a central feature of neoliberal governance has been the dominance of centre-right political coalitions that have used the state to concretize neoliberalism through a transformation of state institutions. In almost every province and territory this has included a centralization of political power in the Premier's Office and privileging government ministries responsible for private-sector accumulation.

A variety of paradoxes and contradictions emerge from these transformations, particularly in the neoliberal era where roll-out strategies have combined increasing state capacity and interventions to discipline and co-opt workers into new competitiveness and productivity alliances within the neoliberal state. In Newfoundland, increased provincial fiscal capacity was strengthened as a result of offshore oil extraction. This economic change allowed the Conservative government of Danny Williams to utilize these resources to improve public services and public-sector compensation. Yet this was not governmental recognition for past injustices but rather an economic incentive to allow the state to restructure the relationship with its public-sector unions by establishing strategic partnerships and thus linking workers directly with the government's competitiveness objectives. In Prince Edward Island the case of the provincial state leading the campaign to establish a gambling industry is further illustration of the shrinking of the political imagination.

Within Atlantic Canada, Nova Scotia reflects a fascinating case study of neoliberal transformation because Liberal, Conservative, and NDP governments each attempted to trigger private-sector industrialization, with little success. In fact, it was the Liberal premiership of John Savage in the early 1990s that pioneered Third Way neoliberalism in Canada with a combination of different rollback and roll-out strategies. Deficit financing was abandoned and public expenditure constraint implemented, including a public-sector wage freeze. Yet this was not a program to shrink the state but rather to reshape it. The Savage government saw the public sector as a stabilizer in turbulent times. Consequently, expenditure cuts were accompanied by tax increases. In these respects, the Rae government in Ontario made similar decisions, but the Savage government was unique in its efforts to depoliticize key policy and delivery fields, especially education, health, and economic development, by creating new arm's-length authorities responsible for policy and program delivery at the regional level. In addition, the Liberals embraced market-driven policy projects through public-private partnerships rather than directly by the government.

The subsequent Hamm Progressive Conservative government turned to a more explicitly neoliberal plan, which sought to create a free trade and investment region, the so-called Atlantica Strategy. The election of the Dexter NDP in 2009 was a departure from these "big idea" strategies because it embraced neoliberalism rather than presenting a social democratic alternative to the Conservatives and Liberals. The Nova Scotia NDP's seven-point election platform was perhaps the most modest in the province's history and reflected the NDP's embrace of fiscal conservatism and anti-tax rhetoric usually associated with the New Right. In material terms, expanding the role of the public sector in social and economic development was not possible in the context of this enthusiam for anti-tax populism.

The anti-tax rhetoric in Nova Scotia was not unique to that province. Throughout the 1990s, increased taxation had become an unspeakable word in Canadian political culture. The Harmonized Sales Tax revolt in BC nearly brought down the Liberal government of Gordon Campbell and eventually forced the premier to resign. In Alberta, the Klein revolution also transformed the state, as anti-tax policy and fiscal orthodoxy became so entrenched that any attempt to break with that tradition, as with Klein's successor, Ed Stelmach, met with significant opposition. In Ontario, the 2003 election of Dalton McGuinty's Liberals was partially secured by the signing of an anti-tax pledge proposed by the right-wing Canadian Tax-Payers Federation. In many ways, McGuinty's natural tendency to embrace neoliberal positions on taxation (despite imposing a health tax in 2004) while also embracing fiscal orthodoxy as premier suggested that the Ontario Liberals did not represent a break with neoliberalism in that province. In practical terms, the McGuinty government accomplished two essential objectives to secure the onward march of neoliberalism. First, the much-needed reinvestment in social policy fields in particular remedied the severe expenditure cuts of the previous government, which destabilized political support for restructuring and further threatened Ontario's competiveness. Second, the McGuinty government embedded neoliberalism more deeply into the Ontario state through a Third Way roll-out strategy that created a variety of new institutions to improve planning and policy capacity. At the same time, McGuinty remained committed to fiscal conservatism and balanced-budget orthodoxy until the Great Recession of 2008 forced significant deficit financing and in particular a major provincial intervention in the auto sector.

The state of resistance to neoliberalism, the fourth general theme running through many of the cases here, is uneven and marked by periods of quietude punctuated by episodic eruptions of protest. The neoliberal era is now older than the "glorious thirty years" of the post-war golden age of capitalism. Between 1945 and 1975 economic and political institutions were constructed that enabled the grand social democratic projects we associate with the Keynesian welfare state. That model began to unravel in the mid-1970s and has never recovered. And it is the durability of the neoliberal paradigm that is so remarkable. Yet if there is no sustained resistance to this economic, political, and social paradigm, then there is no possibility of transformations beyond neoliberalism.

The lesson of the history of resistance to neoliberalism in the Canadian sub-national context is instructive here. As many of the chapters in this volume illustrate, where resistance to austerity measures or state intervention took place, the opposition has typically been limited to the sector under attack, as with nurses in Alberta and Saskatchewan, teachers in Ontario, or government workers in a number of provinces. In Quebec, the Liberal government of Jean Charest was arguably defeated by Quebec students angered by a proposed tuition increases and their skill in broadening this single issue into a expression of a much more broad attack on Quebec social programs. In other cases, however, there was initial opposition and eventual acceptance. The point is that once the specific conflict was concluded in either a victory or defeat for the workers or protestors, generally there was no broader capacity for a sustained mobilization. Even where broad coalitions of resistance were constructed, most notably with the examples of Solidarity in BC in the early 1980s and the Days of Action in Ontario the mid-late 1990s, nothing of an enduring social or political transformation occurred. In both examples, there was internal disagreement on the goal of the opposition. Were opponents of neoliberal restructuring seeking a province-wide general strike? Or were these groups seeking a change in government and a new political program? And what, if an agreement was reached, became of the movement against neoliberalism? In other words, in ideological terms, there was no particularly well-developed program envisioning an alternative to neoliberalism.

In many of the sector-specific cases referenced in this volume, it is not uncommon for some compromise settlement to be reached in order to stop or alter government restructuring. But as we see in the case of New Brunswick Power, when confronted with a broad resistance, governments can be forced to change strategy, at least for a period. Here again, however, once NB Power was saved as a publicly owned provincial utility, resistance melted away. There was no broader effort to raise the political stakes further by initiating a debate on extending public ownership into other sectors or to press the province to develop economic development strategies where the public sector would perform a central role. Opportunities to generate alternatives were not generally exploited for anything more than short-term objectives.

Neoliberalism and the Future of Provincial Political Economy

One of the most notable changes in provincial political economy over the past three decades has been the present dominance of resource extraction over regional well-being. The relationship of the provincial/territorial state to non-renewable resource industries and specifically hydrocarbons, and the role of the state in facilitating exploitation, is likely the most important dimension in the political economy of several provinces and territories. As noted above, in Newfoundland, revenues from offshore oil extraction provided the provincial government with unprecedented fiscal capacity to win labour peace in the public sector. Indeed, the ownership, management, and division of royalties was so fragmented in Newfoundland that premier Danny Williams played the populist neo-nationalism card to great effect, earning him the moniker of "Danny Chavez" in 2008.[5] Similarly in Nova Scotia, the prospect of offshore oil and gas and the division of royalties that would be generated by that project was a major point of contention between the province and the federal government throughout the 2000s.

However, among the provinces, it is in Alberta (and possibly now Saskatchewan) where we see how the oil and gas industry dominates and indeed shapes the political life of provincial governance in unique ways. At the level of political culture and ideology, the hydrocarbon industry has forged the province's very identity and sense of well-being as one and the same. As Steve Patten demonstrates in his chapter, so entrenched has the power of oil and gas become within the province

that it has shaped political culture in a way that there is broad acceptance of the view that "what is good for oil is good for Albertans." So it
is only in Alberta that a conservative government can force a political
split by modestly suggesting that royalty rates should be increased. The
emergence of the Wildrose Party, the first truly competitive opposition
party in Alberta in more than a generation, was very much the response
of an angry section of the oil elite who interpreted the policy modifica-
tion by the Stelmach government as an indicator of their loss of influence in government. Of course, under such conditions, one must then
change the government, and in Alberta, it appears, only the oil industry
has the political and economic capacity to mobilize a sufficient part of
the electorate to threaten government change.

While this single-industry hegemony might be unique to Alberta, all
Canadian governments to some extent have historically been particularly accommodating to the needs of extractive industries. In the 1970s
a lively and informed debate was held in Parliament, the legislatures,
and the media on who should own our natural resources, how or if they
should be exploited, and the need for industrial policy to diversify the
Canadian economy and to add value to our exports. That debate has
largely disappeared, despite a clear need to revive that debate in the
wake of climate change and a shift in the global hierarchy of power.[6]
Nevertheless, the influence of resource extraction is likely to dominate
the study of provincial political economy for decades to come.

The same observation is also true in the Northern territories, which
represent fundamental case studies in the political economy of non-
renewable resources. The presence of large First Nations and Inuit
populations in all three territories, a clear majority in the NWT and
Nunavut, has in all cases placed land claims settlement at the centre
of political life. However, the semi-colonial status of the territories vis-
à-vis the Government of Canada presents a paradox of neoliberalism
in Canada. While the territories lack the constitutional status of provinces, they do exercise many of the policy and taxation powers held by
provinces. However, public lands in the territories are owned and controlled by the Government of Canada. And this is a critical point in land
claims, as this means that royalties from oil, gas, and mineral extraction
belong to the federal government and not the territory. The purpose of
land claim and devolution agreements is to allow indigenous people to
transfer ownership of their lands to the federal government in return
for a range of benefits including cash, governance arrangements, ownership of some lands, and receipt of royalties from resource extraction.

The territorial governments are also critical actors in rolling out new institutions and political arrangements to facilitate capitalist development. Nunavut is particularly striking because its very origin as a separate territory was based in a land claims agreement. Key provisions in this agreement are concerned with governance, and it establishes new state and quasi-state institutions as well as influential non-state organizations that nonetheless play an important role in Nunavut governance. While there are divisions in Nunavut society on how or even if economic development should proceed, quasi-state organizations are leading the development of capitalist relations in the territory.

With respect to the NWT, the move towards devolution began before land claims issues had been resolved, and this sequencing has proven to have been highly problematic. In many ways, devolution has simply allocated the role of colonizer from the federal government to the government of NWT. While a devolution agreement was achieved in 2013, there was little consultation with the peoples of NWT. The political implications are far reaching in that for indigenous citizens of NWT their territorial government lacks legitimacy and is seen to be an agent of the federal government and not representative of their interests. In the case of NWT, devolution is seen to undermine the aspirations of the indigenous population to settle land claims and achieve self-government.

Yukon, by contrast, is well ahead of the other two territories because devolution of powers took place only following the resolution of fourteen of fifteen land claims and self-government agreements that seek to ensure that the indigenous peoples of Yukon benefit directly from any subsequent economic development. And none other than the Fraser Institute, a free market think tank, concluded that successive Yukon governments, whether NDP or Conservative, have created one of the most attractive regulatory environments in the world for mining investment. The Fraser Institute attributed the settlement of most land claims in the territory as a critical part of this success, as they created a stable and predictable economic context.

Somewhat paradoxically, the settlement of land claims is critical not only for the benefit of indigenous peoples but also for capital. Of the three territories, Yukon appears to have gone farthest down this road, but then it has the oldest agreements and may well be a harbinger of Nunavut's future. Of course, Nunavut is vastly different from Yukon, and the political governance arrangements in place there will have an enduring effect in shaping its economy. The role of quasi-state agencies in this process will be defining. And the case of NWT demonstrates that even for capitalist development in the era of neoliberalism, inclusion matters. Without serious movement on the land claims front, one is left questioning if that territory will remain a colonial outpost of Ottawa.

Arguably, the territories present three important case studies that will likely dominate the study of Canadian political economy in the near future. As this volume goes to press, governments throughout the Canadian West and the North are advocating for speedy resolution of environmental disputes in order to construct new pipelines for oil and gas extraction. Meanwhile, in regions as diverse as Newfoundland and Labrador, New Brunswick, Saskatchewan, Alberta, British Columbia, Yukon, NWT, and Nunavut advocates of resource extraction continue to clash with Aboriginal and First Nation communities over questions of ownership, environmental stewardship, and community development. The protests in New Brunswick by the Elsipogtog First Nation against hydraulic fracturing (fracking) are only the most recent clashes in a long-standing dispute. None of these debates is likely to be resolved quickly and certainly points to the contradiction of governments placing all of their economic priorities within the development and shipment of resource commodities.

The transformation of provincial and territorial political economy under the auspices of neoliberalism identified in this volume also highlights new and important areas of research. Throughout the country, Aboriginal and First Nation groups have demonstrated that they are no longer willing to accept the status quo. These communities have signalled that they will no longer sacrifice community autonomy or health for the economic benefits of distant provincial or federal governments. Economic, political, and social struggles are also igniting within the ranks of organized labour as working men and women are increasingly pushing back against government policies that seem to benefit certain classes over others. New research questioning the benefits of market-driven public policy that prioritizes private-sector accumulation over the public good has much to teach us about the institutionalization of neoliberalism across Canada. Finally, there has been a general awakening of young activists since the 2008 financial crisis. Throughout the country, First Nations, students, workers, environmentalists, women's groups, and others have begun challenging neoliberalism in new and creative ways. In many ways, those struggles remain understudied and have much to offer those interested in the study of political economy in Canada's diverse and complicated regions. Whether these movements will create the conditions for a new social transformation remains an open-ended and essential question.

NOTES

1   Leo Panitch and Donald Swartz, *From Consent to Coercion: The Assault on Trade Union Freedoms* (Toronto: Garamond, 2003).
2   Bryan Evans and Ingo Schmidt, eds., *Social Democracy after the Cold War* (Edmonton: Athabasca University Press, 2012).
3   Wolfgang Merkel, Alexander Petring, Christian Henkes, and Christoph Egle, *Social Democracy in Power: The Capacity to Reform* (New York: Routledge, 2008), 6 and 25.
4   Colin Crouch, *The Strange Non-Death of Neoliberalism* (Cambridge: Polity, 2011), 162.
5   "The Making of 'Danny Chavez': Newfoundland's Rebellious Premier Takes On Big Oil and 'Steve' Harper," Canada News Wire, 23 January 2008, http://www.newswire.ca/en/story/330019/the-making-of-danny-chavez-newfoundland-s-rebellious-premier-takes-on-big-oil-and-steve-harper.
6   However, recent research suggests that this debate is still worth having. See Paul Kellogg, "Prairie Capitalism Revisited: Capital Accumulation and Class Formation in the New West" (paper presented to the Canadian Political Science Association, University of Victoria, June 2013), accessed 14 May 2014, http://www.cpsa-acsp.ca/papers-2013/Kellogg.pdf.

Bibliography

Government Documents and Cases

Canada. *Economic Reference Tables*. Ottawa: Department of Finance, August 1992.
- *Income in Canada*. Ottawa: Statistics Canada, 2007.
- *Labour Market Update*. Ottawa: Human Resources and Skills Development Canada, January 2005.
- *National Policy Framework for Strategic Gateways and Trade Corridors*. Ottawa: Transport and Infrastructure, 2009, http://www.canadasgateways.gc.ca/nationalpolicy.html.
- *Report of the Auditor General of Canada to the Legislative Assembly of Nunavut 2010: Human Resource Capacity – Government of Nunavut*. Ottawa: Auditor General of Canada, March 2010.
- *Report of the Royal Commission on Dominion-Provincial Relations (Rowell-Sirois), Book I*. Ottawa: King's Printer, 1940.
- *Understanding the Early Years: Early Childhood Development in Prince Edward Island*. Ottawa: Human Resources and Skills Development Canada, November 2001.
- Senate, Standing Committee on Fisheries and Oceans. *Nunavut Marine Fisheries: Quotas and Harbours*. Ottawa, June 2009.
Government of New Brunswick. *Electricity in New Brunswick and Options for Its Future*. Fredericton: Queen's Printer, 1998.
- "Electricity in New Brunswick beyond 2000: Discussion Paper." Fredericton: Queen's Printer, 1998.
- "New Brunswick Energy Commission." 2011. www.gnb.ca/Commission/mandate-e.asp.
- New Brunswick Forestry Products Association. "Economic Value," 2014, www.nbforestry.com/economy/economic-value/.

– *The New Brunswick Reality Report.* Fredericton: Queen's Printer, 2005.
– *The New Brunswick Reality Report: Part 2; An Export-Driven Economy.* Fredericton: Queen's Printer, 2007.
– *Our Action Plan to Be Self-Sufficient in New Brunswick.* Fredericton: Queen's Printer, 2007.
– *The Road to Self-Sufficiency: A Common Cause.* Fredericton: Queen's Printer, 2007.
– Department of Finance. "Provincial Profiles: New Brunswick, Canada," http://www2.gnb.ca/content/dam/gnb/Departments/ed-de/PDF/ExportTrade-Commerce/NBProfile2014.pdf.
Halifax Gateway Council. "Building the Halifax Gateway: A New Vision of the Future." Halifax: Halifax Gateway Council, February 2006.
New Brunswick Court of Queen's Bench, *Small & Ryan v New Brunswick (Minister of Education)*, NBQB 201 (2008).
New Brunswick Liberal Party. *Getting Results, Together.* Fredericton: Queen's Printer, 2006.
New Brunswick Power. "History," www.nbpower.com/html/en/about/publications/history.html.
– *2007/08 Annual Report*, www.nbpower.com/html/en/about/publications/annual/AnnualReport0708.pdf.
– *2009/10 Sustainability Report*, www.nbpower.com/html/en/about/publications/annual/2009–10AR-ENG.pdf.
Newfoundland and Labrador. *The Economic Review.* St John's: Queen's Printer, 2009.
North Sky Consulting Group. *Qanukkanniq? The GN Report Card: Analysis & Recommendations.* Iqaluit: North Sky, October 2009.
Northwest Territories. *Results of the Public Engagement on the Proposed Northwest Territories Lands and Resources Devolution Agreement.* Iqualuit: Queen's Printer, May 2013.
Nova Scotia. *Addressing Nova Scotia's Fiscal Challenge.* Halifax: Economic Advisory Panel, 2009.
– *Canada's East Coast Gateway via Nova Scotia.* Halifax: Department of Transportation and Public Works, 2006.
– *A Guide: Getting Back to Balance.* Halifax: Queen's Printer, 2009.
– *Report of the Auditor General.* Halifax: Office Auditor General, 2010.
– Department of Finance. "Statistics." www.gov.ns.ca/finance/statistics/economy.
Nova Scotia New Democratic Party. *Better Deal 2009: The NDP Plan to Make Life Better for Today's Families.* Halifax: NDP, 2009.
Nunavut. *Towards a Representative Public Service.* Iqaluit: Department of Human Resources, 2010.

Nunavut Tunngavik Incorporated. *Annual Report on the State of Inuit Culture and Society: Kindergarten to Grade 12 Education in Nunavut.* Iqaluit: Nunavut Tunngavik, 2007.

Ontario. *Breaking the Cycle: Ontario's Poverty-Reduction Strategy.* Toronto: Queen's Printer, 2008.

– *Commission on the Reform of Ontario's Public Services.* Toronto: Queen's Printer for Ontario, 2012.

– *Ministry of Finance Budget Speech 1991.* Toronto: Queen's Printer, 1991.

– *Ontario Economic Outlook and Economic Review 2012.* Toronto: Queen's Printer, 2012.

– *Ontario Economic Outlook and Fiscal Review 1999.* Toronto: Queen's Printer for Ontario, 1999.

– *Ontario Economic Outlook and Fiscal Review 2004.* Toronto: Queen's Printer, 2004.

– *Ontario Economic Outlook and Fiscal Review 2011.* Toronto: Queen's Printer, 2011.

– *Ontario Economic Outlook 1994–1998.* Toronto: Queen's Printer for Ontario, 1994.

– *Open Ontario: Ontario's Plan for Jobs and Growth 2010 Ontario Budget.* Toronto: Queen's Printer, 2010.

– *A Prosperous and Fair Ontario 2013: Ontario Budget.* Toronto: Queen's Printer, 2013.

– *Report of the Premier's Council on Economic Issues· Competing in the New Economy.* Toronto: Queen's Printer for Ontario, 1989.

Ontario Civil Service Commission. *Annual Reports* (various years). Toronto: Queen's Printer, 1947–2005.

Ontario Liberal Party. *Achieving Our Potential: The Ontario Liberal Plan for Economic Growth,* Book 3. Toronto: Ontario Liberal Party, 2003.

Ontario Management Board Secretariat. *Ideas for Organization Renewal: Organizational Renewal of the Ontario Management Board.* Ontario: Queen's Printer, 1991.

Ontario Ministry of Finance. Commission on the Reform of Ontario's Public Services. Toronto: Queen's Printer for Ontario, 2012, http://www.fin.gov .on.ca/en/reformcommission/.

– *Expenditure Estimates of the Province of Ontario* (various years). Toronto: Queen's Printer, 2001–8.

– *Ontario Budget Speech 2005.* Toronto: Queen's Printer, 2005.

– *Ontario Budget 2004: The Plan for Change.* Toronto: Queen's Printer, 2004.

– *Ontario Economic Outlook and Fiscal Review, 1999.* Toronto: Queen's Printer, 1999.

- *Ontario Economic Outlook and Fiscal Review 2011*. Toronto: Queen's Printer, 2011.
- *Ontario Economic Outlook, 1994–1998*. Toronto: Queen's Printer for Ontario, 1994.
- *Ontario Economic Outlook and Economic Review 2010*. Toronto: Queen's Printer, 2010.
- *Ontario Economiic Outlook, 1994–1998*. Toronto: Queen's Printer for Ontario, 1994.
- *Ontario Fiscal Overview and Spending Cuts*. Toronto: Queen's Printer, 1995.
- *Ontario Outlook and Fiscal Review 2004*. Toronto: Queen's Printer, 2004.
- *Open Ontario: Ontario's Plan for Jobs and Growth 2010 Ontario Budget*. Toronto: Queen's Printer, 2010.
- *A Prosperous and Fair Ontario 2013, Ontario Budget*. Toronto: Queen's Printer, 2013.
- *Turning the Corner to a Better Tomorrow: 2011 Ontario Budget*. Toronto: Queen's Printer, 2011.
- Ontario Ministry of Industry, Trade and Technology. *An Industrial Policy Framework for Ontario*. Toronto: Queen's Printer, 1992.
- Ontario Ministry of Public Infrastructure Renewal. *Building a Better Tomorrow: An Infrastructure Planning, Financing and Procurement Framework for Ontario's Public Sector*. Toronto: Queen's Printer, 2004.
- Ontario Ministry of Research and Innovation. *Results-Based Plan Briefing Book 2009–10*. Toronto: Queen's Printer, 2010.
- Ontario Ministry of Treasury and Economics. *Ontario Budget 1987*. Toronto: Queen's Printer for Ontario, 1987.
- *Public Accounts of Ontario, 1970–1985*. Toronto: Queen's Printer for Ontario, various years.
- Ontario Ministry of Treasury and Economics. Sectoral and Regional Policy Branch, Statistics Section. *Ontario Statistics 1986*. Toronto: Queen's Printer, 1986.
- Ontario Progressive Conservative Party. *The Common Sense Revolution*. Toronto: Ontario Progressive Conservative Party, 1995.
- *The Road Ahead*. Toronto: Ontario Progressive Conservative Party, 2003.
- Quebec. Ministère des finances. *Prioriser l'emploi et la solidarité: Plan d'action pour le développement des entreprises d'économie sociale*. Quebec: Government of Quebec, 2003.
- *Québec Objectif Emploi, Vers une Économie d'avant-garde: Une stratégie de développement économique créatrice d'emplois*. Quebec: Government of Quebec, 1998.
- Saskatchewan. *Ministry of Agriculture, Agricultural Statistics 1991*. Regina: Ministry of Agriculture, 1992.

– *A Submission of the Government of Saskatchewan to the Royal Commission on Dominion-Provincial Relations*. Regina: King's Printer, 1937.

Saskatchewan Court of Appeal, *Reference Re Provincial Electoral Boundaries*, (1991), 90 Sask. R. 174, 78 DLR (4th) 449.

Supreme Court of Canada, *Newfoundland (Treasury Board) v NAPE*, [2004] 3 SCR 381.

– *Reference re Prov. Electoral Boundaries (Sask.)*, [1991] 2 SCR 158.

Yukon. Yukon Bureau of Statistics. "Survey of Employment, Payroll and Hours, 2013." http://www.eco.gov.yk.ca/stats/pdf/seph_2013.pdf.

– *Yukon Community Profiles*. Yellowknife: Government of Yukon, 2004.

– *Energy, Mines, and Resources: Regional Land Use Planning*. Yellowknife: Government of Yukon, 2001. http://www.emr.gov.yk.ca/lands/frequently_asked_questions.html.

Presentations and Reports

Aboriginal Justice Implementation Commission. *The Aboriginal Justice Implementation Commission*. 1999. http://ajic.mb.ca/index.html.

Adamson, Agar. "Can the Nova Scotia NDP Stand McEwan's Strong Ale?" Paper presented to the Atlantic Provinces Political Science Association, 1985.

AIMS. "Atlantica: One Region – Two Futures." Halifax: AIMS, 26 October 2003.

– "AIMS Talks about Atlantica with Commons Committee." Halifax: AIMS, 26 February 2002.

Arragutainaq, Lucassie, NIRB chairperson, to Chuck Strahl, minister of Indian and Northern Affairs, 22 February 2010.

Association of University of New Brunswick Teachers. *AUNBT & the New Brunswick Post-Secondary Education Crisis*, 2008.

Atlantic Provinces Economic Council (APEC). *Atlantic Canada Today*. Halifax: Formac, 1987.

– "Building Competitiveness in Atlantic Canada's Forest Industries: A Strategy for Future Prosperity." *APEC Forum on Competitiveness, 2005–2010*, August 2008, https://www.apec-econ.ca/publications/view/?do-load=1&publication.id=167&site.page.id=103004&search-form.theme=Industry%20Specific%20Reports.

Barager, Fletcher. *Report on the Manitoba Economy 2011*. Winnipeg: Canadian Centre for Policy Alternatives – Manitoba, 2001. http://www.policyalternatives.ca/sites/default/files/uploads/publications/Manitoba%20Office/2011/09/2011ReportMbEconBaragar-smaller%20file%20size.pdf.

Bateman, Tom. "The Law and Politics of Public Consultation in New Brunswick: A New Front for Judicial Action." Paper presented at the Canadian Constitution Foundation Conference on Individual Freedom and the Common Good, Toronto, 17–19 October 2008.

Berger, Thomas. *Northern Frontier, Northern Homeland: The Report of the Mackenzie Valley Pipeline Inquiry.* Minister of Supply Services. Ottawa: Supply and Services, 1977.

Black, Errol, and Jim Silver. "Is Labour's Future in the Streets?" CCPA, Fast Facts, 10 October 2004.

Campaign 2000. *2009 Report Card on Child and Family Poverty in Canada: 1989–2009*, 2009, http://www.campaign2000.ca/reportCards/national/2009EnglishC2000NationalReportCard.pdf.

Canadian Centre for Policy Alternatives. *Deficit Mania in Perspective: Ontario Budget 2010.* Toronto: Canadian Centre for Policy Alternatives, 2010.

– *No Time to Lose: An Action Blueprint for Ontario.* Toronto: CCPA, 2007.

– *The Ontario Alternative Budget, 2002.* Toronto: Canadian Centre for Policy Alternatives, 2002, http://www.policyalternatives.ca/sites/default/files/uploads/publications/Ontario_Office_Pubs/oab2002.pdf.

Canadian Centre for Policy Alternatives – Nova Scotia. *Nova Scotia Alternative Budget 2009.* Halifax: Canadian Centre for Policy Alternatives, September 2009, https://www.policyalternatives.ca/publications/reports/nova-scotia-alternative-budget-2009.

Cirtwell, Charles. "Follow or Get Out of the Way." Halifax: AIMS, February 2009.

Coalition pour l'avenir du Québec. *Taking Action for the Future: Action Plan.* Montreal: CAQ, November 2011.

Conference Board of Canada. *Northern Outlook: Economic Forecast.* Ottawa: Conference Board, January 2010.

Conway, J.F. "The Distribution of Benefits of the 1986 Saskatchewan Farm Production Loan Program." Paper presented to the Canadian Association of Rural Studies, Learned Societies, Laval University, June 1989.

– "The Saskatchewan Electoral Boundaries Case, 1990–91." *Proceedings of the Canadian Political Science Association Annual Meetings*, 1993 (microfiche).

Corporate Research Associates. *CRA Atlantic Quarterly* (Winter 2010).

– *CRA Atlantic Quarterly* (Spring 2012).

– Newsroom. Data consolidated from quarterly reports (2006–10), www.cra.ca.

David, Françoise, and Louise Marcoux. *Du pain et des roses.* Montreal: Marche des femmes contre la pauvreté, 1995.

Deloitte and Touche LLP. *Province of Nova Scotia Financial Review: Interim Report*, 7 August 2009.

Eglington, Peter, and Lew Voytilla. *Report re Fiscal and Self-Government Issues in Connection with Devolution*. Prepared for Richard Nerysoo, president Gwich'in Tribal Council. Inuvik, NT. 5 February 2011, www.assembly.gov .nt.ca/_live/.../11–02-28%20158-16(5).pdf.

Ekos Research Associates Inc. *Neighbourhoods Alive! Community Outcomes Evaluation 2010, Final Report*, 24 September 2010, http://www.gov.mb .ca/housing/neighbourhoods/na_bg/pdf/NACommunityOutcomes Evaluation2010.pdf.

Election Almanac. "Complete Coverage of Federal, Provincial and Territorial Elections in Canada," last modified 2012, http://www.electionalmanac .com/ea/.

Enoch, Simon. *Mapping Corporate Power*. Regina: Canadian Centre for Policy Alternatives Saskatchewan Office, 2012.

Fox-Decent, Wally. *Report on Certain Aspects of the Winnipeg Floodway Project*, 2004, http://www.floodwayauthority.mb.ca/pdf/wallyfox_decent_report .pdf.

Groupe de travail sur l'économie sociale. *Osons la solidarité*. Québec: Groupe de travail, 1996.

Hanly, David. "Husky Energy," *Encyclopedia of Saskatchewan*, http://esask .uregina.ca/entry/husky_energy.html.

Hazell, Elspeth, Kar-Fai Gee, and Andrew Sharpe. *The Human Development Index in Canada: Estimates for the Canadian Provinces and Territories, 2000 2011*. Ottawa: Centre for the Study of Living Standards, May 2012.

Irlbacher-Fox, Stephanie. "Gahcho Kué Economic Impacts and NWT Devolution," 4 May 2012, http://www.northernpublicaffairs.ca/index/ irlbacher-fox-gahcho-kué-economic-impacts-and-nwt-devolution/.

– "Governance in Canada's Northwest Territories: Emerging Institutions and Governance Issues." Main paper for Plenary on Arctic Governance, in *Conference Proceedings: 3rd Northern Research Forum*, Yellowknife, September 2004, http://www.arcticgovernance.org/governance-in-canadas-northwest -territories-emerging-institutions-and-governance-issues.4745074-142902.html.

Joint Review Panel for the Mackenzie Gas Project. *Foundation for a Sustainable Northern Future: Report of the Joint Review Panel for the Mackenzie Gas Project*, 30 December 2009, http://www.reviewboard.ca/upload/project _document/EIR0405-001_JRP_Report_of_Environmental_Review _Executive_Volume_I_1263228660.PDF.

Kellogg, Paul. "Prairie Capitalism Revisited: Capital Accumulation and Class Formation in the New West." Paper presented to the Canadian Political Science Association, University of Victoria, June 2013, http://www.cpsa -acsp.ca/papers-2013/Kellogg.pdf.

"Labour Market Sub-Committee of the Strategic Partnership Initiative." Labour Market Symposium, 2006, http://www.labourmarketcommittee.ca/index .htm.

Lau, James C.S. "2007 Annual Meeting of Shareholders," http://www.husky energy.com/downloads/investorrelations/presentations/AGM_0408.pdf.

Linklater, Joe. "The Perspective of a Settled Aboriginal Land Claim 'Stakeholder': Realities to Date in Terms of Oil and Gas Operations and Exploration." Presentation to Conference on Extending Oil & Gas into the Yukon and the NWT, Calgary, September 2000.

MacKinnon, Wayne. "Muddling Through: The Prince Edward Island Legislative Assembly." Ottawa: Canadian Study of Parliament Group, December 2010.

MacMillan, Elizabeth. "Bromley: GNWT Chose Paternalistic Way Typical of Colonizing Govt's, Hey Ppl We Have Authority, We Can Make Decisions w/o Asking #nwtpoli." Twitter post, 5 June 2013, https://twitter.com/ elizmcmillan/status/342399754996695040.

Miner, Rick, and Jacques L'Ecuyer. *Advantage New Brunswick: A Province Reaches to Fulfill Its Destiny*. Fredericton: Commission on Post-Secondary Education in New Brunswick, 2007, www.gnb.ca/cpse-ceps/EN/docs/ CEPNB_cahier_ang_LR.pdf.

Northern Clipper. "#NWT Chamber Cries ... over Yesterday's Sahtu #fracking Pull-out by #MGM #Energy." Twitter post, 10 November 2012, http:// mediamentor-circumpolar.blogspot.ca/2012/11/nwt-chamber-cries-over -yesterdays-sahtu.html.

Nunasi Corporation. *Nunasi Corporation*, 2014, http://www.nunasi.com/wp -content/uploads/2013/06/2014-04-21-nunasi-info-package-sm.pdf.

Nunavummiut Makitagunarningit. "Media Releases," 2013, http:// makitanunavut.wordpress.com/press-releases/.

Nunavut Economic Forum. *2010 Nunavut Economic Outlook: Nunavut's Second Chance*. Iqualuit: October 2010.

Ontario Confederation of Faculty Associations. "Ontario Budget 2009 Backgrounder: Ontario's Post-secondary Spending Plans," Working Paper Series 3. Toronto: OCUFA, 2009.

Parti Québécois. *Québec in a New World*. Toronto: Lorimer, 1994.

Poverty and Employment Precarity in Southern Ontario. *It's More Than Poverty: Employment Precarity and Household Well-being*. February 2013. http://www.unitedwaytoronto.com/document.doc?id=91.

Saskatchewan Institute for Social and Economic Alternatives. "The Privatization of the Potash Corporation of Saskatchewan: A Case Study." Regina, Saskatchewan Institute, June 1996.

Stevenson, Marc. *Traditional Inuit Decision-Making Structures and the Administration of Nunavut*. Ottawa: Royal Commission on Aboriginal Peoples, 1993.

Stewart, David K., and Anthony M. Sayers. "Alienated and Conservative? Continuity and Change in Alberta Political Culture." Paper presented at the Annual Meeting of the Canadian Political Science Association Montreal, Concordia University, 2 June 2010.

"St John's: Strategic Partnership Study Group." *Thunder Bay Chronicle-Journal*, 2004.

Strategic Partnership Study Group. *Strategic Partnership: How Business, Labour and Government Collaborate to Produce Europe's High-Performance Economies*. Strategic Partnership Study Group, 2002.

Timpson, Annis May. "The 2008 Nunavut Territorial Election." Paper presented at the Annual Meeting of the Canadian Political Science Association, Carleton University, June 2009.

Wolfe, David, and Meric Gertler. "Globalization and Economic Restructuring in Ontario: From Industrial Heartland to Learning Region?" Paper presented at the Conference on Regional Innovation Systems in Europe, Donostia – San Sebastian, Spain, 30 September to 2 October 1999.

World Bank. "The State in a Changing World." *The World Development Report 1997*. Washington DC: World Bank, 1997.

Books and Dissertations

Albo, Greg, Sam Gindin, and Leo Panitch. *In and Out of Crisis: The Global Financial Meltdown and Left Alternatives*. Oakland: PM, 2010.

Amagoalik, John. *Changing the Face of Canada: The Life Story of John Amagoalik*, edited by Louis McComber. Iqaluit: Nunavut Arctic College, 2009.

Anastakis, Dimitry. *Auto Pact: Creating a Borderless North American Auto Industry, 1960–1971*. Toronto: University of Toronto Press, 2005.

Apostle, Richard, and Gene Barrett. *Emptying Their Nets: Small Capital and Rural Industrialization in the Nova Scotia Fishing Industry*. Toronto: University of Toronto Press, 1992.

Barrie, Doreen. *The Other Alberta: Decoding a Political Enigma*. Regina: University of Regina, Canadian Plans Research Center, 2006.

Bavington, Dean. *Managed Annihilation: An Unnatural History of the Newfoundland Cod Collapse*. Vancouver: UBC Press, 2010.

Bellay, David J., Jon H. Pammett, and Donald C. Rowat, eds. *The Provincial Political Systems: Comparative Essays*. Agincourt: Methuen, 1976.

Bickerton, James P. *Nova Scotia, Ottawa and the Politics of Regional Development*. Toronto: University of Toronto Press, 1990.

Biggs, Lesley, and Mark Stobbe, eds. *Devine Rule in Saskatchewan*. Saskatoon: Fifth House, 1991.

Blake, Donald E., R.K. Carty, and Lynda Erickson. *Grassroots Politicians*. Vancouver: UBC Press, 1991.

Boismenu, Gérard, Pascale Dufour, and Denis Saint-Martin. *Ambitions libérales et écueils politiques*. Outremont: Athéna Editions, 2004.

Boudreau, Michael, Peter G. Toner, and Tony Tremblay, eds. *Exploring the Dimensions of Self-Sufficiency for New Brunswick*. Fredericton: New Brunswick and Atlantic Studies Research and Development Centre, 2009.

Bourque, Gilles L. *Le modèle québécois de développement*. Sainte-Foy: Presses de l'Université du Québec, 2000.

Brehaut, John H. *Left Arm Missing, Left Leg Missing, Unfit for Service: The Life & Times of Daniel J. MacDonald*. Charlottetown: J.H. Brehaut Publishing, 2009.

Brodie, M. Janine. *The Political Economy of Canadian Regionalism*. Toronto: Harcourt Brace Jovanovich, Canada, 1990.

Brown, Lorne, Joseph Roberts, and John Warnock. *Saskatchewan Politics from Left to Right, 1944–1999*. Regina: Hinterland Publications, 1999.

Brownsey, Keith, and Michael Howlett, eds. *The Provincial State: Politics in Canada's Provinces and Territories*. Mississauga: Copp Clark Pitman, 1992.

– *The Provincial State in Canada: Politics in the Provinces and Territories*. Peterborough, ON: Broadview, 2001.

Brym, Robert J., and R. James Sacouman, eds. *Underdevelopment and Social Movements in Atlantic Canada*. Toronto: New Hogtown, 1979.

Buckner, P.A., and David Frank, eds. *Atlantic Canada after Confederation*. Fredericton: Acadiensis, 1985.

Burgar, Joanna, and Martin Monkman. *Who Heads to the Polls? Exploring the Demographics of Voters in British Columbia*. Victoria: BC Stats, 2010.

Cadigan, Sean T. *Newfoundland and Labrador: A History*. Toronto: University of Toronto Press, 2009.

Carroll, W.K., and R.S. Ratner, eds. *Challenges and Perils: Social Democracy in Neoliberal Times*. Halifax: Fernwood, 2005.

Carty, R. Kenneth, William Cross, and Lisa Young. *Leaders and Parties in Canadian Politics: Experiences of the Provinces*. Toronto: HBJ, 1992.

Chernomas, Robert, and Ian Hudson. *Social Murder: And Other Shortcomings of Conservative Economics*. Winnipeg: ARP, 2007.

Clancy, Peter. *Offshore Petroleum Politics: Regulation and Risk in the Scotian Basin*. Vancouver: UBC Press, 2011.

Clancy, Peter, Jim Bickerton, Rod Haddow, and Ian Stewart. *The Savage Years: The Perils of Re-inventing Government in Nova Scotia*. Halifax: Formac Publishing, 2000.

Clarkson, Stephen. *The Big Red Machine*. Vancouver: UBC Press, 2005.
– *Uncle Sam and the US: Globalization, Neoconservatism and the Canadian State*. Toronto: University of Toronto Press, 2002.
Confédération des Syndicats Nationaux. *Prendre les devants dans l'organisation du travail*. Montreal: CSN, 1991.
Conway, J.F. *The West: The History of a Region in Confederation*. Toronto: Lorimer, 2006.
Cosgrove, James F., and Thomas R. Klassen, eds. *Casino State: Legalized Gambling in Canada*. Toronto: University of Toronto Press, 2009.
Courchene, Thomas J., and Colin R. Telmer. *From Heartland to North American Region State: The Social, Fiscal and Federal Evolution of Ontario*. Toronto: University of Toronto Faculty of Management, 1998.
Dacks, Gurston. *Devolution and Constitutional Development in the Canadian North*. Ottawa: Carleton University Press, 1990.
Dafoe, J.W. *Clifford Sifton in Relation to His Times*. Toronto: Macmillan, 1931.
Denison, Merril. *The People's Power: The History of Ontario Hydro*. Toronto: McClelland and Stewart, 1960.
Dickerson, Mark. *Whose North? Political Change, Political Development, and Self-Government in the Northwest Territories*. Vancouver: UBC Press, 1992.
Dickison, Joshua John. "Making New Brunswickers Modern: Natural and Human Resource Development in Mactaquac Regional Development Plan 1965–1975." MA thesis, University of New Brunswick, 2006.
Distasio, Jino, Michael Dudly, Molly Johnson, and Kurt Sargent. *Neighbourhoods Alive!: Community Outcomes Final Report*. Winnipeg: Institute of Urban Studies, 2005.
Dunn, Christopher. *Provinces: Canadian Provincial Politics*. Peterborough: Broadview, 2006.
Dyck, Rand. *Provincial Politics in Canada: Towards the Turn of the Century*. Scarborough, ON: Prentice-Hall, 1996.
– *Provincial Politics in Canada*. Toronto: Prentice-Hall, 1991.
Earle, Michael, ed. *Workers and the State in Twentieth-Century Nova Scotia*. Fredericton: Acadiensis.
Elkins, David J., and Richard Simeon. *Small Worlds: Provinces and Parties in Canadian Political Life*. Toronto: Methuen, 1980.
Evans, Bryan. "From Pragmatism to Neoliberalism: The Remaking of Ontario's Politics and Administrative State." PhD diss., York University, 2003.
Evans, Bryan, and Ingo Schmidt, eds. *Social Democracy after the Cold War*. Edmonton: Athabasca University Press, 2012.
Ferguson, Barry, and Robert Wardhaugh, eds. *Manitoba Premiers of the 19th and 20th Century*. Winnipeg: Canadian Plains Research Center, 2010.

Ferrar, Katie Shawn. "Power for Progress: The Mactaquac Hydroelectric Development and Regional Development Plans, 1964–1968." MA thesis, University of New Brunswick, 2005.

Florio, Massimo. *The Great Divestiture: Evaluating the Welfare Impact of the British Privatizations 1979–1997.* Cambridge, MA: MIT Press, 2004.

Foot, David. *Provincial Public Finance in Ontario.* Toronto: Ontario Economic Council / University of Toronto Press, 1977.

Forbes, E.R. *The Maritime Rights Movement, 1919–1927: A Study in Canadian Regionalism.* Montreal and Kingston: McGill-Queen's University Press, 1979.

Fredericks H.A., and Allan Chambers. *Bricklin.* Fredericton: Brunswick, 1977.

Gagnon, Alain-G., and Rafaele Iacovino. *Federalism, Citizenship and Québec: Debating Multinationalism.* Toronto: University of Toronto Press, 2007.

Gawthrop, Daniel. *Highwire Act: Power, Pragmatism and the Harcourt Legacy.* Vancouver: New Star, 1996.

Giddens, Anthony. *The Third Way and Its Critics.* Cambridge, UK: Polity, 2000.

– *The Third Way: The Renewal of Social Democracy.* Cambridge, UK: Polity, 1998.

Gilson, C.H.J., and A.M. Wadden. "The Windsor Gypsum Strike and the Formation of the Joint Labour/Management Study Committee: Conflict and Accommodation in the Nova Scotia Labour Movement 1957–79," in *Workers and the State in Twentieth Century Nova Scotia,* edited by Michael Earle, 190–216. Fredericton: Acadiensis, 1989.

Glyn, Andrew. *Capitalism Unleashed: Finance Globalization and Welfare.* Oxford: Oxford University Press, 2006.

Haddow, Rodney, and Thomas Klassen. *Partisanship, Globalization, and Canadian Labour Market Policy: Four Provinces in Comparative Perspective.* Toronto: University of Toronto Press, 2006.

Harvey, David. *A Brief History of Neoliberalism.* Oxford: Oxford University Press, 2005.

Hay, Colin. *Political Analysis.* New York: Palgrave, 2002.

Healy, Teresa. *The Harper Record.* Ottawa: Canadian Centre for Policy Alternatives, 2008.

Henderson, Ailsa. *Nunavut: Rethinking Political Culture.* Vancouver: UBC Press, 2007.

Henderson, Stephen T. *Angus L. Macdonald: A Provincial Liberal.* Toronto: University of Toronto Press, 2007.

Hoy, Claire. *Bill Davis.* Toronto: Methuen, 1985.

– *Clyde Wells: A Political Biography.* Toronto: Stoddart, 1992.

Inwood, Gregory J. *Continentalizing Canada: The Politics and Legacy of the Macdonald Commission.* Toronto: University of Toronto Press, 2005.

Jackson, Robert J., and Doreen J. Jackson. *Politics in Canada: Culture, Institutions, Behaviour and Public Policy.* Toronto: Pearson Prentice Hall, 2006.

Jamieson, Barbara, ed. *Governing Nova Scotia: Policies, Priorities and the 1984–85 Budget.* Halifax: Dalhousie School of Public Administration, 1984.

Jeffrey, Brooke. *Divided Loyalties.* Toronto: University of Toronto Press, 2010.

Jobb, Dean. *Calculated Risk: Greed, Politics and the Westray Tragedy.* Halifax: Nimbus, 1994.

Kavanagh, Peter. *John Buchanan: The Art of Political Survival.* Halifax: Formac Publishing, 1988.

Kealey, Gregory S. *The History and Structure of the Newfoundland Labour Movement.* St John's: Royal Commission on Employment and Unemployment, Newfoundland and Labrador, 1986.

Kealey, Gregory S., and Gene Long. *Labour and Hibernia: Conflict Resolution at Bull Arm, 1990–92.* St John's: Institute of Social and Economic Research, 1993.

Keirstead, B.S. *The Economic Effects of the War on the Maritime Provinces of Canada.* Halifax: Lattimer, 1944.

Knuttila, Murray, and Bob Stirling, eds. *The Prairie Agrarian Movement Revisited.* Regina: University of Regina Press, 2007.

Lawton, Alma. "Urban Relief in Saskatchewan during the Years of the Depression, 1930–37." MA thesis, University of Saskatchewan, 1969.

Laycock, David. *Populism and Democratic Thought in the Canadian Prairies.* Toronto: University of Toronto Press, 1990.

Lee, Marc. *Fair and Effective Carbon Pricing.* Vancouver: CCPA, 2011.

Lee, Philip. *Frank: The Life and Politics of Frank McKenna.* Fredericton: Goose Lane Editions, 2001.

Leys, Colin. *Market Driven Politics: Neoliberal Democracy and the Public Interest.* London: Verso, 2001.

Lipietz, Alain. *Mirages and Miracles. The Crisis of Global Fordism.* London: Verso, 1987.

Lipset, Seymour Martin. *Agrarian Socialism: The Cooperative Commonwealth Federation in Saskatchewan.* Berkeley: University of California Press, 1950.

Lisac, Mark. *Alberta Politics Uncovered: Taking Back Our Province.* Edmonton: NeWest, 2004.

Lisée, Jean-François. *Nous.* Montreal: Boréal, 2007.

Loxley, John, ed. *Transforming or Reforming Capitalism: Towards a Theory of Community Economic Development.* Halifax: Fernwood, 2007.

Loxley, John, Jim Silver, and Kathleen Sexsmith, eds. *Doing Community Economic Development.* Halifax: Fernwood, 2007.

Macdermid, Robert. *Funding the Common Sense Revolutionaries: Contributions to the Progressive Conservative Party of Ontario.* Toronto: Centre for Social Justice, 1999.

MacKinnon, Wayne E. *The Life of the Party: A History of the Liberal Party in Prince Edward Island.* Summerside: Williams and Crue, 1973.

Marx, Karl, and Friedrich Engels. *The Communist Manifesto,* 1848. http://
www.marxists.org/archive/marx/works/1848/communist-manifesto/
ch01.htm#007.

Masters, Donald C. *The Reciprocity Treaty of 1854.* Toronto: McClelland and
Stewart, 1963.

McBride, Stephen. *Dismantling a Nation: The Transition to Corporate Rule in
Canada.* Winnipeg: Fernwood, 1997.

– *Globalization and the Canadian State.* Halifax: Fernwood, 2005.

McCormack, A. Ross. *Reformers, Rebels, and Revolutionaries: The Western Canadian
Radical Movement, 1899–1919.* Toronto: University of Toronto Press, 1977.

McKenna, Peter. *Terminal Damage: The Politics of VLTs in Atlantic Canada.*
Halifax: Fernwood Publishing, 2008.

Meggs, Geoff, and Rod Mickleburgh. *The Art of the Impossible: Dave Barrett and
the NDP in Power 1972–1975.* Vancouver: Harbour Publishing, 2012.

Mellon, Hugh P. "Political Communications and Government Reform: New
Brunswick under Richard Hatfield." PhD diss., Queen's University, 1990.

Milne, William J. *The McKenna Miracle: Myth or Reality?* Toronto: Centre for
Public Management, University of Toronto, 1996.

Mitchell, David J. *W.A.C. Bennett and the Rise of British Columbia.* Vancouver:
Douglas and McIntyre, 1983.

Moody, Kim. *Workers in a Lean World.* London: Verso, 1997.

Norcliffe, Glen. *Global Game, Local Arena: Restructuring in Corner Brook,
Newfoundland.* St John's: Institute of Social and Economic Research, 2005.

Ommer, Rosemary E. *Coasts under Stress: Restructuring and Social-Ecological
Health.* Montreal and Kingston: McGill-Queen's University Press, 2007.

Palmer, Bryan D. *Solidarity: The Rise and Fall of an Opposition in British
Columbia.* Vancouver: New Star, 1987.

Panitch, Leo, and Donald Swartz. *From Consent to Coercion: The Assault on Trade
Union Freedoms.* Toronto: Garamond, 2003.

Parizeau, Jacques. *An Independent Québec.* Montreal: Baraka Books, 2010.

Pasolli, Lisa. "Bureaucratizing the Atlantic Revolution: The Saskatchewan Mafia
and the Modernization of the New Brunswick Civil Service, 1960–1970." MA
thesis, University of New Brunswick, 2007.

Peck, Jamie. *Constructions of Neoliberal Reason.* Oxford: Oxford University Press, 2010.

Persky, Stan. *Bennett II: The Decline and Stumbling of Social Credit Government in
British Columbia.* Vancouver: New Star, 1983.

– *Fantasy Government: Bill Vander Zalm and the Future of Social Credit.*
Vancouver: New Star, 1989.

– *Son of Socred: Has Bill Bennett's Government Gotten BC Moving Again?*
Vancouver: New Star, 1979.

Piotte, Jean-Marc. *Du Combat au Partenariat*. Montreal: Nota Bene, 1998.

Pitsula, James M., and Ken Rasmussen. *Privatizing a Province: The New Right in Saskatchewan*. Vancouver: New Star, 1990.

Plecas, Bob. *Bill Bennett: A Mandarin's View*. Douglas and McIntyre, 2005.

Poitras, Jacques. *The Right Fight: Bernard Lord and the Conservative Dilemma*. Fredericton: Goose Lane Editions, 2004.

Richards, John, and Larry Pratt. *Prairie Capitalism: Power and Influence in the New West*. Toronto: McClelland and Stewart, 1979.

Robin, Martin, ed. *Canada's Provincial Politics*. Toronto: Prentice-Hall, 1978.

– *Pillars of Profit: The Company Province, 1934–1972*. Toronto: McClelland and Stewart, 1973.

– *The Rush for Spoils: The Company Province, 1871–1933*. Toronto: McClelland and Stewart, 1972.

Ross, Stephanie, and Larry Savage, eds. *Rethinking the Politics of Labour in Canada*. Halifax: Fernwood, 2012.

Rouillard, Christian, Éric Montpetit, Isabelle Fortier, and Alain-G. Gagnon. *Reengineering the State: Toward an Impoverishment of Quebec Governance*. Ottawa: University of Ottawa Press, 2006.

Sandberg, L. Anders, and Peter Clancy. *Against the Grain: Foresters and Politics in Nova Scotia*. Vancouver: UBC Press, 2000.

Saunders, S.A. *The Economic History of the Maritime Provinces*. Fredericton: Acadiensis, 1984.

Savoie, Donald J. *Governing from the Centre: The Concentration of Power in Canadian Politics*. Toronto: University of Toronto Press, 1999.

– *La lutte pour le développement: Le cas du Nord-Est Québec*. Quebec City: Les Presses de l'Université du Québec, 1988.

– *Pulling against Gravity: Economic Development in New Brunswick during the McKenna Years*. Montreal: Institute for Research in Public Policy, 2001.

– *Visiting Grandchildren: Economic Development in the Maritimes*. Toronto: University of Toronto Press, 2006.

Silver, Jim. *The Inner Cities of Saskatoon and Winnipeg: A New and Distinctive Form of Development*. Winnipeg: CCPA-Manitoba/Saskatchewan, 2008.

– *In Their Own Voices: Building Urban Aboriginal Communities*. Halifax: Fernwood, 2006.

– ed. *Solutions That Work: Fighting Poverty in Winnipeg*. Halifax: Fernwood, 2000.

Silver, Jim, Cyril Keeper, and Michael McKenzie. *Electoral Participation in Winnipeg's Inner City*. Winnipeg: CCPA-Manitoba, 2005.

Skocpol, Theda, and Morris Fiorina, eds. *Civic Engagement in American Democracy*. Washington, DC: Brookings Institution Press, 1999.

Speirs, Rosemary. *Out of the Blue: The Fall of the Tory Dynasty in Ontario.* Toronto: Macmillian, 1986.

Stevenson, Garth. *Unfulfilled Union: Canadian Federalism and National Unity.* Montreal and Kingston: McGill-Queen's University Press, 2009.

Stewart, Ian. *Roasting Chestnuts: The Mythology of Maritime Political Culture.* Vancouver: UBC Press, 1994.

Strategic Partnership Study Group. *Strategic Partnership: How Business, Labour and Government Collaborate to Produce Europe's High Performance Economies.* St John's, 2002.

Taft, Kevin. *Democracy Derailed: A Breakdown of Government Accountability in Alberta – And How to Get It Back.* Calgary: Red Deer, 2007.

– *Shredding the Public Interest: Ralph Klein and 25 Years of One-Party Government.* Edmonton: University of Alberta Press, 1997.

Teeple, Gary. *Globalization and the Decline of Social Reform.* Toronto: Garamond, 2000.

Thomas, Mark. *Regulating Flexibility: The Political Economy of Employment Standards.* Montreal and Kingston: McGill-Queen's University Press, 2009.

Thomas, Paul, and Curtis Brown, eds., *Manitoba Politics and Government: Issues, Institutions, Traditions.* Winnipeg: University of Manitoba Press, 2010.

Tobin, Brian, and John L. Reynolds. *All in Good Time.* Toronto: Penguin Canada, 2002.

Tomblin, Stephen. *Ottawa and the Outer Provinces: The Challenge of Regional Integration in Canada.* Toronto: Lorimer, 1995.

Vivone, Rich. *Ralph Could Have Been a Superstar: Tales of the Klein Era.* Kingston: Patricia Publishing, 2009.

Walkom, Thomas. *Rae Days: The Rise and Follies of the NDP.* Toronto: Key Porter Books, 1994.

Warnock, John W. *Saskatchewan: The Roots of Discontent and Protest.* Montreal: Black Rose, 2004.

– *The Structural Adjustment of Capitalism in Saskatchewan.* Ottawa: CCPA, 2003.

Warren, Jim, and Kathleen Carlisle. *On the Side of the People: A History of Labour in Saskatchewan.* Regina: Coteau, 2005.

Weale, David. *Whatever You Say: The Talk of Islanders, 1975–2005.* Charlottetown: Tangle Lane, 2005.

Wesley, Jared. *Code Politics: Campaigns and Cultures on the Canadian Prairies.* Vancouver: UBC Press, 2011.

White, Randall. *Ontario since 1985.* Toronto: Eastend Books, 1998.

Whitfield, Dexter. *New Labour's Attack on Public Services.* Nottingham: Spokesman, 2006.

Wilson, H.T. *Capitalism after Postmodernism: Neo-Conservatism, Legitimacy and the Theory of Public Capital.* Leiden: Brill Academic Publishers, 2002.

Workman, Thom. *Banking on Deception: The Discourse of Fiscal Crisis*. Winnipeg: Fernwood Publishing, 1996.

– *If You're in My Way, I'm Walking: The Assault on Working People since 1970*. Halifax: Fernwood, 2009.

– *Social Torment: Globalization in Atlantic Canada*. Halifax: Fernwood, 2003.

Articles and Book Chapters

Acheson, T.W. "The National Policy and the Industrialization of the Maritimes, 1880–1910." *Acadiensis* 1 (1971): 3–28.

Adams, Chris. "Realigning Elections in Manitoba." In *Manitoba Politics and Government: Issues, Institutions, Traditions*, edited by P. Thomas and C. Brown, 159–80. Winnipeg: University of Manitoba Press, 2010.

Agar, Adamson, and Ian Stewart. "Changing Party Politics in Atlantic Canada." In *Party Politics in Canada*, edited by Hugh G. Thorburn, 302–20. Scarborough, ON: Prentice Hall Canada, 2001.

Albo, Greg. "Competitive Austerity and the Impasse of Capitalist Employment Policy." In *Between Globalism and Nationalism: The Socialist Register 1994*, edited by R. Miliband and L. Panitch, 144–70. London: Merlin, 1994.

– "Neoliberalism, the State, and the Left: A Canadian Perspective." *Monthly Review* 54 (2002): 46–55.

– "The 'New Economy' and Capitalism Today." In *Interrogating the New Economy: Restructuring Work in the 21st Century*, edited by Norene J. Pupo and Mark P. Thomas, 3–20. Toronto: University of Toronto Press, 2010.

Alcantara, Chris. "Explaining Aboriginal Treaty Negotiation Outcomes in Canada: The Cases of the Inuit and the Innu in Labrador." *Canadian Journal of Political Science* 40 (2007): 185–207.

– "To Treaty or Not to Treaty? Aboriginal Peoples and Comprehensive Claims in Canada." *Publius* 38 (2007): 343–69.

Alexander, David. "Economic Growth in the Atlantic Region, 1880–1940." *Acadiensis* 8 (1978): 47–76.

Alper, Donald. "The Effects of Coalition Government on Party Structure: The Case of the Conservative Party in BC." *BC Studies* 33 (1977): 40–9.

Barber, Paul. "Manitoba's Liberals: Sliding into Third." In *Manitoba Politics and Government: Issues, Institutions, Traditions*, edited by P. Thomas and C. Brown, 128–58. Winnipeg: University of Manitoba Press, 2010.

Beers, David. "The Big Swerve." In *Liberalized*, edited by David Beers, 3–16. Vancouver: New Star, 2005.

Belkhodja, Chedly. "La dimension populiste de l'émergence et du succès électoral du Parti Confederation of Regions au Nouveau-Brunswick." *Canadian Journal of Political Science* 32 (1999): 293–315.

Belshaw, John Douglas. "Provincial Politics, 1871–1916." In *The Pacific Province: A History of British Columbia*, edited by Hugh M. Johnston, 134–64. Vancouver: Douglas and McIntyre, 1996.

Bercuson, David J. "Labour Radicalism and the Western Industrial Frontier, 1897–1919." *Canadian Historical Review* 58 (1977): 154–77.

Bernstein, Steven, and Benjamin Cashore. "Globalization, Four Paths of Internationalization and Domestic Policy Change: The Case of Eco-Forestry in British Columbia." *Canadian Journal of Political Science* 32 (2000): 67–99.

Black, Erroll, and Paula Mallea. "The Privatization of the Manitoba Telephone System." *Canadian Dimension* 31 (March 1997): 11–13.

Blake, Donald. "Electoral Democracy in the Provinces." *Choices* 7 (2001): 1–37.

– "The Politics of Polarization: Parties and Elections in British Columbia." In *Politics, Policy, and Government in British Columbia*, edited by R.K. Carty, 67–84. Vancouver: UBC Press, 1996.

– "Value Conflicts in Lotusland: British Columbia Political Culture." In *Politics, Policy and Government in British Columbia*, edited by R.K. Carty, 3–17. Vancouver: UBC Press, 1996.

Blake, Raymond B. "The Saskatchewan Party and the Politics of Branding." In *Saskatchewan Politics: Crowding the Centre*, edited by Howard Leeson, 165–88. Regina: Canadian Plains Research Center, 2008.

Borden, Chris. "Electricity in New Brunswick and Options for Its Future: Summary of the New Brunswick Government's Task Force Findings." *Utilities Law Review* 10 (1990): 30–1.

Bouchard, Pier, and Sylvain Vézina. "Modernizing New Brunswick's Public Administration: The Robichaud Model." In *The Robichaud Era, 1960–70: Colloquium Proceedings*, 54–66. Moncton: Canadian Institute for Research on Regional Development, 2001.

Bowler, Shaun, and David J. Lanoue. "Strategic and Protest Voting for Third Parties: The Case of the Canadian NDP." *Political Research Quarterly* 45 (1992): 485–99.

Bradford, Neil. "Renewing Social Democracy: Beyond the Third Way." *Studies in Political Economy* 67 (2002): 145–61.

Bradford, Neil, and Glen Williams. "What Went Wrong? Explaining Canadian Industrialization." In *The New Canadian Political Economy*, edited by W. Clement and G. Williams, 54–76. Montreal and Kingston: McGill-Queen's University Press, 1989.

Brown, Paul Leduc. "Déjà Vu: Thatcherism in Ontario." In *Open for Business, Closed to People: Mike Harris's Ontario,* edited by D.S. Ralph, A. Régimbald, and N. St-Amand, 37–44. Halifax: Fernwood, 1997.

Brownsey, Keith. "The Post-Institutionalized Cabinet: The Administrative Style of Alberta." In *Executive Styles in Canada: Cabinet Structures and Leadership Practices in Canadian Government,* edited by Luc Bernier, Keith Brownsey, and Michael Howlett, 208–24. Toronto: University of Toronto Press, 2005.

Brownsey, Keith, and Michael Howlett. "Class Structure and Political Alliances in an Industrialized Society." In *The Provincial State: Politics in Canada's Provinces and Territories,* edited by K. Brownsey and M. Howlett, 147–74. Mississauga, ON: Copp Clark Pitman, 1992.

Cadigan, Sean T. "Boom, Bust and Bluster: Newfoundland and Labrador's 'Oil Boom' and Its Impacts on Labour." In *Boom, Bust, and Crisis: Work and Labour in 21st Century Canada,* edited by John Peters, 68–83. Halifax: Fernwood Publishing, 2011.

– "The Moral Economy of Retrenchment and Regeneration in the History of Rural Newfoundland." In *Retrenchment and Regeneration in Rural Newfoundland,* edited by Reginald Byron, 14–42. Toronto: University of Toronto Press, 2002.

– "Organizing Offshore: Labour Relations, Industrial Pluralism and Order in the Newfoundland and Labrador Oil Industry, 1997–2006." In *Work on Trial: Cases in Context,* edited by Judy Fudge and Eric Tucker, 143–72. Toronto: Osgoode Society and Irwin, 2010.

Cameron, David, and Richard Simeon. "Ontario in Confederation: The Not-So-Friendly Giant." In *The Government and Politics of Ontario,* edited by Graham White, 158–88. Toronto: University of Toronto Press, 1997.

Cameron, Kirk, "There Is a Northern Crown." *Policy Options* (March 2000): 57–8.

Camfield, David. "Renewal in Canadian Public Sector Unions: Neoliberalism and Union Praxis." *Relations Industrielles* 62 (2007): 282–304.

Carroll, William K. "The NDP Regime in British Columbia, 1991–2001: A Post-Mortem." *Canadian Review of Sociology and Anthropology* 42 (2005): 167–96.

Carroll, W.K., and R.S. Ratner. "Ambivalent Allies: Social Democratic Regimes and Social Movements." *BC Studies* 154 (2007): 41–66.

– "The NDP Regime in British Columbia, 1991–2001: A Post-Mortem." *Canadian Review of Sociology and Anthropology* 42 (2005): 167–96.

– "Social Democracy, Neo-Conservatism and Hegemonic Crisis in British Columbia." *Critical Sociology* 16 (1989): 29–53.

Carty, R. Kenneth, and Munroe Eagles. "Party Activity across Electoral Cycles: The New Brunswick Party System, 1979–1994." *Canadian Journal of Political Science* 36 (2003): 381–99.

Cerny, Philip G., George Menz, and Susanne Soederberg. "Different Roads to Globalization: Neoliberalism, the Competition State, and Politics in a More Open World." In *Internalizing Globalization: The Rise of Neoliberalism and the Decline of National Varieties of Capitalism*, edited by Philip G. Cerny, George Menz, and Susanne Soederberg, 1–32. Houndmills, UK: Palgrave Macmillan, 2005.

Chalmers, Ron. "Insults to Democracy during the Lougheed Era." In *Socialism and Democracy in Alberta: Essays in Honour of Grant Notley*, edited by Larry Pratt, 172–85. Edmonton: NeWest, 1986.

Chung, Huhnsik, and Gregory Hoffnagle. "The Risks of Hydrofracking." *Risk Management* 58 (2011): 32–4.

Clancy, Peter. "Concerted Action on the Periphery? Voluntary Economic Planning in 'The New Nova Scotia.'" *Acadiensis* 26 (Spring 1997): 3–30.

– "Politics by Remote Control: Historical Perspectives on Devolution in Canada's North." In *Devolution and Constitutional Development in the Canadian North*, edited by Gurston Dacks, 13–42. Ottawa: Carleton University Press, 1990.

Clement, Wallace. "Introduction: Whither the New Canadian Political Economy?" In *Understanding Canada: Building on the New Canadian Political Economy*, edited by Wallace Clement, 3–18. Montreal and Kingston: McGill-Queen's University Press 1997.

Coates, David. "Labour Governments: Old Constraints and New Parameters." *New Left Review* 219 (1996): 62–78.

Coates, Ken. "Yukon and Northwest Territories: The Emerging North of Native and Non-Native Societies." In *The Challenge of Northern Regions*, edited by Peter Jull and S. Roberts, 147–82. Darwin: Australian National University of Northern Australia, 1991.

Cohen, Marcy. "The Privatization of Health Care Cleaning Services in BC." *Antipode* 38 (June 2006): 626–44.

Collins, Lyndhurst. "Environmental Performance and Technological Innovation: The Pulp and Paper Industry as a Case in Point." *Technology in Society* 16 (1994): 427–46.

Confédération des Syndicats Nationaux. *Prendre les devants dans l'organisation du travail* (Montreal: CSN, 1991).

Conrad, Margaret. "The 1950s: The Decade of Development." In *The Atlantic Provinces in Confederation*, edited by E.R. Forbes and D.A. Muise, 382–420. Toronto: University of Toronto Press, 1993.

Conway, J.F. "Agrarian Petit-Bourgeois Responses to Capitalist Industrialization: The Case of Canada." In *The Petite Bourgeoisie: Comparative Studies of the Uneasy Stratum*, edited by Frank Bechhofer and Brian Elliot, 1–37. London: Macmillan, 1981.

– "The Devine Regime in Saskatchewan, 1982–1991: The Tory Caucus Fraud Scandal and Other Abuses of Power." In *(Ab)Using Power: The Canadian*

Experience, edited by Dorothy E. Chunn, Susan C. Boyd, and Robert Menzies, 95–109. Halifax: Fernwood, 2001.

– "From 'Agrarian Socialism' to 'Natural' Governing Party." In *The Prairie Agrarian Movement Revisited,* edited by K. Murray Knuttila and Robert Sterling, 228–9. Regina: University of Regina Press, 2007.

– "Labour and the CCF/NDP in Saskatchewan." *Prairie Forum* 31 (Fall 2006): 389–426.

– "Populism in the United States, Russia and Canada: Explaining the Roots of Canada's Third Parties." *Canadian Journal of Political Science* 11 (March 1978): 99–124.

– "The Prairie Populist Resistance to the National Policy: Some Reconsiderations." *Journal of Canadian Studies* 14 (Fall 1979): 77–91.

– "Wall Declares War on Organized Labour in Saskatchewan." *Bullet,* Socialist Project, e-bulletin no. 239, 13 July 2009. http://www.socialistproject.ca/bullet/239.php.

Cross, William. "Leadership Selection in New Brunswick: Balancing Language Representation and Populist Impulses." In *Political Parties, Representation, and Electoral Democracy in Canada,* edited by William Cross, 37–54. Don Mills, ON: Oxford, 2002.

Dacks, Gurston. "From Consensus to Competition: Social Democracy and Political Culture in Alberta." In *Socialism and Democracy in Alberta,* edited by Larry Pratt, 186–204. Edmonton: NeWest, 1986.

– "Implementing First Nations Self-Government in the Yukon: Lessons for Canada." *Canadian Journal of Political Science* 37 (2004): 671–94.

Davidson, Alan. "Sweet Nothings: The BC Conversation on Health." *Health Policy* 3 (May 2008): 33–40.

Desserud, Don. "The 2006 Provincial Election in New Brunswick." *Canadian Political Science Review* 2 (2008): 51–63.

Dobrowolsky, Alexandra. "Rhetoric versus Reality: The Figure of the Child and New Labour's Strategic Social Investment State." *Studies in Political Economy* 69 (2002): 43–73.

Drummond, Robert. "Ontario 1980." In *The Canadian Annual Review of Politics and Public Affairs,* edited by R.B. Byers, 172–80. Toronto: University of Toronto Press, 1983.

Dufour, Pascal. "L'adoption du projet de loi 112 au Québec: Le produit d'une mobilisation ou une simple question de conjoncture politique." *Politique et sociétés* 23 (2004): 159–82.

Eagles, D. Munroe. "The 1988 Nova Scotian Election." *Canadian Political Views and Life* 1 (October 1988): 1–4.

Erickson, Lynda. "Electoral Behaviour in British Columbia." In *British Columbia Politics and Government,* edited by Michael Howlett, Dennis

Pilon, and Tracy Summerville, 131–50. Toronto: Emond Montgomery Publications, 2010.

Evans, Bryan. "Capacity, Complexity and Leadership: Secretaries to Cabinet and Ontario's Project of Modernization at the Centre." In *Searching for Leadership: Secretaries to Cabinet in Canada*, edited by P. Dutil, 121–60. Toronto: University of Toronto Press, 2008.

Evans, Bryan, Janet Lum, and Duncan MacLellan. "From 'Gurus' to Chief Executives? The Contestable Transformation of Ontario's Deputy Ministers, 1971 to 2007." In *Deputy Ministers: Comparative and Jurisdictional Perspectives*, edited by Jacques Bourgault and Christopher Dunn, 148–200. Toronto: IPAC / University of Toronto Press, 2013.

Fédération des travailleurs et travailleuses du Québec. *Face aux changements, de nouvelles solidarités*. Montreal: FTQ, 1993.

Feehan, James P. "Natural Resource Devolution in the Territories: Current Status and Uresolved Issues." In *Northern Exposure: Peoples, Powers and Prospects in Canada's North*, edited by F. Abele, T. Courchene, L. Seidle, and F. St-Hilaire, 344–72. Montreal: Institute for Research on Public Policy, 2009.

Fodor, Matt, "The Dexter NDP: Old Wine, New Bottle?" *Bullet*, no. 294, 3 January 2010, http://www.socialistproject.ca/bullet/294.php.

Forbes, E.R. "Consolidating Disparity: The Maritimes and the Industrialization of Canada during the Second World War." In *Atlantic Canada after Confederation*, edited by P.A. Buckner and David Frank, 383–407. Fredericton: Acadiensis, 1988.

– "Misguided Symmetry: The Destruction of Regional Transportation Policy for the Maritimes." In *Canada and the Burden of Unity*, edited by David J. Bercuson, 60–86. Toronto: University of Toronto Press, 1977.

Fudge, Judy. "Substantive Equality, the Supreme Court of Canada, and the Limits to Redistribution." *South African Journal of Human Rights* 23 (2007): 235–52.

Gertler, Meric. "Grouping towards Reflexivity: Responding to Industrial Change in Ontario." In *The Rise of the Rustbelt*, edited by P. Cooke, 231–45. London: University College London Press, 1995.

Graefe, Peter. "The Québec *Patronat*: Proposing a Neoliberal Political Economy after All." *Canadian Review of Sociology and Anthropology* 41 (2004): 171–93.

– "The Social Economy and the American Model: Relating New Social Policy Directions to the Old." *Global Social Policy* 6 (2006): 197–219.

– "State Restructuring and the Failure of Competitive Nationalism: Trying Times for Québec Labour." In *Canada: The State of the Federation 2005*, edited by Michael Murphy, 153–76. Kingston: Institute of Intergovernmental Relations 2007.

– "Whither the Québec Model? Boom, Bust and Québec Labour." In *Boom, Bust and Crisis: Labour, Corporate Power and Politics in 21st Century Canada*, edited by John Peters, 125–41. Halifax: Fernwood 2012.

Haddow, Rodney. "How Malleable Are Political-Economic Institutions? The Case of Labour-Market Decision-Making in British Columbia." *Canadian Public Administration* 43 (December 2008): 387–411.

Hall, David, Emanuele Lobina, and Robin de la Motte. "Public Resistance to Privatisation in Water and Energy." *Development in Practice* 15 (2005): 286–301.

Harrison, Trevor W. "The Best Government Money Can Buy? Political Contributions in Alberta." In *The Return of the Trojan Horse: Alberta and the New World (Dis)Order*, edited by Trevor W. Harrison, 95–114. Montreal: Black Rose Books, 2005.

Hart, Susan M. "The Pay Equity Bargaining Process in Newfoundland: Understanding Cooperation and Conflict by Incorporating Gender and Class." *Gender, Work and Organization* 9 (2002): 355–71.

Hatfield, Robert. "Extreme Organising: A Case Study of Hibernia." *Just Labour* 2 (2003): 14–22.

Hayter, Roger. "The War in the Woods: Post-Fordist Restructuring, Globalization, and the Contested Remapping of British Columbia's Forest Economy." *Annals of the Association of American Geographers* 93 (2003): 706–29.

Hicks, Jack. "Toward More Effective Evidence-Based Suicide Prevention in Nunavut." In *Northern Exposure: Peoples, Powers and Prospects in Canada's North*, edited by Frances Abele, Thomas J. Courchene, and F. Leslie Seidle, 467–95. Montreal: Institute for Research on Public Policy, 2009.

Houle, François. "Economic Strategy and the Restructuring of the Fordist Wage-Labour Relationship in Canada." *Studies in Political Economy* 11 (1983): 127–47.

House, J.D. "Premier Peckford, Petroleum Policy, and Popular Politics in Newfoundland and Labrador." *Journal of Canadian Studies* 17, no. 2 (1982): 12–31.

Howlett, Michael, and Keith Brownsey. "British Columbia: Politics in a Post-Staples Political Economy." In *The Provincial State in Canada: Politics in the Provinces and Territories*, edited by Keith Brownsey and Michael Howlett, 309–34. Peterborough, ON: Broadview, 2001.

Hum, Derek, and Wayne Simpson. "Manitoba in the Middle: A Mutual Fund Balanced for Steady Income." In *Manitoba Politics and Government: Issues, Institutions, Traditions*, edited by Paul Thomas and Curtis Brown, 293–305. Winnipeg: University of Manitoba Press, 2010.

Hyslop-Margison, E.J., and A. Sears, "The Neoliberal Assault on Democratic Learning," *UCFV Research* 2, no. 1 (2008): 28–38.

Hyson, Stewart. "Governing from the Centre in New Brunswick." In *Executive Styles in Canada: Cabinet Decision-Making Structures and Practices at the Federal and Provincial Levels,* edited by Luc Bernier, Keith Brownsey, and Michael Howlett, 75–90. Toronto: University of Toronto Press, 2005.

– "The Horrible Example: New Brunswick's 58-to-0 Election Result Is a Clear Argument for the Advantages of Proportional Representation." *Policy Options* 9 (1988): 25–7.

– "Where's 'Her Majesty's Loyal Opposition' in the Loyalist Province?" *Canadian Parliamentary Review* 11, no. 2 (1988), 22–5.

Irlbacher-Fox, Stephanie. "Governance in Canada's Northwest Territories: Emerging Institutions and Governance Issues." Main paper for Plenary on Arctic Governance, in *Conference Proceedings: 3rd Northern Research Forum,* Yellowknife, September 2004.

– "Northern Governance and the Economy: Thinking about the Big Picture." *Northern Public Affairs,* 13 November 2012, http://www.northernpublicaffairs .ca/index/irlbacher-fox-northern-governance-and-the-economy-thinking -about-the-big-picture/.

Jackson, Andrew. "Rowing against the Tide: The Struggle to Raise Union Density in a Hostile Environment." In *Paths to Union Renewal: Canadian Experiences,* edited by P. Kumar and C. Schenk, 61–77. Peterborough, ON: Broadview, 2006.

Jenson, Jane. "'Different' but Not 'Exceptional': Canada's Permeable Fordism." *Canadian Review of Sociology and Anthropology* 26 (1989): 69–94.

– "Rolling Out or Backtracking on Québec's Child Care System? Ideology Matters." In *Public Policy for Women: The State, Income Security and Labour Market Issues,* edited by Marjorie Griffin Cohen and Jane Pulkingham, 50–70. Toronto: University of Toronto Press, 2009.

Jessop, Bob. "Hollowing Out the 'Nation-State' and Multi-Level Governance." In *A Handbook of Comparative Social Policy,* edited by Patricia Kennett, 11–26. Northampton: Edward Elgar Publishing, 2004.

Juteau, Danielle. "The Citizen Makes an Entrée: Redefining the National Community in Québec." *Citizenship Studies* 6 (2007): 441–58.

Karabegovic, Amela, Charles Lammam, and Milagros Palacious. "Fiscal Performance of Canada's Premiers." *Fraser Forum* 4 (January/February 2011): 10–13.

Karabegovic, Amelam, Charles Lammam, Milagros Palacious, Niels Velduls. "Measuring the Fiscal Performance of Canada's Premiers." *Fraser Forum* 10 (January/February 2011), http://www.fraserinstitute.org/research -news/display.aspx?id=2147483714.

Kenny, James L. "A New Dependency: State, Local Capital, and the Development of New Brunswick's Base Metal Industry, 1960." *Canadian Historical Review* 78 (1997): 1–39.

Kenny, James L., and Andrew Secord. "Public Power for Industry: A Re-Examination of the New Brunswick Case, 1940–1960." *Acadiensis* 30 (2001): 84–108.

Kirk Laux, Jeanne. "How Private Is Privatization?" *Canadian Public Policy* 19 (1983): 398–411.

Kristianson, G.L. "The Non-partisan Approach to B.C. Politics: The Search for a Unity Party – 1972–1975." *BC Studies* 33 (Spring 1997): 13–29.

Laforest, Rachel. "The Politics of State / Civil Society Relations in Québec." In *Canada: The State of the Federation 2005*, edited by Michael Murphy, 177–98. Kingston: Institute for Intergovernmental Relations, 2007.

Langille, Brian. "Canadian Labour Law Reform and Free Trade." *Ottawa Law Review* 22 (1991): 581–622.

Langille, David. "The Business Council on National Issues and the Canadian State." *Studies in Political Economy* 24 (1987): 41–85.

Larner, Wendy. "Neoliberalism: Policy, Ideology, Governmentality." *Studies in Political Economy* 63 (2000): 5–25.

Leeson, Howard. "The Rich Soil of Saskatchewan Politics." In *Saskatchewan Politics: Into the Twenty-First Century*, edited by H. Leeson, 3–13. Regina: University of Regina Publications, 2001.

– "The 2007 Election: Watershed or Way Station?" In *Saskatchewan Politics: Crowding the Centre*, edited by H. Leeson, 119–40. Regina: Canadian Plains Research Center, 2008.

Loree, D.J., and D.R. Pullman. "Sociopolitical Facets of a Plural Province: Reasons for the Failure of 'Third Parties' in New Brunswick, Canada." *Plural Societies* 10 (1979): 85–102.

MacArthur, Doug. "The Changing Architecture of Governance in the Yukon and the Northwest Territories." In *Northern Exposure: Peoples, Powers and Prospects in Canada's North*, edited by Frances Abele, Thomas Courchene, Leslie Seidle, and France St-Hilaire, 187–232. Montreal: Institute for Research on Public Policy, 2009.

MacDermid, Robert, and Greg Albo. "Divided Province, Growing Protests: Ontario Moves Right." In *The Provincial State in Canada: Politics in the Provinces and Territories*, edited by Keith Brownsey and Michael Howlett, 163–202. Toronto: Broadview, 2001.

Mansell, Robert L., and Ron C. Schlenker. "Energy and the Alberta Economy: Past and Future Impacts and Implications." Paper No. 1 of the Alberta Energy Future Project of the Institute for Sustainable Energy, Environment and Economy, 2006.

Manuel, John. "EPA Tackles Fracking." *Environmental Health Perspectives* 118, no. 5 (2010): A199.

Marland, Alex. "Masters of Our Own Destiny: The Nationalist Evolution of Newfoundland Premier Danny Williams." *International Journal of Canadian Studies* 42 (2010): 155–81.

– "The 2007 Provincial Election in Newfoundland and Labrador." *Canadian Political Science Review* 1 (2007): 75–85.

Martin, Geoffrey R. "We've Seen It All Before: The Rise and Fall of the Confederation of Regions Party of New Brunswick, 1988–1995." *Journal of Canadian Studies* 33 (1998): 22–38.

Martinello, F. "Correlates of Certification Application Success in British Columbia, Saskatchewan, and Manitoba." *Relations Industrielles / Industrial Relations* 51 (1996): 544–62.

McBride, Stephen. "Domestic Neoliberalism." In *Working in a Global Era,* edited by Vivian Shalla, 257–77. Toronto: Canadian Scholars', 2006.

– "Quiet Constitutionalism: The International Political Economy of Domestic Institutional Change." *Canadian Journal of Political Science* 36 (2003): 251–73.

McGrane, David. "The 2007 Provincial Election in Saskatchewan." *Canadian Political Science Review* 2 (March/April 2008): 64–71.

– "Which Third Way? A Comparison of the Romanow and Calvert NDP Governments from 1991 to 2007." In *Saskatchewan Politics: Crowding the Centre,* edited by Howard Leeson, 143–64. Regina: Canadian Plains Research Center, 2008.

McLaughlin, Mark. "Power Tools as Tools of Power: Mechanization in the Tree Harvest of the Newfoundland Pulp and Paper Industry." *Newfoundland Studies* 2, no. 21 (2006): 235–54.

McMahon, Fred, and Miguel Cervantes. *Fraser Institute Annual: Survey of Mining Companies 2010/2011.* Fraser Institute, 2011. http://www.fraserinstitute.org/uploadedFiles/fraser-ca/Content/research-news/research/publications/mining-survey-2010-2011.pdf.

McMartin, Will. "Fiscal Fictions." In *Liberalized,* edited by David Beers, 119–71. Vancouver: New Star Books, 2005.

Milne, David A. "Prince Edward Island: Politics in a Beleaguered Garden." In *The Provincial State in Canada,* edited by Keith Brownsey and Michael Howlett, 111–38. Peterborough: Broadview, 2001.

Minow, Martha. "Public and Private Partnerships: Accounting for the New Religion." *Harvard Law Review* 116 (2003): 2–42.

Morissette, René, Grant Schellenberg, and Anick Johnson. "Diverging Trends in Unionization." *Perspectives on Labour and Income* 6 (April 2005): 5–12.

Muise, Del. "'The Great Transformation': Changing the Urban Face of Nova Scotia, 1871–1921." *Nova Scotia Historical Review* 11 (December 1991): 1–29.

NB Power. *Serving You ... Today and Tomorrow, 2009/10, Sustainability Report.* www.nbpower.com/html/en/about/publications/annual/2009-10AR -ENG.pdf.

Nesbitt, Doug, and Andrew Stevens. "Waiting for a Walkout: The End of McGuinty?" *Bullet*, 8 October 2012. http://www.socialistproject.ca/ bullet/709.php.

Noël, Alain. "Québec's New Politics of Redistribution." In *The Fading of Redistributive Politics*, edited by Keith Banting and John Myles, 256–84. Vancouver: UBC Press, 2014.

Noel, Sid. "Ontario's Tory Revolution." In *Revolution at Queen's Park*, edited by Sid Noel, 1–17. Toronto: Lorimer, 1997.

O'Byrne, Nicole, and Gregory Ericson. "Is There a Future for the NDP in New Brunswick?" *Inroads: The Canadian Journal of Opinion* 28 (2011): 20–3.

Pal, Leslie. "The Political Executive and Political Leadership in Alberta." In *Socialism and Democracy in Alberta*, edited by Larry Pratt, 1–30. Edmonton: NeWest, 1986.

Panitch, Leo. "Neoliberalism, Labour, and the Canadian State." In *Working in a Global Era: Canadian Perspectives*, edited by Vivian Shalla, 347–78. Toronto: Canadian Scholars', 2006.

Parks, A.C. "The Atlantic Provinces of Canada." *Journal of Industrial Economics* 13 (1965): 76–87.

Peck, Jamie, and Adam Tickell. "Neoliberalizing Space." *Antipode* 34 (2002): 380–404.

Penikett, Tony. "Destiny or Dream Sharing Resources, Revenues and Political Power in Nunavut Devolution." In *Polar Law Textbook II*, edited by N. Loukacheva, 199–214. Copenhagen: Nordic Council of Ministers, 2013.

Pentland, H. Clare. "The Western Canadian Labour Movement, 1897–1919." *Canadian Journal of Political and Social Theory* 3 (1979): 53–78.

Phillips, Stephen. "Party Politics in British Columbia: The Persistence of Polarization." In *British Columbia Politics and Government*, edited by Michael Howlett, Dennis Pilon, and Tracy Summerville, 109–30. Toronto: Emond Montgomery, 2009.

Pierson, Paul, and Theda Skocpol. "American Politics in the Long Run." In *The Transformation of American Politics: Activist Government and the Rise of Conservatism*, edited by P. Pierson and T. Skocpol, 3–16. Princeton: Princeton University Press, 2007.

Pilon, Dennis. "Assessing Gordon Campbell's Uneven Democratic Legacy in British Columbia." In *The Campbell Revolution: Power and Politics in British Columbia from 2001 to 2011*, edited by Tracy Summerville and Jason Lacharite. Vancouver: UBC Press, forthcoming.

- "Democracy, BC Style." In *British Columbia Politics and Government*, edited by Michael Howlett, Dennis Pilon, and Tracy Summerville, 87–108. Toronto: Emond Montgomery, 2010.
- "The Long Lingering Death of Social Democracy." *Labour / Le Travail* 70 (Fall 2012): 245–60.

Pilon, Dennis, Stephanie Ross, and Larry Savage. "Solidarity Revisited: Organized Labour and the New Democratic Party." *Canadian Political Science Review* 5 (January 2011): 20–37.

Pratt, Larry. "The State and Province-Building: Alberta's Development Strategy." In *The Canadian State: Political Economy and Political Power*, edited by Leo Panitch, 133–64. Toronto: University of Toronto Press, 1977.

Praud, Jocelyn, and Sarah McQuarrie. "The Saskatchewan CCF-NDP from the Regina Manifesto to the Romanow Years." In *Saskatchewan Politics: Into the Twenty-First Century*, edited by Howard Leeson, 143–68. Regina: Canadian Plains Research Center Press, 2001.

Prince, Michael. "At the Edge of Canada's Welfare State: Social Policy-making in British Columbia." In *Politics, Policy and Government in British Columbia*, edited by R.K. Carty, 236–271. Vancouver: UBC Press, 1996.

Prudham, Scott. "Sustaining Sustained Yield: Class, Politics, and Post-war Forest Regulation in British Columbia." *Society and Space* 25 (2007): 258–83.

Rasmussen, Derek. "Forty Years of Struggle and Still No Inuit Right to Education in Nunavut." *Our Schools / Ourselves* 19 (Fall 2009): 67–86.

Rasmussen, Ken. 2001. "Saskatchewan: From Entrepreneurial State to Embedded State." In *The Provincial State in Canada: Politics in the Provinces and Territories*, edited by Keith Brownsey and Michael Howlett, 241–76. Peterborough, ON: Broadview, 2001.

Rasmussen, Merrilee, and Howard Leeson, "Parliamentary Democracy in Saskatchewan, 1982–1989." In *Devine Rule in Saskatchewan*, edited by Leslley Bigg and Mark Stobbe, 49–66. Saskatoon: Fifth House, 1991.

Reitsma-Street, Marge, and Bruce Wallace. "Resisting Two-Year Limits on Welfare in British Columbia." *Canadian Review of Social Policy* 53 (Spring/Summer 2004): 170–7.

Resnick, Phillip. "Neo-Conservatism on the Periphery: The Lessons from B.C." *BC Studies* 75 (1987): 3–23.
- "Social Democracy in Power: The Case of British Columbia." *BC Studies* 34 (Summer 1977): 3–20.

Richmond, Ted, and John Shields. "Reflections on Resistance to Neoliberalism: Looking Back on Solidarity in 1983 British Columbia." *Socialist Studies* 7, nos. 1–2 (Spring/Fall 2011): 216–37.

Riddell, Chris. "Union Certification Success under Voting versus Card-Check Procedures: Evidence from British Columbia, 1978–1998." *Industrial and Labor Relations Review* 57 (2004): 493–517.

Robin, Martin. "British Columbia: The Politics of Class Conflict." In *Canadian Provincial Politics,* edited by Martin Robin, 27–68. Scarborough, ON: Prentice-Hall Canada, 1972.

Robinson, Ian. "Neoliberal Trade Policy and Canadian Federalism Revisited." In *New Trends in Canadian Federalism,* edited by François Rocher and Miriam Smith, 197–242. Peterborough, ON: Broadview, 2003.

Ross, George, and Jane Jenson. "Post-War Class Struggle and the Crisis of Left Politics." In *Socialist Register, Social Democracy and After,* edited by R. Miliband, J. Saville, M. Liebman, and L. Panitch, 23–49. London: Merlin, 1986.

Rossiter, David, and Patricia K. Wood. "Fantastic Topographies: Neoliberal Responses to Aboriginal Land Claims in British Columbia." *Canadian Geographer* 49 (2005): 352–66.

Ruff, Norman. "The Cat and Mouse Politics of Redistribution: Fair and Effective Representation in British Columbia." *BC Studies* 87 (Autumn 1990): 48–84.

– "Executive Dominance: Cabinet and the Office of Premier in British Columbia." In *British Columbia Politics and Government,* edited by Michael Howlett, Dennis Pilon, and Tracy Summerville, 205–16. Toronto: Emond Montgomery, 2010.

Salée, Daniel. "The Québec State and the Management of Ethnocultural Diversity." In *Belonging? Diversity, Recognition and Shared Citizenship in Canada,* edited by Keith Banting, Thomas Courchene, and F. Leslie Seidle, 105–42. Montreal: IRPP, 2007.

– "Transformative Politics, the State, and the Politics of Social Change in Québec." In *Changing Canada: Political Economy as Transformation,* edited by Wallace Clement and Leah Vosko, 25–50. Montreal and Kingston: McGill-Queen's University Press, 2003.

Sampert, Shannon. "King Ralph, the Ministry of Truth, and the Media in Alberta," In *The Return of the Trojan Horse: Alberta and the New World (Dis)Order,* edited by Trevor W. Harrison, 37–51. Montreal: Black Rose Books, 2005.

Savoie, Donald J. "Governing a 'Have-Less' Province: Unravelling the New Brunswick Budget Process in the Hatfield Era." In *Budgeting in the Provinces: Leadership and the Provinces,* edited by Allan M. Maslove, 31–54. Toronto: Institute of Public Administration of Canada, 1989.

– "New Brunswick: Let's Not Waste a Crisis." *Journal of New Brunswick Studies* 1 (2010): 54–63.

– "Rural Redevelopment in Canada: The Case of Northeast New Brunswick." *Journal of Rural Studies* 5 (1989): 185–97.

Schrier, Dan. "Mind the Gap: Income Inequality Growing." *British Columbia Statistics Business Indicators* 12 (January 2012): 1–4.

Shaffir, William, and Steven Kleinknect. "The Trauma of Political Defeat." *Canadian Parliamentary Review* (Autumn 2002): 16–21.

Sheldrick, Byron, "The British Labour Party: In Search of Identity between Labour and Parliament." In *Social Democracy after the Cold War*, edited by Bryan Evans and Ingo Schmidt, 149–82. Vancouver: UBC Press, 2012.

– "The Contradictions of Welfare to Work: Social Security Reform in Britain." *Studies in Political Economy* 62 (2000): 99–122.

– "New Labour and the Third Way: Democracy, Accountability and Social Democratic Politics." *Studies in Political Economy* 67 (2002): 133–43.

Sheldrick, Byron, Harold Dyck, Claudette Michell, and Troy Myers. "Welfare in Winnipeg's Inner City: Exploring the Myths." *Canadian Journal of Urban Research* 15 (2006): 54–85.

Sheldrick, Byron, and Kevin Warkentin. "The Manitoba Community Economic Development Lens: Local Participation and Democratic State Restructuring." In *Doing Community Economic Development*, edited by John Loxley, Jim Silver, and Kathleen Sexsmith, 209–19. Halifax: Fernwood Publishing, 2007.

Sigurdson, Richard. "The British Columbia New Democratic Party: Does It Make a Difference?" In *Politics, Policy and Government in British Columbia*, edited by Kenneth Carty, 310–38. Vancouver: UBC Press, 1997.

Silver, Jim. "Segregated City: A Century of Poverty in Winnipeg." In *Manitoba Politics and Government: Issues, Institutions, Traditions*, edited by Paul Thomas and Curtis Brown, 331–57. Winnipeg: University of Manitoba Press, 2010.

Sinclair, Peter R. "An Ill Wind Is Blowing Some Good: Dispute over Development of the Hebron Oilfield off Newfoundland," 2008, http://www.ucs.mun.ca/~oilpower/documents/illwind.pdf.

Sinclair, Peter R., Martha MacDonald, and Barbara Neis. "The Changing World of Andy Gibson: Restructuring Forestry on Newfoundland's Great Northern Peninsula." *Studies in Political Economy* 78 (2006): 177–99.

Slinn, Sara. "The Effect of Compulsory Certification Votes on Certification Applications in Ontario: An Empirical Analysis." *Canadian Labour and Employment Law Journal* 367, no. 10 (2003): 367–97.

Slowey, Gabrielle. "America, Canada and ANWR: Bilateral Relations and Indigenous Struggles." *Native Americas* 18 (2001): 26–32.

Smith, Charles W. "The 'New Normal' in Saskatchewan: Neoliberalism and the Challenge to Workers' Rights." In *New Directions in Saskatchewan Public Policy*, edited by David McGrane, 121–52. Regina: Canadian Plains Research Center, 2011.

Smith, Peter J. "Alberta: Experiments in Governance – From Social Credit to the Klein Revolution." In *The Provincial State in Canada: Politics in the Provinces and Territories*, edited by Keith·Brownsey and Michael Howlett, 277–308. Peterborough, ON: Broadview, 2001.

Smith, Patrick J., and Marshall W. Conley. "'Empty Harbours, Empty Dreams': The Democratic Socialist Tradition in Atlantic Canada." In *Building the Cooperative Commonwealth: Essays on the Democratic Socialist Tradition in Canada*, edited by J. William Brennan, 227–51. Regina: Canadian Plains Research Center, 1984.

Soron, Dennis. "The Politics of De-Politicization: Neoliberalism and Popular Consent in Alberta." In *The Return of the Trojan Horse: Alberta and the New World (Dis)Order*, edited by Trevor Harrison, 65–81. Montreal: Black Rose Books, 2005.

Speca, Anthony. "Nunavut, Greenland and the Politics of Resource Revenue." *Policy Options* (May 2012): 62–7.

Stanley, Della. "The 1960s: The Illusions and Realities of Progress." In *The Atlantic Provinces in Confederation*, edited by Ernest Forbes and D.A. Muise, 421–59. Fredericton: Acadiensis, 1993.

Steuter, Erin, and Geoff Martin. "The Irvings Cover Themselves: Media Representations of the Irving Oil Refinery Strike, 1994–1996." *Canadian Journal of Communication* 24 (1999): 1–18.

Stewart, David. "Klein's Makeover of the Alberta Conservatives." In *The Trojan Horse: Alberta and the Future of Canada*, edited by Trevor Harrison, 24–47. Montreal: Black Rose Books, 1995.

Stewart, David K., and R. Kenneth Carty. "Many Political Worlds? Provincial Parties and Party Systems." In *Provinces: Canadian Provincial Politics*, edited by Christopher Dunn, 97–113. Peterborough, ON: Broadview, 2006.

Stirling, Bob, and J.F. Conway. "Fractions among Prairie Farmers." In *The Political Economy of Agriculture in Western Canada*, edited by G.S. Basran and D.A. Hay, 73–86. Saskatoon: University of Saskatchewan Social Research Unit, 1988.

Stobbe, Mark. "Political Conservatism and Fiscal Irresponsibility." In *Devine Rule in Saskatchewan: A Decade of Hope and Hardship*, edited by Lesley Biggs and Mark Stobbe, 15–32. Saskatoon: Fifth House Publishers, 1991.

Summerville, Tracy. "The Political Geography of BC." In *British Columbia Politics and Government*, edited by Michael Howlett, Dennis Pilon, and Tracy Summerville, 69–84. Toronto: Emond Montgomery, 2010.

Taagepera, Rein. "Party Size Baselines Imposed by Institutional Constraints: Theory for Simple Electoral Systems." *Journal of Theoretical Politics* 3 (2001): 331–54.

Tennant, Paul. "The NDP Government of British Columbia: Unaided Politicians in an Unaided Cabinet." *Canadian Public Policy* 3 (Autumn 1977): 489–503.

Tenove, Chris. "In the Hurtland." In *Liberalized*, edited by David Beers, 38–70. Vancouver: New Star Books: 2005.

Tester, Frank. "Iglutaasaavut (Our New Homes): Neither 'New' nor 'Ours': Housing Challenges of the Nunavut Territorial Government." *Journal of Canadian Studies* 43 (2009): 137–58.

Timpson, Annis May. "Reconciling Settler and Indigenous Language Interests: Language Policy Initiatives in Nunavut." *Journal of Canadian Studies* 43 (2009): 159–80.

Tupper, Allan, Larry Pratt, and Ian Urquhart. "The Role of Government." In *Socialism and Democracy in Alberta*, edited by Larry Pratt, 31–66. Edmonton: NeWest, 1986.

Turnbull, Lori. "The Nova Scotia Election of 2009." *Canadian Political Science Review* 3 (September 2009): 69–76.

– "The 2006 Provincial Election in Nova Scotia." *Canadian Political Science Review* 1 (December 2007): 63–8.

Wedley, John R. "Laying the Golden Egg: The Coalition Government's Role in Post-War Northern Development." *BC Studies* 88 (Winter 1990): 58–92.

Wesley, Jared. *Code Politics: Campaigns and Cultures on the Canadian Prairies.* Vancouver: UBC Press, 2011.

– "Political Culture in Manitoba." In *Manitoba Politics and Government: Issues, Institutions, Traditions*, edited by Paul Thomas and Curtis Brown, 43–72. Winnipeg: University of Manitoba Press, 2010.

– "Stalking the Progressive Centre: An Ideational Analysis of Manitoba Party Politics." *Journal of Canadian Studies* 45 (Winter 2011): 143–77.

Whitaker, Reg. "Images of the State." In *The Canadian State: Political Economy and Political Power*, edited by Leo Panitch, 28–70. Toronto: University of Toronto Press, 1977.

Wilbur, Richard. "New Brunswick." In *Canadian Annual Review of Politics and Public Affairs 2002*, edited by David Muttimer, 213–24. Toronto: University of Toronto Press, 2002.

Wilson, John, and David Hoffman. "Ontario: A Three-Party System." In *Canadian Provincial Politics: The Party Systems of the Ten Provinces*, edited by Martin Robin, 198–239. Scarborough, ON: Prentice Hall, 1972.

Wiseman, Nelson. "The Success of the New Democratic Party." In *Manitoba Politics and Government: Issues, Institutions, Traditions*, edited by Paul G. Thomas and Curtis Brown, 73–95. Winnipeg: University of Manitoba Press, 2010.

Wishlow, Kevin. "Rethinking the Polarization Thesis: The Formation and Growth of the Saskatchewan Party, 1997–2001." In *Saskatchewan Politics: Into the Twenty-First Century*, edited by Howard Leeson, 169–98. Regina: University of Regina Press, 2001.

Wolfe, David, and Meric Gertler. "Globalization and Economic Restructuring in Ontario: From Industrial Heartland to Learning Region." *European Planning Studies* 9, no. 5 (2001): 575–92.

Yates, Charlotte A.B. "Staying the Decline in Union Membership: Union Organizing in Ontario, 1985–1999." *Relations industrielles / Industrial Relations* 640, no. 55 (2000): 640–71.

Young, Nathan. "Radical Neoliberalism in British Columbia: Remaking Rural Geographies." *Canadian Journal of Sociology* 33 (2008): 1–36.

Young, R.A. "'And the people will sink into despair': Reconstruction Policy in New Brunswick." *Canadian Historical Review* 69 (1988): 127–66.

Contributors

Sean T. Cadigan has been a professor of history at Memorial University since 2001 and served as head of the History Department from 2010 to 2013. Cadigan's research interests include working-class history, the social and ecological history of fishers and fishing communities, management and development policies in cold-ocean coastal areas, and the history of labour relations in the Newfoundland and Labrador offshore oil and gas industry. He is the author of *Newfoundland and Labrador: A History* (2009).

Peter Clancy teaches political science at St Francis Xavier University. His research focuses on business politics and natural resource management. He is the author of *Freshwater Politics in Canada* (2014).

Aidan D. Conway works as a research and policy analyst for a major Saskatchewan trade union and is a PhD candidate at York University. His research focuses on the politics of labour and finance in relation to key themes in Canadian and comparative political economy.

J.F. Conway is a professor of sociology and chair of the Department of Sociology and Social Studies at the University of Regina. His research interests focus on labour, the Left, and Saskatchewan politics. He is the author of *The West: The History of a Region in Confederation* (2005).

Don Desserud teaches political science at the University of Prince Edward Island. His research focuses on parliamentary institutions and constitutional conventions. He is the author of *Bringing New Brunswick's Legislative Assembly into the 21st Century* (2012).

Bryan M. Evans teaches in the Department of Politics and Public Administration at Ryerson University in Toronto. His research is focused on neoliberal restructuring, policy engagement, and labour and economic policy. He is the author of *From Pragmatism to Neoliberalism: The Remaking of Ontario's Politics and Administrative State* (forthcoming).

Peter Graefe teaches political science at McMaster University. His research focuses on the politics of social and economic development in Ontario and Quebec. He is the editor (with Julie Simmons and Linda White) of *Overpromising and Underperforming: Understanding and Evaluating New Intergovernmental Accountability Regimes* (2013).

Ailsa Henderson is professor of political science and head of Politics and International Relations at the University of Edinburgh. She is the author of *Hierarchies of Belonging: National Identity and Political Culture in Scotland and Quebec* (2007) and *Nunavut: Rethinking Political Culture* (2007).

Peter McKenna is professor and chair of political science at the University of Prince Edward Island in Charlottetown. He has published widely on Canadian foreign policy, politics on Prince Edward Island, and Canada's relationship with Latin America. He is the editor of *Canada Looks South: In Search of an Americas Policy* (2012).

Steve Patten is an associate professor in the Department of Political Science at the University of Alberta. He teaches and researches contemporary Canadian politics. He is the editor (with Lois Harder) of *The Chrétien Legacy: Politics and Public Policy in Canada* (2006).

Dennis Pilon teaches political science at York University. His research focuses on democratization, electoral reform, working-class politics, and British Columbia. He is the author of *Wrestling with Democracy: Voting Systems as Politics in the Twentieth-Century West* (2013).

Byron M. Sheldrick is the chair of the Department of Political Science at the University of Guelph. His research interests include the politics of social democracy, social welfare policy, and social movement mobilization around law and legal issues. His most recent book is entitled *Blocking Public Participation: The Use of Strategic Litigation to Silence Political Expression* (2014).

Gabrielle A. Slowey is an associate professor in the Department of Political Science at York University in Toronto. She teaches courses in Canadian, Aboriginal, and Arctic politics. Her research investigates the intersection between governance, resource extraction, indigenous development, the environment, and the state in multiple regions (Northern Alberta, Northern Quebec, Yukon, NWT, Ontario, the United States, Australia, and New Zealand). Her current research concentrates on pressures to develop shale gas reserves and investigates the variation in response by local communities. She is the author of *Navigating Neoliberalism: Self-Determination in an Era of Globalization (The Case of the Mikisew Cree First Nation)* (2007).

Charles W. Smith is an assistant professor of political studies at St Thomas More College, University of Saskatchewan in Saskatoon. He teaches courses in Canadian, provincial, and constitutional politics, political economy, and social justice. He has written several articles on the Canadian labour movement and is a recent recipient of a SSHRC grant on the Canadian labour movement's interaction with the Charter of Rights and Freedoms (with Larry Savage).

Graham White is professor of political science at the University of Toronto Mississauga. His teaching and research focus on Canadian legislatures and Cabinets and on the politics of the Canadian Arctic. He is a former president of the Canadian Political Science Association and is currently English co-editor of the *Canadian Journal of Political Science.* His most recent published book is *Cabinets and First Ministers* (2005), and he has recently completed a manuscript about the creation of Nunavut (co-authored with Jack Hicks).

Studies in Comparative Political Economy and Public Policy